CAMBRIDGE UNIVERSITY PRESS

CAMBRIDGE EN[GLISH]
Language Assessment
Part of the University of Cambridge

MW01709846

Cambridge English

CAMBRIDGE OFFICIAL PREPARATION MATERIAL

The **Official** Cambridge Guide to

IELTS

FOR ACADEMIC & GENERAL TRAINING

STUDENT'S BOOK WITH ANSWERS

Pauline Cullen Amanda French Vanessa Jakeman

Cambridge University Press
www.cambridge.org/elt

Cambridge English Language Assessment
www.cambridgeenglish.org

First published 2014
China reprint edition 2014
Reprinted 2015

Printed in China by Golden Cup Printing Co., Ltd.

ISBN 978-1-107-69491-0 Student's Book with Answers with DVD-ROM China reprint edition

Contents

IELTS Writing p91

IELTS Speaking p134

Practice Tests

Introduction

Who is this book aimed at?

This book is designed for candidates of any level hoping to take the IELTS test. It is suitable for students working alone or in a classroom situation. The materials can be used for self-study, or can be integrated into an IELTS preparation course. The book is also a valuable resource for teachers who are preparing IELTS candidates.

How can students of different levels use this book?

The IELTS test has two modules: the Academic Module and the General Training Module (see the following pages for an explanation of the two). Each Academic Module candidate will take the same test, no matter what his or her English level is. Similarly, each General Training candidate will take the same General Training test. So, the information in this book is useful and important to students of every level.

Lower-level language students generally need more guided practice and there are exercises in this book to provide this. However, they also need experience and practice in expressing themselves more freely, as this is what IELTS requires them to do. Similarly, more advanced students need frequent opportunities for self-expression, but they also need to become more self-critical and aware of their own common mistakes. Corpus research has shown that even high-level candidates make careless slips, so all levels can benefit from both controlled and free practice.

What are the aims of this book?

This book aims to provide an official, comprehensive guide to IELTS as well as a range of authentic practice tests.

The skills section of the book provides

- a detailed explanation of each paper and each section of IELTS;
- examples of the different types of question candidates can expect to find in each section;
- an analysis of the language skills and strategies needed for each type of question;
- study tips and test tips that can help you to achieve your best score.

This book also contains eight complete Practice Tests, to give you thorough preparation.

How is the book organised?

At the beginning of the book, there is a summary of each IELTS paper. Then, there are four sections dealing with the four skills covered in IELTS: Listening, Reading, Writing and Speaking. These are divided into units, which focus on key areas aiming to build your abilities and confidence, and provide authentic test practice. The second half of the book contains eight complete Practice Tests, each with a comprehensive answer key. The first practice test contains hints and reminders to guide you. At the end of the book, you will find the Answer Key and complete Recording Scripts.

How do I use this book?

For the skills sections, it is best to work through each unit in order. This is because the tasks and information are graded, developing your skills as the units progress. However, the different skills can be covered in any order. For example, you may decide to concentrate on only one skill at a time, or you may want to work on all four skills to provide a more balanced course. You should study all of the skills units before taking the Practice Tests.

When taking the Practice Tests, try to use the tips and strategies recommended in the skills units. You should also try to take the tests under exam conditions and stick closely to the time limits in the test.

How is this book different from other books?

The skills units and Practice Tests have been written by IELTS exam writers, so you can be sure they contain authentic, accurate and up-to-date information and advice. For the first time, we have also included a DVD showing IELTS Speaking tests, along with a commentary to explain the candidates' scores. Our writers have used the Cambridge Learner Corpus to help choose the most appropriate language and skill areas to focus on.

What is the Cambridge Learner Corpus?

The Cambridge Learner Corpus is the world's largest learner corpus. It is made up of thousands of exam scripts written by students from all over the world who have taken Cambridge ESOL exams. The corpus allows us to see the types of error candidates commonly make in the IELTS exam at each different level.

What is 'paraphrase' and why is it important?

Paraphrase is the use of different words to express the same idea. In order to test whether you have understood the Reading and Listening texts, the questions in IELTS will paraphrase the words used in the texts. In the Writing and Speaking sections of the test, being able to use paraphrase, instead of simply repeating and copying the words in the question, will show that you have a wide vocabulary and help you to achieve a higher score. So, using and understanding paraphrase is important in every part of the test.

IELTS Summary

IELTS Academic Module

The IELTS Academic Module can be used for undergraduate or postgraduate study or for professional reasons.

Academic Reading

Time: one hour

N.B. This includes the time needed to transfer your answers to an answer sheet. There is no extra time for this.

The Reading paper consists of three different texts and a total of 40 questions.

The texts are authentic and academic in nature, but written for a non-specialist audience. They are similar to the types of texts you may find in newspapers or magazines. The style may be descriptive or argumentative and at least one text contains detailed logical argument. Texts may contain illustrations. If a text contains technical terms, a simple glossary is provided. The three texts are graded from easiest to most difficult. Each text will have 12–14 items.

Overview of task types

Task type	What do I have to do?
1 multiple choice	• Choose one answer from alternatives A–D. • Choose two answers from alternatives A–E. • Choose three answers from alternatives A–G.
2 identifying information (T/F/NG)	Say whether a statement is True, False or Not Given.
3 identifying the writer's views/ claims (Y/N/NG)	Say whether a statement agrees with claims or views (Yes), disagrees with the views/claims (No) or whether there is no information on this (Not Given).
4 matching information	Match information to a paragraph in the text.
5 matching headings	Match a heading from a list of possible answers to the correct paragraph or section of the text.
6 matching features	Match a list of statements to a list of possible answers in a box (e.g. specific people or theories or dates).
7 matching sentence endings	Complete a sentence by choosing a suitable ending from a box of possible answers.
8 sentence completion	Complete a sentence with a suitable word or words from the text within the word limit given.
9 notes/summary/table/flow-chart completion	Complete notes/a summary/a table/flow-chart with a suitable word (or words) from a text.

10 labelling a diagram	Label a diagram with a suitable word (or words) from the text or from a box of possible answers.
11 short-answer questions	Answer questions using words from the text.

Assessment: each question is worth one mark.

Academic Writing

Time: one hour

This test consists of two separate writing tasks. You must answer both tasks.

Task	Timing	Length	What do I need to do?
Writing Task 1	20 minutes	150 words	You need to accurately describe and summarise visual information. The information may be presented in a diagram, map, graph or table.
Writing Task 2	40 minutes	250 words	You need to write a discursive essay. You will be given an opinion, problem or issue that you need to respond to. You may be asked to provide a solution, evaluate a problem, compare and contrast different ideas, or challenge an idea.

You will be assessed on the following criteria:

- Task Achievement
- Coherence and Cohesion
- Lexical Resource
- Grammatical Range and Accuracy

Writing Task 2 is worth twice as much as Writing Task 1.

Listening

Time: approximately 30 minutes (plus an additional 10 minutes to transfer your answers)

Academic and General Training candidates take the same Listening test. This consists of four separate sections and a total of 40 questions. Sections 1 and 2 are set in a social context and Sections 3 and 4 are set in an academic context. In the IELTS Listening, you will hear the text **ONCE ONLY**. Each test is divided up as follows.

Section	What kind of text will I hear?
1	A conversation between two people about a general topic with a transactional purpose (e.g. finding out information about travel).
2	A monologue or prompted monologue on a general topic with a transactional purpose (e.g. giving information about events in the community).
3	A conversation between two or three people in an academic context (e.g. a student and a tutor discussing an academic problem).
4	A monologue in an academic context (e.g. a lecture).

There are ten questions for each section in the listening test. Below are the task types that you may find in any section. You may have between one and three different tasks per section.

Task type	What do I have to do?
notes/summary/table/flow-chart completion	Complete notes/a summary/table/flow-chart with a suitable word or words within the word limit given.
multiple choice	Choose one answer from alternatives A–C. Choose two answers from alternatives A–E.
short-answer questions	Answer questions in the word limit given.
sentence completion	Complete a sentence with a suitable word or words within the word limit given.
labelling a diagram, plan or map	Label a diagram/plan or map with a suitable word (or words) or by choosing from a box of possible answers.
classification	Classify the information given in the question according to three different criteria (A, B or C). These may be dates, names, types, etc.
matching	Match a list of statements to a list of possible answers in a box (e.g. people, theories or dates).

Assessment: each question is worth one mark.

Speaking

Time: 11–14 minutes

This test consists of an interview with a trained examiner. The interview is recorded and has three separate parts.

Part	Timing	What will I need to talk about?
1	4–5 minutes	Questions on familiar topics (e.g. hobbies, likes and dislikes, etc.).
2	3–4 minutes	You will be given a booklet with a topic (e.g. describe a good friend) and some suggestions. You need to talk about the topic for 1–2 minutes. You have about one minute to write notes before you begin.
3	4–5 minutes	The examiner will ask you more detailed and more abstract questions about the topic in Part 2 (e.g. How important is friendship?).

You will be assessed on the following criteria:

- Fluency and Coherence
- Lexical Resource
- Grammatical Range and Accuracy
- Pronunciation

General Training Module

The General Training Module is commonly used for vocational training programmes (not at degree level) or for immigration purposes.

Candidates for the General Training Module take the same Listening and Speaking test as the Academic Module. Only the Reading and Writing papers are different.

General Training Reading

Time: one hour

N.B. This includes the time needed to transfer your answers to a separate answer sheet. There is no extra time given for this.

This test consists of three different sections and a total of 40 questions.

The texts are about more general topics or related to work. The General Training Reading paper has three sections, each of increasing difficulty. The sections are organised as follows.

Section	Reading texts
1	two or three short texts or several shorter ones (e.g. advertisements)
2	two texts related to the workplace (e.g. information for staff)
3	one long discursive text

The General Training Reading paper has a total of 40 questions.
Section 1 has 14 items. Sections 2 and 3 each have 13.

Task type	What do I have to do?
1 multiple choice	• Choose one answer from alternatives A–D. • Choose two answers from alternatives A–E. • Choose three answers from alternatives A–G.
2 identifying information (T/F/NG)	Say whether a statement is True/False or Not Given in the text.
3 identifying the writer's views/claims (Y/N/NG)	Say whether a statement agrees with claims or views in a text (Yes), disagrees with the views/claims in the text (No) or whether there is no information on this in the text (Not Given).
4 matching information	Match the information in the question to the correct paragraph in the text.
5 matching headings	Match a heading from a list of possible answers to the correct paragraph or section of the text.
6 matching features	Match a list of statements to a list of possible answers in a box (e.g. specific people or theories or dates).
7 matching sentence endings	Complete a sentence by choosing a suitable ending from a box of possible answers.
8 sentence completion	Complete a sentence with a suitable word or words from the text within the word limit given.
9 notes/summary/table/ flow-chart completion	Complete notes/a summary/table/flow-chart with a suitable word (or words) from the text within the word limit given.
10 labelling a diagram	Label a diagram with a suitable word (or words) from the text or by choosing from a box of possible answers.
11 short-answer questions	Answer questions using words from the text in the word limit given.
12 multiple matching	Match the information in the question to the correct short text or advertisement.

Assessment: each question is worth one mark.

General Training Writing

Time: one hour

This test consists of two separate writing tasks. You must answer both tasks.

Task	Timing	Length	What do I need to do?
Writing Task 1	20 minutes	150 words	Write a letter in response to a given situation.
Writing Task 2	40 minutes	250 words	You need to write a discursive essay. You will be given an opinion, problem or issue that you need to discuss. You may be asked to provide a solution, evaluate a problem, compare and contrast different ideas or opinions, or challenge an argument or idea.

You will be assessed on the following criteria:

- Task Response
- Coherence and Cohesion
- Lexical Resource
- Grammatical Range and Accuracy

N.B. Writing Task 2 is worth twice as many marks as Writing Task 1.

IELTS Listening

How long is the Listening paper?

The Listening paper is the same in both the Academic and the General Training modules of the IELTS test. It lasts approximately 30 minutes and you are given an extra 10 minutes to write your answers onto a separate answer sheet.

What type of information will I hear?

The Listening paper has four separate sections. Each section is a little more difficult than the one before. They feature speakers from a variety of English-speaking countries. Each section has a different focus.

- In **Section 1**, you will hear a conversation between two people (e.g. finding out information about travel).
- In **Section 2**, you will hear a monologue on a general topic (e.g. a radio broadcast).
- In **Section 3**, you will hear a conversation between two or three people in an academic context (e.g. discussing an assignment).
- In **Section 4**, you will hear a monologue in an academic context (e.g. a lecture).

Will I hear the recording more than once?

It is important to remember that you will hear the recording **only once**. To help you prepare, you will be given some extra time at the start of each section. During this time, you should read the questions carefully.

How is the Listening paper assessed?

You will be asked a total of 40 questions. In order to assess how much of the recording you understand, the questions will usually paraphrase (use different words with a similar meaning) the words that are in the text.

What types of question will I need to answer?

There are 10 questions in each section, and there is a variety of question types. For some types, you need to write words or numbers that you hear.

- forms/notes/table/flow-chart/summary completion
- short-answer questions
- sentence completion

For other tasks, you need to choose an option from a list and write a letter on your answer sheet.

- labelling a diagram/plan/map
- matching
- multiple choice

How do I answer the questions?

The instructions and the questions will tell you what type of information you need to listen for, and the type of answer you need to give. Listen carefully to any instructions you hear on the recording. Follow the instructions on the question paper carefully. In this unit, you will be able to practise all of these question types.

How can I improve my Listening paper score?

You can improve your score by following the instructions carefully, and remembering the Test Tips in this unit. This unit will also tell you the skills you need in order to achieve your highest score. Before the test, try to listen to accents from a variety of English-speaking countries. Studying all aspects of English (including vocabulary and grammar) will also help improve your IELTS score. If you make any mistakes in the practice exercises, make sure that you listen to the recording again and check your answers carefully in the Answer Key.

Listening skills

1 Getting ready to listen

In this unit you will practise:

- understanding the context
- using correct spelling
- listening for specific details
- understanding numbers

1 Understanding the context

In the introduction to the Listening section, you will be told who the people are, what they are talking about and why. This information is called the context. It helps you understand the topic. It is not written on the question paper.

After the introduction, you will be given a short time to look at the questions. Studying the questions before you listen can help you predict what the speakers will talk about.

Test Tip Before you do each section, you will be given 30–45 seconds to look at the questions. Use this time to study the questions and try to predict what you might hear.

1.1 ▶ 2 **You are going to hear the introductions of four IELTS Listening sections. Before you listen, try to predict the context by reading the questions in the table below. Choose FOUR answers from the box and write the correct letter, A–F, in the table.**

Section	Listening test questions	context
1	• Total number of guests: ______ • Susie will organise invitations and ______	C
2	What type of gift does the speaker recommend for a child's birthday?	
3	The students chose this topic because **A** they have a lot of information about it. **B** they would like to learn more about it. **C** they think they will get a higher mark.	
4	**Aim:** To assess the impact of loss of habitat on native animals **Methods:** • Calculate the current numbers of native animal species • Study their movements by attaching ______	

Contexts

A shopping for food	**D** describing a research project
B discussing an assignment	**E** buying presents
C organising a party	**F** explaining how something works

1.2 **Listen again. Decide how many speakers you will hear in each of these sections. Try to write down who the speakers will be.**

2 Using the correct spelling

In Listening Section 1, you may need to listen for the name of a person or a place. Often, the names will be spelt out for you. You need to recognise the letters of the English alphabet well, so that you can write the letters you hear quickly. You will only hear the spelling once.

Any spellings that you hear will be in the context of a normal conversation, so you need to be able to hear the difference between letters and words.

2.1 ▶ 3 Listen and write the letters you hear.

1 ________ 4 ________

2 ________ 5 ________

3 ________

> **Test Tip** Always check your spelling. If you make a spelling mistake in the IELTS Listening paper, your answer will be marked wrong.

2.2 ▶ 4 There are several ways to help you spell a word. Listen to five short conversations and complete notes 1–5 with *NO MORE THAN ONE WORD AND/OR A NUMBER.*

1 Name: Mr Andrew ________________

2 Address: 63 ________________ Road, Birmingham

3 Website address: www.________________.com

4 Meet at the ________________ Hotel

5 Registration number: ________________

> **Test Tip** Listen carefully, as there are several ways of helping people to spell a word without simply spelling it out. If you need to write something that is not a name (e.g. the registration number of a car), you may hear a combination of numbers and letters.

2.3 Listen again and complete extracts a–f from the conversations.

Conversation 1

a Is that ____ ____ ____ ____ ____ colour?

b Yes, but ____ ____ ____ ____ ____ ____ .

Conversation 2

c Sorry, ____ ____ ____ ____ N or M?

Conversation 3

d That's right, ____ ____ ____ ____ ____ lower case.

Conversation 4

e Oh, it's the Rose Hotel, ____ ____ ____ .

Conversation 5

f It's just ____ ____ ____ ____ ____ .

It's HLP 528.

> **Study Tip** Practise saying the letters of the English alphabet. For example, spell words out for a friend to write down.

3 Writing numbers

In Section 1 of the Listening paper, you need to listen for specific details.

3.1 ▶ 5 **Listen and circle the number you hear in each pair (a–j).**

a	1st / 3rd	**f**	15 / 50
b	$10.50 / $10.15	**g**	52 / 62
c	6th / 5th	**h**	£110 / £810
d	17 / 70	**i**	31st / 33rd
e	19 / 90	**j**	22nd / 27th

3.2 **Listen again and practise saying the numbers.**

3.3 ▶ 6 **Listen and complete the information below.**

1 How much does the woman pay for her room? £______

2 New students need to bring $______

3 Garage width: ______ m height: ______ m

4 How much does the woman pay for the bus tickets?
A $25 **B** $55 **C** $75

5 Party date: ______

3.4 **Listen again and write the other numbers you hear and the reason they are incorrect.**

1 *£80* *this is the amount she paid last time*

3.5 ▶ 7 **Listen to extracts from four different talks and choose the correct answer (A, B or C).**

1 The survey found that the majority of students drink
A water. **B** coffee. **C** tea.

2 What point does the speaker make about skiing?
A A small percentage of the US is suitable for skiing.
B A surprisingly large number of Americans like skiing.
C A relatively small proportion of Americans have tried skiing.

3 The number of wild elephants in Africa is estimated to be at least
A 53,000. **B** 470,000. **C** 690,000.

4 According to the speaker, which two can weigh the same?
A the tongue of a blue whale and an elephant
B an elephant and a blue whale
C a bus and an elephant

Listening skills

2 Following a conversation

In this unit you will practise:

- identifying the speakers
- identifying function
- understanding categories
- matching items
- completing notes
- completing a table

Test Tip In the IELTS Listening paper, Sections 1 and 3 are conversations between two or three people. Sections 2 and 4 are monologues with only one main speaker. Sometimes, you may hear another speaker introducing the talk or asking questions.

1 Identifying the speakers

For Sections 1 and 3, each speaker will have a different voice to help you tell them apart (e.g. male/female; younger/older). Both speakers will talk equally, and you will hear answers from **both** speakers.

For Section 1, there is normally one person who has to find out information from the other.

1.1 ▶ 8 You will hear three short extracts from Listening Section 1. Listen and identify what makes each speaker different, and what information they want to find out.

	people	description	information wanted
1	travel agent	*older female*	The customer would like information about …
	customer		
2	hotel receptionist		The receptionist needs to find out the guest's …
	guest		
3	interviewer		The applicant would like to know about …
	job applicant		

Study Tip You will hear native speaker accents from several English-speaking countries in the test. These may include British, American, Canadian, Australian and New Zealand accents. Search online for **non-commercial national radio stations** in these countries, and try to listen to a variety of them. National stations often have talk or current affairs programmes that can help you practise for IELTS.

1.2 ▶ 9 You need to listen to both speakers carefully. Listen to the rest of the conversations from 1.1 and answer the questions below. Ignore the final column for now.

1	**NOTES:** • No need to book the **1** ____________ from the airport	travel agent customer
	• the customer wants me to organise **2** ____________	travel agent customer
2	**1** How many nights will the man stay? **A** one night **B** two nights **C** three nights	hotel receptionist guest
	2 Which of the following is on the 10th floor? **A** the gym **B** the business centre **C** the restaurant	hotel receptionist guest
3	**1** Which country has the applicant worked in most? ____________	interviewer job applicant
	2 What department would the applicant like to work in? ____________	interviewer job applicant

1.3 Listen again and look at the final column in the table. Circle the person who provided the answer. Sometimes both are possible.

2 Identifying function

Each speaker has a specific purpose in mind when they talk. We say their language has a **function**. We use different language for different functions.

2.1 ▶ 10 Listen to seven short extracts from different conversations. Complete extracts 1–7.

1 ________ ________ getting her a new bike?

2 ________ ________ . We arrive on 22nd July.

3 That sounds great. ________ ________ ________ .

4 ________ ________ ________ I'd enjoy that one.

5 You said you'd prefer to have the party outside, ________ ________ ________ ?

6 ________ , it's just gone up to $250.

7 ________ , ________ ________ accommodation? Where would you like to stay?

2.2 What is the function of the phrases you wrote in 2.1? Match extracts 1–7 to the correct function (A–H). There is one extra letter that you do not need to use.

Functions

A agreeing	**E** confirming
B correcting	**F** moving to a new topic
C rejecting an idea	**G** checking information
D suggesting	**H** showing anger

2.3 ▶ 11 Listen to extracts from two conversations: one from Section 1 and one from Section 3. Choose the correct answers (A, B or C).

Listening Section 1

1 What food do the speakers decide to prepare for the party?

A pizza
B sandwiches
C hot dogs

2 What will they do next?

A go shopping
B decide on the music
C sort out the invitations

Listening Section 3

3 What aspect of pollution do the students decide to concentrate on?

A water pollution
B air pollution
C industrial pollution

4 What do the students decide to do next?

A contact their tutor for more help
B visit the library to find more resources
C check which topic other students have chosen

2.4 Look at the phrases below. Listen again and decide whether the phrases are in Extract 1 or Extract 2.

a That's a good idea.
b Actually, I think we're better off looking online.
c Why don't we … ?
d We could look at …
e What about a … ?
f Let's ask them.
g Pizzas it is, then!
h Shall we go to … ?
i You're right …
j That's right.
k So we could just do that?
l We'd better not.
m We'd better start …
n Now, we also need to …
o So, what else do we need to do?
p But we always do that.

3 Understanding categories

In the Listening paper, you may be asked to complete a table. The headings in the table tell you the type of information you will hear and need to listen for. They can also help you to follow a talk or conversation.

3.1 Complete the table below with the correct words from the box.

juice	picnic	tent	barbecue	tram
coffee	cabin	flat	theatre	lemonade
coach	cinema	buffet	concert	ferry

accommodation	transport	entertainment	food	drink

To complete a table or a set of notes or a sentence, you need to write words that you hear in the recording. You will be told how many words to write.

3.2 ▶ 12 Listen to an extract from a conversation and answer the question below.

Complete the sentence below with ***NO MORE THAN ONE WORD AND/OR A NUMBER.***

The expo will be useful because there will be more than ________________ experts there.

3.3 Now look at the answers that different candidates wrote. Tick the correct answers. Why are the other answers incorrect?

- two hundred and fivety computer
- 250 computer
- two hundred and fifty computers
- over 250 computer
- 250 computer experts
- over 250 experts
- two hundred and fifty computer
- 250

Test Tip Pay attention to the number of words you need to write. **NO MORE THAN TWO WORDS** means that you may need to write one word or two words. **NO MORE THAN ONE WORD AND/OR A NUMBER** means that if you write two words or more, then your answer will be wrong. Each of the following is an example of **ONE WORD AND/OR A NUMBER:** 16th June / three books / 6.11.12 / twenty-four cats / $450.50.

Listening skills

3 Recognising paraphrase

In this unit, you will practise:

- identifying distractors
- recognising paraphrase
- selecting from a list
- matching items
- sentence completion

1 Identifying distractors

Distractors are the incorrect answers to a question. Identifying distractors helps you to choose the correct answer and shows you have understood the Listening text.

Test Tip For most questions in the Listening paper, you will hear two or more potential answers to each question, but only one will be correct. The incorrect answers are called distractors.

1.1 ▶ 13 Listen to extracts from each Section of the Listening paper. Answer the questions in the table below.
Write *ONE WORD AND/OR A NUMBER*.

	questions	distractors
1	What date will they leave? ______	
2	What day will the tour visit a farm? ______	
3	The students decide to do a project about ______ .	
4	Problems: • poor weather • a lack of ______	

Study Tip To improve your concentration, when you are doing the Practice Tests in this book, try to write down each possible answer. Cross out the incorrect answers as you listen, based on what the speakers say. (Note that you may not have time to do this in the exam, however.)

1.2 Listen to the extracts again. Write down each possible answer and cross out the incorrect ones. Write the distractors in the table.

2 Recognising paraphrase

The speakers you will hear in the Listening paper often use different words to those in the questions. For example, you may hear a **synonym** (a word with a similar meaning).

2.1 Match words/phrases 1–8 with their synonyms a–h.

1	a price	**a**	money
2	a location	**b**	to carry
3	funding	**c**	a drawback
4	dangerous	**d**	a fee
5	a solution	**e**	a place
6	to transport	**f**	risky
7	disadvantage	**g**	an impact
8	an effect	**h**	an answer

The questions may **paraphrase** an idea that you will hear (express the same idea in a different way).

2.2 ▶ 14 Listen to more extracts from each Listening Section. Complete the first column by choosing the correct answer.

		synonyms/paraphrase	reasons the other options are incorrect
1	What do they decide to organise first? **A** a place to stay **B** their airfares **C** car hire		
2	What change will they make in the garden? **A** improve the shade **B** remove plants **C** add a water feature		
3	What do the students agree they need to do with their project? **A** do more research **B** make some cuts **C** add some visual effects		
4	The scientists are studying **A** how snow forms in different conditions. **B** the effect that snow has on our climate. **C** the effect different clouds have on snow.		

2.3 Listen again and complete the table on the previous page. First, write the synonyms or paraphrases you hear for the underlined words and phrases. Then explain why the other possible answers are incorrect.

3 Selecting from a list

Sometimes, you need to choose an answer from a longer list. All of the ideas in the list will be mentioned, but only two or three options are correct. To help you concentrate, it can help to underline key words before you listen. **Key words** are important words in the question (or the words or phrases in an option that make it different to the others).

3.1 Look at the question and list of possible answers. Before you listen, underline the key ideas you need to listen for.

What TWO disadvantages of the new mobile phone does the speaker mention?

A it isn't very user-friendly
B it is very expensive
C it can't take photographs
D it has a short battery life
E it is quite big

3.2 ▶ 15 To help practise scanning a list, listen and put options A–E in the order they are mentioned. Don't answer the question yet. Remember, the ideas will be paraphrased, so you may not hear the same words you see in the options.

A it isn't very user-friendly

B it is very expensive

C it can't take photographs

D it has a short battery life

E it is quite big *1*

3.3 Listen again and put a ✓ or a ✗ next to each option A–E, depending on whether or not it matches the information in the recording. Which TWO options are correct?

Test Tip The questions in the Listening paper are in the same order as the information you hear. This means that you will hear the information you need for Question 1 before you hear the information for Question 2, etc. However, in questions where you have to choose an **option** from a list, (e.g. multiple choice or matching items) the list of possible options will be in random order.

Test Tip Make sure that you pay close attention to any negatives in the options, as well as any adjectives. With matching or multiple choice tasks, pay careful attention to the question, as well as the options. The question will tell you how many answers you have to choose, as well as what you need to listen for (e.g. problems, solutions, advantages, etc.).

Listening skills

4 Places and directions

In this unit, you will practise:

- understanding a description of a place
- following directions
- labelling a map
- multiple choice

1 Describing a place

For some questions in the Listening paper, you need to look at a map of a place, or a plan of a building.

Test Tip For labelling a map or plan in IELTS, you may need to follow directions, or you may hear a description of a location.

1.1 Look at drawings A–F and decide what the images are.

A

D

B

E

C

F

Test Tip You should study the map or plan carefully **before** you listen. Having a clear image in your mind will help you understand what you hear.

1.2 Study the map in section 3.3 for 30 seconds.

1.3 Try to answer questions 1–4 without looking back at the map.

1 What is it a map of?
2 Name three landmarks on the map.
3 Where is the entrance?
4 What is in the centre of the map?

Features already on the map are often used as landmarks to help you find your way.

1.4 ▶ 16 Listen to extracts from the four sections of the Listening test. Complete the first column in the table by choosing the correct letter (A, B or C).

		landmark(s)	locating words/phrases
1	Where is the gift shop? 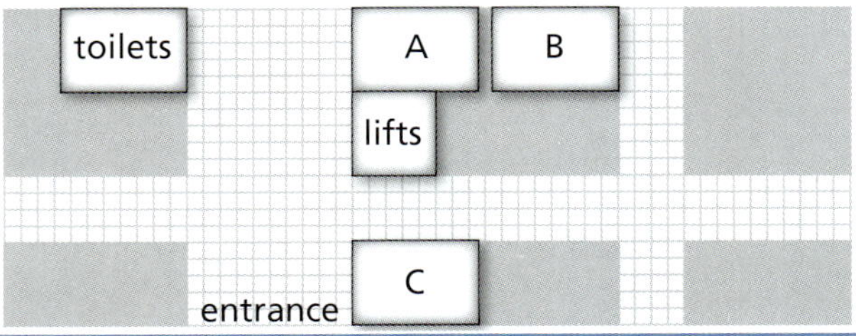	*lifts*	• The entrance is ______ ______ ______ ______ • Then go ______ ______ • The shop you want is ______ ______ ______ • ______ ______ ______ lifts
2	Where can you buy stamps? 		• In ______ ______ ______ ______ resort, you'll see a … • ______ ______ ______ ______ ______ courtyard, you'll find a … • It's just ______ ______ tree
3	What is the proposed location of the new bridge? 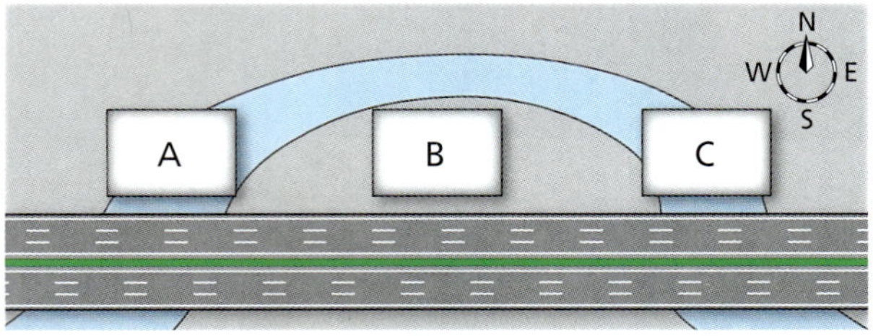		• I was thinking of putting it ______ ______ ______ ______ • I think it would be better if it's ______ ______ ______ ______ ______ motorway
4	Where is the ideal habitat for the Traviston Frog? 		• … it is unable to live in ______ ______ of a pond • … it does need to live in ______ ______ ______ to water • … in a tiny burrow ______ ______ bushes

1.5 Listen again and complete the table on the previous page. Write down the landmarks mentioned and fill in the gaps in the phrases that help you to locate the correct answer.

> **Test Tip** You may need to follow directions to locate a place on the map or plan. Marking the way directly on the map can be helpful.

2 Following directions

2.1 ▶ 17 Listen and decide which diagram (A, B or C) shows the directions described by the speaker.

A

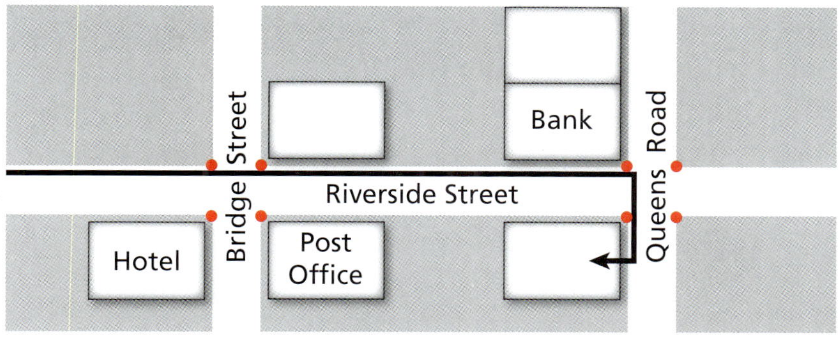

B

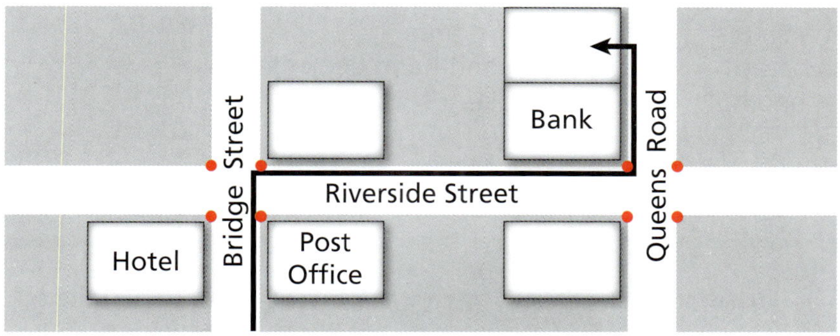

> **Test Tip** The distractors for this type of task might be extra buildings marked on the map, or they might be extra options in a list of possible answers.

C

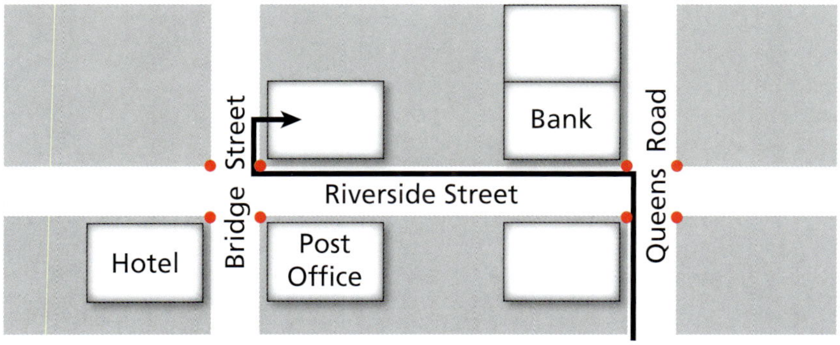

2.2 Listen again and make a note of any words or phrases that are used to give directions.

3 Labelling a map

Sometimes, a map completion task asks you to identify an area on a map then choose an answer from a list. For this type of question, you need to familiarise yourself with both the list of options and the features on the map before you start.

3.1 Look at this map completion task. Which landmarks might be used to help you to find your way around?

3.2 ▶ 18 Listen and label the map with the correct letter (A–F).

3.3 Check your answers, then listen again.

Test Tip Before you listen, read the options several times so that you become familiar with the information you need to listen for. Don't cross out any options unless you are sure they are wrong. If you can't decide between two answers, write both down and decide later.

Questions 1–4

Label the map below.

*Choose the correct letter **A–F** and write the answers next to questions 1–4.*

A	farm animals	**D**	picnic area
B	fresh bread	**E**	second-hand book stall
C	ticket booth	**F**	cookery shows

Brookside Market

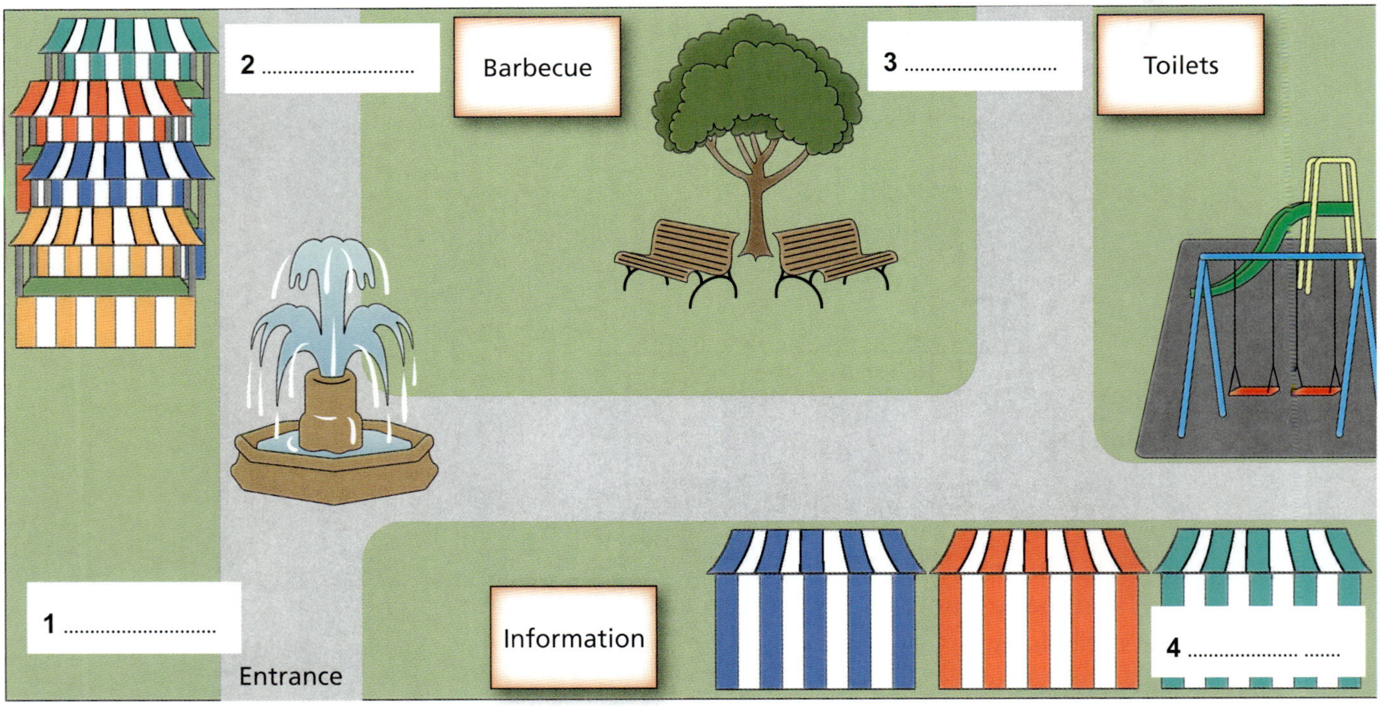

Listening skills

5 Listening for actions and processes

In this unit you will practise:

- understanding mechanical parts
- describing actions
- describing a process
- labelling a diagram

1 Understanding mechanical parts

For diagram completion tasks, you may need to listen and label the parts of a machine or device.

1.1 Look at the images below. What machine parts can you see?

1

2

3

4

5

6

1.2 ▶ 19 Listen to extracts A–F from different talks. Match them to pictures 1–6 and check your answers to 1.1.

A At the bottom of the system there is a storage tank …

B A small spring in the centre causes the toy …

C The water passes through the pipe and …

D The water in the pool was becoming quite polluted so a pump …

E There is a very fine grille at different points …

F There is a wheel on the side, which is attached to …

1.3 Look at the diagram completion task below.

1 Look at options A–F. How many extra answers are there?

2 Look carefully at the device. Think about how it might work.

3 Decide which verbs in the box you might hear.

spin	turn	pop	hold	wind	generate	wrap	pull
explode	push	rotate	hit	drag	activate	force	

1.4 ▶ 20 Listen and complete the diagram.

Questions 1–4

Write the correct letter, ***(A–F)****, next to questions 1–4 below.*

Parts

A cooling fan
B storage
C detonator
D party starter
E motor
F winder

The Party Popper Machine

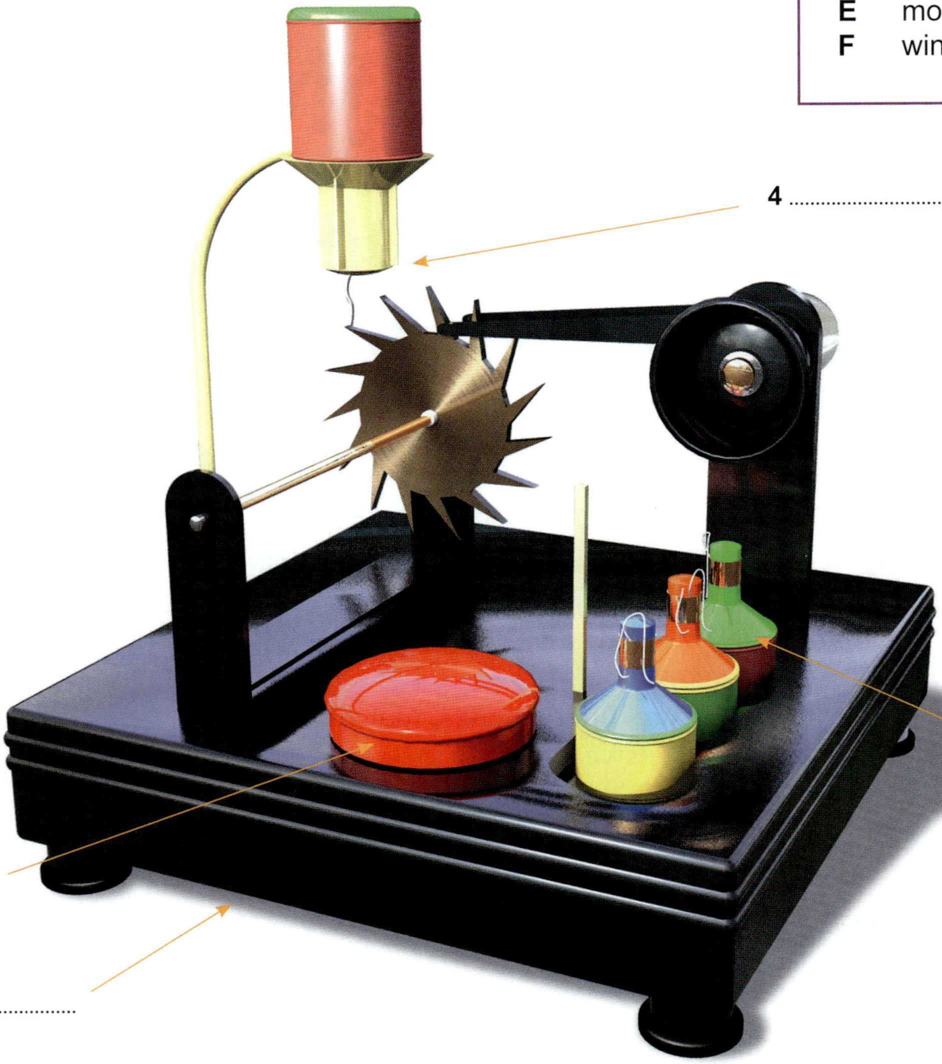

4 ....

3 ....

1 ....

2 ....

1.5 Which were the distractors? Listen again and decide why these answers were wrong.

1.6 Which verbs from the box in 1.3 did you hear?

2 Describing an action or process

When we describe how something works, we often use prepositions or adverbs to explain movement.

2.1 Draw an arrow on the following images to represent the words that have been underlined. The first one has been done for you.

1 Put it <u>inside</u> the box …

2 It then passes <u>through</u> a pipe …

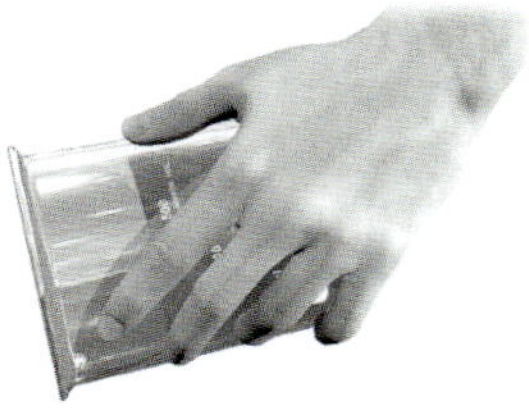

3 Turn the container <u>upside down</u>, then …

4 The trolley moves <u>along</u> the tracks and …

5 The area <u>beneath</u> the table was …

6 The paper was then wrapped <u>around</u> the …

7 This then forces the air <u>upwards</u> …

8 Cut the paper <u>diagonally</u> …

Describing how a machine works often involves verbs that you do not commonly use.

2.2 **Match objects A–D with the words in the box. Then complete the description of each object.**

scales	thermometer	speedometer	calculator

A

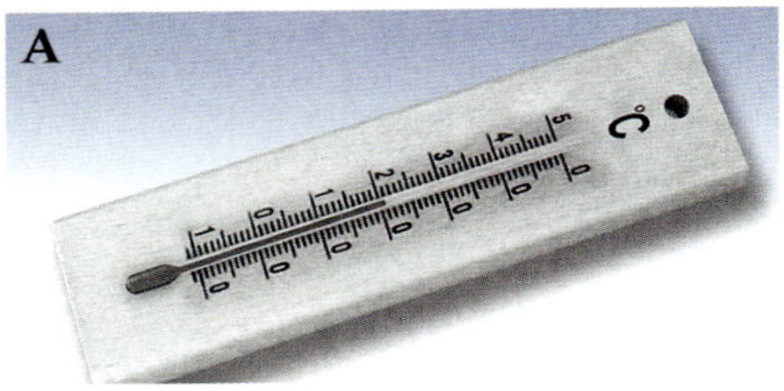

It is used to ________ ________ .

B

It is used to ________ figures.

C

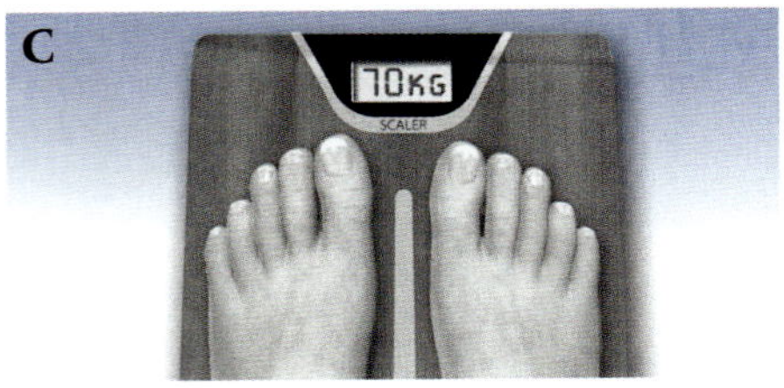

They are used to ________ things.

D

It is used to ________ ________ .

2.3 ▶ 21 **Listen and check your answers to 2.2.**

3 Describing a process

3.1 **Think about the different stages involved in wrapping a present. How would you use the words in the box?**

First,	Then,	Next,	Then, neatly	Finally,

3.2 ▶ 22 **Listen to a description of the process and fill in the gaps. Then circle all the verbs used to describe the process.**

Here's how to wrap a present. First, gather together all of the things you need: wrapping paper, sticky tape, scissors, some ribbon and, of course, a present. Then, **1** ________ your present on the opened wrapping paper and **2** ________ a suitable amount using the scissors. Next, **3** ________ the paper around the present and **4** ________ it down with sticky tape. Then, neatly **5** ________ up each of the ends of the paper and **6** ________ them down. Finally, **7** ________ the ribbon around your present. It's now ready to present!

Listening skills

6 Attitude and opinion

In this unit you will practise:

- identifying attitudes and opinions
- persuading and suggesting
- reaching a decision
- multiple choice
- matching items

1 Identifying attitudes and opinions

In Listening Sections 1 and 3, the speakers are often trying to make a decision or reach an agreement. Identifying the speakers' opinions can help you to answer the questions correctly.

1.1 ▶ 23 **Listen to eight extracts. What does each speaker show?**

a strong agreement
b neither complete agreement nor complete disagreement
c complete disagreement

1.2 **Listen again and complete the extracts.**

1 Well, I ________ ________ ________ ________ ________ .
2 I think that's a ________ ________ ________ .
3 Well, I'm ________ ________ ________ about that.
4 I think you're ________ ________ .
5 Hmm, that's a bit ________ ________ ________ .
6 I think that's ________ ________ .
7 That seems ________ to me.
8 I have to admit I don't like the ________ ________ ________ ________ ________ .

1.3 **In Listening Sections 3 and 4, you may be asked to identify a speaker's attitude. Match words 1–7 with synonyms a–g.**

1	worried	**a**	dubious
2	enthusiastic	**b**	hesitant
3	afraid	**c**	annoyed
4	confused	**d**	concerned
5	irritated	**e**	scared
6	reluctant	**f**	puzzled
7	doubtful	**g**	eager

1.4 ▶ 24 **Listen to an extract from a Listening Section 3 task. What aspect of the research did the students find surprising? Choose the correct answer (A, B or C).**

A The amount of time it took to achieve results.
B The reaction of the public to the research.
C The findings that the research produced.

1.5 **Listen again and write down all the words/phrases the speakers use to mean 'surprising' or 'unsurprising'.**

2 Persuading and suggesting

In Listening Sections 1 and 3, in order to reach a decision, you will hear the speakers make suggestions, agree, disagree or try to persuade each other.

2.1 **Look at the Listening Section 3 task below. Before you listen, complete these tasks.**

1. Try to think of a synonym or paraphrase for the underlined words/phrases.
2. Read through decisions A–F in the box several times so that you are familiar with the different options to choose from.
3. Decide whether you will hear the decisions or the presentation sections in order.

Test Tip For matching tasks like this, the topics in the questions will be discussed in the same order as they are listed. But you will hear the different options in the box in a random order. As you listen, you need to keep looking at the list of options.

2.2 ▶ 25 **Listen and complete the task.**

Questions 1–4

What do the students decide to do with the different sections of their project?

*Write the correct letter, **(A–F)**, next to questions 1–4 below.*

Presentation Sections

1. Introduction
2. Advantages
3. Disadvantages
4. Conclusion

Decisions

A reduce the length
B change the method of presentation
C write some more
D make it more interesting
E check the sources are reliable
F make sure they have current data

2.3 Check your answers and then listen again. Which synonyms of the underlined words/phrases are used?

2.4 Look at Recording script 25 and find phrases which are used to do the things below.

- make a suggestion
- agree with an idea
- disagree

Study Tip Search online for national radio stations from the UK, the US, Canada, Australia or New Zealand. These often have programmes that discuss topical issues and you will hear people suggesting ideas and discussing possible solutions. This is useful for Listening Section 3.

3 Reaching a decision

In Listening Sections 1 and 3, you will often hear people discussing a problem, suggesting solutions and then reaching a decision. A discussion like this might focus on the advantages and disadvantages of each suggestion.

3.1 Look at these questions and try to think of possible advantages and disadvantages you might hear. Write them in the table.

	possible advantages/disadvantages
Section 1 The speakers decide to travel to the airport by **A** taxi **B** bus **C** car	
Section 3 What do the students decide to do next? **A** ask their tutor for help **B** do more research on the topic **C** produce a typed copy of their notes	

3.2 ▶ 26 Listen and answer the questions in 3.1.

3.3 Listen again and make a note of any language that the speakers use to show they reach a decision or agreement.

Sometimes the speakers may need to decide on what action to take. A discussion like this might focus on the reasons why one course of action is necessary or important.

Listening skills

7 Following a lecture or talk

In this unit you will practise:

- identifying main ideas
- understanding how ideas are connected
- understanding an explanation
- completing a summary
- short-answer questions

1 Identifying main ideas

The questions in the Listening paper will focus on the main points made by the speakers, so it is important to be able to identify the main points of a talk.

Test Tip At the start of each talk, you will be told who the speaker is and why they are talking. You won't be tested on this, but you can use this information to get a clear idea of the situation. This can help you to concentrate and follow the information in the talk.

1.1 ▶ 27 **Listen to part of a talk by Paul, an Australian palaeontologist (a scientist who studies dinosaurs and fossils). To help practise keeping track of the talk, put the phrases below in the order you hear them.**

- The very first field trip I went on
- It's an ancestor of the modern Australian wombat
- I found a funny-looking piece of rock
- an old professor studying dried-up dinosaur bones
- I immediately changed courses
- I had to do a compulsory unit on extinction

1.2 **Which of the following describes the main topic of the talk?**

a Important lectures Paul has given
b Describing the process that led to Paul's current role
c Explaining how ancient Australian animals became extinct

The questions in the IELTS Listening paper focus on the **main points** of the talk. In between the points, the speaker may also mention things that are not directly related to the main purpose of the talk.

1.3 ▶ 27 **Think about your answer to 1.2 and listen again. Which three phrases in 1.1 are used to give information that is directly related to the main purpose of the talk?**

You may be asked to complete a summary in the Listening paper. This can look difficult, so it will help to break down the information.

1.4 Look at the summary below and write questions related to the information missing from each gap.

> **Summary**
>
> Paul was interested in the **1** .... so took an ecology course at university. The course included a section on **2** .... and an interesting lecture caused him to quickly change his degree.
>
> Paul says working in palaeontology can be difficult and he describes the conditions as **3** .... However, the discovery of a **4** .... from an ancient animal made him realise he had made the right choice.

1 *What was Paul interested in? / Why did Paul take an ecology course?*

1.5 ▶ 27 Listen to the talk again and complete the summary with **ONE WORD ONLY**. Check your answers, paying attention to your spelling.

1.6 The information in the Listening summary can help you to keep track of a talk. Look at Recording script 27 and compare it to the summary.

1 Is the information in the summary in the same order as the script?
2 Complete the table below with the correct phrases from the script or the summary.

audio script	summary
My main interest has been …	**1** *Paul was interested in …*
2	The course included a section on …
a lecturer … I was fascinated	**3**
4	change his degree
I found a …	**5**
6	a tooth from an ancient animal

2 Understanding how ideas are connected

The topics and language in Listening Sections 3 and 4 are more complex. Here are some examples of the information you may hear.

A the methods used in a particular study
B the effects of an action
C the reason an action was carried out
D the conclusions that can be drawn from research
E the findings of an experiment

2.1 ▶ 28 **Listen to four extracts from Listening Sections 3 and 4. Decide what type of information above (A–E) you hear in each.**

1 ______ **2** ______ **3** ______ **4** ______

2.2 ▶ 29 **Listen to the second part of Paul's talk. Answer questions 1–4 with NO MORE THAN TWO WORDS.**

1 What information does Paul get from the machine he mentions?
2 What did the government recently give Paul?
3 What modern-day problem does he say ancient animals can help with?
4 What two causes of mega-fauna extinction does Paul hope to study?

3 Understanding an explanation

Test Tip Don't be worried if you see technical terms in the Listening questions. These will usually be explained to you.

To help you prepare for the listening, read the information in the questions carefully and try to predict what information you will hear.

3.1 **Read the two multiple-choice questions below. Use the information in the questions to complete the notes on the right.**

1 What did the researchers find in their experiments on mice? **A** A lack of exercise made them appear older. **B** Their cells remained the same as they aged. **C** Their cells were unaffected by changes in diet.	*The talk is most likely about research done on* **1** ______ *. The talk will probably mention* **2** ______ *,* ______ *and* ______ *.*
2 What new discovery have scientists made about pigeons? **A** They use the Earth's magnetic field to navigate. **B** Their beak plays an important role when flying. **C** A part of their ear helps them find their way.	*During this talk, we will probably hear about what we already know about* **3** ______ *as well as some* **4** ______ *information. I need to listen for whether pigeons use the* **5** ______ *, or their* **6** ______ *or* ______ *to stop them getting lost.*

3.2 ▶ 30 **Listen to the two extracts and answer the questions in 3.1 by choosing the correct answer, A, B or C.**

3.3 **Why were the other options incorrect?**

Listening skills

8 Contrasting ideas

In this unit you will practise:

- signposting words
- comparing and contrasting ideas
- using notes to follow a talk
- table completion
- notes completion

1 Signposting words

For Listening Section 4, you will hear a talk by a student or an expert on an academic subject. Speakers often use signposting words to move from one topic to another, or to help connect their ideas.

Test Tip A shift in topic often indicates that you should move on to the next question. Use signposting words (as well as headings) in the notes to help guide you through the topics and the questions.

1.1 ▶ 31 **Listen to six short extracts from different Listening Section 4 talks. Complete the extracts below.**

1 OK, ________ ________ ________ ________ the late 19th century, when a great deal of changes were taking place.

2 Now, ________ ________ ________ , I wanted to give you some background information.

3 So, ________ ________ ________ ________ ________ some possible reasons for this.

4 ________________ , I'd like to talk about some future projects.

5 So, ________ ________ did we reach?

6 I'll ________ ________ ________ what this machine can do.

1.2 **Match the extracts 1–6 in 1.1 to uses A–C below.**

A to start off a topic
B to change to a new topic
C to finish off a topic

1.3 **Here are some words you might hear in a talk. Match words 1–8 to their synonyms A–H.**

1 results	**A** background
2 definition	**B** benefits
3 challenges	**C** solutions
4 history	**D** findings
5 advantages	**E** conclude
6 disadvantages	**F** meaning
7 answers	**G** drawbacks
8 summarise	**H** problems

Test Tip Remember, you may hear synonyms of the words written on the question paper.

2 Comparing and contrasting ideas

Sometimes, the focus of a talk will be comparing or contrasting (saying what is the same or different about) several different things. The information may be organised as a table that you need to complete.

Test Tip The information in a table is always read from left to right. The different examples will be described in order. Notice that there is often a title or a heading at the top of the table to give you more information.

2.1 **You are going to do a table completion task. First, study the table and then answer questions 1–5 below.**

1 Which of the following do you think you will hear?

- **A** the names of all the plants, then all of their origins, then finally, a discussion of all the positives and negatives
- **B** a full description of one plant that also contains some references to the other plants listed
- **C** a complete analysis of one plant at a time, describing its origins, then finally its positives and negatives

2 What type of information will you need to write for Question 1?

3 In which column will the questions focus on the benefits?

4 In which column do the questions focus on the drawbacks?

5 What information will you need to listen for in Question 8?

Plants that changed the world

Plant	**Origins**	**Positives**	**Negatives**
potatoes	Central and South America Brought to **1** .... by the Spaniards in 16th century	It led to • changes in **2** .... • people moving to another country to find new **3**	• In Ireland, the **4** .... became dependent on potatoes. • Disease led to mass **5** ....
tobacco	The Americas	• It played an important role in US history. • Known as the first **6** .... crop in the US.	• Led to increases in slavery • Became a cause for **7** ....
8	China	Helped bring about independence in the US.	The **9** .... imposed on it became a key event in American Revolution.
White Mulberry	China	It started **10** .... between East and West.	It led to increases in the spread of disease.

2.2 ▶ 32 Listen and complete the table with ONE WORD ONLY.

3 Using notes to follow a talk

The headings in a set of notes can help you in the same way as the headings in a column.

3.1 Read the notes below and answer questions 1–4 below.

1 How is the information organised differently, in comparison with the table in 2.1?
2 How will this help you to follow the talk?
3 What **new** topic will you hear about, which was not in the table in 2.1?
4 For which question do you need to write a nationality?

Plants that changed the world

Prehistory: flowering plants

- arrived about 130 million years ago
- became an essential source of **1** ....

2737 BC: tea

- discovered in China, played a key role in USA, China & UK
- led to financial problems in Britain – a Chinese ruler insisted all tea was paid for with **2** .... , which had to be sourced from other countries

202 BC: White Mulberry

- in demand from 202 BC when it was essential in the production of **3** ....
- trade routes led to the spread of different **4** .... but also made more people ill and encouraged the exchange of dangerous products (e.g. **5** ....)

16th century: the potato

- originated in Central and South America, brought to Europe by the **6** ....
- it was rapidly accepted because it was cheap and contained lots of **7** ....
- helped prevent one specific **8** ....
- 1845–1849 – large-scale failure of potato crops led to a million deaths in Ireland and the **9** .... of another million people

3.2 ▶ 33 Listen and complete the notes with ONE WORD ONLY.

3.3 Check your answers, then listen again and notice how the notes help to guide you through the talk.

IELTS Reading

What's the difference between Academic Reading and General Training Reading?

There are two separate reading tests, one for Academic candidates and one for General Training candidates. Before enrolling for the test, you need to decide which test is best for you. See www.ielts.org for advice.

How long does the IELTS Reading paper last?

The test lasts 60 minutes. Within that time, you must complete three separate sections with a total of 40 questions. You must also transfer your answers onto a separate answer sheet (there is no extra time given for this).

What type of information will I read?

The Reading paper has three separate sections. Each section is a little more difficult than the one before and features authentic reading passages. The Academic module contains three long texts of an academic nature. The General Training module features a mixture of long and short texts of a more general nature, as well as texts related to work situations.

How is the Reading paper assessed?

You will be asked a total of 40 questions. In order to assess how much of the reading passages you understand, the questions will usually paraphrase (use different words with the same meaning) the words that are in the text. The questions test a variety of reading skills including your ability to do the following.

- Identify the writer's overall purpose.
- Follow key arguments in a text.
- Identify opinions and attitudes.
- Locate specific information.
- Distinguish main ideas from supporting details.
- Extract information from a text to complete a diagram, summary, table or set of notes.

What type of questions will I need to answer?

There are 12–13 questions in each section, and you will be asked 1–3 different types of question in any section. There are several possible types of question. For some tasks, you need to write words or numbers from the reading passage.

- sentence completion
- summary, note, table, flow-chart completion
- short-answer questions
- diagram label completion

In other tasks, you need to choose one option from a list and write a letter on your answer sheet.

- multiple choice
- matching information
- matching headings
- matching features
- matching sentence endings
- summary completion

You may also need to decide if sentences are True/False/Not Given or Yes/No/Not Given, based on the information that you read.

How do I answer the questions?

The instructions and the questions will tell you what type of information you need to locate in the texts, and the type of answer you need to write. Carefully follow all of the instructions on the question paper. In this unit, you will be able to practise all of these question types.

How can I improve my Reading paper score?

You can improve your score by following the instructions exactly and remembering the Test Tips in this unit. Managing your time so that you can complete all of the questions is an important part of the Reading paper. This unit will also tell you the reading skills you need to practise in order to achieve your best score. Before the test, try to read a variety of texts and improve your speed-reading skills. Studying all aspects of English (including vocabulary and grammar) will also help improve your IELTS score. If you make any mistakes in the Practice Tests in this book, make sure that you read the texts again carefully and use the Answer Key to help you identify any problems.

Reading skills

1 Reading strategies

In this unit you will practise:

- using the features of a passage
- understanding explanations
- skimming a text and speed reading
- global understanding of a passage

1 Using the features of a Reading passage

1.1 Label the reading passage with the correct letters in the box (A–G).

Features of a Reading passage

A	footnote	**E**	heading
B	subheading	**F**	caption
C	column	**G**	paragraph
D	figure / illustration		

1 ....

2 ....

3 ....

Health-Tea

Sid Cowans looks at the health properties of a favourite drink

If you are a tea drinker you have probably heard of **tannins**, which are plant based chemicals found in tea. They are responsible for the **astringent** bitter taste sometimes associated with tea. When you drink a cup of tea, it usually dissolves and remains clear unless the water is too cold or too **alkaline**.

Tannins occur in many different types of plants and food, but are especially present in **oak galls**, which have been used for centuries in Chinese medicine due to their health giving properties. Tannins are often present in drinks and medicine because they are **soluble** in water, but how much they dissolve depends on factors like temperature and the chemical make up of the liquid.

Tannins exist in all types of tea

[1] In chemistry, an alkali is the opposite of an acid.
[2] Abnormal growths on oak trees

6 ....

5 ....

4 ....

Most Reading passages will have a heading and a subheading. The subheading is used to give you the context to the passage.

1.2 Match headings A–D from four Reading passages with subheadings 1–5. There is one extra subheading that you do not need.

A Alpine Glacial Lakes
B Clean Dream
C Virtual Connections
D Creating Young Scientists

1 *Researchers disagree about whether social media is making us more isolated.*
2 *Climatologists are assessing the impact of climate change on high-altitude bodies of water.*
3 *James Clegg identifies two current trends that are expanding the role of science in high schools.*
4 *Alan Parker outlines a recent breakthrough in technology.*
5 *In the 19th century, a schoolgirl and a former travelling salesman helped turn the humble soap bar into an $18 billion industry.*

Understanding the context can help you to predict the type of information contained in the Reading passage.

1.3 Match the types of information 1–6 to Reading headings A–D. You will need to use the information in the subheadings to help you and you may use any letter more than once.

1 arguments put forward by several different experts
2 a description of a project in mountainous areas
3 a discussion about the impact of technology on society
4 research linked to trends in weather patterns
5 a historical look at a successful business venture
6 an argument presented from one expert's point of view

An IELTS Reading passage might contain *footnotes*. These help explain technical terms. Some terms are explained in the passage. Other terms can be understood by reading the text carefully.

Test Tip Timing is an important part of the Reading test. Try to finish each section in **less than 20 minutes.**

Read the passage as quickly as possible (up to three minutes).
Look at the questions to see what type of information you need to find (up to one minute).
Spend 12–13 minutes reading the passage in detail and answering the questions.
If a question is taking too long, move on.
Use your last 3–4 minutes to transfer your answers, checking and filling in any gaps in your answers.

1.4 The passage in 1.1 contains several explanations and definitions. Read the passage and match terms (1–5) with meanings A–F.

1 tannin
2 astringent
3 alkaline
4 oak gall
5 soluble

A a taste similar to a lemon
B a chemical found in certain plants
C able to dissolve in liquid
D the opposite of acidic
E becoming cloudy
F a problem found on a type of tree

1.5 What helped you to identify the definition of each word?

A a footnote in the text
B an explanation in the text
C the surrounding context

2 Skimming a passage and speed reading

Skimming a passage means reading it quickly (concentrating on content words, like nouns and verbs) to find the main points. It is not reading for detail. Skimming a text will also give you a general idea of how the information is organised, which can help you locate information more easily later on. In your own language, you can probably skim read 100 words in 20 seconds. In the exam, you should aim to skim read 100 words in 30 seconds.

2.1 This passage has four paragraphs of around 100 words each.

1 Using a timer, skim read the text to get the general idea of what it is about.
2 After 30 seconds, jump to the start of the next paragraph.

A The diets of children have changed dramatically over the last century due to the effect of technologies (such as improved transport, canning and refrigeration), social changes (such as the establishment of boarding schools) and evolving ideas about the nutritional needs of growing bodies. Before World War I, the meals of children and adults alike would typically consist of vegetables (often potatoes), large amounts of bread (often 0.5 kg/day) and soups with small amounts of meat.

B Imagine a 12-year-old Australian boy from 1970 standing next to a 12-year-old boy from 2010. The boy from 2010 will probably be 3–5 cm taller and 7 kg heavier than his counterpart in 1970. He will also be 25% fatter. A lot of that fat will be around the waist. The 2010 school trousers won't fit the boy from 1970: they will be 10 cm too big around the waist. Now imagine that the two boys have a running race of over 1,600 metres: the boy from 1970 will finish 300 metres ahead of his mate from 40 years in the future.

C There are two chances in three that the boy from 1970 walked to school each day; there are three chances in four that the boy from 2010 is driven to school by mum or dad. There are four chances in five that in 1970 the boy was allowed to play unsupervised in the neighbourhood; there is only one chance in four that in 2010 the boy will be allowed to go down to the park on his own. The boy in 1970 probably played three or four different sports; the boy from 2010 plays one or none. It is 30 times more likely that the local river was the favourite play space of the boy from 1970 than it is for the boy today.

D What has caused these dramatic changes in the space of a single generation? There are two main theories. Increasing overweight is caused by an energy imbalance: either energy intake (food) increases, or energy expenditure decreases, or both. The 'Gluttony Theory' argues that children are fatter because they are eating more than they used to, and more bad food (high energy density, high in fat and sugar, high in saturated fats). The 'Sloth Theory' argues that children are fatter because they are less active than they used to be. The two theories have battled it out in nutrition and physical activity journals for the last 10 years.

2.2 Now look at questions 1–3 and, without looking at the passage, try to remember whether this information was

A near the beginning.
B in the middle.
C near the end.

1 a comparison of children now and in the past
2 different hypotheses for the changes in weight
3 a list of factors that brought about changes in our diet

2.3 Questions 1–3 in 2.2 each give the main idea of the paragraphs in the passage. Read the questions again and decide which paragraph (A–D) they relate to.

3 Global understanding

Sometimes, you may be asked a question that focuses on the whole Reading passage. This type of question may ask you to choose a suitable title for the passage.

3.1 Which title (A–D) would be the most suitable for the Reading passage in 2.1?

A Children's eating patterns mimic those of their parents
B The rapid transformation occurring in children's body size
C A demonstrated positive link between diet and health in children
D The impact of modern technology on today's food production

Skim reading a passage can also give you a sense of the attitude of the writer. Global questions can sometimes focus on this.

3.2 Read the passage again and answer the global question below. Which of the following describes the writer's tone in this passage?

A He is giving a neutral account of recent scientific research.
B He is shocked that so many children are becoming overweight.
C He feels enthusiastic about the progress that is being made.
D He is doubtful that the situation will change in the near future.

Reading skills

2 Descriptive passages

In this unit you will practise:

- scanning for specific details
- recognising paraphrase
- completing notes or a flow-chart
- labelling a diagram

1 Scanning for detail

The passages in the IELTS Reading paper gradually become more difficult, with Section 1 being the easiest.

1.1 Spend one minute skim reading the following passage to get a sense of the overall meaning. What is the main topic?

A new discoveries in chemistry
B the discovery of ancient objects
C how international scientific teams work

Ochre find reveals ancient knowledge of chemistry

The oldest ochre-processing toolkits and workshop ever found have been unearthed, indicating that as far back as 100,000 years ago, humans had an understanding of chemistry.

South Africa's Blombos Cave lies within a limestone cliff on the southern Cape coast, 300 km east of Cape Town. It's known for its 75,000-year-old rich deposits of artefacts such as beads, bone tools and ochre engravings. Some engravings date as far back as 100,000 years.

Archaeologist Christopher S. Henshilwood from the University of Witwatersrand in Johannesburg and University of Bergen, Norway has been excavating at the site since 1992, and has reported the discovery of a mixture, rich in ochre, stored in two abalone shells. It dates back to the Middle Stone Age – 100,000 years ago. Ochre is a term used to describe a piece of earth or rock containing red or yellow oxides or hydroxides of iron. It can be used to make pigments, or paints, ranging from golden-yellow and light yellow-brown to a rich red. Its use spans the history of humans – from those living more than 200,000 years ago, to modern indigenous communities.

Made from an array of materials, this mixture, which could have functioned as wall, object and skin decoration or skin protection (acting in a similar way to modern-day sunscreen), indicates the early developments that occurred in the people who originally used the site.

"[Judging from] the complexity of the material that has been collected from different parts of the landscape and brought to the site, they [the people] must have had an elementary knowledge of chemistry to be able to combine these materials to produce this form. It's not a straightforward process," said Henshilwood.

1.2 Scanning involves searching a text quickly for a specific piece of information. Practise scanning the passage for the words/numbers in the box.

75,000	100,000	200,000	artefacts	ochre

2 Using words from the passage

There are several types of question that ask you to write a word and/or number from the passage.

- You will be told the maximum number of words to write.
- You must only write words that are in the passage. Make sure you copy the spelling correctly.
- You do not need to change the words in the passage and you do not need to join words together.
- If you write too many words or make a spelling mistake, your answer will be marked wrong.

Test Tip If the question asks you to write TWO WORDS AND/OR A NUMBER, this means the answer may be:

- one word
- one word + a number
- two words
- two words + a number

Remember that even if a number is written as a word, it counts as a number (e.g. *twenty five trees* = one word and a number). You do not need to write full sentences or join words together. For example:

Answer the question with ***NO MORE THAN TWO WORDS*** from the reading passage.

What **TWO** colours did the painter use?

(Answer: *black, white* not ~~*black and white*~~)

Short answer questions and sentence completion tasks

Short answer questions test your ability to find specific details in a passage. Use the words in the questions to:

- help locate the relevant part of the passage
- find out exactly what details you are looking for.

2.1 In questions 1–3 below, the key words that you need to locate in the passage are in bold, and the details you need to find out are underlined. Use these words to help you locate the relevant parts of the text and then answer the questions.

Choose ***NO MORE THAN TWO WORDS AND/OR A NUMBER*** from the passage for each answer.

1 Which of the **artefacts** mentioned are <u>the oldest</u>?

2 <u>When</u> was the material **Henshilwood** found <u>originally made</u>?

3 What <u>two common materials</u> did ancient humans use to obtain their **ochre**?

2.2 Look at the remaining questions, 4–6. Underline the words that will help you locate the information in the passage and highlight the details you need to find. Then answer the questions.

4	What did the ancient people use to keep their ochre mixture in?
5	Nowadays, who makes use of ochre?
6	Apart from painting, what else might ancient humans have used ochre for?

3 Notes/flow-chart/diagram completion

The questions in **3.1** all focus on paraphrase. Paraphrase is the use of different words with the same meaning. This helps to test how much of the Reading passage you understand.

3.1 Look again at Questions 4–6.

1. For Question 4, which word/s in the passage mean the same as 'keep … in'?
2. For Question 5, which word in the passage helped you to identify what happens 'nowadays'?
3. For Question 6, which word/s in the passage mean the same as 'used for'?

Sentence completion questions also test your ability to find specific details or information in the passage. You must fill in the gaps in the sentences with appropriate words from the passage. The sentences will paraphrase the words and ideas. They also contain details that help you find the part you need to read in detail.

3.2 Spend 30 seconds skim reading the next part of the Reading passage to get the general meaning.

> The Blombos Cave discovery is the earliest-known example of a pigment- or paint-producing workshop. All of the materials were discovered at the same site, and they included an array of raw materials including samples of bone and charcoal, as well as pigment-producing equipment such as grindstones and hammerstones. Judging by the equipment, which shows signs of wear, Henshilwood and his team were able to deduce the process used to produce the ochre mixture.
>
> First, the pieces of ochre were rubbed on quartzite slabs and crushed to produce a red powder. This was combined with ground-up mammal bone, the traces of which show signs that it was heated before being ground. The ochre powder and the bone pieces were mixed with charcoal, stone chips, quartz grains and a liquid (perhaps water) and was then transferred to abalone shells to be gently stirred before being ready for application.

3.3 Look at the sentence completion task below. Find words in the passage in 3.2 that are paraphrases of the underlined words.

> *Choose* ***NO MORE THAN THREE WORDS*** *from the passage for each answer.*
>
> **1** Two <u>ingredients</u> used to make paint found in the cave were .... and ....
>
> **2** Two examples of <u>tools</u> used to <u>make</u> the <u>paint</u> that were found in the cave are .... and ....
>
> **3** The <u>scientists</u> used the .... on the equipment to help <u>work out how</u> the paint was made.

3.4 Carefully read the text, before and after the words you have found. Then complete Questions 1–3.

> **Test Tip** Make sure you read the whole passage so that you can locate any key words and paraphrases from the questions. Take highlighter pens into the exam with you. Use a different colour for each task, to highlight important parts of the text. This will help save time when checking answers.

Flow-chart and Note completion tasks

A **flow chart** is a diagram that shows the sequence of events in a process. In **flow-chart completion** questions, the information may not be presented in the same order as in the passage.

3.5 Study the flow-chart completion task below. For Questions 1–6, decide what type of information you need to find.

1 *a noun – something colourful that is created by rubbing ochre against quartzite*

Choose ***ONE WORD ONLY*** *from the passage for each answer.*

How pigment was made in ancient times

A <u>colourful</u> **1**.. was <u>created</u> by rubbing the ochre against <u>pieces of</u> quartzite

↓

Animal bones were **2** .... and then <u>crushed</u> and added to the ochre

↓

The bones and ochre were mixed with <u>other solids</u> and <u>the researchers</u> believe **3** .... was then added

↓

The mixture was <u>poured into</u> **4** .... then <u>mixed</u> by hand

↓

The final mixture was ready to use for either **5** .... of walls or as an early type of **6** .... for <u>the body</u>

3.6 Look at the **two** Reading passages in 1.1 and 3.2. Which words or ideas are paraphrases of the underlined words in the flow chart? Highlight the parts you need to read in detail.

3.7 Carefully read the passages in 1.1 and 3.2 and complete the flow chart. Make sure you use ONE WORD ONLY from the passages.

> **Test Tip** If you are asked to choose **ONE WORD ONLY** from the passage, make sure you do not add extra information such as adjectives or adverbs (e.g. ~~bone~~ *tools;* ~~*abalone*~~ *shells;* ~~*gently*~~ *stirred*) or articles (~~*the*~~ *ochre*). If you write more than one word, your answer will be marked as wrong.

Note completion tasks are similar to flow-chart completion, but may cover a larger part of the Reading passage. Again, the information may not be presented in the same order as the information in the passage. Use the headings in the notes to help you find the information in the passage.

3.8 Study the note completion task below. For Questions 1–7, decide what type of information you need to find.

1 *a specific year or the date when digging began*

2, 3, 4 ....

5 ....

6 ....

7 ....

Complete the notes below.

*Choose **NO MORE THAN ONE WORD AND/OR A NUMBER** from the passage.*

Blombos Cave discovery

Background
- location: South Africa
- the date <u>digging</u> began: **1** ....

- Previous <u>ancient objects</u> found in this area
  - **2** ....
  - **3** ....
  - **4** ....

Recent findings
- a mixture containing a substance called **5** .... (used to provide colour)
- equipment
- a <u>range</u> of additional **6** .... including animal bone and charcoal

Conclusion
- in prehistoric times, humans <u>knew basic</u> **7** ....

3.9 Read the passages in 1.1 and 3.2 and complete the notes. Use the same techniques you have learned from previous exercises.

Diagram completion tasks

In **labelling a diagram** tasks, you will see a diagram and a description of a process. You need to carefully read the part of the passage that describes the process and complete the diagram with words from the passage.

3.10 Look at the diagram. Try to imagine how the hydropower plant would work. Pay attention to how the parts are connected.

Write ***ONE WORD ONLY*** from the text for each answer.

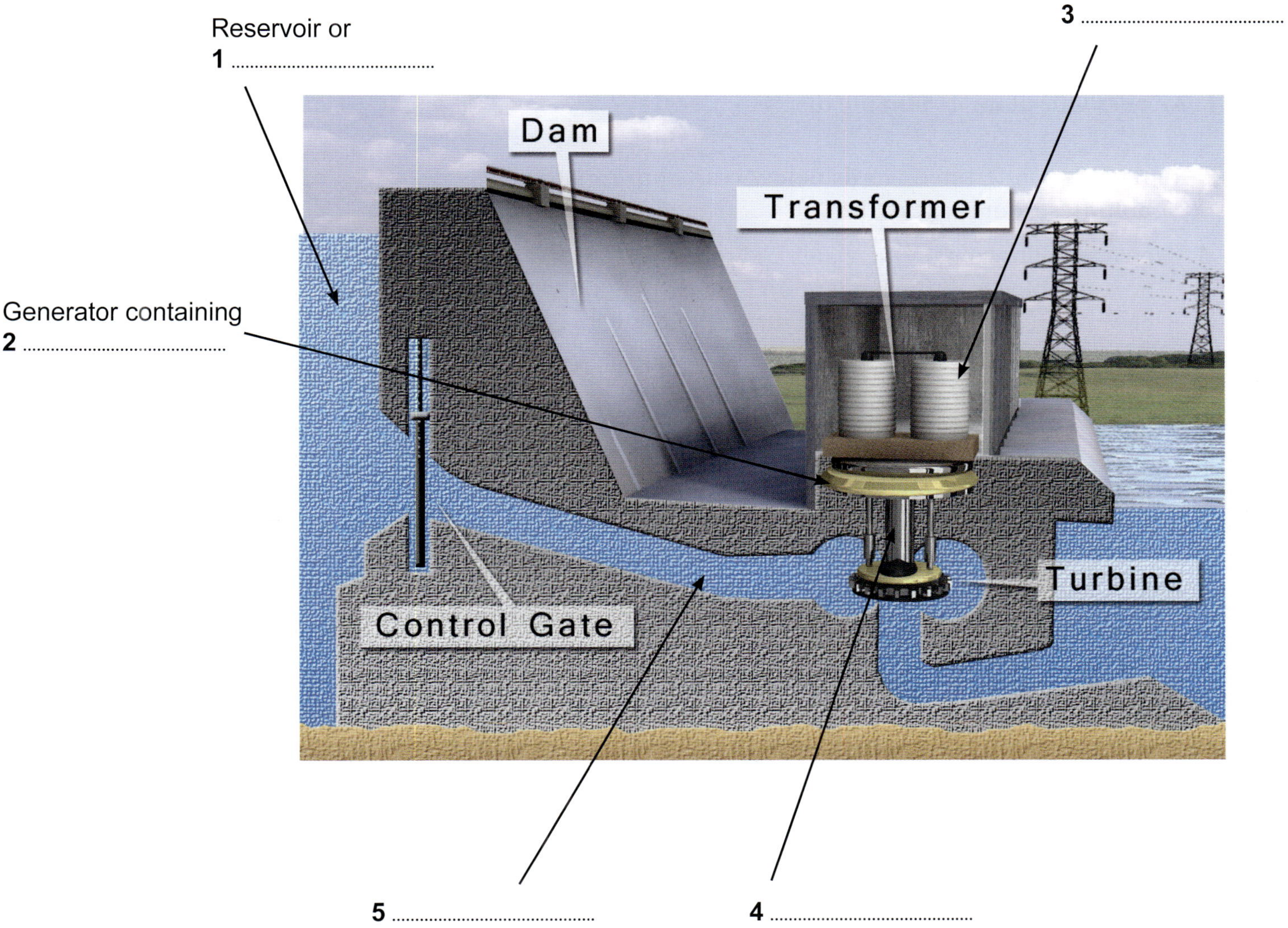

3.11 Read the passage and underline the words that are already marked on the diagram.

The power of water

Most hydropower plants rely on a dam that holds back water, creating a large reservoir behind it. Often, this reservoir is used as a recreational lake and is also known as the intake. Gates on the dam open and gravity pulls the water through the penstock, a line of pipe that leads to the turbine. Water builds up pressure as it flows through this pipe. The water strikes and turns the large blades of a turbine, which is attached to a generator above it by way of a shaft. As the turbine blades turn, so do a series of magnets inside the generator producing alternating current (AC) by moving electrons. The transformer, located inside the powerhouse, takes the AC and converts it to higher-voltage current.

3.12 Answer Questions 1–5 on the diagram.

3.13 Replace the underlined words below with appropriate paraphrases from the text.

1 The dam <u>helps contain</u> the water and <u>produces</u> a reservoir.
2 The water <u>moves</u> through a pipe and <u>increases in</u> pressure.
3 The water <u>rotates</u> the blades of a turbine that is <u>connected</u> to a generator.
4 The transformer <u>changes</u> the AC current <u>into</u> a more powerful one.

Reading skills

3 Understanding the main ideas

In this unit you will practise:

- distinguishing main ideas from supporting ideas
- understanding the main points
- identifying information in a Reading passage
- matching headings
- multiple choice
- True / False / Not Given

1 Identifying the main idea

In the IELTS Reading paper, you may be asked to match a list of headings with the correct paragraph or section of a passage. The headings summarise the main idea of the paragraph or section.

The passage may be divided into paragraphs or sections (i.e. with more than one paragraph in a section). **Matching headings** questions are always placed before the passage on the question paper.

1.1 Read headings i–vii. What topic do all of the headings have in common? Underline the main points in each heading.

List of headings

i The future of urban planning in America
ii Conflicting ideas through the history of urban planning
iii Urban planning has a long and varied history
iv Financial problems helped spread an urban planning concept
v The background to one particular planned community
vi Political change obstructs progress in urban planning
vii An urban plan to reduce traffic

Test Tip Use this approach when matching headings.

1. Read the headings so that you are familiar with them.
2. Skim read the whole passage to get the overall meaning.
3. Read the first paragraph and decide which headings might fit.
4. Re-read the paragraph and choose the heading that best summarises it.
5. Repeat steps 3 and 4 for the remaining paragraphs.

1.2 Skim read the passage below to get the overall meaning.

Planned communities: garden cities

A

The notion of planning entire communities prior to their construction is an ancient one. In fact, one of the earliest such cities on record is Miletus, Greece, which was built in the 4th century BC. Throughout the Middle Ages and the Renaissance, various planned communities (both theoretical and actual) were conceived. Leonardo da Vinci designed several cities that were never constructed. Following the Great Fire of London in 1666, the architect Christopher Wren created a new master plan for the city, incorporating park land and urban space. Several 18th-century cities, including Washington D.C., New York City, and St Petersburg, Russia, were built according to comprehensive planning.

B

One of the most important planned city concepts, the Garden City Movement, arose in the latter part of the 19th century as a reaction to the pollution and crowding of the Industrial Revolution. In 1898, Ebenezer Howard published the book *To-Morrow: A Peaceful Path to Real Reform* in which he laid out his ideas concerning the creation of new economically viable towns. Howard believed that these towns should be limited in size and density, and surrounded with a belt of undeveloped land. The idea gained enough attention and financial backing to lead to the creation of Letchworth, in Hertfordshire, England. This was the first such 'Garden City'. After the First World War, the second town built following Howard's ideas, Welwyn Garden City, was constructed.

C

In the early 1920s, American architects Clarence Stein and Henry Wright, inspired by Howard's ideas and the success of Letchworth and Welwyn, created the city of Radburn, New Jersey. Conceived as a community which would be safe for children, Radburn was intentionally designed so that the residents would not require automobiles. Several urban planning designs were pioneered at Radburn that would influence later planned communities, including the separation of pedestrians and vehicles, and the use of 'superblocks', each of which shared 23 acres of commonly held parkland.

D

In America, following the stock market crash of 1929, there was great demand for both affordable housing and employment for workers who had lost their jobs. In direct response to this, in 1935 President Roosevelt created the Resettlement Administration, which brought about a total of three greenbelt towns: Greenbelt, Maryland; Greenhills, Ohio; and Greendale, Wisconsin. These towns contained many of the elements of the Garden City Movement developments, including the use of superblocks and a 'green belt' of undeveloped land surrounding the community.

1.3 Read Paragraph A and choose the best summary:

A Past, present and future examples of urban planning
B The history of urban planning
C Problems associated with urban planning

1.4 Create a shortlist of possible answers for Paragraph A.

1 Decide which headings (i–vii) you can confidently say are not connected to the main topic of paragraph A.
2 Look at your shortlist again and choose the heading that best summarises **the main idea of all of paragraph A.**

1.5 Read Paragraphs B–D again, and repeat the steps above.

1.6 Look again at headings i–vii. For headings i, ii and vi, explain why they don't match any paragraphs.

Test Tip Don't try to match words in the headings to words in the passage. You need to focus on the whole idea of each paragraph.

2 Understanding the main points

Another type of question that can focus on the main point of a paragraph is multiple choice. This type of question often requires you to carefully read more than one sentence in the paragraph.

2.1 Look at this question, based on the passage in 1.2.

1 In Paragraph A, what is the main point that the writer makes?

A Some urban designs are better in theory than in practice.
B The urban-planning concept itself is not restricted to modern times.
C Urban planning should be carried out by professionals.
D Some planned ancient cities are more successful than modern ones.

2.2 **The parts of Paragraph A relating to each option are underlined below. Read the paragraph carefully and choose the correct option, A–D.**

[B] The notion of planning entire communities prior to their construction is an ancient one. [D] In fact, one of the earliest such cities on record is Miletus, Greece, which was built in the 4th century BC. [A/D] Throughout the Middle Ages and the Renaissance, various planned communities (both theoretical and actual) were conceived. [C] Leonardo da Vinci designed several cities that were never constructed. Following the Great Fire of London in 1666, the architect Christopher Wren created a new master plan for the city that incorporated park land and urban space. [C] Several 18th-century cities, including Washington D.C., New York City, and St Petersburg, Russia, were built according to comprehensive planning.

2.3 **Read the questions below. Underline the parts of the passage that each question relates to. Then read the text in detail and choose the correct letter, A–D.**

2 According to the second paragraph, the Garden City Movement
A came just before the Industrial Revolution.
B was held back by a war and a lack of funds.
C resulted in cities that were larger than they had been before.
D was designed to combat problems caused by modernisation.

3 What was one aim in designing the city of Radburn?

A to create something totally different from cities elsewhere.
B to reduce the danger for families living in the area.
C to make sure people could park their cars close to their home.
D to increase green spaces by designing houses with gardens.

4 What do the towns of Greenbelt, Greenhills and Greendale all have in common?

A The residents were affected by the stock market collapse.
B The towns were built for the wealthiest people in America.
C The towns were each surrounded by natural parkland.
D They were all constructed in the same year.

3 Identifying information in a passage

For **True / False / Not Given** tasks, you need to look at a list of sentences or statements and decide whether they are:

- **True** (the statement agrees with the information in the text)
- **False** (the statement is incorrect and does not agree with the information in the text)
- **Not Given** (you cannot say whether the statement is true or false because there is no information about this in the text)

> **Test Tip** Remember that you are being tested on your ability to understand the information you read **in the passage**. So you should ignore anything you already know about the topic.

3.1 Skim read this passage to get the general idea of the content.

Urban heat

In 1818, Luke Howard published *The Climate of London* in which he identified an emerging problem: urban development was having a direct impact on the local weather. The early 1800s was a time of great expansion for London and [1] Howard noticed that temperatures in the city were gradually becoming higher than those in rural areas. We now refer to these areas as Urban Heat Islands. [2] The difference in temperature is usually greater at night and the phenomenon occurs in both winter and summer. [3] Experts agree that this is due to urban development, when open green spaces are replaced with asphalt roads and tall brick or concrete buildings. These materials retain heat generated by the Sun and release it through the night. In Atlanta, in the US, this has even led to thunderstorms occurring in the morning rather than, as is more common, in the afternoon. Officials there are advising builders to use light-coloured roofs in a bid to reduce the problem.

Large cities around the world are adopting strategies to combat this issue and it is not uncommon to find plants growing on top of roofs or down the walls of large buildings. In Singapore, the government has pledged to transform it into a 'city within a garden' and, in 2006, they held an international competition calling for entries to develop a master plan to help bring this about. One outcome was the creation of 18 'Supertrees'. These metal constructions are made to resemble very tall trees and range in height from 25m to 50m. Each one is a vertical freestanding garden and is home to exotic plants and ferns. Their structure allowed the designers to create an immediate rainforest canopy without having to wait for trees to reach such heights. They contain solar panels used to light the trees at night and also containers to collect rainwater, making them truly self-sufficient.

3.2 Decide if statements 1–3 are *True, False* or *Not Given* according to the underlined parts of the text.

1. Luke Howard invented the term 'Urban Heat Island'.
2. City temperatures are higher than country temperatures regardless of the season.
3. Experts have failed in their efforts to create heat-reflecting concrete and brick.

3.3 Read statements 4–8, then underline the relevant parts in the text. Are the statements *True, False* or *Not Given*?

4. Atlanta has experienced more dramatic weather change than other areas of the US.
5. Roofs that are dark in colour help address the issue of Urban Heat Islands.
6. Singapore's Supertrees are made entirely from natural materials.
7. The designers of the Supertrees originally planned to plant very tall trees.
8. The Supertrees require regular maintenance.

3.4 Read statements 1–8 again and correct any that were false.

Reading skills

4 Locating and matching information

In this unit you will practise:

- identifying types of information
- locating and matching information
- connecting ideas
- matching sentence endings
- matching information

1 Identifying types of information

For **matching information** tasks, you need to locate an idea or piece of information in the text and match it to a phrase that accurately describes it.

1.1 Read the extracts from two separate paragraphs of a Reading passage. What type of information has been underlined?

A a description of an animal's habitat
B the issues that can cause something to happen
C an argument for a type of action

A	B
Meerkats devote a significant part of their day to foraging for food with their sensitive noses. When they find it, they eat on the spot. Primarily, meerkats are insectivores, which means their diet is mainly made up of insects.	These animals are transient by nature and move if their food is in short supply or if they're forced out by a stronger gang. The group's dominant male, the alpha male, marks the group's territory to protect the boundary from rivals and predators.

1.2 Look at this matching information task based on the extracts above.

Which paragraph contains the following information?

1 two situations that force meerkats to change where they live
2 how meerkats generally spend their time

1 For this type of question, do you need to look for individual words or a whole idea?

2 Question 1 matches the information underlined in the paragraph above, so the answer is B. Underline the part of paragraph A that matches the information in Question 2.

These questions **describe the information** you need to find.

1.3 Look at extracts A–H from different Reading passages and match them to the type of information that best describes them.

A Water is forced at pressure through a narrow pipe. The water hits the top of the water wheel, causing it to turn.	**B** The water is warm thanks to a natural hot spring beneath the riverbed.	**C** Our study looked at the surrounding environment while previous researchers have concentrated on diet.	**D** We achieved this by weighing the animals both before and after periods of exercise.
E They live in dark, humid areas and so tend to be found in and around tropical rainforests.	**F** A month later, we were able to test it again and the results showed a significant change in temperature when the insulation was used.	**G** After ten years, they gave up. The experiment had failed and, as a result, the public grew angry at the waste of public funds.	**H** It takes 35 days for the chick to leave the nest and fly.

Types of information

1 the findings of a study
2 the method used in a research study
3 the reaction to something
4 a description of a habitat
5 the difference between current and past studies
6 a description of how something works
7 the cause of something
8 the amount of time needed for something

2 Locating and matching information

Just like matching headings, **matching information** questions are not in the same order as the passage.

Study Tip Some examples of the type of information you may be asked to find are:

- a number
- a date
- a measurement
- a reason
- a cause
- an effect
- a conclusion
- the problems
- a finding
- an account
- a reaction
- a description.

When you are reading different passages in this book, think about whether the information matches any of these types.

2.1 **Spend two minutes skim reading the passage below, so that you are familiar with the type of information it contains.**

What is the main purpose of the passage?

A to describe the habitat and eating habits of one specific animal
B to explain the background to a proposed study into tropical animals
C to argue that scientists can learn a great deal from studying nature
D to give the findings of new research into an animal's behaviour

How geckos cope with wet feet

A Geckos are remarkable little lizards, clinging to almost any dry surface, and Alyssa Stark, from the University of Akron, US, explains that they appear to be equally happy scampering through tropical rainforest canopies as they are in urban settings. 'A lot of gecko studies look at the very small adhesive structures on their toes to understand how the system works at the most basic level', says Stark. She adds that the animals grip surfaces with microscopic hairs on the soles of their feet, which make close enough contact to be attracted to the surface by the minute forces between atoms.

B However, she and her colleagues Timothy Sullivan and Peter Niewiarowski were curious about how the lizards cope on surfaces in their natural habitat. Explaining that previous studies had focused on the reptiles clinging to artificial dry surfaces, Stark says 'We know they are in tropical environments that probably have a lot of rain and geckos don't suddenly fall out of the trees when it's wet'. Yet, the animals do seem to have trouble getting a grip on smooth, wet, artificial surfaces, sliding down wet vertical glass after several steps. The team decided to find out how geckos with wet feet cope on both wet and dry surfaces.

C First, they had to find out how well their geckos clung onto glass with dry feet. Fitting a tiny harness around the lizard's pelvis and gently lowering the animal onto a plate of smooth glass, Stark and Sullivan allowed the animal to become well attached before connecting the harness to a tiny motor and gently pulling the lizard until it came unstuck. The geckos hung on tenaciously, and only came unstuck at forces of around 20N – about 20 times their own body weight. 'In my view, the gecko attachment system is over-designed,' says Stark.

D Next, the trio sprayed the glass plate with a mist of water and re-tested the lizards, but this time the animals had problems holding tight. The droplets were interfering with the lizards' attachment mechanism, but it wasn't clear how. And when the team immersed the geckos in a bath of room-temperature water with a smooth glass bottom, the animals were completely unable to anchor themselves to the smooth surface. 'The toes are super-hydrophobic,' (i.e. water repellent) explains Stark, who could see a silvery bubble of air around their toes. But, they were unable to displace the water around their feet to make the tight contact that usually keeps the geckos in place.

E Then the team tested the lizard's adhesive forces on the dry surface when their feet had been soaking for 90 minutes, and found that the lizards could barely hold on, detaching when they were pulled with a force roughly equalling their own weight. 'That might be the sliding behaviour that we see when the geckos climb vertically up misted glass', says Stark. So, geckos climbing on wet surfaces with damp feet are constantly on the verge of slipping and Stark adds that when the soggy lizards were faced with the misted and immersed horizontal surfaces, they slipped as soon as the rig started pulling. Therefore geckos can walk on wet surfaces, as long as their feet are reasonably dry. However, as soon as their feet get wet, they are barely able to hang on, and the team is keen to understand how long it takes geckos to recover from a drenching.

2.2 Look at this task based on the Reading passage. For each question, underline the type of information you need to scan for. The first two have been done for you.

> *Which paragraph contains the following information?*
>
> *N.B. You may use any letter more than once*
>
> *Write the correct letter, A–E, next to questions 1–7 below.*
>
> **1** visual evidence of the gecko's ability to resist water
>
> **2** a question that is yet to be answered by the researchers
>
> **3** the method used to calculate the gripping power of geckos
>
> **4** the researcher's opinion of the gecko's gripping ability
>
> **5** a mention of the different environments where geckos can be found
>
> **6** the contrast between Stark's research and the work of other researchers
>
> **7** the definition of a scientific term

2.3 It is important to fully understand what you are looking for in the passage. Answer these questions, based on Question 1 in the task above.

1 Which of the following do you think is 'visual evidence'?

- **A** something the researchers believe
- **B** something the researchers have seen
- **C** something the researchers have read about

2 Which of the following means the same as 'ability to resist water'?

- **A** soaks up water
- **B** sinks in water
- **C** stops water getting in

3 Scan the passage to find 'visual evidence' of an ability to resist water. Which paragraph contains this information?

Test Tip Make sure to note any plurals in the questions (e.g. ***two** examples of the different **environments***, etc). There may be parts of the passage that refer to only one of the things mentioned, so you need to find the paragraph that has more than one.

2.4 Study Questions 2–7 in 2.2 carefully and match them to paragraphs A–E. Remember, the questions are not in the same order as the passage. This is because your task is to find out where the information is.

2.5 Look again at Questions 2–7 and underline the parts of the passage that gave you your answer.

3 How ideas are connected

Another type of question that requires you to match information is **matching sentence endings.** For this type of task, you need to understand how ideas are connected within the Reading passage.

3.1 Complete each sentence below with the correct ending, A–F.

1 When I pressed the switch,
2 If you heat ice,
3 The respondents to the survey
4 Children who attend small schools
5 Parents with overactive children

A all came from similar economic backgrounds.
B tend to need more sleep at night.
C the light came on.
D reported that she has been successful.
E generally get more individual attention.
F it melts.

You were able to complete this task using only logic and your knowledge of grammar. In the IELTS Reading paper, you can do this to confirm or check your answers, but you will **not** be able to answer the questions without reading the passage.

3.2 Look at these matching sentence endings questions based on the passage in 2.1. Try using these techniques to answer the questions.

1 Scan the passage in **2.1** to locate the information in the sentence beginnings (1–4).

2 Read the relevant part of the passage carefully, then choose the best sentence ending (A–F).

1 Other researchers have aimed to discover how

2 The work of Stark and her team is different because they wanted to find out how

3 Stark's experiments revealed that

4 The researchers would still like to know when

A geckos struggle to grip onto dry glass as well as wet glass.
B the gripping mechanism of geckos actually works.
C geckos have a weaker gripping mechanism than previously thought.
D geckos are able to grip in rainforest settings.
E geckos are able to recover their gripping abilities after getting wet.
F geckos can grip more easily if their feet are not damp.

Reading skills

5 Discursive passages

In this unit you will practise:

- reading discursive passages
- identifying theories and opinions
- matching features

1 Discursive passages

The texts in the Reading paper gradually become more difficult. They may present contrasting points in an argument or explain a complex theory. All Reading passages contain cohesive devices to help explain how the ideas are connected together.

1.1 Write the cohesive devices in the box into the correct column of the table to show why a writer would use them.

~~moreover~~	such as	although	for instance	
indeed	therefore	despite	consequently	
in spite of	in addition	thus	as a result	
similarly	to illustrate this	nonetheless	in fact	
whilst	hence	furthermore	though	

to add more / clarify a point	to show contrast / present the opposite view	to give an example	to draw a conclusion / introduce a result
moreover			

1.2 Skim read the passage below. Find nine of the cohesive devices from the table in 1.1.

Aesop's fable 'The crow and the pitcher' more fact than fiction

New research indicates that rooks, members of the crow family, are able to solve complex problems using tools.

In Aesop's fictional fable 'The crow and the pitcher', a thirsty crow uses stones to raise the level of water in a jug to quench its thirst. A recent study demonstrates that rooks, birds belonging to the *corvid* (or crow) family, are in fact able to solve complex problems using tools and can easily master the same technique used in the story.

Christopher Bird of the University of Cambridge, who led the study, highlighted the importance of the findings, stating: 'Corvids are remarkably intelligent, and in many ways rival the great apes in their physical intelligence and ability to solve problems. The only other animal known to complete a similar task is the orang-utan. This is remarkable considering their brain is so different to the great apes. Although it has been speculated in folklore, empirical tests are needed to examine the extent of their intelligence and how they solve problems.'

In their first experiment, the researchers varied the height of the water in a tube and the four rooks, which were the subject of the research, used stones to raise the water level to reach a worm floating on top. The clever birds proved very adept and were highly successful, regardless of the starting level of the water or the number of the stones needed. Two of the birds were successful on their first attempt in raising the water to the correct height whilst the other two birds needed a second try.

In addition to the speed with which they completed the task, the birds were also highly accurate in their ability, adding the exact number of stones needed to reach the worm. Furthermore, rather than attempting to reach the worm after each stone was dropped in, they apparently estimated the number needed from the outset, and waited until the appropriate water level was reached before dipping their beaks into the tube.

In the second experiment, the rooks were presented with stones that varied in size. Here, the rooks selected larger stones over smaller ones (though they didn't do this straight away). The scientists speculate that the birds quickly realised that the larger stones displaced more water, and they were thus able to obtain the reward more quickly than by using small stones.

According to the team, in the final experiment, the rooks recognised that sawdust could not be manipulated in the same manner as water. Therefore, when presented with the choice between a tube half-filled with either sawdust or water, rooks dropped the pebbles into the tube containing water and not the sawdust.

Despite the fact that the study clearly demonstrates the flexible nature of tool use in rooks, they are not believed to use tools in the wild. 'Wild tool use appears to be dependent on motivation,' remarked Bird. 'Rooks do not use tools in the wild because they do not need to, not because they can't. They have access to other food that can be acquired without using tools.' As Bird noted, that fits nicely with Aesop's maxim, demonstrated by the crow: 'Necessity is the mother of invention.'

1.3 Read the passage again and complete sentences 1–6 with endings A–H.

1 A new study has actually

2 The intelligence of birds has been suggested in stories, but

3 Half of the birds in the experiment were immediately successful; however,

4 The birds promptly realised the advantage of using big stones, and so

5 The research showed rooks can use tools with ease, though

6 The rooks worked out the properties of different materials and as a result,

A	others needed several attempts.
B	experts think that they don't do this in their natural habitat.
C	they achieved their goal sooner.
D	confirmed a fictional account.
E	helped us to understand a mysterious event.
F	only scientific studies can prove this.
G	they were able to protect themselves.
H	consistently rejected one particular type.

Study Tip There are several ways of linking ideas in a text. Look at the following examples: *the findings*; *This is remarkable ...*; *Here, the rooks ...* .

Remember, it is important to study all aspects of language when preparing for the IELTS exam. As you read through longer, complex passages, try to be aware of how the ideas are connected. This can also help improve your writing.

1.4 Find synonyms in the passage for the cohesive devices that are underlined in questions 1–6.

2 Identifying theories and opinions

Many academic texts contain the theories or views of different people or experts. Direct quotations are easily recognised by quotation marks, but a person's views or ideas can also be referred to indirectly.

In this extract from the Reading passage. the verbs *highlighted* and *stated* are both used to draw attention to the words of Christopher Bird.

Christopher Bird of the University of Cambridge, who led the study, highlighted the importance of the findings, stating: 'Corvids are remarkably intelligent, and in many ways rival the great apes in their physical intelligence and ability to solve problems.'

Bird's views could also be expressed indirectly.

2.1 Which verb in this sentence tells us that this is Bird's view and not the writer's?

Christopher Bird of the University of Cambridge, who led the study, believes that Corvids are remarkably intelligent, and in many ways rival the great apes in their physical intelligence and ability to solve problems.

2.2 Find three more verbs and one preposition in the passage that refer to the views or theories of an expert.

2.3 Statements A–F paraphrase opinions or theories that appear in the Reading passage. Match them to the same idea in the passage, then put them in the order they appear.

A We imagine that the rooks were soon able to appreciate the advantage of using different-sized tools.

B Tool use in rooks demonstrates a common English saying.

C Using tools in their natural habitat is simply not necessary for rooks.

D Rooks are as intelligent as the most intelligent of animals.

E In their natural setting, rooks can obtain food without using tools.

F The ability of rooks is surprising, given the lack of similarities between the brains of birds and mammals.

Study Tip Look online or find out if your local library has copies of international newspapers and magazines. Read the Education, Health or Science sections of newspapers such as *The Times*, *The Guardian*, *The Australian*, *The New Zealand Herald*, *The New Yorker* and *The Washington Post* for reports on academic studies.

3 Matching features

Matching features tasks are used with Reading passages that contain theories or comments about different people, places, years and things.

For these tasks, the different options are listed in a box and you need to match them to the questions (sentences that paraphrase the information in the passage). The questions will **not** be in the same order as the passage.

For some questions, you may need to match a person to a study or an action, rather than a theory or opinion.

3.1 Scan the passage on the following page for these names and highlight them each time they appear.

- Page 1
- Lieberman
- Gray

3.2 Look at the following statements (Questions 1–5) and the list of researchers below. Match each statement with the correct researcher, A, B or C.

Researchers
A Pagel
B Lieberman
C Gray

1 We are able to recognise certain words used by people in other cultures.
2 Regardless of what happens in the world, there appear to be fixed rules that govern the way words alter over time.
3 Words that don't follow a standard pattern will remain that way if they are used often.
4 Certain words have kept a similar sound across many years and many countries.
5 We focused on the historical changes that have occurred in one particular language.

3.3 Put Questions 1–5 in the order they appear in the passage.

Test Tip For matching features tasks, the questions will not be in the same order as in the passage. The people mentioned may appear in several different sections. You need to scan the whole passage carefully. Some of the people in the list may be distractors, and you may not need to use all of the letters.

3.4 Remember that some of the questions are based on comments made about the researchers.

1 For which question in 3.2 did you need to match a person to the study that they carried out?

2 Which verbs in the text are used to show that a person other than the writer expressed a particular theory or idea?

3.5 For further practice in matching sentence endings, complete sentences 1–3 with endings A–E.

1 For a long time, language experts have asked why
2 The English verb 'help' proves that
3 While cultures vary a great deal around the world,

A regular and irregular verbs change at different rates.
B there are surprising similarities in the way different languages evolve.
C eventually, some irregular verbs become regular.
D some words stay the same over hundreds of years while others change quite quickly.
E some verbs gradually become irregular over time.

Maths shows why words persist over time

In a finding that parallels the evolution of genes, researchers have shown that the more frequently a word is used, the less likely it is to change over long periods of time.

The question of why some words evolve rapidly through time while others are preserved – often with the same meaning in multiple languages – has long plagued linguists. Two independent teams of researchers have tackled this question from different angles, each arriving at a remarkably similar conclusion.

"The frequency with which specific words are used in everyday language exerts a general and law-like influence on their rates of evolution," writes Mark Pagel, author of one of two studies published this week.

Anyone who has tried to learn English will have been struck by its excess of stubbornly irregular verbs, which render grammatical rules unreliable. The past tense of regular verbs is formed by adding the suffix '-ed', but this luxury is not afforded to their irregular kin. Over time, however, some irregular verbs 'regularise'. For instance, the past tense of 'help' used to be 'holp', but now it is 'helped'.

Mathematician Erez Lieberman, from Harvard University in Massachusetts, US, performed a quantitative study of the rate at which English verbs such as 'help' have become more regular with time. Of the list of 177 irregular verbs they took from Old English, only 98 are still irregular today. Amazingly, the changes they observed obey a very precise mathematical description: the half-life of an irregular verb is proportional to the square root of its frequency. In other words, they found that the more an irregular verb is used, the longer it will remain irregular.

A separate group of academics, led by evolutionary biologist Mark Pagel from the University of Reading, in the UK, used a statistical modelling technique to study the evolution of words from 87 different Indo-European languages.

"Throughout its 8,000-year history, all Indo-European-language speakers have used a related sound to communicate the idea of 'two' objects – duo, due, deux, dos, etc." Pagel commented. "But," he adds, "there are many different and unrelated sounds for the idea of, for example, a bird – uccello, oiseau, pouli, pajaro, vogel, etc."

Before now, however, nobody had proposed a mechanism for why some words should evolve more quickly than others. According to Pagel, "our research helps us to understand why we can still understand bits of Chaucer [a medieval poet]" and points out that this likely explains "why we can instinctively recognise words in other Indo-European languages, just from their sounds".

Psychologist and language expert Russell Gray, from the University of Auckland in New Zealand, was impressed by both findings.

"Despite all the vagaries and contingencies of human history, it seems that there are remarkable regularities in the processes of language change," he commented.

Reading skills

6 Multiple-choice questions

In this unit you will practise:

- understanding longer pieces of text
- different types of multiple-choice questions
- answering multiple-choice questions
- identifying a writer's purpose

1 Understanding longer pieces of text

To answer **multiple choice questions**, you often need to carefully read two or more connected sentences or several connected sentences.

1.1 Look at this extract from an IELTS Reading passage. Read it quickly to find out the main points and then re-read it more carefully to get a more detailed understanding.

> Linguists agree that language is needed during reading, but at which stage language becomes a necessity has come under debate. Past research has shown that animals have the ability to discriminate letters from one another, but previously, experts thought the ability to recognise written words was dependent on an ability to understand language. Findings recently published in the journal *Science* challenge this long-held notion, showing that despite having no linguistic skills, monkeys are able to tell the difference between sequences of letters that form real English words, and those that do not.

1.2 Without looking back at the extract, try to explain what it is about, in your own words.

Some multiple-choice questions begin with a direct question and then have four possible answers. Some begin with an incomplete sentence and then have four possible endings.

1.3 Look at the question below and choose the best answer, A–D.

1 According to the paragraph, what point do linguists have different views on?

A animals are intelligent enough to learn how to read
B our ability to read words is linked to our writing ability
C when our language ability begins to affect reading ability
D when early humans developed the ability to read and write

2 Different types of multiple choice

Sometimes you may be asked to choose two correct answers from five options. You will need to read and consider even more text.

2.1 Spend 45 seconds skim reading this Reading passage to find out the main points.

What do hurricanes mean for dolphins?

Hurricanes are typically associated with loss of life, loss of property and economic devastation. Hurricane Katrina, which blew through the gulf coast of North America in 2005, brought all those things and more. It also brought lots of baby dolphins. Hurricanes tend to be related to increased strandings of marine mammals, so why might a hurricane be associated with *more* dolphins, rather than fewer?

Scientist Lance J. Miller reasoned that there were probably several related phenomena that, combined, could explain the apparent increase. Firstly, after a female dolphin loses her calf, she can give birth again much sooner than if her calf had matured to adulthood. "If a large number of calves perished as a result of Hurricane Katrina, this would allow for a greater percentage of females to become reproductively active the following year." By itself, this didn't seem to adequately explain the increase in dolphin calves. Something else was going on. That something was distinctively human.

When Hurricane Katrina blew through the gulf, the local shrimping, crabbing and fishing industries were ravaged. In Mississippi, according to one estimate, 87% of commercial fishing vessels were damaged or destroyed. This meant a decrease in the amount of seafood brought into shore, of nearly 15%. Despite the common notion that dolphins enjoy playing in the wakes created by boats, there is plenty of evidence that dolphins actually avoid them. Miller deduced that, with a reduction in the number of boats in the water, both commercial and recreational, dolphins may have been able to spend more time eating, and less time travelling or diving in an effort to avoid boats.

2.2 Look at this task. What information do you need to find in the passage?

*Which **TWO** possible issues did Miller believe may have caused the rise in dolphin numbers?*

A More female dolphins survived the hurricane than males.
B Female dolphins were able to breed earlier than usual.
C The dolphins had access to greater numbers of shrimp and fish.
D There was a decrease in the number of dolphins being caught for sport or food.
E The dolphins had less contact with humans after the hurricane.

2.3 Read the passage again and highlight the parts that introduce the idea of a first and second issue. Read the options A–E in 2.2 carefully and decide which two options are correct.

3 Identifying a writer's purpose

Sometimes, multiple-choice questions ask you to consider the writer's purpose or aim. You may be asked to identify:

- why the writer made a particular reference
- what the purpose of a part of the text is
- the opinion or attitude of the writer.

3.1 Look at this extract from a Reading passage to get the main idea and then re-read it more carefully to understand it in detail.

> One of the reasons *Jurassic Park* was so successful – as a novel and a blockbuster film – is that it presented a plausible way to bring dinosaurs back to life. The idea that viable dinosaur DNA might be retrieved from bloodsucking prehistoric insects seemed like a project that could actually succeed. Even though the actual methodology is hopelessly flawed and would never work, the premise was science-ish enough to let us suspend our disbelief and revel in the return of the dinosaurs.

3.2 Read these questions and consider how you would answer them.

1 What is the writer's purpose in this paragraph?
2 What is the writer's opinion of *Jurassic Park*?

To answer these questions, you need to consider more than the surface meaning of the words in the Reading passage. You need to consider the writer's tone or attitude.

3.3 Scan the extract in 3.1 and find the following words or phrases: *blockbuster, hopelessly flawed, revel in*. Do they suggest a positive or a negative tone?

3.4 Answer the questions by choosing the correct letter (A, B, C or D).

1 What is the writer's purpose in this paragraph?

A to suggest that scientists should look to science fiction for inspiration
B to argue that people may choose to believe the improbable in order to be entertained
C to persuade us that art and science can be skilfully linked
D to demonstrate that scientific research can provide a source of entertainment

2 What is the writer's opinion of *Jurassic Park*?

A the film was not a faithful rendition of the original book
B it shows how important thorough research is for successful writers
C in spite of its inaccuracies, it was a successful novel and film
D it is a good example of the importance of science fact in science fiction novels

Reading skills

7 Opinions and attitudes

In this unit you will practise:

- dealing with argumentative texts
- identifying a writer's views/claims
- identifying grammatical features
- Yes / No / Not Given questions
- summary completion with a box
- summary completion without a box

1 Argumentative texts

The most difficult and complex texts are in Reading Section 3. These passages may feature arguments for or against a specific idea or theory. Or, they may present a discussion of different arguments. In texts like this, it is important to be aware of the writer's overall tone. A writer's choice of words often indicates their attitude towards a topic.

1.1 Put the adjectives into the correct column, to show whether they suggest a positive or negative tone.

diverse	disastrous	unspoilt	biased
accomplished	vulnerable	productive	realistic
confusing	irrelevant	sophisticated	harsh
catastrophic	efficient	monotonous	distorted
thorough	influential	prominent	dated

positive	negative

1.2 Spend two minutes skim reading the following passage to get the main ideas. Then read it again and underline any adjectives that you think might indicate a personal opinion or attitude.

Living with Mies

Lafayette Park is a group of modernist townhouses in the US designed by the architect Mies van der Rohe.

A few blocks east of downtown Detroit sits Lafayette Park, an enclave of single- and two-storey modernist townhouses set amid a forest of locust trees. Like hundreds of developments nationwide, they were the result of postwar urban renewal; unlike almost all of them, it had a trio of world-class designers behind it: Ludwig Hilbersheimer as urban planner; Alfred Caldwell as landscape designer; and Mies van der Rohe as architect.

The townhouses were built between 1958 and 1962 on land previously occupied by a working-class neighbourhood. While much of Detroit began a steep decline soon after, Lafayette Park stayed afloat, its residents bucking the trend of suburban flight. Lafayette Park today is one of the most racially integrated neighbourhoods in the city. It is economically stable, despite the fact that Detroit has suffered enormous population loss.

We wanted to know what residents think about this unique modernist environment created by a famous architect, and how they confront and adapt it to meet their needs. During our research, we were struck by the casual attitude that many residents have toward the architecture. Then again, Detroit has an abundance of beautiful housing options: one can live in a huge Victorian mansion, a beautiful arts and crafts house or a cavernous loft-conversion space in a former factory. Living in a townhouse built by a renowned architect isn't as noteworthy as one might think. At the same time, such nonchalance is a mark of success: the homes are great because they work, not because they come affixed with a famous name.

Indeed, their beauty isn't always obvious. There is a kind of austere uniformity to the Lafayette Park townhouses when viewed from the outside. Some visitors find them unappealing; one contractor described them as 'bunkers'. The interior layouts are nearly identical. The units are compact in size and some people find them too small, though the floor-to-ceiling windows on the front and back of each building open the living spaces to the outside.

While they may have strong aesthetic preferences, the residents we spoke with do not necessarily favour mid-century modernism in their interiors or architecture. But they make it work: several people remarked on the way the interiors in the Lafayette Park townhouses can function as blank canvases for a variety of decorating styles. Indeed, the best design doesn't force a personality on its residents. Instead, it helps them bring out their own.

2 Identifying the writer's views/claims

In **Yes / No / Not Given** tasks, you will be asked whether the statements in the questions match the views or claims of the writer. A **view** is a personal opinion. A **claim** is a statement made by the writer and presented as a fact.

2.1 Look at these extracts and decide whether you think they are *views* or *claims*.

1. Like hundreds of developments nationwide, they were the result of post-war urban renewal.
2. While much of Detroit began a steep decline soon after, Lafayette Park stayed afloat.
3. Detroit has an abundance of beautiful housing options.
4. There is a kind of austere uniformity to the Lafayette Park townhouses when viewed from the outside.
5. Indeed, the best design doesn't force a personality on its residents.

There are a lot of similarities between **True / False / Not Given** questions and **Yes / No / Not Given** questions. But the main difference is that True / False / Not Given questions are based on factual information in the Reading passage. Yes / No / Not Given questions ask you to interpret the views or claims of the writer.

2.2 Look at the statements below and write

YES if the statement agrees with the views or claims in the Reading passage,
NO if the statement contradicts the views of the writer,
NOT GIVEN if it is impossible to say what the writer thinks.

1. It is the era in which Lafayette Park was developed that makes it special.
2. Since 1962, many people have moved away from Detroit.
3. Mies van der Rohe's designs influenced other architects in Detroit.
4. The exterior of each building in Lafayette Park has a distinct style.
5. Good architecture allows its occupants to reveal their identity.

2.3 For each question in 2.2, if you wrote

YES – give supporting evidence from the passage
NO – correct the statements so that they match the views of the writer
NOT GIVEN – say what you **do** know from the passage and say which part of the passage gave you your answer.

3 Identifying grammatical features

There are two types of **summary completion** tasks: one with a box of possible answers, and one without a box, where you need to choose word/s from the passage to complete the summary.

With a box of possible answers, the options may be actual words from the passage, or synonyms of words in the passage.

3.1 Look at the box of possible answers (A–F) and decide what type of word each one is (noun, verb, etc.). There may be more than one possible answer.

A	settled
B	adapt
C	neutral
D	poor
E	afford
F	strongly

3.2 Read the summary below and decide what type of word (noun, verb, etc.) you need for gaps 1–4.

The residents of Lafayette Park

Lafayette Park was originally quite a **1** .... area of Detroit. Nowadays, the area is unusual because its residents are more **2** .... than those in other areas of the city. In general, the residents of Lafayette Park feel quite **3** .... about the famous architecture they live in. But the residents do appreciate the fact that they can **4** .... the townhouses and make them their own.

3.3 Read the relevant part of the passage in 1.2 and complete the summary using the list of words (A–F) in 3.1.

Test Tip A summary is different from a set of notes, because it consists of complete sentences that are connected together grammatically. You need to

- carefully read and understand the summary.
- decide what type of word is needed to complete each gap in the summary.
- locate and carefully read the relevant part of the passage.
- choose the word or phrase (either from a box of answers or from the passage) that accurately fills each gap.

For **summary completion tasks without a box** of answers

- consider the grammatical features of the summary.
- choose words from the text that accurately complete the summary.

Test Tip Use the title of the summary to help you find the part of the passage you need to read in detail to find your answers.

3.4 Skim read this passage to understand the main points.

Meerkat study

Dr Alex Thornton from the University of Cambridge recently led a study into meerkat society. Meerkats are highly social mongooses that live in large social groups and take turns foraging for food and standing guard to look out for predators. Research has shown that the animals have their own traditions within their group. For example, while members of one meerkat troop will consistently rise very early, those of another will emerge from their burrows much later in the morning.

In an attempt to assess whether meerkats simply copy these behavior patterns or are taught them, Thornton and his team travelled to the Kalahari Desert and set a series of tests for a group in the wild. One test involved putting a scorpion (the meerkats' favourite food) into a transparent container. The meerkats had to work out how to open the opaque lid of the container in order to reach the scorpion inside. The tests showed that the more subordinate juvenile members of meerkat troops are the most innovative when it comes to foraging - these low-ranking males were best at solving problems and obtaining the treat. However, Dr Thornton conceded that the meerkats didn't ever appear to work out that it was the opaque surface of the box that they should attack in preference to the transparent ones. So, this may simply be evidence of persistence rather than actual intelligence.

3.5 Look at this summary completion task.

1 What types of word will you need to fill in the gaps in the summary?

A recent study at Cambridge University discovered that different meerkat groups **1** .... at different times of the day. This demonstrates that each group has distinct customs. They also learned that young, male meerkats were more **2** .... than other members of their social groups when it came to problem solving. The researchers conducted an experiment where the meerkats had to try to open a container. If they did, they were rewarded with a **3** .... However, they also found that the meerkats never learned that it was the **4** .... part of the container that they needed to open.

3.6 Read the text in 3.5 carefully and choose ONE WORD ONLY from the text to complete each answer in the summary.

Test Tip For any questions where you need to write words from the passage, a hyphenated word (e.g. *long-term*) counts as one word.

Reading skills

8 General Training Reading

In this unit you will practise:

- understanding the different sections of the test
- scanning a passage for specific details
- recognising paraphrase
- dealing with multiple passages
- understanding work-related passages
- matching questions to parts of a text

1 The General Training Reading paper

The paper is divided into three sections, each with a different theme or focus.

1.1 Look at the table and the list of example texts below. Match the examples (A–H) with the correct section of the Reading paper. Write your answers in the final column of the table.

	theme	texts	examples of texts
Section 1	Social survival	up to five short factual texts	
Section 2	Workplace survival	two work-related texts that are descriptive and informational	
Section 3	General reading	one longer text that is descriptive and instructive, rather than argumentative	

Examples of texts

A staff-training manual
B train timetable
C magazine article about modern travel
D job description
E shop advertisements
F job application procedures
G an extract from a novel
H travel brochures

The Reading passages in each section gradually become more difficult. Section 1 is the easiest and Section 3 is the most difficult.

> **Test Tip** Try to spend no more than 15–20 minutes on Section 1, so that you have enough time for the more difficult texts and questions in Sections 2 and 3. Remember you only have 60 minutes to complete 40 questions, and you need to transfer your answers onto a separate sheet in that time. Aim to spend less than 20 minutes on each section so you have time to check your answers at the end.

1.2 Read extracts 1–8 and match them to texts A–H.

1 This position involves communicating effectively with patients and health care personnel. The chosen applicant will have proven skills in problem solving and assisting in the smooth running of a hospital admissions department.

2 The airport is planning a digital revolution over the next decade. Among the ideas under consideration are talking holograms. These virtual staff would greet passengers on arrival and direct them to the relevant areas of the terminal.

3 Passengers travelling into the city should change trains at Bardon.

4 When we finally arrived at the hotel we were too exhausted to notice just how run-down it was. It wasn't until the next morning, as the sun shone brightly through the gaps in the broken shutters, that I took a good look around me.

5 Sick leave: any member of staff who is ill and unable to come to work should immediately contact their department supervisor so that any necessary arrangements can be made.

6 Your application form will be processed by the Human Resources team, who will contact you to arrange an interview if you meet our criteria.

7 We're passionate about travel and because we're travellers too we have loads of experience and knowledge we'd love to share with you.

8 **Opening Times**
Weekdays 9:00 – 17:00
Weekends 10:00 – 19:00
Public holidays 10:00 – 16:00

There are 40 questions to complete in 60 minutes. The question types are the same as in the Academic Reading paper. Study the information in units 1–7 for more tips and advice on how to answer the different questions.

General Training Reading – Section 1

1.3 Read the Section 1 passage about recycling.

1 Who is the text written by?
2 Who is likely to read this?

Recycling

Recycling tips and hints

- Use separate bins or bags for waste and recyclables in the kitchen – it makes recycling easy.
- Remember to recycle items from other rooms in your house. Try placing a separate bin in the bathroom, laundry or study.
- Your normal household waste is collected every week and should go in the bin with the black lid. Place all recyclable items in your bin with a yellow lid. This will be emptied every two weeks. Make sure you do not include plastic shopping bags in with your recyclables.
- You can find out your collection day by contacting the council on 3403 8888. You can also get a free reusable bag and use it to collect recyclables around the house or take it shopping and cut down on plastic bags.
- You do not need to remove staples or the plastic window from envelopes, as this is done in the recycling process.
- Tree trimmings, grass clippings and flowers are not recyclable, even though paper is made from woodchip. These items should either be turned into compost or placed in your general waste bin.

Why recycle?
For every tonne of waste paper that gets recycled, 13 trees are saved. One job is created for every 500 tonnes of paper collected for recycling. Every year in Australia, we use about 3.5 million tonnes of paper and cardboard – enough to fill 160,000 semi-trailers. Paper can be recycled six times before it needs new fibres added.

Want to know more about recycling?
Visit our website or call 3467 9809 to talk to our experts at the recycling centre.

There are several types of questions that ask you to write words and/or numbers from the Reading passage. For these questions:

- you will be told the maximum number of words to write.
- you must only write words that are in the text (make sure you copy the spelling correctly).
- you do not need to change the words in the text and you do not need to join the words together.

Scanning for detail

1.4 Scanning a text involves searching it quickly for specific information. The information may appear only once or several times (e.g. the name of a hotel). Scan the passage in 1.3 to find seven different numbers.

1.5 Answer these short-answer questions. Choose *NO MORE THAN ONE WORD AND/OR A NUMBER* from the passage for each answer.

1 What will you help to protect if you recycle one tonne of waste?
2 How many tonnes of paper products do Australians use each year?
3 What is the telephone number of the recycling centre?

You might also be asked to complete sentences using words from the Reading passage.

Recognising paraphrase

There may be key words in each question that you can locate in the Reading passage. However, some parts of the question will **paraphrase** (use another word that has the same meaning) the words in the passage. This tests how much you understand.

1.6 Complete the following sentences with NO MORE THAN TWO WORDS AND/OR A NUMBER from the passage.

1 You should put special bins for collecting recyclables in different ____________ .
2 Plastic shopping bags should be put in the bin with the ____________ top.
3 The council will collect your recyclables every ____________ .
4 If you call the council, they will tell you your ____________ .

1.7 Which words in the Reading passage in 1.3 are paraphrases of the underlined words in 1.6?

Test Tip When answering short-answer questions, you do not need to write full sentences or join words together. Look at this example.

Answer the question with ***NO MORE THAN TWO WORDS*** *from the reading passage.*

What ***TWO*** *colours did the painter use?*

Answer: *black, white* (not *black ~~and~~ white*)

For **identifying information** tasks, you need to look at several sentences or statements and decide whether they are:

True (the statement agrees with the information in the passage)
False (the statement is incorrect and does not agree with the information in the passage) or
Not Given (you cannot say whether the statement is true or false because there is no information about this in the passage)

1.8 Look at the identifying information task below.

Questions 1–5

Do the following statements agree with the information given in the reading passage?
In boxes 1–5 on your answer sheet, write

TRUE	if the statement agrees with the information
FALSE	if the statement contradicts the information
NOT GIVEN	if there is no information on this

1 Envelopes with a plastic window are unsuitable for your recycling bin.
2 Staples often damage the recycling machinery.
3 Garden waste should be thrown away with food waste.
4 Recycling can help to reduce unemployment.
5 Paper that has already been recycled is unsuitable for recycling.
6 The fibres that are added to recycled paper are environmentally friendly.

Not given is not the same as False.

In Question 1, *unsuitable for your recycling bin* means 'you cannot put it in the recycling bin'.

The passage says *You do not need to remove staples or the plastic window from envelopes as this is done in the recycling process.* This means you **can** put envelopes with a plastic window in your recycling bin. So the statement in the question is **False**.

In Question 2, you need to find out from the passage if *staples often damage the recycling machinery.* The passage tells us that *staples will be removed in the recycling process,* but there is no information about staples causing damage to the machinery. We cannot check this fact in the text, so this is **Not Given**.

Test Tip Remember that you are being tested on your ability to understand the information you read **in the passage**. So, you should ignore anything you already know about the topic.

1.9 Decide if the statements in Questions 3–6 are *True, False* or *Not Given*. For each question, justify your answer using the relevant parts of the passage.

2 Dealing with multiple texts

In Section 1 of the General Training Reading paper, you may be given three or more short texts. The texts will all be based on a similar topic. The questions will focus on what is different about the information in each text. You need to scan all of the texts to locate the answers to the questions.

2.1 Look at these four texts. What are they all about?

A

Hampshire University Open Day

10:00 till 21:00

Interested in film? Check out our visual effects studio with all the latest software.

Watch students and staff demonstrate their own games in the Animation and Games studio. (15:00–16:00)

Food and drink stalls.

Free balloons and children's play area.

All finished off with our popular fireworks display!

B

Lexington College Open Day

11:00–16:00

Creative arts market – crafted by our third-year students – all reasonably priced.

International food fair.

Digital photography – workshops on photographing animals in the wild!

Entertainment, prizes and giveaways!

You'll feel like you're flying on our trapeze!

C

Come and join the fun at our

Open Day!

Bellingham House College

Interested in becoming a vet? Visit our working farm and chat to our lecturers and students.

A fun day out for all the family

Marine biology exhibit – come and find out about our fascinating sea creatures.

Open from 8:00 to 16:00.

Parking available at discounted prices.

D

Open Day!

South Bank University

11:00–18:00

Come along and test your skills in our flight simulator.

Enter the draw to win a free flying lesson!

Meet tutors from eight different countries!

Hot dog stand and barbecue from 12:00.

Free parking available.

2.2 Read questions 1–6 and choose the correct text (A–D).

At which open day can you

1 eat food from around the world?
2 see live animals?
3 learn about becoming a pilot?
4 learn how to use a camera?
5 buy work created by students?
6 watch evening entertainment?

2.3 Underline the parts of the texts that gave you your answer.

2.4 Match the words/phrases 1–5 from the text with paraphrases A–E used in the questions.

1	fireworks display	**A**	from around the world
2	international	**B**	animals
3	digital photography	**C**	learn how
4	creatures	**D**	evening entertainment
5	workshop	**E**	use a camera

Study Tip To achieve the best IELTS score, focus on learning vocabulary, grammar and building your reading, writing, listening and speaking skills as a part of your preparation. Don't just focus on test-taking strategies.

3 Understanding work-related texts

Section 2 of the General Training Reading paper contains two separate passages related to work situations. Make sure that you study vocabulary related to work.

3.1 Match the work-related words 1–12 with definitions A–L.

1	hospitality	**A**	to stop working – usually because of age
2	retail	**B**	the type of work done with your hands
3	redundancy	**C**	to hire or employ a person for a job
4	retire	**D**	the industry related to shops
5	consumer	**E**	the person who provides you with work
6	customer	**F**	the industry related to hotels and restaurants
7	manual	**G**	the loss of a job due to a business closing
8	shift	**H**	a person who uses goods
9	employee	**I**	a staff member
10	employer	**J**	the time by which work must be completed
11	deadline	**K**	a person who buys goods
12	recruit	**L**	a person's scheduled period of work

3.2 Spend 40 seconds reading the passage below to understand the main points. Who do you think would read a text like this?

A a person wanting to apply to become an inspector
B the owner of a business
C a new temporary employee at a company
D an experienced inspector

Workplace health and safety

Workplace health and safety is the legal responsibility of all employers. There are rules and regulations governing workplace health and safety to help ensure the safety of workers in all industries. Workplace Health and Safety inspectors are employed by the government to carry out regular workplace inspections and ensure current safety standards are being met.

Inspector training

All inspectors complete a rigorous nine-month program of classroom training and field experience with a qualified inspector. New inspectors also receive training on the regulations specific to their respective programs (i.e. construction, mining, healthcare, industrial and diving). Each inspector is issued a comprehensive manual of policies and procedures to be used when carrying out workplace inspections.

Powers of an inspector

Inspectors are employed to monitor employers and workers and ensure that they comply with the laws concerning Workplace Health and Safety. Inspectors' powers include the ability to enter any workplace without giving notice.

Once an inspector has begun a workplace inspection, he or she is permitted to:

- question any employee
- handle, use or test any equipment, machinery and materials and take away any samples
- look at any documents or records and take them from the workplace in order to make copies, and
- take photographs.

What to expect from a workplace health and safety visit

Workplace visits by an inspector are typically unannounced and, by law an inspector must be granted access to enter and access all areas of the workplace. When a workplace health and safety inspector arrives at your workplace, he or she will introduce themselves and ask to speak with either the workplace health and safety representative or the most senior member of management available. If the staff concerned are not available, the inspector may continue with a limited inspection based on available information and/or arrange a follow-up visit later that day or on the following day.

When all relevant staff have been assembled, the inspector will check that all of the required documentation is in place. This includes the employer's written occupational health and safety policy, and the health and safety-awareness poster. These must be displayed in an area accessible to all employees. Any other documentation that shows workers have been provided with instructions on how to carry out specific tasks may also be requested. Finally, the inspector may ask to see where the documents are posted, and verify that a copy of the law and regulations is also displayed.

Following the documentation review, the inspector will inspect the workplace to determine if staff are maintaining a safe work environment. Short videos describing the specific hazards that inspectors look for during an inspection can be obtained from the Department of Labour.

If the inspector finds any fault within the workplace, then they may issue what is known as a compliance order. Compliance orders describe actions the employer is obliged to take in order to meet the current regulations. If the inspector believes there is immediate risk of injury to a worker, a 'stop work' order will be issued to prevent work from continuing until the problem is solved.

3.3 Read these questions based on the passage. For each question:

- read the 'stem' (the first line of the question) and use it to locate the relevant part of the passage.
- read each of the options and carefully read the relevant part of the passage.
- choose the best answer (A–D).

1 When a new inspector is trained, they

A spend a year learning all of the rules and regulations.
B need to learn about rules concerning several different industries.
C spend some time working with an experienced inspector.
D can carry out inspections as soon as they have completed theoretical training.

2 According to the passage, a workplace health and safety inspector has the power to

A take away all faulty equipment they find.
B photocopy paperwork they find in the workplace.
C ask employees about the company's recruitment process.
D warn employees that they are going to carry out an inspection.

3 If the company's workplace health and safety representative is not present

A the inspection must be postponed.
B the inspector may issue a complaint to management.
C the inspector might simply collect the information they need.
D the inspector may partially inspect the premises and return later.

Test Tip Quickly read the whole passage to get the general idea before you begin answering questions. This will help to give you an overall understanding of the passage and will help you to locate relevant parts of the text more quickly.

Summary, Flow-chart or **Note completion** questions all have spaces that you need to fill using words from the text. Because these types of questions are organised into a summary, a set of notes or a flow chart rather than separate sentences, the information may not be organised in the same order as the information in the passage.

3.4 Look at the flow-chart completion task below. Which part of the passage will you need to read to complete it?

3.5 Complete the flow chart using ONE WORD ONLY from the passage in each gap.

What happens during an inspection?

The workplace health and safety inspector arrives and <u>identifies themselves</u>.

↓

The inspector asks <u>to meet</u> the company's relevant **1** .... (if they are <u>absent</u>, the inspection may be postponed for up to a **2** ....).

↓

The inspector asks to see the following documents:

- the company's **3** .... and **4** .... concerning workplace health and safety
- any **5** .... given to workers to help <u>do a job</u>.

↓

The inspector will inspect <u>the premises</u> – (<u>you can get</u> **6** .... to help prepare your staff for this).

↓

If there are any problems, the staff will be given a written warning.

If the problems may lead to **7** .... , the company will be forced to stop work.

3.6 Which words in the passage mean the same as the words that are underlined in the flow chart?

Test Tip If you are asked to choose **ONE WORD ONLY** from the passage, make sure you do not add extra information such as adjectives or adverbs (e.g. ~~short~~ videos). If you write more than one word, your answer will be marked as wrong.

General Training Reading – Section 3

Section 3 contains one long passage that is more difficult than the previous ones. Timing is an important part of the IELTS test, so make sure you leave at least 20 minutes for this section.

3.7 **Spend three minutes reading the passage on the following page to understand the main points.**

For some tasks, you need to match the information in the question to specific parts of the text. This is similar to the task in **2.2**. Instead of separate short texts, you will need to scan separate paragraphs or sections of one passage.

For **matching headings** tasks, you need to match the headings to the correct paragraph or section. The correct heading will accurately summarise **all** of the ideas within the section or paragraph.

3.8 **Look at the headings in the box below. In the IELTS Reading paper, you will need to consider every paragraph. For this exercise, the headings only relate to paragraphs A–C in the passage.**

1. Read paragraph A carefully, then read each of the headings in the box.
2. Choose the heading that correctly summarises the ideas in the paragraph.
3. Do the same for paragraphs B and C.

Headings

i Industry insiders welcome the change
ii The city votes for major change
iii Advertisements are more than marketing tools
iv How one man changed a city
v Professionals warn of the consequences of change

3.9 **Explain why you chose each answer.**

For **matching information** tasks, you need to match individual ideas to the correct paragraph.

Banned Branding

Has São Paulo's advertising experiment worked?

A When you think of São Paulo, Brazil, a city of 12 million residents and the 7th largest in the world, you probably picture a gritty, sprawling metropolis, with skyscrapers rising like islands in a sea of giant billboards and neon signs. But all of that changed in 2007 when São Paulo became the first major city in the world to ban all outdoor advertising. The 'Clean City Law' was the brainchild of Mayor Gilberto Kassab who, in a bid to combat all forms of pollution in the city, decided to begin by tackling the most obvious – the 'visual pollution' created by billboards and signs advertising brands of all kinds. The move was hailed by writer Roberto Pompeu de Toledo as "a rare victory of the public interest over private'.

B However, reactions in São Paulo were not all positive. Marketing executives were convinced that the new law would prove a terrible blow to the advertising industry and representatives drove their cars up and down in front of city hall to protest against the ruling. *Border*, the Brazilian Association of Advertisers, was incensed over the move, pointing out that tens of thousands of small businesses would have to bear the cost of altering their shop fronts under the new regulations. In the press, a US$133m loss in advertising revenue was forecast, while the São Paulo outdoor media association, *Sepex*, predicted job losses of up to 20,000.

C Others were concerned with the aesthetic impact of the move and that, rather than cleaning up the city, it would look even worse. Would removing the colourful, though chaotic, billboards turn it into a bland concrete jungle? Dalton Silvano, the only city councillor to vote against the law, believed it would: 'Advertising is both an art form and, when you're in your car or on foot, a form of entertainment that helps relieve solitude and boredom,' he claimed. Adding, 'I think this city will become a sadder, duller place.'

D Nevertheless, the council pressed ahead with its plans. 'What we are aiming for is a complete change of culture,' spokesman Roberto Tripoli said. 'Yes, some people are going to have to pay a price, but things were out of hand and the population has made it clear that it wants this.' Eventually, the law was passed and businesses were given 90 days to take down any signs that did not meet the new regulations or pay a fine of up to $4,500 per day. Throughout that period, the city's workmen dismantled around 100 sites per day, occasionally supervised personally by Kassab.

E 15,000 billboards – some the size of the buildings they adorned – huge outdoor video screens, and even posters and ads on the side of buses and taxis, were all quickly removed across the city. To help police, Kassab set up telephone hotlines so that citizens could report instances of advertisers breaking the law. 'Some days we had 3,000 calls on those lines,' he said proudly. Even giving out pamphlets in public spaces was made illegal. Extraordinarily, six years later, it is extremely difficult to find outdoor advertising anywhere in the city.

F Equally remarkable is the speed with which big advertisers adapted to this new environment. 'It was really dramatic ... Big companies had to change their focus and strategies,' says Marcello Queiroz, editor of the newspaper *Propaganda and Marketing*. Marketing directors soon found new areas to spend their advertising budgets on. The move forced them to be more creative and find innovative methods of indoor advertising such as inside elevators and bathrooms. Other businesses were even more creative. Big banks and stores began painting their buildings in eye-catching colours, creating a visual pattern that consumers could associate their brand with, even from a distance. But, according to advertising executive Marcio Oliveira, 'The internet was the really big winner.' Although, at the time, there was already a worldwide move towards social media, the new law gave Brazilian ad agencies an extra incentive.

G For now then, the scheme has worked, and surveys conducted by local newspapers indicate it is extremely popular, with more than 70% of residents showing their approval. It has also brought some unforeseen advantages. When the hoardings were removed, many locals were shocked at the state of the buildings and houses beneath. As a result, renovation work in the city has increased considerably and its cultural heritage is now more visible. As journalist Vincenze Galvao commented about finding his way around the city, 'My old reference was a big Panasonic billboard, but now my reference is an art deco building that had been covered by it. The city's now got new language, a new identity.'

3.10 **Look at the following statements. In the first question, the type of information you need to find in the text has been underlined. Do the same for questions 2–6.**

Which paragraph, A–G, contains the following information? You can use any of the letters more than once.

1 <u>some unexpected benefits</u> of banning outdoor advertising
2 the deadline businesses were given to clear away their advertising material
3 the public's reaction to the new proposal
4 advertising techniques that emerged as a result of the ban
5 an action carried out to try to stop the law being passed
6 examples showing the wide range of advertising material that was banned

3.11 **Scan the text for the following names and highlight them each time they appear in the text.**

People
A Gilberto Kassab
B Roberto Pompeu de Toledo
C Dalton Silvano
D Roberto Tripoli
E Marcello Queiroz
F Marcio Oliveira
G Vincenze Galvao

3.12 **Match the people (A–G) with the following statements. You can use any of the letters more than once.**

1 Removing the billboards has made us more aware of local architecture.
2 The changes led to more people advertising their business online.
3 Billboards can be interesting to look at.
4 Businesses quickly adjusted after the law change.
5 The public was very keen to report businesses that ignored the new rules.
6 Although it might hurt certain businesses, this is a necessary change.

IELTS Writing

How long is the Writing paper?

The Writing paper lasts one hour. Within that time, you must complete two writing tasks. Writing Task 2 carries more marks than Writing Task 1.

What will I need to write about?

There are two separate writing tests, one for Academic candidates and one for General Training candidates. Before enrolling, you need to decide which test is best for you. See the website www.ielts.org for advice on this. You will be given two specific writing tasks as follows.

Task		**Timing**	**What do I have to do?**
Academic Writing	**1**	20 minutes	Describe visual information (e.g. a diagram, chart, graph or table).
	2	40 minutes	Write an essay. You may be asked to: • provide a solution • evaluate a problem • compare and contrast different ideas or opinions • challenge an argument or idea.
General Training Writing	**1**	20 minutes	Respond to a given situation (e.g. by writing a letter). You may be asked to request information or explain a situation.
	2	40 minutes	Write an essay in response to a point of view, argument or problem.

How is the Writing paper assessed?

A trained assessor will read your answers and award a mark based on the following criteria.

Task	Criteria	What do these criteria mean?
Writing Task 1	**Task Achievement**	Did you answer the question fully and write 150 words?
Writing Task 2	**Task Response**	• Did your answer address all of the points in the question? • Did you provide a balanced argument and support your ideas with evidence and examples? • Were all of your ideas relevant to the question? • Did you write 250 words?
Both tasks	**Coherence and Cohesion**	• Is your writing easy to understand? • Are your ideas well organised and clearly linked?
	Lexical Resource	Did you use a wide range of vocabulary accurately and effectively?
	Grammatical Range and Accuracy	Did you use a wide range of grammatical structures accurately and effectively?

Writing Task 2 is worth more marks than Writing Task 1. The assessor will combine your two scores to obtain one final score.

How can I improve my Writing paper score?

You can improve your score by making sure you answer each question fully and remembering the test tips in this unit. This unit will also tell you the writing skills you need to practise in order to achieve your best score. Before the test, practise writing quickly and neatly and make sure you **do not** use bullet points, notes or abbreviations or prepared answers. Studying all aspects of English, including vocabulary and grammar, will also help improve your score.

Writing skills

1 Academic Writing Task 1 – Describing a chart, table or graph

In this unit you will practise:

- understanding Academic Writing Task 1
- understanding charts, tables and graphs
- identifying relevant information
- improving your Task Achievement score

1 Understanding graphs, tables and charts

IELTS Writing Task 1 presents you with visual information that you need to describe.

1.1 Label examples of visual information 1–6 with words A–F.

A diagram	**D** table
B map	**E** bar chart
C pie chart	**F** graph

1

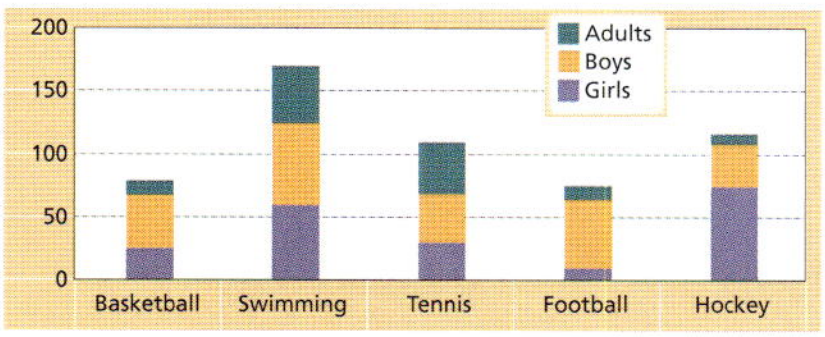

4

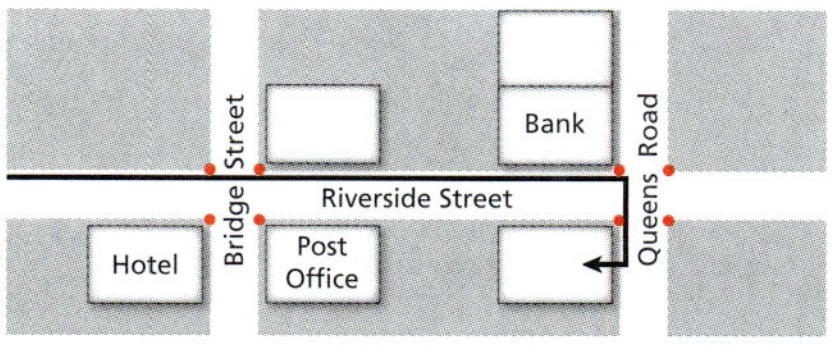

2

WINNING TEAMS	GOLD	SILVER
USA	929	729
Soviet Union	395	319
UK	207	255
France	191	212
Germany	163	163
Italy	190	157
Sweden	142	160

5

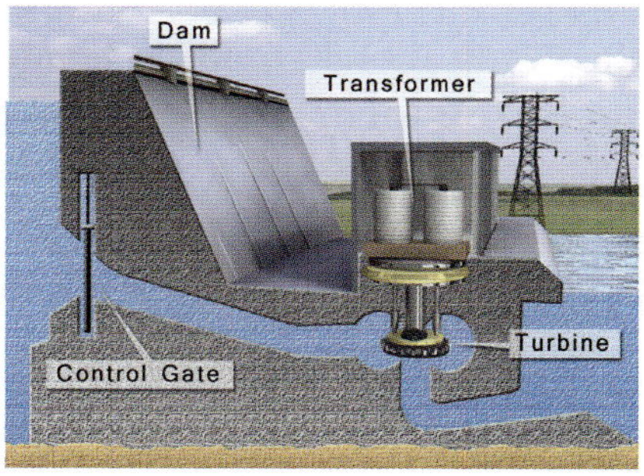

3

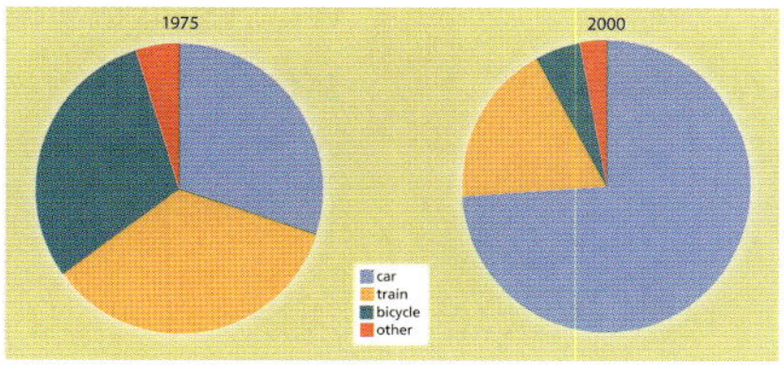

6

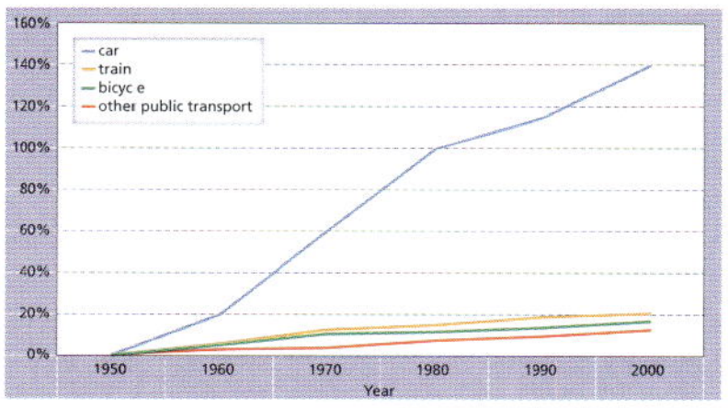

You only have 20 minutes to complete this task, so practise reading and understanding this type of information quite quickly.

1.2 Spend a minute looking at the graph below. Mark any information you think is important with a highlighter or pencil.

1.3 Answer these questions.

1 What is being measured and how? (e.g. is the information in millions or as a percentage?)
2 Is there a time element to the information? (If yes, what is the gap between each year shown?)
3 Are two or more things being compared? (What are they?)

Traffic growth in the Netherlands since 1950

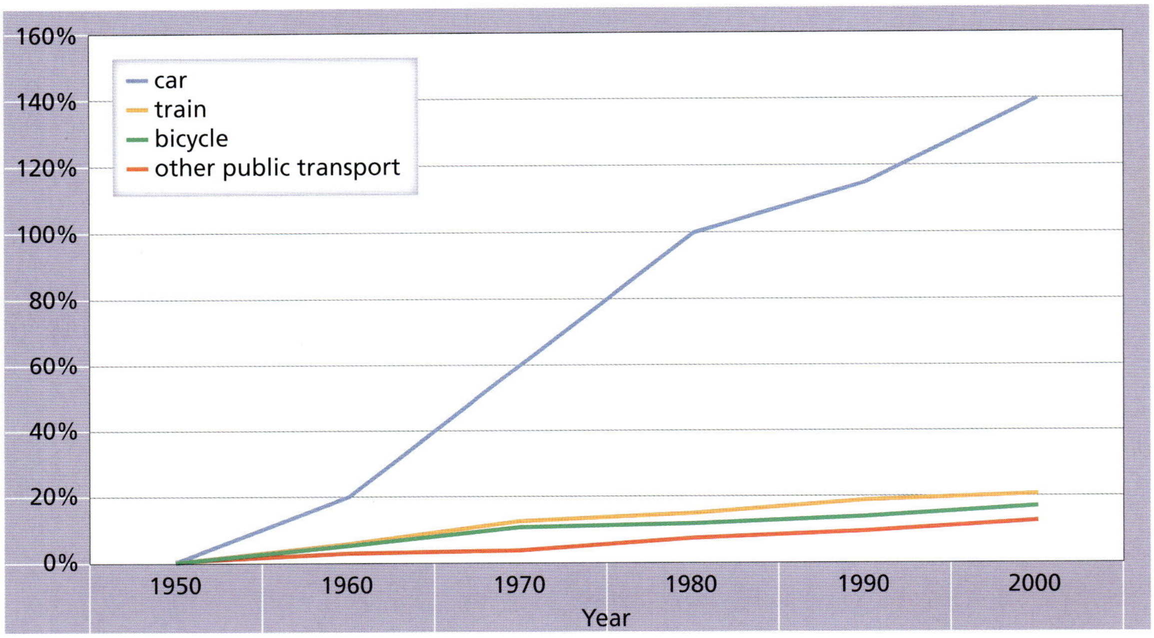

1.4 This description of the graph in 1.3 contains seven mistakes. Find the mistakes and correct them.

The graph shows the increases in traffic in England from 1960 to 2010. During this time, car traffic increased by just over 150%, while train traffic increased by 40 percent, bicycle traffic increased by approximately 20%, and other public transport traffic actually decreased by about 20%.

Test Tip You will be assessed on the type of information you write about, as well as the language that you use. If you give information that is incorrect or inaccurate, then you will receive a lower score.

The visual information may also be presented in a bar chart, table or a pie chart. You must limit your description to the information presented to you.

1.5 Study the information presented in these pie charts carefully, then complete the task.

Proportion of journeys made in the Netherlands according to transport type

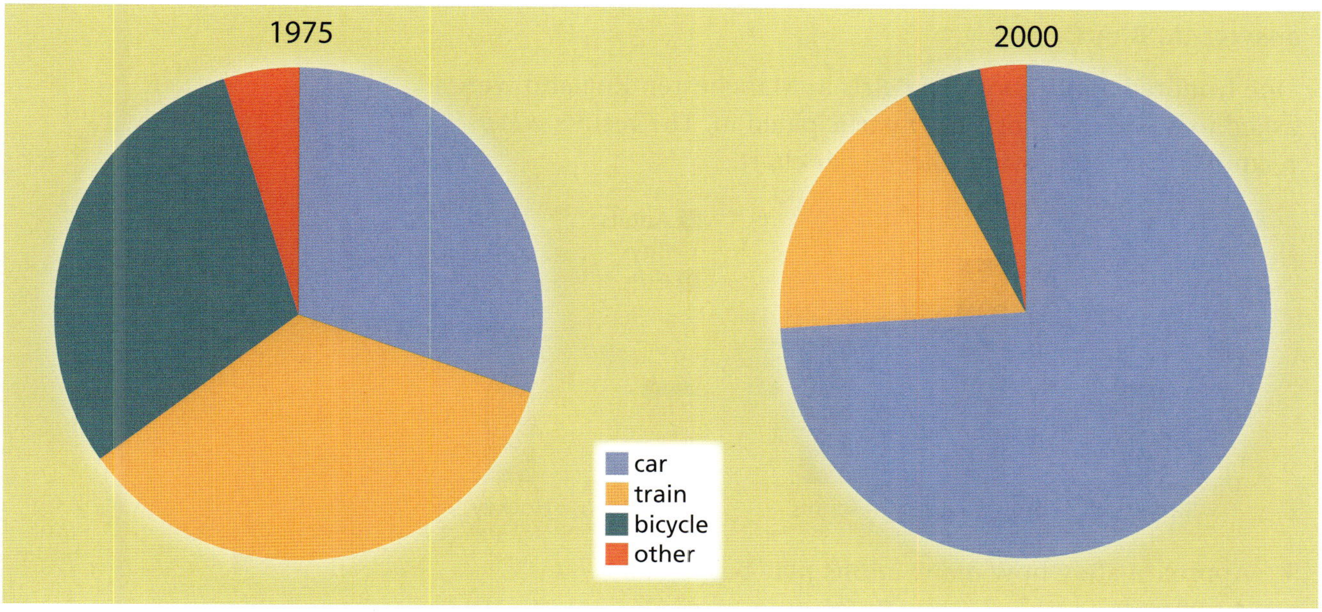

Look at statements 1–6 and say whether the information

A *is **true** according to the data*

B *is **incorrect** according to the data*

C ***cannot be verified** from the data*

1 The two pie charts tell us the number of vehicles being used in the Netherlands in 1975 and 2000.

2 As many people travelled by train as by car in the Netherlands in 1975.

3 Fewer people travelled by train than by bicycle in the Netherlands in 2000.

4 In 2000, people in the Netherlands were making most of their journeys by car.

5 A larger percentage of people bought new cars in 2000 than in 1975.

6 We can see from this information that travelling by train and by bicycle was far less common in 2000 than in 1975.

Test Tip Your answer must **accurately** describe the information presented in the visual. Don't draw conclusions that are not supported by the information you are given.

2 More complex charts

The visual information you are given in Writing Task 1 often asks you to compare or contrast different information. One way of allowing you to compare information is through a bar chart.

2.1 Study the bar chart below. Notice that you have to estimate some of the numbers. Answer the questions by choosing the best answer, A, B or C.

One hundred adults, boys and girls in Manchester, England were asked to name the sports they participated in. The results were recorded in the following stacked bar chart.

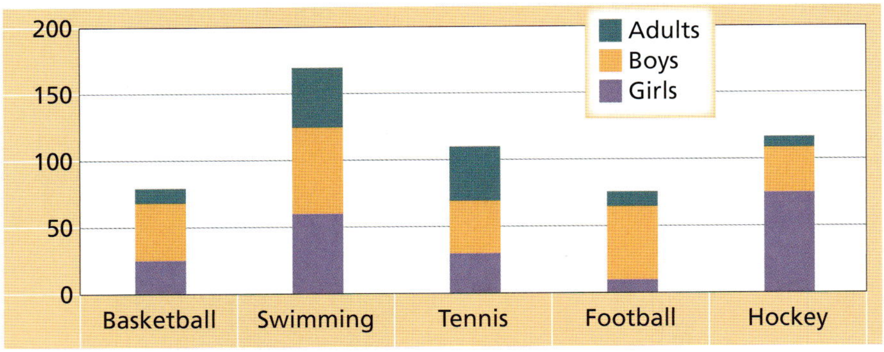

1 Approximately how many adults play basketball?
A 80 **B** 25 **C** 10

2 How many boys enjoy swimming?
A about 40 **B** about 60 **C** about 170

3 Which sport is enjoyed by the same number of adults as girls?
A basketball **B** tennis **C** football

4 Which group seems to participate in the most sport overall?
A adults **B** boys **C** girls

2.2 Some charts are used to show predictions of the future. Study the graph below and decide what the information is telling you.

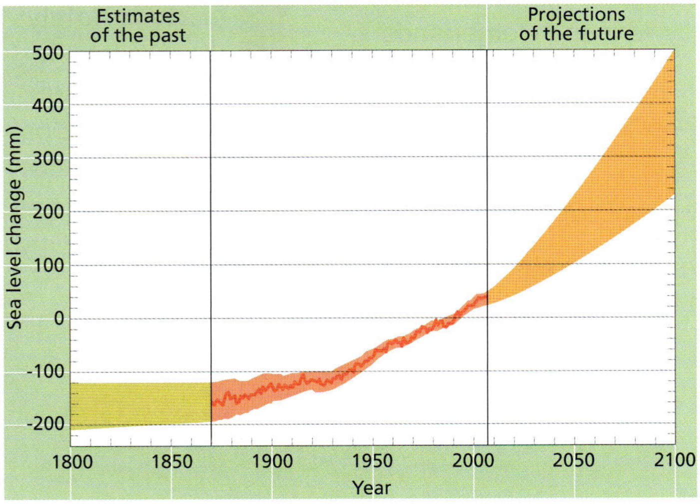

Using the passive voice helps to show you are **describing** the visual information, rather than giving your own ideas. To describe future predictions, we often use the passive form of the verbs *estimate, predict,* and *forecast*. These sentences often start with *It*.

2.3 Rewrite these sentences, describing the graph in 2.2.

1 I predict that sea levels will continue to rise.

It is predicted that ______________________

2 I estimate that sea levels will have increased by 200mm by the year 2050.

It ______________________

3 I forecast that sea levels will rise more rapidly between 2050 and 2100.

Sea levels ______________________

4 I estimate that by 2100, sea levels will be 500 mm higher than they are at present.

By 2100, sea levels ______________________

Test Tip Each time you come across any form of graph, chart or table, study it carefully and practise picking out the major changes that the figure shows. Imagine that you are explaining to someone else what you have noticed from the graph.

3 Improving your Task Achievement score

When the examiner assesses your writing, one of the criteria they will use is called **Task Achievement**. Look at the wording of this Writing Task 1 question.

> *Summarise the information by selecting and reporting the main features, and make comparisons where relevant.*
>
> *Write at least 150 words.*

This means that, to achieve a good score for Task Achievement, you need to

1 give an overview of the main information in the graph (summarise the information).

2 describe **all** the most relevant and significant information (select and report the main features).

3 point out the key differences and similarities in the data (make comparisons where relevant).

4 only include information that is represented in the data.

5 produce an answer that is at least 150 words.

It is **very important** to give a one-sentence overview or summary of the **main trends** in the chart or graph. **You will not achieve a good Task Achievement score if your answer does not include an overview sentence.**

3.1 The bar chart below shows the reduction in traffic accidents in Bridgewater following the introduction of extra lanes on busy roads. Look at the chart and try to identify the main trend(s).

Accident reductions per kilometre in Bridgewater following the introduction of extra lanes on busy motorways

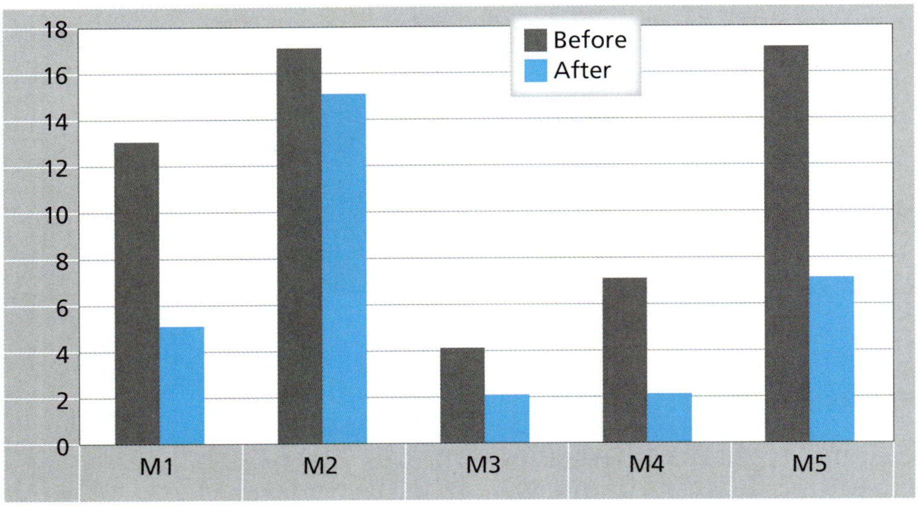

3.2 Which of the following sentences is an accurate overview sentence of the bar chart?
(You must summarise the main trend(s).)

A There were mixed results following the introduction of the new traffic system in Bridgewater.
B On some roads the extra lanes were more popular than on others.
C The roads with the largest amount of traffic are the M1 and M5.
D In every case, adding an extra lane on main roads had a positive effect on traffic incidents.
E All cities should incorporate this system on their main roads.

For Writing Task 1, you need to write 150 words describing and summarising the **main features.** The visual information may contain minor details that should not be included. For example:

Main feature: *Extra lanes were introduced to five main roads.*

Minor detail: *Before the new lane was introduced, almost eight cars had accidents on the M4 per kilometre per year.*

> **Test Tip** You will **lose marks** for Task Achievement if you
> - leave out data that is important.
> - speculate on reasons for the data.
> - add information not included in the data.
> - write less than 150 words.
>
> **Don't** do these things.

3.3 Look at sentences 1–6 and decide if the information is

A a main feature (it should be included)
B a minor detail (it can be left out)

1 The M2 and the M3 showed the smallest reduction in accidents.
2 Approximately four accidents per kilometre occurred on the M3 prior to the peak lane being introduced.
3 About 17 accidents per kilometre occurred each year on the M2 following the introduction of extra lanes on busy roads.
4 The greatest reduction in accident numbers occurred on the M1, the M4 and the M5.
5 The introduction of the new system cut the number of accidents occurring on the M1 and the M5 by half.
6 Each year, the greatest number of accidents occur on the M1, the M2 and the M5.

3.4 Look again at the bar chart in 2.1 and read the model answer below. Check the Task Achievement of the model answer.

1 Find a sentence that gives an overview of the main information.
2 Find four examples of the **main features** of the data that have been selected and reported.
3 Check the word count.

> The chart shows the responses of a group consisting of 100 boys, 100 girls and 100 adults in Manchester, England, when asked whether they participated in four sports: basketball, swimming, tennis and football. From their responses, it is clear that swimming is the most popular sport among all groups, and that from these three groups, boys participated in the most sports. In fact, for three out of the four sports, boys were the major participants. The only sport not enjoyed by the boys surveyed was hockey, a sport that the vast majority of the girls who were interviewed participated in. Other sports enjoyed by girls were tennis and basketball. However, only a very small number, approximately 10 of the 100, participated in football. We can conclude from this that girls in Manchester enjoy hockey a lot and that they don't particularly like football.

3.5 Improve the Task Achievement score of the model answer.

1 Find one piece of information that should be deleted.
2 Decide what details are missing.
3 Complete the answer so that there are 150 words.

Writing skills

2 Academic Writing Task 1 – Comparing and contrasting graphs and tables

In this unit you will practise:

- avoiding repetition
- comparing and contrasting data
- describing changes in numbers
- grammatical range and accuracy
- describing numbers and figures accurately

1 Avoiding repetition

As well as Task Achievement, another criterion the examiner will use is called **Lexical Resource.** This assesses the accuracy and range of the vocabulary you use. To display a wide range of vocabulary, you must make sure not to simply repeat your own words or the words from the question.

1.1 A good way to avoid repetition is to use synonyms. Which words A–F could be used to replace the underlined words in sentences 1–6?

1 There was a sharp <u>decrease</u> in sales between 2007 and 2010
2 The figures <u>fell</u> steadily over the next 10 years.
3 It is predicted that the numbers will begin to <u>increase</u> from 2025.
4 It is predicted that the numbers will <u>remain</u> the same for the next ten years.
5 The charts <u>show</u> how many people travelled by train in 1950 and 2000.
6 According to the <u>data</u> in the table, 2005 was the most successful year.

A stay
B indicate
C information
D dropped
E rise
F reduction

You need to write an introductory statement for your description. For this, it is particularly important to use your own words instead of copying words and phrases directly from the question. You can do this by

- using a synonym of the words in the question.
- changing the form of a word (e.g. changing a verb into a noun).

1.2 Look at these extracts from Writing Task 1 questions, and candidates' introductory statements. Replace the underlined words in the candidates' answers with a suitable phrase from the box to improve the range of vocabulary.

A *how many*
B *a group of people of a range of ages*
C *the countries they come from*
D *the number of vehicles on the road*
E *have taken courses at*
F *different sports preferred by*
G *how much people spent*

1 The graph shows traffic growth in the Netherlands between 1960 and 2010.
The graph indicates the changes in traffic in the Netherlands from 1960 to 2010.

2 The bar chart shows the sporting preferences of 100 adults, boys and girls in Manchester.
The bar chart tells us the sporting preferences of 100 adults, boys and girls in Manchester.

3 The graphs show the number of students that have attended the college since 1980 and their different nationalities.
From the graphs, we can see the number of students that have attended the college since 1980 as well as their different nationalities.

4 The two pie charts show the average household expenditure in the US in 1900 and in 2000.
The pie charts reveal the average household expenditure in the US in 1900 and 2000.

1.3 Look at the candidates' statements again. Which other examples of paraphrase can you find?

2 Comparing and contrasting data

When you are describing a chart or graph, you are actually describing the patterns in the data. Before you begin to write, spend one or two minutes noticing the different features of the visual information.

Test Tip Remember that, to achieve a high score for Writing Task 1, you need to **select and report on the main features and make comparisons where relevant.**

2.1 Look at this Writing Task and then answer the questions.

The bar chart below shows the net worth of the UK from 2000 to 2010 according to three different sectors.

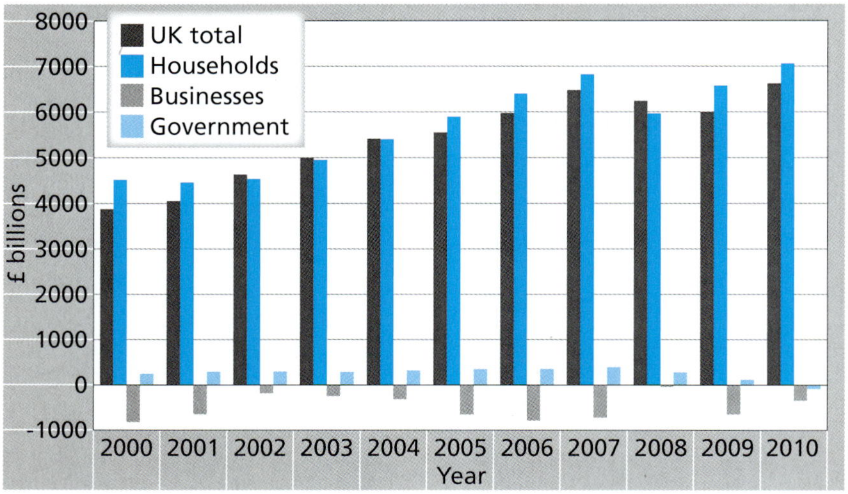

1 What do the figures on the left measure?
2 Why does the number 1,000 appear twice?
3 Which set of figures shows what is happening in the country as a whole?

To help identify the patterns, you need to look for the

- **peaks** (high points) and **troughs** (low points)
- periods when the figures **remain steady** (show little or no change)
- periods when the figures **fluctuate** (show a lot of changes)

You also need to notice which different figures you can **compare** (show that they are similar) and **contrast** (show that they are different)

2.2 Look at the patterns in the data and answer these questions.

1 Over which span of time did the UK government's wealth remain steady?
2 Over which period did its wealth decline?
3 In which three separate years did business wealth show a marked improvement?
4 In which two years was the total wealth of the UK worth more than household wealth?
5 Which three sets of data generally followed the same pattern?
6 Which sector fluctuated the most between 2000 and 2010?

Usually, changes occur over time. So, to describe these changes accurately, you must use the appropriate tense.

2.3 **Complete the sentences with the most appropriate tense of the verbs in brackets.**

1 The figures for UK households __________ (remain) fairly steady between 2000 and 2002 then __________ (begin; increase). By 2007, UK household wealth __________ (rise) from £4,500 billion to just under £7000 billion.

2 Between 2000 and 2007, both the government and household wealth __________ (show) positive figures that gradually __________ (increase) over time.

3 While both the household and government net wealth __________ (drop) significantly in 2008, the government's net worth __________ (fall) so much that it actually __________ (go) into negative figures in 2010.

4 Between 2000 and 2010, the total net worth of the UK __________ (follow) a similar pattern to that of the households and the government.

5 Although the net worth of businesses in the country __________ (improve) from 2000 to 2002, this trend __________ (not last) long and __________ (begin; worsen) again only a year later.

6 From 2005 to 2007, although the rest of the country __________ (experience) continued growth, the wealth of businesses __________ (return) to the levels of 2000.

7 The data for the business community __________ (reveal) the opposite trend to that of the rest of the country. At the same time that the wealth of households and the government __________ (grow), the wealth of businesses __________ (decline).

2.4 **Look at the sentences in 2.3 again. Which sentences are**

A describing a pattern or trend in one sector?
B pointing out the similarities in data for two or more sectors?
C contrasting data from two or more sectors?

2.5 **Study the language used in the sentences in 2.3 and make a note of any new vocabulary.**

3 Grammatical Accuracy – describing numbers and figures accurately

Another criterion the examiner will use to assess your writing is **Grammatical Range and Accuracy**.

After your introductory sentence and your overview sentence, you need to select relevant data to report on. To do this, you need to be able to accurately describe numbers and figures.

3.1 Read this extract from a description of the bar chart in 2.1 and the underlined information.

The chart shows that the maximum net worth of all UK households reached a little over £7000 billion. In six of the ten years represented in the chart, UK households were worth approximately 5% to 10% more than the UK total. For just under a third of this period, in the years 2002 to 2004, the UK total was equal to or greater than the total worth of UK households.

1 Which information is written as numerals (1, 2, 3, etc.)?

2 Which information is written in words?

3.2 Replace the relevant numerals in the following sentences with the correct word from the box.

three and a half billion	a quarter	half
a third	one million dollars	

1 ½ of the people who attended in 1961 had never attended a concert before.

2 They reduced the budget by $1m 40 years later.

3 60% of students report using the library in term time only and ¼ of those use the library at night.

4 The population rose by 3½ billion in the next 15 years.

5 Over 15 million planes landed at the airport in the last seven months; this is an increase of ⅓.

A common problem for candidates is in deciding whether or not a noun or a number should have a final 's'.

3.3 Complete the sentences with the correct form of the words in brackets.

1 There were approximately three hundred ____________ on the roads in 1970. (thousand; car)
2 Current figures show that this has now risen to over twelve ____________ . (million)
3 ____________ of people travel by plane every year. (million)
4 According to the chart, four ____________ were manufactured in the factory last month. (hundred; bed)
5 Approximately 40% of all ____________ admitted to working through the night before exams. (student)

Another common mistake that candidates make when describing numbers is missing out the preposition or using the wrong one.

3.4 Choose the correct preposition from the box to complete the sentences below. You may use some prepositions more than once.

in	of	to	for	from

1 The increase ________ car use was accompanied by a decline in the use of public transport.

2 The table shows the number ________ students enrolled at the school between 1960 and 1990.

3 Approximately 70% ________ women have experienced this as compared to only 30% ________ men.

4 The figures ________ train and bicycle use reveal a steady drop in these types of transport.

5 The figures had increased ________ 35% ________ over 60% within five years.

Study Tip When you are practising this type of writing, say your answer aloud to help you decide whether your language is too repetitive. Do your sentences sound very similar? Think about the sentence structures you have used, as well as the vocabulary.

The **coherence** (how easy your writing is to understand) and **cohesion** (how the ideas in your answer are connected together) of your answer are also assessed in Writing Task 1. You need to take the time to organise your ideas into paragraphs. You can practise this in Units 3, 4 and 6.

Test Tip Make sure that you leave time at the end to check your writing. You need to make sure that your facts and your language are both accurate.

Writing skills

3 Academic Writing Task 1 – Describing diagrams

In this unit you will practise:

- understanding a diagram
- describing a process
- improving coherence and cohesion
- understanding Lexical Resource
- being accurate

1 Understanding a diagram

Another form of visual information is a diagram. Again, you need to spend a little time studying and understanding the diagram before you begin to write. Remember, you need to include **all** of the most relevant information.

Test Tip Try drawing your own diagram of an everyday machine in your home (e.g. a washing machine). Divide the process up into different stages and describe it.

1.1 Look at the diagram below for one minute.

How to make recycled paper from old newspapers.

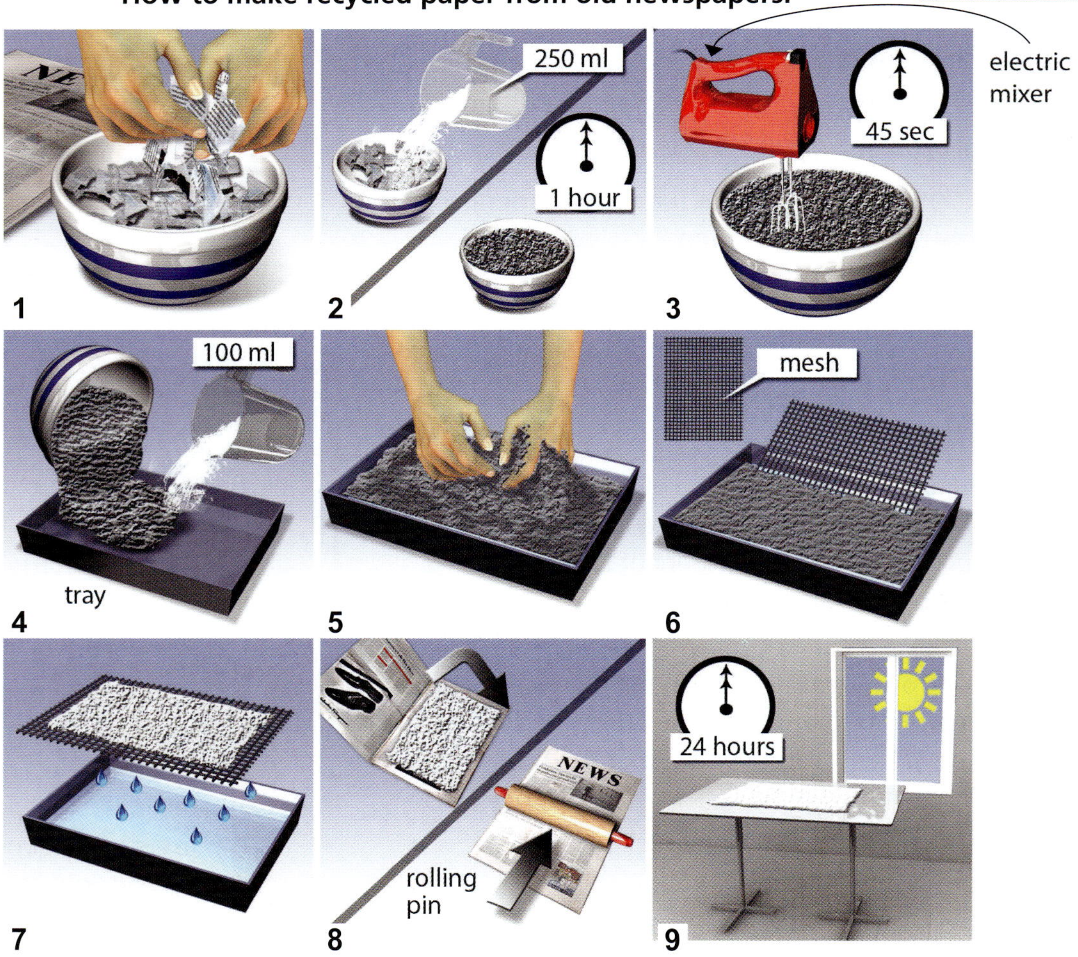

1.2 Match the verbs to parts 1–9 in the diagram. You may use more than one verb for each image.

lift	pour	leave	drain	add	put	tear
mix	press	soak	dry	place	slide	beat

There may be some labels included in the diagram. These are usually the names of different objects that you are not expected to know. You should use these in your description.

Test Tip Remember, you have only 20 minutes to complete Writing Task 1, so you need to identify the most important information in only one or two minutes. To help plan your answer, write the different verbs you will use to describe each stage on the diagram itself. This will help to make sure you don't miss out any important steps in your description.

1.3 Study the diagram again and complete these sentences.

1 You need old newspapers, a ________ to hold the mixture and a ________ containing 250 ml of water.

2 An ________ is used to form the mixture into a pulp.

3 The pulp is poured into a ________ .

4 Some ________ is used to lift the pulp out of the water.

5 A ________ is used to flatten the pulp and press the water out.

2 Describing a process – coherence and cohesion

Your Writing Task answer will be assessed based on its **coherence** (is it easy to understand?) and its **cohesion** (are the ideas connected well?). For every Writing Task answer, your ideas must be organised in a logical way and be connected together. Your answer must not be a list of individual sentences.

2.1 Complete sentences 1–9 with endings A–I.

1 The diagram explains how to
2 First,
3 Then, add 250 ml of water and
4 Next, using an electric mixer,
5 When it is ready,
6 Then, use a piece of mesh, to carefully
7 Next, open up an old newspaper and
8 Then, use a rolling pin to
9 Finally,

A place the pulp mixture inside.
B beat the mixture for about 45 seconds until it forms a pulp.
C leave your new paper to dry in a warm place for at least 24 hours.
D make recycled paper from old newspapers.
E tear some newspaper into small pieces and put them in a bowl.
F lift the pulp mixture out of the tray, allowing the water to drain.
G press the paper down and force out any excess water.
H leave the paper to soak for up to an hour.
I pour the pulp into a shallow tray and add a further 100 ml of water. Mix it together by hand.

To describe a process, we usually use the passive voice.

Active voice
First, tear some newspaper into small pieces.

Passive voice
First, some newspaper is torn into small pieces.

2.2 **Now complete the description below by changing the sentences in 2.1 to the passive voice.**

The diagram explains how recycled paper is made from old newspapers. First, some newspaper is torn into small pieces and put into a bowl. Then, ______________________________

____

____

____

____

____

2.3 **Look at the complete description in the Answer Key. The beginning of each sentence helps to organise the information and link it together. Complete the list of words/phrases below that help do this.**
First, ... Then, ...

3 Lexical Resource – being accurate

Common spelling mistakes

3.1 **Accuracy in vocabulary includes using the correct spelling. The sentences below each contain one spelling mistake. Find the mistakes and correct them.**

1 The goverment increased spending in 1988 and again in 1998.
2 The chart shows the persentage of students who have access to the internet in their home.
3 From the pie charts, we can see the diffrent sports enjoyed by each age group.
4 These figures remained steady untill 1990, when they rose steeply.
5 The charts show the energy use of four different contries over a 50-year period.
6 The highest rise occurred betwen 1970 and 1990.
7 This figure had dicreased by 50% by the end of this decade.
8 While the amount of money spent on education remained the same, the budget for transport incresed considerably over this time.

Test Tip Remember, your answer for Writing Task 1 will be marked against specific criteria. One of these is Lexical Resource. To get a good score, you need to use a wide range of vocabulary (not repeating the same common words) and use vocabulary accurately (without mistakes).

Using the wrong noun

3.2 **Accuracy in vocabulary also involves using the most appropriate words. Improve the accuracy of the sentences below by replacing the underlined words with one of the nouns from the box.**

percentage	number	means	method
amount	factors	figures	

1 The <u>number</u> of traffic on the road continues to increase.
2 The diagram shows the <u>way</u> for making canned food.
3 The <u>amount</u> of children who do not have access to a computer at home is higher in Newtown than in Westbridge.
4 The chart shows figures for four different <u>ways</u> of transport in The Netherlands.
5 Another significant figure is the <u>percent</u> of the budget that the school spent on recruiting staff.
6 The chart clearly shows the <u>reasons</u> that led to the current energy problems.

Using the wrong form

3.3 **Another accuracy problem occurs when you choose the right word but use it in the wrong form. Complete these sentences with the correct form of the words in brackets.**

1 The ________ between the two is only 9%. (different)
2 This involved a great deal of hard ________ . (work)
3 The chart shows several of the areas we tend to take for granted in our ________ . (live)
4 In the older group, there was a dramatic ________ in 2000. (increase)
5 The graph shows that the ________ rate of women increased far more than that of men. (attend)
6 There was a ________ decrease from 2005 to 2010, but overall it remained the same. (slight)
7 The figures show how many people in the area make use of the local ________ centre. (sport)
8 We often go on ________ trips to museums and art galleries. (education)

Writing skills

4 Academic Writing Task 1 – Describing maps

In this unit you will practise:

- describing a map
- describing changes in a place
- being accurate

1 Describing a map

1.1 Look at the following Writing Task 1. Then complete the list of changes below.

Test Tip Work out how much space 150 of your words take on a page. This can save you having to count. Make sure your handwriting is neat and legible.

The following maps show the changes that have taken place in the centre of a town since 1700.

Summarise the information by selecting and reporting the main features, and make comparisons where relevant.

Town centre, 1700

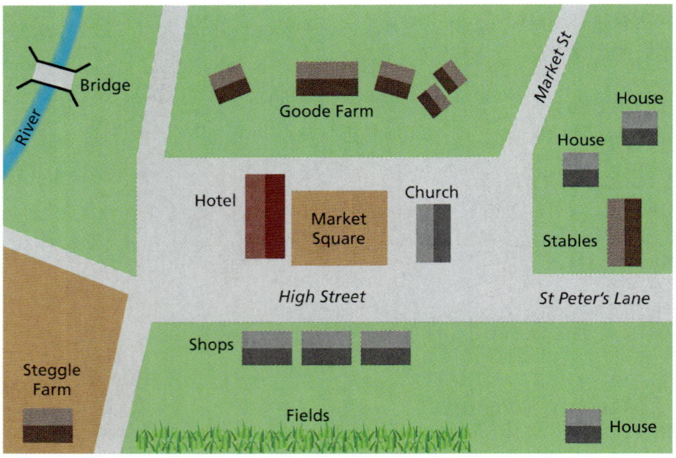

Town centre today

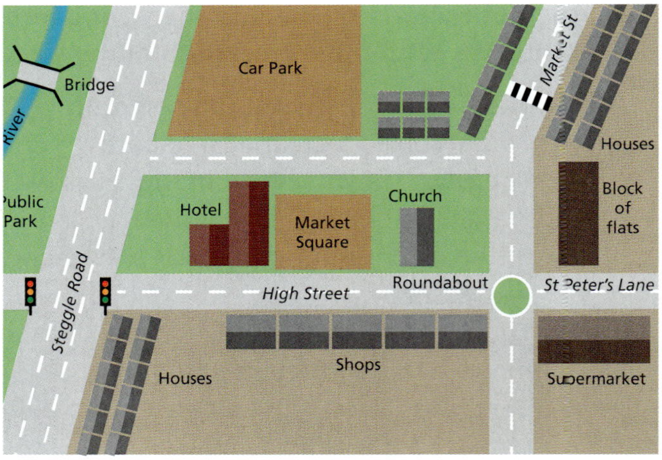

Write at least 150 words

changes:

- the hotel *has been expanded / extended.*
- Steggle Farm
- the roads
- the shops
- the houses
- Goode Farm
- the house in St Peter's Lane
- the stables

1.2 **Complete the sentences with the correct feature.**

1 The ________ , which is right in the centre of the town, has not changed in 300 years.

2 According to the 1700s map, there was a ________ in the bottom right-hand corner.

3 Another feature that has remained the same is the ________ , located in the centre, to the right of the market square.

4 The row of ________ that can be seen in the bottom centre of both maps, has changed little over the years.

1.3 **Complete the sentences with the correct location.**

1 Steggle Farm, which can be seen ________ of the 1700s map, is no longer there.

2 To ________ the market square is the hotel, which has changed considerably over the years.

3 In the ________ ________ both maps, there is a bridge.

4 In the 1700s, there were stables located ________ the church.

2 Describing changes in a place

2.1 **Match the verbs in the box to definitions 1–10.**

add	remove	modernise	extend	replace
reconstruct	expand	improve	renovate	
reduce	develop			

1 make something bigger: ________ or ________

2 make something new again: ________

3 make something modern: ________

4 take something away and put something else in its place: ________

5 make something better: ________

6 make something smaller: ________

7 build several buildings in an area where there was nothing: ________

8 put in something totally new: ________

9 take something away: ________

10 build something again: ________

2.2 Complete these sentences with the correct form of verbs from 2.1.

1 Goode Farm has now been ____________ with a car park.

2 The hotel has been ____________ , and is now almost twice the size it was in 1700.

3 Though many of their names have remained the same, all of the roads ____________ .

4 The traffic lights, roundabout and zebra crossing, which were not needed in 1700, ____________ now ____________ , and the road surfaces ____________ .

5 The stables ____________ and replaced with a block of flats.

Test Tip Get an old map of your own town centre and write about some of the changes that have happened.

3 Grammatical Accuracy

Your answer for Writing Task 1 will be marked against specific criteria. One of these is Grammatical Accuracy. To obtain a good score, you need to produce writing that is grammatically accurate.

3.1 Correct the 10 mistakes underlined in the answer below.

> The two maps 1 allows us to see the changes in one small town over a 300-year period. In the 1700s, the town was relatively small and 2 consists of a few farms and houses gathered around a central market place and church. Transport 3 restricted to horses at that time so the roads were very basic. Having said that, the roads were clearly marked and the river had a bridge running across it.
>
> In the present-day town, a great deal 4 changing. Perhaps the most noticeable changes are those relating to transportation. Our modern-day needs are very different and so the roads 5 are improving and traffic lights, a roundabout and a zebra crossing 6 been adding, as well as an extra road. Increased traffic means that a car park 7 now replaced Goode Farm and the fields that 8 are locate at the top of the 1700 map. Housing is another area where many changes 9 are made. While in 1700 there were few houses, now there are rows of houses and a block of flats instead of the stables. A further development is the supermarket and the hotel, which 10 is extending.

It is important to use paragraphs in your Writing Task 1 answer. Paragraphs show that your answer is well organised.

3.2 Look at the answer in 3.1 again and explain how it is organised.

Study Tip Practise writing with a timer set for 15 minutes so that you get a good feel for how long this is.

Writing skills

5 General Training Writing Task 1 – A letter

In this unit you will practise:

- understanding the task
- organising your response
- improving your score
- checking and correcting

1 Understanding the task

For General Training Writing Task 1, you will be asked to write a letter. The letter must be written in the correct style:

- informal (if you are writing to family or friends)
- semi-formal (if you are writing to a work colleague you know well)
- formal (if you are writing to a business or a local newspaper)

Test Tip In the General Training Writing Test, you must manage your time well. Writing Task 2 is worth twice as many points as Writing Task 1, so you must only spend 20 minutes on Writing Task 1. Take a reliable watch into the exam with you. You won't be allowed to take your mobile phone into the exam room.

1.1 Complete the table with these phrases, according to which part of a letter they belong to and what style they are.

1 Hi Mum.
2 I look forward to your reply
3 Dear Mike
4 Lots of love
5 I'm afraid I won't be able to attend the meeting next week.
6 Thanks for the parcel, it just arrived!
7 Yours sincerely
8 Dear Sir or Madam
9 Kind regards
10 I'm writing in response to your advertisement.
11 I can't wait to see you next week.
12 I'm looking forward to getting back to work.

	informal	semi-formal	formal
greeting			
opening statement			
closing statement			
ending			

In your letter, you might be asked to

A request information.
B give personal or factual information.
C explain a problem or situation.
D explain wants or needs / make a request.
E complain about a service.
F make a suggestion or recommend something.

1.2 Match phrases 1–6 to ideas A–F.

1 I think it would be better if you opened at the weekend as well.
2 Could you please send me a brochure and an application form?
3 Because I'm a student, I need a quiet place to study at night.
4 I'm very unhappy about the dinner we ate in your restaurant last night.
5 I finished high school last year and I am currently taking a computer course.
6 I'm unable to go to the meeting myself because I have to look after my son.

1.3 Look at this General Training Writing Task 1 question.

> You should spend about 20 minutes on this task.
>
> You rent a four-bedroom house, which you share with two other students. However, there are several problems with this house that need fixing. You also find it expensive and would like to find another student to share the spare bedroom.
>
> Write a letter to the estate agency. In the letter
>
> - explain your situation
> - describe the problems with the house
> - say what you would like to happen
>
> Write at least 150 words. You do NOT need to write any addresses. Begin your letter as follows: *Dear Sir or Madam,*

This part explains the situation.

The bullet points tell you what to write about.

This tells you how to begin.

1.4 Look again at the situation described in the question.

1 Do you think this situation is informal, semi-formal or formal?
2 Can you change these details and write about your own personal situation?
3 Should you write your own address at the top of your letter?

2 Improving your score

Your answer will be assessed based on the following criteria.

- **Task Achievement** Does your letter answer all the parts of the question? Are all your ideas relevant?
- **Coherence and Cohesion** Are your ideas well organised, clear and well connected?
- **Lexical Resource** Have you avoided repeating the same words and copying words from the question?
- **Grammatical Range and Accuracy** Have you made few grammatical mistakes and shown a range of grammatical structures?

The information in the exam task will tell you what to write about. To achieve a good Task Achievement score, include all of these points in your letter and only include relevant ideas. To improve your score for Coherence and Cohesion, use the information in the exam task to help plan and organise your ideas.

2.1 Look at the suggested plan below for a letter to answer the question in 1.3. Think about what you would write for parts 2–6.

1 Greeting	*Dear Sir or Madam,*
2 Opening statements (introduce yourself, say why you are writing)	
3 Explain the situation	
4 Describe the problems with the house	
5 Say what you would like to happen	
6 Closing statements (signal the end of the letter)	
7 End the letter	

2.2 Look at a candidate's notes below for their letter.

1 Are all the ideas relevant to this question?
2 Match the relevant ideas (A–F) with parts 2–6 of the plan.
N.B. You may not be able to fill in each part.

A The upstairs shower seems to be leaking into the kitchen below and this is dangerous.
B We would be grateful if you could get the problems fixed as soon as possible.
C We're also worried as there is no front gate, which makes the house less secure.
D We have exams soon and my computer is broken.
E I look forward to hearing from you very soon.
F My friends and I rent one of your properties and I am writing to inform you of some problems that we are having.

2.3 Which two parts of the plan still need ideas?

To achieve a good score for Lexical Resource, you need to avoid copying words from the question.

2.4 Look at the following explanation of the situation. Why do you think it would receive a low mark?

We rent a four-bedroom house. However, there are several problems with the house that need fixing and we also find it expensive.

2.5 Help to improve the explanation below by filling in the blanks. Then add the paragraph into the correct part of the plan on the previous page.

The house we are **1** ________________ four bedrooms and there are three of us sharing it. Our rent was recently increased and, as we are all students, it is a little difficult for us to **2** __________ . It's a very nice house that suits us perfectly but at the moment some **3** __________ are needed.

2.6 What extra details does this second explanation include?

2.7 Which ideas (A–C) would help to complete the plan?

A I would like to ask permission to invite my friends to the house.
B Finally, we would like to ask if it is possible to invite a friend of ours to share the rent and occupy the spare bedroom.
C To summarise, there are many problems with the house and we are unhappy with your service.

To finish off a formal letter, we use

- *Yours sincerely* – if you know the name of the person you are writing to.
- *Yours faithfully* – if you do not know the name of the person.

2.8 Which ending is the most appropriate for this letter?

A Best wishes **B** Lots of love **C** Yours faithfully

Study Tip Study the Academic Writing sections of this book for extra help with improving coherence, cohesion and accuracy.

3 Checking and correcting

Your writing will be assessed for grammatical and lexical accuracy. This means using vocabulary correctly, not making grammatical mistakes and using the correct spelling. Below are some common mistakes.

Common mistakes with tenses

3.1 **Correct the underlined mistakes.**

1. I hope that the above information would be helpful to you.
2. I will be grateful if you could think about the situation.
3. However, there were a few things I have to comment on.
4. On the bus, I spend the entire journey trying to make myself warm with the help of my shawl.
5. Secondly, I want to describe the kind of area I like to move to.
6. I am look forward to hear from you.
7. My uncle is going away on holiday, so, he need someone to help run his business.
8. I hope that help you with the identification of my parcel.
9. I writing you this letter regarding doing a computer course.

Common mistakes with prepositions

3.2 **Complete these sentences with the correct preposition. You may use any preposition more than once.**

in	of	on	at	with	about	to	for

1. The reason that I didn't take part is that I had an important examination in Marketing ________ the following day.
2. On the night ________ last Sunday, I was playing games on the computer with my classmate.
3. Yesterday, I noticed an advertisement ________ the newspaper.
4. The main reason ________ my trip is to meet my nephews who are living there.
5. I am looking forward ________ your reply and ________ having more details of this project.
6. You can contact me ________ my phone at home ________ 5467 4539.
7. I can support the project ________ a lot of ways.
8. I have lots of experience ________ cooking and cleaning.
9. I am really interested ________ this job and also have the ability to do this job very well.

Test Tip Leave at least three minutes at the end to check your writing. Check your spelling, punctuation and grammar.

Test Tip To help with your tenses when you are writing, remember that you are writing in the present about something that

- **happened** in the **past**.
- **has happened recently.**
- **is** true **now** or **is happening now**.
- will happen **in the future**.
- you **would like to** happen in the future.

Common spelling mistakes

3.3 **Find and correct the common spelling mistakes.**

1 I am writing to you becouse I'd like to attend the computer course at your college.
2 I'm studying biology and I saw the advertisment at the university.
3 I think this is good for our sociaty.
4 Is that course avaible part time?
5 Finally, the liberary needs more workers to help out at the weekend.
6 She has a degree in bussiness and marketing.
7 This resturant is situated at the centre of the city and is therefore accessible from any point in the city.
8 I'm going to change my job soon, and it's neccessary for me to improve my computer skills.
9 Yours sincerly.

Study Tip If you have trouble spotting these spelling mistakes, perhaps they are mistakes you make yourself! Make a note of any words you often spell incorrectly and study them often. Writing the words out many times can help you to learn the spelling.

Common punctuation mistakes

3.4 **Find and correct the common punctuation mistakes.**

1 I was on my way to my office when i noticed your advertisement on a billboard.
2 However; there is one certain thing which I see as a fault.
3 Yours Sincerely,
4 However, I would like to ask you about the party?
5 Please dont take a taxi, just wait for me.
6 Im available every Monday and Tuesday and every other weekend.
7 Dear Sir:

Writing skills

6 Writing Task 2 – Getting ready to write

In this unit you will practise:

- understanding the task
- planning and organising your ideas
- improving your Task Response score
- writing an introduction

1 Understanding the task

Writing Task 2 consists of

- one or two statements on a topic OR a direct quotation giving someone's opinion on a topic
- a specific task or question for you to answer
- the types of idea you need to include in your answer.

1.1 The words and phrases 1–8 are often used in Writing Task 2. Match them with their correct meanings A–H.

1 to what extent	**A** connected to the topic
2 positive trend	**B** to give a summary of
3 a factor	**C** a means of achieving something
4 an approach	**D** to consider the different sides
5 to regard	**E** how far or how much
6 to outline	**F** to view or judge
7 to discuss	**G** a change for the better
8 relevant	**H** an element or condition

1.2 Read statements 1–6 carefully and make sure that you understand them. Then match the statements to questions A–E.

1. Children have to be educated, but they also have to be allowed to learn things for themselves.
2. 'Advertisements spoil our enjoyment of today's entertainment.' 'I think the adverts are often more enjoyable than the programmes they interrupt.'
3. The world would be a happier place if we all enjoyed our work.
4. Computers allow us to stay connected with each other. However, they also encourage people not to go out and socialise.
5. Some countries reduce inner-city traffic by increasing public transport. Others impose a tax on people who drive in the city.
6. Nowadays, more people are travelling to remote places, spreading their own language and culture as a result.

Questions

A What are the advantages and disadvantages of each system?

B Discuss both statements and give your own opinion.

C To what extent do you think this is a positive trend?

D How realistic do you think this is?

E To what extent do you agree or disagree with this view?

2 Planning and organising your ideas

Before you begin to write, it's important to make a plan. If you don't do this, your ideas will be disorganised and you will lose marks.

Step 1: decide on your own position or attitude

2.1 Look at the statements from 1.2 again.

1 For statements 1, 3 and 6, decide how much you agree.

2 For the statements in 2, 4 and 5, decide which one you agree with.

3 For each of the statements in 1.2, explain why you agree or disagree. Then give your own opinion on the topic.

2.2 Study the following Writing Task 2 question.

> *The internet allows us to stay connected with each other no matter where we are. On the other hand, it also isolates us and encourages people not to socialise.*
>
> *To what extent do you agree or disagree with these statements?*
>
> *Give reasons for your answer and include any relevant examples from your own knowledge or experience.*

The final part of the question is very important. It tells you what you must include in your answer.

You **must** include
- your own opinion about the statements.
- the reasons for your opinion.

You **can** include
- examples from your own personal experience. BUT these must be relevant to the question.

2.3 Look at the question in 2.2 again.

1 Decide on your own point of view.

2 Think about your own personal experience of this topic. Make notes.

My own opinions and experience

Test Tip The score you get for Writing Task 2 is **two thirds** of your total writing score, so it is very important that you spend a full 40 minutes on this part of the IELTS Writing paper. You are given more time than for Writing Task 1 because you need to write 250 words, and also because you have to use **your own ideas**. Spend at least four or five minutes planning your ideas before you start writing.

Step 2: note down any ideas about the topic

The examiner will mark your Writing Task 2 based on specific criteria. One of these is **Task Response.** To achieve a good Task Response score, you must

- explain your own opinions on the topic
- support your opinions (e.g. with personal examples or your knowledge of the world)
- include **only relevant** ideas
- write 250 words.

2.4 You will lose marks if you include ideas that are not relevant to the question. Look at these ideas that a candidate noted to answer the question in 2.2. Cross out **four** ideas that are not relevant to the task and should not be included.

1 Instant communication (e.g. emails/text messages) means that it is difficult to escape from work.
2 The internet makes it easier to do your homework.
3 In my company, computers have replaced many staff and have caused more unemployment
4 A friend of mine uses a social-networking site a great deal but we rarely see her.
5 Virtual friends made on the internet cannot be compared to our actual friends and family.
6 I learned to type using a computer program, these programs make it easy to understand computers and make learning fun
7 My cousin travelled for a year but kept in touch with his family every day.
8 With more and more technological advances, our society will continue to develop faster and faster.
9 Through the internet, we can share memories with people who are far away.

2.5 Check your answers, then look back at your own ideas from 2.3. Are there any you need to cross out?

Study Tip Articles that contain opinions can help give you ideas to use in the Writing tasks. The letters page of a newspaper usually contains people's personal opinions about different topics. Read them and decide whether you agree or disagree. Decide what your own opinion is.

Step 3: organise your ideas into paragraphs

It is important to produce a balanced answer that looks at both sides of the question equally. It is also important to organise your ideas into separate paragraphs.

2.6 Decide which of the remaining ideas from 2.4 can be put together into the same paragraph. Put the ideas from 2.4 into the correct box below.

For: the internet helps us to stay connected:	Against: the internet isolates us

> **Test Tip** Your answer will also be marked on **coherence** (are your ideas clearly linked?). You need to make sure your ideas are organised into separate paragraphs. To help group your ideas together logically, make notes under different headings that show both sides of the discussion. These can then form the middle paragraphs of your answer.

Step 4: check that you have enough ideas

If you do not have enough ideas for both sides of the question, then your ideas will not be fully developed.

2.7 Which side of the argument do we need to add more to?

2.8 Which of the following ideas would be best to add?

A The business world benefits from the immediate contact provided by the internet.
B The internet has both advantages and disadvantages.

3 Getting started – writing an introduction

Once you have your ideas planned out, you can begin to write. Your answer must be clearly developed, and so it needs a clear start. The best way to start is by restating the question **in your own words**.

3.1 Match introductory sentences A–D below to Writing Task 2 statements 1–6 in 1.2.

A Each year, there are more and more cars on our streets creating congestion and causing delays. There are several ways that local governments can try to solve these problems.
B Unless we are born into wealth, we all need to find a way to earn a living. For many, our working life takes up most of our waking hours and this can make us very unhappy indeed.
C As a society, we have a duty to teach our young people. However, there are some lessons that we need to learn for ourselves.
D Marketing involves teaching as many people as possible about a product. There is no better way to reach people than through television, popular culture and the internet.

3.2 In this introduction for the Writing Task in 2.2, too many words have been copied from the question. Improve the introduction by replacing the underlined phrases. Use the words from the box.

keep in touch	however	anywhere in the world
obsession	stay at home	see their friends

The internet is a wonderful tool that helps us to stay connected with each other no matter where we are. On the other hand, some websites encourage us not to socialise.

> **Test Tip** You will lose marks if you copy words from the question. Make sure to paraphrase the ideas.

Once you have restated the question, the rest of your introduction could

1 give your interpretation of the words or ideas used in the question
2 explain what you intend to write about
3 give a brief reaction to the question
4 summarise the question or topic through a new question

3.3 What suggestions above (1–4) do sentences A–D relate to?

A Does the internet really help us to develop relationships?
B We need to consider both the benefits and the drawbacks of the internet.
C I think the word 'tool' is important here. In my view it shows how impersonal this contact is.
D These statements summarise my own mixed feelings towards the internet.

3.4 Look at sentences 1–4 below and decide which would make a good final sentence for the introduction.

1 It seems clear that the internet brings a lot of problems.
2 Is the internet a positive or a negative influence on our lives?
3 How can we ensure that the internet does not cause widespread problems?
4 Let us consider the arguments for and against computers.

> **Study Tip** Don't learn whole answers and expect to use them in the exam. You will receive a very low score if you do this. Candidates who receive a higher band score in writing are able to show **flexible** use of language. The more you practise writing and reading, the more flexible your writing will become.

Writing skills

7 Writing Task 2 – Expressing your ideas clearly

In this unit you will practise:

- linking your ideas
- being accurate with vocabulary
- avoiding repetition
- using the correct style
- expressing a personal view
- reaching a conclusion

1 Linking ideas – cohesion

Cohesion means linking your ideas together clearly. Without cohesion, you will have a list of sentences, rather than a connected paragraph or essay.

Test Tip The examiner will assess the **Coherence and Cohesion** of your answer. They will judge how your ideas are organised and how you link information. Planning before you write is the best way to make sure your ideas are organised in a logical way.

1.1 The following words and phrases are all used to connect sentences and ideas together. Put them into the correct place in the list, according to how they are used.

that is	because of	however	in spite of	
furthermore	in addition	on the other hand		
consequently	while	so	despite	such as
as a result	whereas	for instance		
not only … but also	although	also	in fact	

- Connecting similar ideas: *similarly,*
- Connecting different ideas: *but,*
- Clarifying an idea: *in other words,*
- Giving examples: *for example,*
- Giving a reason or conclusion: *therefore,*

1.2 Choose the correct words.

1 Advertisements provide vital revenue for the entertainment industry. *Consequently / Despite*, without adverts we could lose certain forms of entertainment altogether.

2 Nowadays, the internet has become an indispensable business tool. *Although / In fact*, we would find it very difficult to get through a working day without it.

3 The internet brings the world into our home. *Also / However*, we sometimes want to shut out the outside world from time to time.

4 Schools can give our children academic knowledge. *Whereas / Furthermore*, at school, children can learn social skills.

5 Many people today spend time on social networking sites. *As a result / For example*, Facebook and Twitter are both used around the world to help people stay connected.

1.3 Which connectors in the box could also be used to link the ideas in 1.2?

In addition	On the other hand	In other words
For instance	As a result	

2 Lexical Resource – avoiding repetition

To achieve a high band score in the IELTS Writing paper, you need to show a wide variety of vocabulary and sentence structure.
You can avoid repeating words by

- using a synonym
- using a pronoun to refer back to an idea (*This* + noun / *These* + plural noun)
- using a group noun (*This/these type(s) of* / *kind(s) of* + noun)

For example
Settlers introduced several new animals, such as ***the cat. This predator*** *preyed on the local wildlife.*
Settlers often ***introduce new crops and animals*** *to an area.* ***This type of activity*** *can be disastrous.*

Test Tip Just like Writing Task 1, your Writing Task 2 answer will be assessed based on the lexical resources or vocabulary you use. This means that you need to avoid repeating words from the question and use as wide a variety of words and phrases to discuss the topic as you can.

2.1 Extracts 1–5 repeat the same vocabulary. Improve them by replacing the underlined phrases with a suitable synonym from the box and the appropriate pronoun.

funding	system	natural resources	facilities
method	technology		

1. We depend on oil, coal and gas for the majority of our energy needs. However, oil, coal and gas will one day run out.
2. Remote and rural areas may initially seem like idyllic places to live but they often lack hospitals, shops and schools. Living without easy access to hospitals, shops and schools can make life very difficult indeed.
3. Governments sometimes try to encourage innovation by offering grants. This isn't always effective because special grants are often difficult to obtain.
4. Some teachers ask students to simply copy down texts from a blackboard. But copying down texts does not help students to become independent or flexible in their use of language.
5. In my country, cars driving through the city centre are charged a toll. Charging a toll has been a success because the traffic has decreased considerably.

Using the correct style

The language you choose must be as accurate as possible and must suit this formal task.

> **Test Tip** Writing an essay like this is a formal situation and so your language must be formal or neutral as well. Never use notes or bullet points. You will lose marks if you use abbreviations or language that is too casual.

2.2 **Sentences 1–6 contain one example of incorrect style. Find the mistakes and correct them.**

1. Children with no access to education are most likely gonna end up in manual jobs.
2. Two of the major problems we are facing today are global warming & increased pollution.
3. A lot of our modern conveniences are contributing to our unhealthy lifestyle, e.g. we often use a car instead of walking to the local shops.
4. Some businesses think it is OK to simply dump toxic waste and pay the necessary fine.
5. Kids of any age need the right type of guidance.
6. I find that the internet helps me a lot when I travel. I can use it to book flights, find a hotel, get maps, etc.

> **Study Tip** Think about your own language when you are studying English. Make a note of important differences such as vocabulary or grammar. Noticing these will help you to avoid making the mistakes that are common for people with the same first language as you.

2.3 **Some words are commonly confused. Circle the correct word or phrase in each sentence.**

1. I don't think it is necessary for children to *learn / study* about ancient history.
2. I do think it is important for us to try to *understand / know* different cultures.
3. Before I travel to a new country, I always take the time to *find out about / know* the local customs and rules.
4. It is almost impossible to get a good office job without up-to-date computer *skills / knowledge*.
5. I don't think we will be able to *stop / solve* this problem in our lifetime.
6. I believe today's younger generation are more attracted by flexible working hours than by the thought of earning *money / wages*.
7. Sadly, not all *employers / employees* receive sick pay and holiday pay.
8. A great deal of *advertising / advertisement* is now done as we surf the internet.

3 Expressing a personal view

Remember that your Writing Task 2 answer should give your own **views on** or **attitude to** the topic. One way to show this is by using

A adverbs such as *personally* or *probably*.
B modals such as *might* or *could*.
C phrases such as *in my view*.
D verbs such as *appear to be* or *seem to be*.

These can also help to stress your ideas or change them from a simple fact to a personal opinion.

For example
Travelling is dangerous. → *Travelling* ***can be*** *dangerous.*
Most people agree with me. → ***I think*** *most people* ***would*** *agree with me.*

3.1 Match these examples to suggestions A–D.

1 As far as I'm concerned, we have not done enough to address the problem.

2 Perhaps the current strategy will work.

3 People seem to spend a lot more time at work than with their families nowadays.

4 Following a vegetarian diet can help you save money.

3.2 Underline the words or phrases in sentences 1–9 that show opinion and attitude. Then rewrite them using the words in brackets.

1 Perhaps this is because today's teachers are not trained as well as they used to be. (might)
This ***might be*** *because today's teachers are not trained as well as they used to be.*
2 Personally, I don't think this is a good idea. (view)
3 I certainly wouldn't like to have to do a job I didn't enjoy. (personal)
4 I think this could be a bad idea. (probably)
5 In my view, life is much more complicated for young people nowadays. (can)
6 Personally, I think every situation is different. (opinion)
7 Nowadays, young people probably use their mobile phones for multiple tasks. (generally)
8 In my opinion, schools are more crowded than in the past. (seem)
9 My city is less crowded now and people generally enjoy walking through the streets. (appear)

Try to avoid repeating *'I think'* or *'I know'* too often. The following verbs can be used instead: *realise, feel, believe, imagine, can see.*

3.3 Match the words in bold in sentences 1–8 with the most appropriate definition, A–C.

A this is my strong belief
B this is my understanding of the situation
C this is a guess, I don't really know for sure

1 **I feel** it's important for everyone to play an active role in reducing this type of pollution.
2 **I realise** that it could be difficult to cut costs like this.
3 **I can see** that for people who have a disability, the internet provides an essential lifeline.
4 **I suppose** that allowing adverts to be placed on a football pitch might help reduce the cost of tickets.
5 **I believe** that if we all made a positive effort then we could make real progress.
6 **I imagine** that people with high-powered jobs find it difficult to escape from work.
7 **I am convinced** that there is a connection between computer use and obesity.
8 **I suspect** that the rich are not as happy as we think they are.

Reaching a conclusion

To finish off your writing, you need to write a conclusion. Your conclusion should be a brief summary of your argument and ideas and is often a good place to give your own opinion.

3.4 These concluding sentences all contain a mistake. Find the mistakes and correct them.

1 In conclusion, I completely disagree this view.
2 As far as I am concern, this is a problem without any real solution.
3 To summarise, even there is a clear downside to our dependence on technology, I honestly feel we have to find a way to cope with it because the internet is definitely here to stay.
4 In conclude, there are both negatives and positives to this system, but the negatives seem to far outweigh the positives.
5 In my point of view, education is a vital part of every child's life.

Writing skills

8 Writing Task 2 – Checking and correcting

In this unit you will practise:

- developing your ideas clearly
- grammatical accuracy
- assessing your language level
- checking and correcting
- using correct punctuation

1 Developing your ideas clearly

When you have completed your writing, make sure you allow at least three or four minutes to check and read through your answer. First check your ideas against your plan.

- Did you include all of your ideas?
- Are your ideas organised and connected logically?

Test Tip The examiner will assess the **Grammatical Accuracy** of your answer. They will judge how accurate your sentence structures are, and also whether you have shown a **range** of structures and not limited yourself to basic ones. Make sure you vary your sentences in the exam.

1.1 Read the answer to this Writing Task on the following page.

> *'The internet allows us to stay connected with each other no matter where we are. On the other hand, it also isolates us and encourages people not to socialise.'*
>
> *To what extent do you agree or disagree with these statements?*
>
> *Give reasons for your answer and include any relevant examples from your own knowledge or experience.*

1.2 Before checking the spelling and grammar, consider the ideas and organisation of the answer.

1 Look at underlined words 1–10 in the answer. What ideas do these words refer back to? Why does the writer use them?

2 Find a word or phrase that is used to

- **a** introduce what you want to talk about first
- **b** introduce a contrasting idea
- **c** add a supporting idea
- **d** show you are giving an example
- **e** show you are giving a personal opinion
- **f** explain the result of an action or situation
- **g** introduce a summary of the ideas in the answer

3 Write the plan the candidate might have used before beginning to write.

The internet is a wonderful tool that helps us to keep in touch wherever we are. However, I do think that some people can find [1]it quite addictive. Progress often comes at a price, and there are many who is concerned about the impact the internet has on our daily life.

First, let us consider the benefits the internet brought. Undoubtedly, the greatest of [2]these is the case with wich [3]it allows us to make contact with people anywhere in the world. Nowdays, the business world makes use of this every day. Without the internet, companies would find it extremely difficult to expand or meet the needs of [4]their customers. This same ability to keep in touch extends into our personal lives. For example, when my cousins were backpacking around the world [5]they were able to reassure thier family and friends that all was well and also share memories almost immediately, using social networking sites.

Progress comes at a price, however, and there is another side to the coin. [6]This convenience that the internet brings means that our work is only ever a mouse click away. Consequently, many people find it difficult to ever escaping from work. In addition, the websites that encourage us to keep in touch may, ironically, lead to anti-social behaviour in some users. [7]These people end up with more virtual friends than actual friendships. In reality, [8]their feeling of connectedness may only be an illusion as [9]they become more and more isolated in their homes.

To summarise, I completely agree that, although there are clear benefits to the internet, there are also certain risks. Having said that, I belive that [10]these can be minimise through education. As far as I'm concern, something that can bring the world into the home of a person who is disabled and essentially housebound, is more indispensable than intrusive.

Study Tip We use handwriting less and less these days, so make sure that you practise writing quickly and neatly. Ask others to read your writing to make sure it is legible. There may not be time in the exam to write and then rewrite your answer. It is better to spend time planning and then checking at the end.

2 Grammatical Accuracy

To achieve a high band score in the IELTS test, you need to show a range of vocabulary and grammatical structures and use them accurately.

2.1 Look again at the answer and find

1 four common spelling mistakes.
2 five problems with verbs.
3 a phrase that is repeated (decide which one to delete).

When you are writing quickly, it is easy to make silly mistakes. Use the final few minutes to carefully check what you wrote.

Check:

- **your spelling** – Check for careless spelling mistakes.
- **your grammar** – Check verb and subject agreement and check your tenses.
- **your punctuation** – Have you marked the end of a sentence with a full stop? Do any of your words need a capital letter?
- **your handwriting** – Are any words unclear that you need to write more clearly?

2.2 **These words are some of the words most commonly misspelt by IELTS candidates. The parts of the words that often cause problems have been underlined. Look at the words in A for one minute, then cover them and try to correct the mistakes in the words in B.**

A	B
government	govenment
until	untill
nowadays	nowdays
believe	belive
because	becuse
countries	contries
people	peopl
opportunities	oppotunities
between	betwen
environment	enviroment
technology	tecnology
important	importent
experience	expereince
competition	compettion
their	thier
modern	morden
conclusion	concluson
children	chidren
restaurant	resturant
society	soceity

Don't forget to check your punctuation. The most common mistakes are

- with capital letters.
- full stops.
- commas.

2.3 Correct the punctuation in these sentences.

1 According to the survey, the population will grow more and more, it is predicted that by 2050 the population will have increased by 30%.
2 Many famous film stars are american.
3 My conclusion; therefore is that teaching children to be good members of society is the job of both parents and the school.
4 the pie chart gives us information about the causes of land degradation worldwide.
5 Many children spend hours playing video games which can lead to health problems.
6 However, we can see that the rate of both National and international calls increased from 1995 to 2010.
7 Nowadays in many universities around the world university students can study any subject they like.

Study Tip Students often repeat the same mistakes. Get to know your own common mistakes and make sure you deliberately practise these – especially if the mistakes are spelling mistakes you repeatedly make.

3 Assessing your language

3.1 To help you try to assess the different band scores on the IELTS Writing paper, read these features of Bands 4, 6 and 8.

Band 4
- ideas are clear but there may be a lot of repetition
- uses only basic vocabulary which may be used repetitively
- uses only a very limited range of grammatical structures and rarely accurately
- makes frequent spelling mistakes
- errors may cause problems for the reader

Band 6
- organises information and ideas clearly
- uses an adequate range of vocabulary for the task
- uses a mix of simple and complex sentence forms
- attempts to use less common vocabulary but with some mistakes
- makes some errors in grammar, punctuation and spelling but they don't cause problems for the reader

Band 8
- uses a wide range of vocabulary fluently and flexibly
- uses a wide range of structures and the majority of sentences are accurate
- makes only very occasional mistakes
- skilfully uses uncommon vocabulary but there may be occasional mistakes
- errors in spelling are rare

3.2 Now look at these extracts from three different Writing Task 2 answers. Match extracts A–C to the band score you think they received (4, 6 or 8).

A

Television in general is one of the most important tools of our daily life now. From children to adults, every age group enjoys watching the television programmes of their interest. TV in its early days was mainly used for news broadcasting and other important awareness for the public. But now it heavily influences our lives and it almost became an addiction.

In today's world, with the discovery of satellite television, almost every channel reaches our home and we have plenty of choice. In my opinion TV plays a great role in our lives as its a major source of information of happenings around the world and one has enough information about another country before they have a chance to visit the place physically. In today's household one keeps track of programmes and can record them to watch it at a later more convenient time. So TV is not only a great tool for the enhancement of knowledge on every subject but also its an entertainment package as without it life would be very dull and monotonous.

B

Nowdays, with the developing of science and technology, more an more people use computers, computers are getting popular, people use computer to tapy their essaies, get information from internet, and computers are used in everywhere such as bank supermaket and so on. however, it has been widely noted that some people don't know how to use computers. it make them inconvenient and uncomfortable in their lives. people who do not know how to use computs are become more and more disadvantaged. Some people believe that goverment should make means to solve this problem. In my opinion, people who don't know how to use computers make them disadvantaged in three ways.

C

Nowadays, technology is an esstential part of education. The use of computers in a classroom is so common that it is almost impossible to students follow their studies if they do not have computer skills. However, if the computer dominate the major role of education, what should be done with the teachers?

Firstly, not all schools can provide computers for their students. In this case, colleges situated far away from big center or better, in small towns, depend on teachers as the main source of knowledge for their children. Another point to be considered is the fact that not all the students are keen on working with computers or have enough skills to work with these modern machines.

3.3 Look again at the band score descriptions. Which do you think is closer to a description of your own writing?

IELTS Speaking

How long is the Speaking paper?

The Speaking test is an interview with an examiner that lasts between 11 and 14 minutes.

What will I need to talk about?

The interview has three separate parts and is divided up as follows.

Part	Timing	What will I need to talk about?
1	4–5 mins	The examiner will ask you questions about familiar topics (e.g. hobbies, likes and dislikes, daily routine).
2	3–4 mins	The examiner will give you a booklet showing a topic and some suggestions on it. You need to talk about the topic for 1–2 minutes. You have one minute to write notes before you begin. The examiner may ask you some follow-up questions.
3	4–5 mins	The examiner will ask you more detailed and more abstract questions linked to the topic in part 2.

How is the Speaking paper assessed?

The examiner will listen carefully to your answers and will assess your speaking according to the following criteria.

Criteria	What do these criteria mean?
Fluency and Coherence	Do you speak in a fluent way that is easy to understand? Do you link your ideas together clearly?
Lexical Resource	Can you accurately use or attempt to use a wide range of vocabulary accurately and effectively? Can you explain your ideas even if you do not know a particular word? Can you use or attempt to use higher-level vocabulary accurately?
Grammatical Range and Accuracy	Can you use a wide range of grammatical structures rather than repeating basic structures? Are your sentences accurate, or do you often make grammatical mistakes?
Pronunciation	Is your spoken language clear and easily understood? Do you use stress and intonation to add extra meaning? With individual words, do you use stress accurately?

How can I improve my Speaking paper score?

You can improve your score by making sure you answer each question fully and remembering the test tips in this unit. This unit will also tell you the speaking skills you need to practise in order to achieve your best score. Before the test, practise speaking as often as you can and make sure that you can talk for two minutes on a topic. **Do not** try to learn answers for the test. Studying all aspects of English including pronunciation, vocabulary and grammar will also help improve your IELTS score.

Speaking skills

1 The Speaking Test – Part 1

In this unit you will practise:

- getting ready to speak
- talking about familiar topics
- using the correct tense
- Grammatical Range and Accuracy

1 Getting ready to speak

The test has three different parts (Part 1, Part 2 and Part 3) and the examiner will use a script. This helps to make sure that the Speaking tests all follow the same pattern.

1.1 Video 1 Watch the video and focus on what the examiner says. Complete part of the examiner's script below.

> Can you tell me your **1** .... , please?
>
> Thank you. And what **2** .... ?
>
> And can you tell me **3** .... ?
>
> Can I see your **4** .... , please?
>
> Thank you, OK, that's fine.
>
> Now, in this first part, I'd like to ask you **5** ....
>
> Let's talk about **6** ....

1.2 What do you need to bring to the Speaking test?

1.3 Watch again and this time, focus on Sanem, the candidate. As you watch, answer the questions below.

1 Choose the best adjectives to describe Sanem: shy, anxious, friendly, tense, calm, abrupt, confident.

2 Which **TWO** descriptions below (A–E) apply to Sanem?

A She often looks down and avoids looking at the examiner.
B She makes good eye contact with the examiner.
C Her body language shows she is listening carefully.
D Her body language shows how nervous she is.
E The way she is sitting makes her seem a little rude.

> **Test Tip** Make good eye contact with the examiner from the moment you enter the room, and answer in a polite and friendly way. Your body language is an important part of communicating.

The Speaking test is a formal situation, so it is important to use appropriate body language.

1.4 Put a tick (✓) or a cross (✗) to show which of these would be appropriate in the Speaking test.

A chewing gum because it helps you to stay calm
B drinking from a bottle of water
C checking your mobile phone
D using your mobile phone to time your interview
E wearing jeans and a T-shirt
F asking the examiner your score at the end of the test
G shrugging your shoulders to show you don't know or understand
H asking to leave the room for a moment during the test

Test Tip Make sure you arrive early for your test, so that you are not hurrying and have time to relax. If possible, visit the test centre before the day of your test, so that you are familiar with where you need to go.

1.5 If you can, video yourself being interviewed and think about your own body language. Are there any things you can improve?

2 Part 1 – talking about familiar topics

Part 1 will last for approximately five minutes. The examiner will ask you about familiar topics such as your family, or likes and dislikes.

2.1 Look at the questions below on the topic of home, and think about how you would answer them.

> Let's talk about where you live.
>
> - What do you like most about your home town/city? [Why?]
> - Is your home town/city a popular place for tourists to visit? [Why/Why not?]
> - Do you think your home town/city has changed much in recent years? [Why/Why not?]

2.2 At the end of each question, there are follow-up questions in brackets. Why do you think the examiner sometimes uses them?

2.3 Video 2 Watch a candidate called Emanuele answering the questions. As you listen, decide which statement below applies to Emanuele's answers.

A His answers are a little too short – the examiner needs to ask follow-up questions.
B He is clearly giving a prepared speech.
C He answers naturally and fully.

Test Tip The Speaking test should be a natural conversation. If you try to give a prepared speech, the examiner will interrupt you and ask you a different question.

2.4 Practise by answering the questions below. Record yourself if possible. Don't use any notes or learn a prepared answer.

- What food is typical of your home country? [Why do you think that is?]
- Are there any special festivals or celebrations in your town/city? [Can you tell me about that?]
- What advice would you give to a visitor to your town/city? [Why?]

2.5 Listen back to your answers. Did you answer the questions fully? Would an examiner need to have used the questions in brackets?

3 Using the right tense – Grammatical Range and Accuracy

Your examiner will use four different criteria to assess your speaking level. One of these is Grammatical Range and Accuracy. To achieve a high score in this criterion, you need to use a range of tenses and structures accurately. In Part 1 of the Speaking test, you will be asked questions about two or three familiar topics. The questions will feature a variety of tenses.

3.1 **Video 3** Watch a candidate called Saida answering questions about writing and music. As you listen, complete the examiner's questions below. You may need to watch more than once.

1 What different types ______________________?
2 Do you prefer ______________________?
3 Do you write ______________________?
4 Do you like to ______________________?
5 Let's talk about ______________________?

3.2 What tense should you use to answer each question? Listen again to see if Saida showed a range of tenses.

Test Tip It's important to listen carefully to the examiner's questions so that you can answer in the correct tense. When answering yes / no questions, it is important to answer the question and then give reasons for your answer. Don't simply answer *Yes* or *No*.

3.3 Look at these extracts from Saida's answers. Three of them contain a grammatical error. Find the mistakes and correct them.

1 I prefer to email.
2 If you send a letter by yourself, it means you are very appreciate this person.
3 It depends on the situation. For example, for my studies, I prefer to type on a computer, but for my essays, I prefer to write by hand.
4 I think less, because technology nowadays are really go fast.
5 Not actually.
6 I listen to music because it gives me energy.

Here are some other familiar topics that you may be asked about.

- computers
- hobbies
- reading
- studying
- food
- music

3.4 Try to say one sentence about your past, present and future experiences of each of the topics above. Pay attention to tenses.

Study Tip Spoken language is different to written language, and you may make more grammatical mistakes when you are speaking because there is less thinking time. Try recording yourself as you give the answers to the questions in these units. Then, write out your answers to see the type of mistakes you are making.

3.5 Think about how you would answer these questions.

1 Do you like to read the newspaper? [Why/Why not?]
2 Did you enjoy studying when you first started school? [Why/ Why not?]
3 Would you like to do any further study? [Why/Why not?]
4 Do you often go out at the weekends?
5 Have you always liked the same kind of music? [Why/Why not?]

3.6 Which of the answers in the box can be used with questions 1–5?

Not really.	Yes, I do.	No, I didn't.	No, I haven't.
Yes, I have.	Yes, there is.	No, there aren't.	
Yes, I would.	No, I wouldn't.	Yes, I did.	No, I don't.

The answers in the box are a good start, but you need to give more detail and explain your answer.

3.7 **Video 4** Watch Emanuele giving full answers to the following questions about music. As you listen, make a note of the information that he gives, and the different tenses that he uses. Correct any mistakes you hear.

1 Let's talk about music. How often do you listen to music?
2 Why?
3 So, do you prefer to buy CDs or download music from the internet?
4 Have you always liked the same kind of music?
5 And is there a musical instrument that you would like to learn to play?

3.8 Answer each of the questions in 3.5 and 3.7 for yourself using an appropriate answer from the box. Give specific details.

Speaking skills

2 Part 2 – Giving a talk

In this unit you will practise:

- understanding the task
- keeping going
- improving your Fluency and Coherence
- organising your notes and your talk

1 Understanding the task

In Part 2 of the Speaking test, you will be asked to talk about a specific topic. The examiner will give you a booklet showing your question, and the ideas you need to talk about. You will have time to make notes first.

1.1 **Video 5** Watch the video and answer the following questions.

1. How long should you speak for?
2. How long will you have to make notes?
3. Will you need to bring paper and a pen?
4. Can you write on the booklet?
5. How will you know when to stop talking?

There are four instructions on your booklet telling you what to talk about. It is important to address each one. You will usually be asked to choose a person, place, time or thing and explain why you chose them. Also, you may be asked to describe one or two specific examples and talk about your own feelings or reactions.

1.2 Look at the task that Emanuele was given.

> Describe a time when you helped someone.
> You should say:
> who you helped and why
> how you helped this person
> what the result was
> and explain how you felt about helping this person.

Before your talk, you will be given extra paper to make notes on. You need to make sure your notes cover **each** of the points listed. Writing down the key words in the task will help you to organise your thoughts and ideas.

1.3 Fill in the notes below using key words from 1.2.

Notes: a time when I helped someone

- Who I helped
- **1** ....
- How
- **2** ....
- How I **3** ....

1.4 **Video 6** Check your answers to 1.3, set a timer and watch Emanuele giving his talk. As you listen, make notes on what he says about each of the points in the task.

1.5 How long did Emanuele speak for? Look at the notes you made from Emanuele's talk. What would you add to make his talk longer?

1.6 **Video 7** Some candidates run out of ideas after only one minute. Watch Saida's response. How does the examiner help?

If you run out of ideas after only one minute, you can

- look quickly at your notes.
- look at the question again (did you miss any details out?).
- refer back to an earlier point in your talk and add more.
- keep talking while you think.

1.7 The words in the box are useful to help you keep talking. Complete phrases 1–6 with a suitable word from the box. You may use any of the phrases more than once.

add	mentioned	said	described	as
else	forgot			

1 ____________ I said earlier …

2 At the beginning I ____________ …

3 I don't think I've ____________ …

4 Now, what ____________ can I say?

5 I'd just like to ____________ something about …

6 One thing I ____________ to mention …

1.8 **Video 8** Watch Sanem completing the task in 1.2. Does she cover all of the points in the task?

1.9 **Video 9** Watch Sanem and Emanuele, talking at the end of Part 2. Write down the question the examiner asks.

1 Sanem's rounding-off question: ______________________________ ?

2 Emanuele's rounding-off question: ______________________________ ?

1.10 It is important to answer all of the questions fully. Watch again and make a note of how the candidates extend their answer.

Test Tip As you talk, you should only look at your notes briefly. **Don't** read directly from your notes. Notice how each of the candidates in the videos keeps eye contact with the examiner.

Test Tip If you run out of ideas after one minute, give yourself a fresh start by looking at your notes or looking at the task in the booklet again.

2 Improving Fluency and Coherence

Two of the criteria your examiner will use to assess your speaking are **Coherence** and **Fluency**. Coherence means how easy it is for the listener to follow and understand your ideas. Just as in writing, your notes can help you to organise and link your ideas in a logical way.

2.1 Video 10 Watch Melanie giving her talk. As you listen, look back at the task in 1.2.

1 How does Melanie begin her talk?
2 Fill in the blanks in Melanie's first sentences.

> You ________ ________ ________ ________ a time when I ________ ________.
>
> To that aim, ________ ________ ________ ________ ________ Aniseto.

3 How does she use the information in the question to help organise her ideas?

One way of linking your ideas is by using words and phrases like *after that, because of this, but, also,* etc. We also connect ideas using pronouns.

2.2 Below there are some examples of good coherence from Melanie's talk. The words and phrases she uses to connect her ideas are in bold. Complete extracts 1–8 with endings A–H.

> **A** I decided to take English lessons.
> **B** I helped him.
> **C** I could help him a little.
> **D** he couldn't speak English at all.
> **E** it wasn't just for him, it was also for me.
> **F** it wasn't a good thing.
> **G** he was very friendly.
> **H** I've chosen to talk about Aniseto.

1 You asked me to describe a time when I helped someone. ***To that aim ...***
2 I went to visit my uncle just as a tourist ***but then ...***
3 I met a Venezuelan boy ***and ...***
4 I'm not very good at English ***but ...***
5 So, ***that's it, that's how ...***
6 I wanted to do that ***because ...***
7 I could practise my English ***too, so ...***
8 Some people say that ***now*** he has a French accent, ***so maybe ...***

2.3 Watch again to check your answers.

2.4 It is important to use a variety of language. Do you think Melanie uses a variety of connecting words and phrases or does she repeat the same ones?

2.5 Melanie also connects her ideas using pronouns. Look again at the sentence endings A–H and highlight all of the pronouns.

Fluency refers to the speed of your delivery and how hesitant you are. Candidates who are hesitant often say *er* … a lot.

2.6 **Video 11** Watch Saida's talk and think about coherence and fluency.

1 What words and phrases does Saida use to link her ideas?
2 What other connecting words could Saida have used?
3 Does she use pronouns?
4 Does Saida talk fluently, or is she quite hesitant?

3 Organising your notes and your talk

Making notes can help you to plan your ideas and to give you a fresh start during your talk. Your notes will help you to

- start you thinking about the topic.
- organise your ideas (improve your coherence).
- keep going during your talk (improve your fluency).

3.1 Read this Part 2 task and look at two different candidates' notes.

> Describe a person who has been an important influence in your life.
> You should say
> who this person is and how long you have known him or her
> why you chose this person
> how this person has influenced your life
> and explain how you feel about him or her.

Candidate 1

> **Who and how long?** *older brother / 36 years old / a lawyer / lives in America / not see often / known him all my life*
>
> **Why I chose him** *when young had problems at school / learning difficulties / his dream – to be a lawyer / failed many times / finally succeeded*
>
> **How he has influenced my life** *taught me to keep going / have a clear goal / don't give up / last year: I failed important test / disappointed but didn't give up / trying again soon*
>
> **My feelings** *grateful / admiration / proud*

Test Tip When you are making your notes, try not to write too much. It is important to use this time to think and note down ideas or words, but you also need to be able to quickly look at your notes during your talk and easily find your next idea. Try to find a way that helps you do this (e.g. organise your ideas clockwise on your page, rather than in a random order).

Candidate 2

My Grandmother

1 **How long?** Known her all my life

2 **Why?** Looked after me when young – parents working

3 **Influence** – calm, taught me to read & write, to work hard, about my culture

4 **Feelings** – love, respect, admiration, sometimes worry!

3.2 Think about your own notes.

1 When you make notes, do you write them

  A in a list?
  B scattered randomly on the page?
  C in a mind map or diagram?

2 Do you write

  A single words?
  B long phrases?
  C whole sentences?

3 Try to decide which style of notes would be most helpful for you during the exam.

3.3 Use the two sets of notes in 3.1 to give a talk about the different people. Use all of the details, and time yourself. Concentrate on connecting your ideas and use the ideas below to help you.

- I've decided to talk about …
- I've known him/her …
- I chose him/her because …
- I think s/he has influenced my life by …
- When I think of him/her, I feel …

3.4 Choose the style of notes you feel most comfortable with and write detailed notes about a person who has influenced you. Then, give a talk about him or her. Make sure you time yourself. Record or video yourself if possible.

3.5 Were your notes helpful? Did you write too much or not enough?

3.6 Answer the rounding-off question below. Try to expand on your answers in the same way as Sanem and Emanuele did.

- Who do you think has the most influence in your life: your family or your friends? Why?

Speaking skills

3 Part 3 – Talking about abstract topics

In this unit you will practise:

- talking about abstract topics
- giving your personal opinion
- agreeing and disagreeing
- improving your Lexical Resource score

1 Talking about abstract topics

In Parts 1 and 2 of the Speaking test, the topics and questions are familiar and personal. In Part 3, the topics and questions are more general and more abstract. The questions gradually become more difficult.

Test Tip Listen carefully to the examiner's questions to make sure that you answer them fully and appropriately.

1.1 Video 12 **Listen to how the examiner introduces Part 3. Complete the paragraph below. You may need to watch more than once.**

We've been talking about **1** ______________ , and I'd like to **2** ______________ one or two more **3** ______________ .
So, let's consider first of all **4** ______________ .

The examiner has a list of topics and ideas to guide them, but they will also adapt their questions to your answers.

1.2 Video 13 **Watch and complete the questions the examiner asks.**

A Can you tell me some of the practical things ______________ ?

B Why should ______________ ?

C You live in quite a small town … Do you think ______________ ?

D So why don't they ______________ ?

E Let's go on and think about ______________ .
Some people don't ______________ ?

F Do you think that the ______________ ?

G But doesn't that sometimes mean that ______________ ?

H So, Emanuele, do you think that some people ______________ ?

Test Tip In each part of the test, it is very important to answer all of the questions as fully as possible so that the examiner can assess your language. This will also help improve your score. Make sure to expand on your answers as much as possible.

1.3 **▶ Video 13** **Watch Emanuele answering the questions from 1.2. Match the extracts 1–8 from his answers to questions A–H.**

1 I think governments should create … the right base.
2 But sometimes I understand that it's difficult to help some people.
3 You may have a problem some day and if there is someone that can help you, it's a good thing.
4 I think the most common action you can do would be to lend him something he doesn't have.
5 Life in cities is quite stressful.
6 I think that everyone should help each other first, then the government can create the structure and can act in the right way to allow people to be helpful.
7 I think it depends on the country. For example, the experience I had here in England showed me that people are much more helpful here.
8 You should always try to be helpful because you can't base your attitude on a past experience.

1.4 **Emanuele gave full answers to the questions. Look at these techniques for expanding on your answers in Part 3.**

Techniques
A stating or explaining your own view
B giving relevant examples
C explaining how or why something happens
D saying what would, could, should or might happen
E suggesting a solution to a problem
F explaining another side to the issue

1.5 **Match the sentence beginnings 1–6 to the correct technique A–F in 1.4. You may use any letter more than once.**

1 For instance, when we …
2 If that happened, then …
3 Well, I think …
4 On the other hand, some people believe …
5 This happens because …
6 One way of dealing with this is …

1.6 **Match techniques A–F with Emanuele's answers 1–8 above.**

1.7 **The questions in Part 3 often ask for your opinion. Look at the questions 1–5 and answer them in your own words. Make sure you expand on your answer using techniques from 1.4.**

1 Do you think it's more important to earn a large salary or to be happy in your job?
2 Do you think some people spend too much time on their computers these days? (Why?)
3 Do you think the government should try to control the internet, or should people be able to write whatever they want?
4 Pollution is a problem in many countries. What do you think governments can do about it?
5 Do you think newspapers and books will eventually disappear?

Test Tip For Part 3, it is important to have your own opinion. Try to read newspapers and watch the news to keep up with current issues.

2 Agreeing and disagreeing

2.1 **Sometimes the examiner will give you an opinion and then ask 'Would you agree with that?' Look at the following responses to this question. Put the different answers into the correct column according to their meaning.**

1 Oh no, not at all.
2 Well, I think there are valid points for both.
3 I totally agree with that.
4 I think I would probably have to say no.
5 To a certain extent, yes.
6 I completely disagree.
7 I can see your point, but …
8 Yes, I think that's absolutely right.
9 Actually, I think it depends on the situation/country/person
10 It seems to me that there are two sides to consider.

Test Tip Don't be afraid to disagree with the opinions the examiner expresses. These are not necessarily what the examiner thinks or believes. It is simply a chance for you to showcase your language and ideas.

Strongly disagree	Disagree to some extent	Neither agree nor disagree	Agree to some extent	Strongly agree

2.2 Look at the statements 1–5 and decide whether you agree.

1 Video games in general are a lot more violent nowadays.
2 People should be made to retire earlier so that younger people have a better chance of getting a job.
3 Robots will play a more important role in our lives in the future.
4 We don't do enough to protect the environment.
5 Everyone should take some sort of further education.

3 Improving your Lexical Resource score

Another of the criteria your examiner will use to assess your speaking is called **Lexical Resource**. You will score well if you use a wide range of vocabulary and don't limit yourself to basic words and phrases. During the Speaking test, try not to repeat the same words too often and use some idiomatic expressions if you can.

3.1 Create idiomatic expressions by completing phrases 1–6 with endings A–F.

1	I felt as though I didn't have	**A**	louder than words.
2	I couldn't keep	**B**	a bit of a slave driver.
3	Actions speak	**C**	a care in the world.
4	My boss was	**D**	by its cover.
5	My sister and I are like	**E**	a straight face.
6	You can't judge a book	**F**	two peas in a pod.

3.2 Match the completed expressions in 3.1 with the correct meaning.

A I was made to work very hard.
B We're very similar.
C Appearances can be deceiving.
D I was very relaxed.
E What we do matters more than what we say.
F I found it difficult not to laugh.

3.3 Below are some words/phrases that Emanuele used in Part 3. Are they basic or higher-level vocabulary? Circle the higher-level words.

holiday help it depends on experience
attitude small base (something) on
create the structure personal responsibility children
act in the right way allow people to everybody deserves
bad more or less house

3.4 Emanuele was given a score of 7 for Lexical Resource. Why do you think that is?

3.5 Video 13 Watch again and tick the words/phrases in 3.3 as you hear them.

3.6 Look again at the questions in 1.2 and answer them yourself.

Speaking skills

4 Checking, correcting and assessing

In this unit you will practise:

- dealing with problems
- pronunciation and intonation
- running words together (chunking)
- assessing your level

1 Dealing with problems

1.1 Video 14 Watch five extracts from different interviews and decide which of the problems (A–D) each candidate is experiencing. There may be more than one possible answer and you may use any letter more than once.

Problems
A the candidate doesn't understand the question
B the candidate hasn't heard the question properly
C the candidate has made a mistake
D the candidate isn't sure how to answer

1 Emanuele:
2 Saida:
3 Melanie:
4 Saida:
5 Melanie:

1.2 Watch again and notice how the candidate responds to the problem. Choose the correct letter (A–D).

Candidate's response to the problem
A the candidate stays silent
B the candidate attempts an answer but is hesitant
C the candidate asks a question to check
D the candidate corrects him/herself

1.3 Which of these ways of dealing with problems do you think could give you a lower mark? Why?

1.4 What did the examiner do in extracts 1 and 2 to help keep the candidate talking?

1.5 Here are some useful phrases you can use to deal with problems in the test. Match the phrases to the problems (A–D) in 1.1. You can use any of the phrases more than once.

Sorry, I meant to say …	I'm sorry, could you repeat the question?
I honestly have no idea.	I'm not really sure what you mean.
I've never really thought about that before.	

2 Pronunciation, intonation and 'chunking'

Study Tip If you are unsure which individual sounds you are saying incorrectly, try reading a short passage from this book aloud and asking another student to write down what you say. Are there any words or sounds that they have difficulty understanding? Or, record yourself and listen back. How easy is it to write what you hear?

The fourth criterion your examiner will use to assess your English level is **Pronunciation.** This includes:

- pronouncing individual sounds clearly.
- using intonation and stress to help communicate your ideas.
- 'chunking' (running your words together naturally and clearly – not in a robotic way).

Individual sounds

Hearing the difference between sounds you find difficult can be the first step to **saying** them correctly.

2.1 ▶ 34 To help you identify which English sounds you may have a problem with, listen and circle the word that you hear.

1 it / eat
2 look / luck
3 full / fool
4 bad / bed
5 workmen / workman
6 fur / far
7 board / bird
8 spot / sport
9 ankle / uncle
10 stairs / stars
11 heart / hot
12 knee / near
13 chest / chased
14 crawl / cruel
15 con / coin
16 could / code
17 fur / fair
18 back / bike
19 can't / count
20 day / they
21 breathe / breeze
22 depend / defend
23 bland / brand
24 sort / thought
25 close (adj) / close (v)
26 save / shave
27 hair / air
28 bet / vet

2.2 ▶ 35 Listen and practise saying all of the words correctly.

2.3 Read one word from each pair in 2.1 to a friend and ask them to write down the word they hear. Did they write the correct word?

Make sure to focus on the way you pronounce word endings as well.

2.4 Put the words into the correct column depending on how the ending is pronounced.

based	played	laughed	changed	waited
arrived	acted	chased	increased	learned
hoped	wanted	poured	decided	washed

/t/	/d/	/ɪd/

2.5 ▶ 36 Listen and check your answers.

2.6 Listen again and practise saying the words aloud.

2.7 ▶ Video 15 Watch extracts from Saida and Melanie's talks. What problems can you hear with individual sounds?

Stress, intonation, and running words together

Stress is used to accurately pronounce a word.

2.8 Which part of these words should be stressed? Underline the correct syllable.

contact	respect	equal	practice	depend
develop	environment	technique	expert	
difficult	expensive			

2.9 ▶ 37 Listen and check your answers, then practise saying the words with the correct stress.

Stress is also used to give emphasis to a word and add extra meaning to it.

2.10 ▶ 38 **You will hear part of a talk about conducting a job interview. As you listen, follow the script below and underline the words that the speaker stresses to give emphasis.**

> Over the years // I've interviewed hundreds of candidates // for jobs at many different levels. // The point of every job interview is to make sure a candidate has the skills necessary to do the work. Hiring the wrong person can be an expensive mistake. But, apart from references, how can you determine if the candidate actually knows what he says he knows? A very effective way to sort out the good candidates from the bad is by asking 'How did you do that?' and 'Why did you do that?' at appropriate stages in the interview.

Intonation is an important part of your pronunciation. Good intonation stops your speech sounding too monotonous.

Chunking, or running words together, also helps to make your language sound more natural.

2.11 **The first few lines of the script above have // marks to show how the speaker chunks words and phrases together. Listen again and add // marks to show where the speaker naturally pauses.**

2.12 **Look at this extract from Sanem's video and say it aloud.**

1 underline the words that you think should be stressed
2 use // marks to show which phrases or groups of words should be chunked together.

EXAMINER: Let's talk about music. How often do you listen to music?

SANEM: Every day. I love music, yeah I'm a fan of music every type of music especially rock music and classical music and I like to search from the internet, new groups, new bands, new type of genres. Yeah, every day.

2.13 ▶ Video 16 **Watch the extract from Sanem's video.**

1 Does she show a good use of stress and chunking?
2 Does she show a good use of intonation or does she sound monotonous?

> **Study Tip** A good way to practise intonation and fluency is by copying the rhythm of native speakers. Choose a recording from the listening section and play it at a low volume. Read aloud from the script and try to keep the same time and intonation patterns as the speaker on the recording.

3 Assessing yourself and improving your score

Study Tip Record yourself being interviewed, on video if possible, and try to assess your own performance. Decide which areas you need to work on and improve.

3.1 **Video 17** Watch the whole of Saida's test. As you watch, look at the comments made by an examiner below and the score she received.

Criteria	Examiner comments	Band awarded
Fluency and Cohesion	Slow speech and frequent hesitation. A range of spoken discourse markers (*well; so; it depends; actually; I think so; first of all*).	5
Lexical Resource	Some good vocabulary (*architectural design, last two decades, cooperative and tolerant, look after their children, help people become healthy again*), but limited flexibility is demonstrated by lack of range, repetition of certain items (*cooperative and tolerant*) and inappropriacies (*it's very actual, some cookings and housekeeping works, she always says me*).	Between a 5 and 6
Grammatical Range and Accuracy	Quite accurate on basic forms, but little range. Some good examples of complex forms (*help people to become healthy again, try to encourage it, I prefer to write letters by myself, my mother asked me to go to her home and help*), but most of these involve infinitive structures. Examples of errors (*technology nowdays are really go fast, she become healthy, now I proud, they are more closer, think about yourselves/themselves*). However, in general, these do not impede communication.	Between a 5 and a 6
Pronunciation	At times, her slow speech interferes with chunking and rhythm and she has a problem with 'th'. However, control is variable and when more confident, she demonstrates good rhythm and chunking (*if I can help someone, explain some things which I want to say*) and has some good use of intonation and stress (*not only nurses, also teachers*).	6

3.2 Saida's overall score was 5.5. Look at the comments again and decide what Saida would need to do to improve her band scores for each of the criteria.

3.3 Look back at any of the videos or recordings you have made of yourself. Compare your own performance with Saida's. What areas do you need to improve in your own performance?

Test 1

LISTENING

SECTION 1 *Questions 1–10*

Questions 1–6

Complete the notes below.

Write ***NO MORE THAN TWO WORDS AND/OR A NUMBER*** *for each answer.*

PRESTON PARK RUN

Details of run

Example

Day of Park Run: ......Saturday......

Start of run:	in front of the **1** ....
Time of start:	**2** ....
Length of run:	**3** ....
At end of run:	volunteer scans **4** ....
Best way to register:	on the **5** ....
Cost of run:	**6** £..................

Questions 7–10

Complete the notes below.

Write ***NO MORE THAN TWO WORDS AND/OR A NUMBER*** for each answer.

Volunteering

Contact name: Pete **7** ....

Phone number: **8** ....

Activities: setting up course

9 .... the runners

10 .... for the weekly report

Test Tip Remember that you only hear the recording once.

Check how many words you can use for each answer.

Read through the notes to get an overall idea of their content.

Test Tip You can write a time in figures or words, but figures are quicker and easier.

Study Tip 3 The answer is a distance. Make sure you include the unit of measurement – you can write this in an abbreviated form, e.g. 'km' for kilometres or 'm' for miles.

Test Tip If part of the answer is given (e.g. $, £, etc.) remember not to repeat it in your answer.

Test Tip Names are often spelled out on the recording. Make sure you know how all the letters of the English alphabet are pronounced. Listen carefully and write down the letters as you hear them.

Test Tip Check that you have spelled all the answers correctly.

SECTION 2 *Questions 11–20*

Questions 11–14

Complete the table below.

*Write **NO MORE THAN THREE WORDS AND/OR A NUMBER** for each answer.*

PACTON-ON-SEA BUS TOUR		
Bus stops	**Location**	**Things to see**
Bus stop 1	train station	start of tour
Bus stop 2	the aquarium	dolphins and **11** ....
Bus stop 3	**12**	yachts and power boats
Bus stop 4	**13** .... centre	very old **14** ....

Test Tip Look carefully at the table before you listen. Note the headings at the top – they tell you what you need to listen for. Use all the information provided in the table to help you predict answers.

You hear the answers in the same order as the questions.

Use the words that you hear to answer the questions.

Study Tip
11 'dolphins' is plural so the answer to this question is also likely to be plural – don't forget the 's'.

Study Tip 14 You may hear a synonym of 'very old' on the recording (e.g. 'ancient'). Don't repeat it in your answer.

Questions 15–20

Complete the sentences below.

Write ***NO MORE THAN TWO WORDS AND/OR A NUMBER*** *for each answer.*

15 You need to have a .... to buy a ticket for £10.

16 The bus tour lasts .... in total.

17 The cost of the bus ticket includes entrance to the ....

18 You can listen to an audio commentary which has been made by the ....

19 If the weather is wet, it is a good idea to bring ....

20 Don't forget to bring your .... when you book online.

Test Tip Read the sentences through in the preparation time and think about what type of information is missing.

Study Tip 18 If you do not know the phrase 'audio commentary', use the context and other words in the sentence to help you decide what it means, e.g. 'It is something you listen to on a tour bus'.

Study Tip Check that all the sentences are grammatically correct and make sense, e.g. don't repeat 'the' before your answer to Question 18.

SECTION 3 *Questions 21–30*

> **Study Tip** Read the questions through and underline important words that tell you what to listen for, e.g. 'main problem' in Question 22.

Questions 21–26

*Choose the correct letter, **A**, **B** or **C**.*

21 Dave Hadley says that the computer system has

A too many users.
B never worked well.
C become outdated.

22 The main problem with the computer system is that it

A is too slow.
B stops working.
C displays incorrect data.

23 Timetabling has become an issue because

A there is not enough time for anyone to do it.
B the system does not handle course options.
C the courses are constantly changing.

> **Study Tip 23** In addition to noting important words in the question ('Timetabling', 'issue'), you need to pick out the important words in the options ('not enough time', 'system', 'not handle', 'options', 'courses', 'changing').

24 To solve the timetabling issues, Randhir suggests that

A students should create their own timetables.
B Dave should have someone to assist him.
C the number of courses should be reduced.

25 Randhir says that a new system may

A need to be trialled.
B still have problems.
C be more economical.

> **Study Tip 25** Are any of the options positive or negative? Do the speakers' voices sound positive or negative? This may help you answer the question.

26 Improving the existing system will take

A a few weeks.
B four or five months.
C nine months.

Questions 27–30

Complete the flow-chart below.

Write ***NO MORE THAN TWO WORDS*** *for each answer.*

Next steps

Get approval from **27** ....

↓

Complete a **28** .... form

↓

Book a **29** .... with the systems analyst

↓

Set up a **30** .... with technologies team

Test Tip Check the number of words you can use, and read through the flow-chart to understand the process.

What type of information is missing in each gap? Are the answers likely to be plural or singular?

Study Tip 29 & 30 You can predict answers before you listen, but be careful! Why is 'appointment' incorrect for Question 29? What other answers are possible?

Test Tip Read back through the flow-chart and check your answers for both meaning and spelling.

SECTION 4 *Questions 31–40*

Complete the sentences below.

Write ***NO MORE THAN TWO WORDS AND/OR A NUMBER*** *for each answer.*

Ceramics

31 Ceramics date back approximately ....

32 The first figurines were made in the area of ....

33 Early humans could not use their pots to store ....

34 The Chinese improved the quality of ceramics by mixing .... with the clay.

35 Chinese porcelain was also called ....

36 Bottger added quartz and .... to clay to make porcelain.

Glass

37 Glass production is similar to clay ceramics apart from the rate of ....

38 The Romans introduced the use of glass to make ....

Concrete

39 The discovery of concrete is probably due to observing reactions of water and ....

40 The ability to build large .... contributed to the success of the Roman Empire.

Test Tip There is no break in this section. Read all ten sentences carefully in the preparation time.

Study Tip 31 Think of the sentences as questions, e.g. 'When did ceramics start?' This can help you think of words and phrases to listen for.

Study Tip 32–34 The answer to Question 32 is a place. What type of information is missing in the next two questions?

Study Tip Use the headings 'Ceramics', 'Glass' and 'Concrete' to help you keep your place as you listen.

Test Tip Make sure that the grammar of the completed sentences is correct.

Check there are no unnecessary words.

Check spellings and use of plural 's'.

Test Tip Aim to complete the questions in the recommended time.

There are usually two or three sets of questions in each section.

Each correct answer scores one mark.

READING

READING PASSAGE 1

You should spend about 20 minutes on ***Questions 1–13****, which are based on Reading Passage 1 below.*

The Dover Bronze-Age Boat

A beautifully preserved boat, made around 3,000 years ago and discovered by chance in a muddy hole, has had a profound impact on archaeological research.

It was 1992. In England, workmen were building a new road through the heart of Dover, to connect the ancient port and the Channel Tunnel, which, when it opened just two years later, was to be the first land link between Britain and Europe for over 10,000 years. A small team from the Canterbury Archaeological Trust (CAT) worked alongside the workmen, recording new discoveries brought to light by the machines.

At the base of a deep shaft six metres below the modern streets a wooden structure was revealed. Cleaning away the waterlogged site overlying the timbers, archaeologists realised its true nature. They had found a prehistoric boat, preserved by the type of sediment in which it was buried. It was then named the Dover Bronze-Age Boat.

About nine metres of the boat's length was recovered; one end lay beyond the excavation and had to be left. What survived consisted essentially of four intricately carved oak planks: two on the bottom, joined along a central seam by a complicated system of wedges and timbers, and two at the side, curved and stitched to the others. The seams had been made watertight by pads of moss, fixed by wedges and yew stitches.

The timbers that closed the recovered end of the boat had been removed in antiquity when it was abandoned, but much about its original shape could be deduced. There was also evidence for missing upper side planks. The boat was not a wreck, but had been deliberately discarded, dismantled and broken. Perhaps it had been 'ritually killed' at the end of its life, like other Bronze-Age objects.

With hindsight, it was significant that the boat was found and studied by mainstream archaeologists who naturally focused on its cultural context. At the time, ancient boats were often considered only from a narrower technological perspective, but news about the Dover boat reached a broad audience. In 2002, on the tenth anniversary of the discovery, the Dover Bronze-Age Boat Trust hosted a conference, where this meeting of different traditions became apparent. Alongside technical papers about the boat, other speakers explored its social and economic contexts, and the religious perceptions of boats in Bronze-Age societies. Many speakers came from overseas, and debate about cultural connections was renewed.

Within seven years of excavation, the Dover boat had been conserved and displayed, but it was apparent that there were issues that could not be resolved simply by studying the old wood. Experimental archaeology seemed to be the solution: a boat reconstruction, half-scale or full-sized, would permit assessment of the different hypotheses regarding its build and the missing end. The possibility of returning to Dover to search for the boat's unexcavated northern end was explored, but practical and financial difficulties were insurmountable – and there was no guarantee that the timbers had survived the previous decade in the changed environment.

Detailed proposals to reconstruct the boat were drawn up in 2004. Archaeological evidence was beginning to suggest a Bronze-Age community straddling the Channel, brought together by the sea, rather than separated by it. In a region today divided by languages and borders, archaeologists had a duty to inform the general public about their common cultural heritage.

The boat project began in England but it was conceived from the start as a European collaboration. Reconstruction was only part of a scheme that would include a major exhibition and an extensive educational and outreach programme. Discussions began early in 2005 with archaeological bodies, universities and heritage organisations either side of the Channel. There was much enthusiasm and support, and an official launch of the project was held at an international seminar in France in 2007. Financial support was confirmed in 2008 and the project then named BOAT 1550BC got under way in June 2011.

A small team began to make the boat at the start of 2012 on the Roman Lawn outside Dover museum. A full-scale reconstruction of a mid-section had been made in 1996, primarily to see how Bronze-Age replica tools performed. In 2012, however, the hull shape was at the centre of the work, so modern power tools were used to carve the oak planks, before turning to prehistoric tools for finishing. It was decided to make the replica half-scale for reasons of cost and time, and synthetic materials were used for the stitching, owing to doubts about the scaling and tight timetable.

Meanwhile, the exhibition was being prepared ready for opening in July 2012 at the Castle Museum in Boulogne-sur-Mer. Entitled 'Beyond the Horizon: Societies of the Channel & North Sea 3,500 years ago', it brought together for the first time a remarkable collection of Bronze-Age objects, including many new discoveries for commercial archaeology and some of the great treasure of the past. The reconstructed boat, as a symbol of the maritime connections that bound together the communities either side of the Channel, was the centrepiece.

Questions 1–5

Complete the flow-chart below.

*Choose **ONE WORD ONLY** from the text for each answer.*

Write your answers in boxes 1–5 on your answer sheet.

Key events

1992 – the boat was discovered during the construction of a **1** ....

↓

2002 – an international **2** .... was held to gather information

↓

2004 – **3** .... for the reconstruction were produced

↓

2007 – the **4** .... of BOAT 1550BC took place

↓

2012 – the Bronze-Age **5** .... featured the boat and other objects

Test Tip Quickly read through the flow-chart to understand the process. Note that in this task you can only write one word for each answer.

Test Tip Dates are easy to find in the passage because they stand out. Use them to help you quickly find the right part of the passage for each question.

All the answers must be words that are in the passage.

Questions 6–9

Do the following statements agree with the information given in the text?

In boxes 6–9 on your answer sheet, write

TRUE	*if the statement agrees with the information*
FALSE	*if the statement contradicts the information*
NOT GIVEN	*if there is no information on this*

6 Archaeologists realised that the boat had been damaged on purpose.

7 Initially, only the technological aspects of the boat were examined.

8 Archaeologists went back to the site to try and find the missing northern end of the boat.

9 Evidence found in 2004 suggested that the Bronze-Age Boat had been used for trade.

Test Tip The questions are in passage order, but the answers may not be evenly spread across the passage.

The difference between a FALSE and a NOT GIVEN statement is that a FALSE statement says the opposite of what is stated in the passage.

Questions 10–13

Answer the questions below.

*Choose **NO MORE THAN THREE WORDS AND/OR A NUMBER** from the text for each answer.*

Write your answers in boxes 10–13 on your answer sheet.

10 How far under the ground was the boat found?

11 What natural material had been secured to the boat to prevent water entering?

12 What aspect of the boat was the focus of the 2012 reconstruction?

13 Which two factors influenced the decision not to make a full-scale reconstruction of the boat?

Study Tip Which words in the statement are important and help you find the answer?

Test Tip You may have to go back to the beginning of the passage when you start a new set of questions.

Note how many words you can use in your answers.

READING PASSAGE 2

*You should spend about 20 minutes on **Questions 14–26**, which are based on Reading Passage 2 below.*

Test Tip Read the title and introduction of the passage and decide what the main topic is.

Some passages are divided into paragraphs that have clear themes. You may have to match paragraphs to headings or find information in the paragraphs. Always do a quick read of these questions first. Then quickly read the passage to get an overall idea of the content.

The changing role of airports

Airports continue to diversify their role in an effort to generate income. Are business meeting facilities the next step? Nigel Halpern, Anne Graham and Rob Davidson investigate.

A

In recent times developing commercial revenues has become more challenging for airports due to a combination of factors, such as increased competition from Internet shopping, restrictions on certain sales, such as tobacco, and new security procedures that have had an impact on the dwell time of passengers. Moreover, the global economic downturn has caused a reduction in passenger numbers while those that are travelling generally have less money to spend. This has meant that the share of revenue from non-aeronautical revenues actually peaked at 54% at the turn of the century and has subsequently declined slightly. Meanwhile, the pressures to control the level of aeronautical revenues are as strong as ever due to the poor financial health of many airlines and the rapid rise of the low-cost carrier sector.

B

Some of the more obvious solutions to growing commercial revenues, such as extending the merchandising space or expanding the variety of shopping opportunities, have already been tried to their limit at many airports. A more radical solution is to find new sources of commercial revenue within the terminal, and this has been explored by many airports over the last decade or so. As a result, many terminals are now much more than just shopping malls and offer an array of entertainment, leisure, and beauty and wellness facilities. At this stage of facilities provision, the airport also has the possibility of taking on the role of the final destination rather than merely a facilitator of access.

C

At the same time, airports have been developing and expanding the range of services that they provide specifically for the business traveller in the terminal. This includes offering business centres that supply support services, meeting or conference rooms and other space for special events. Within this context, Jarach (2001) discusses how dedicated meetings facilities located within the terminal and managed directly by the airport operator may be regarded as an expansion of the concept of airline lounges or as a way to reconvert abandoned or underused areas of terminal buildings. Previously it was primarily airport hotels and other facilities offered in the surrounding area of the airport that had the potential to take on this role and become active as a business space (McNeill, 2009).

D

When an airport location can be promoted as a business venue, this may increase the overall appeal of the airport and help it become more competitive in both attracting and retaining airlines and their passengers. In particular, the presence of meeting facilities could become one of the determining factors taken into consideration when business people are choosing airlines and where they change their planes. This enhanced attractiveness itself may help to improve the airport operator's financial position and future prospects, but clearly this will be dependent on the competitive advantage that the airport is able to achieve in comparison with other venues.

E

In 2011, an online airport survey was conducted and some of the areas investigated included the provision and use of meeting facilities at airports and the perceived role and importance of these facilities in generating income and raising passenger numbers. In total, there were responses from staff at 154 airports and 68% of these answered 'yes' to the question: Does your airport own and have meetings facilities available for hire? The existence of meeting facilities therefore seems high at airports. In addition, 28% of respondents that did not have meeting facilities stated that they were likely to invest in them during the next five years. The survey also asked to what extent respondents agreed or disagreed with a number of statements about the meeting facilities at their airport. 49% of respondents agreed that they have put more investment into them during recent years; 41% agreed that they would invest more in the immediate future. These are fairly high proportions considering the recent economic climate.

F

The survey also asked airports with meeting facilities to estimate what proportion of users are from the local area, i.e. within a 90-minute drive from the airport, or from abroad. Their findings show that meeting facilities provided by the majority of respondents tend to serve local versus non-local or foreign needs. 63% of respondents estimated that over 60% of users are from the local area. Only 3% estimated that over 80% of users are from abroad. It is therefore not surprising that the facilities are of limited importance when it comes to increasing use of flights at the airport: 16% of respondents estimated that none of the users of their meeting facilities use flights when travelling to or from them, while 56% estimated that 20% or fewer of the users of their facilities use flights.

G

The survey asked respondents with meeting facilities to estimate how much revenue their airport earned from its meeting facilities during the last financial year. Average revenue per airport was just $12,959. Meeting facilities are effectively a non-aeronautical source of airport revenue. Only 1% of respondents generated more than 20% non-aeronautical revenue from their meetings facilities; none generated more than 40%. Given the focus on local demand, it is not surprising that less than a third of respondents agreed that their meeting facilities support business and tourism development in their home region or country.

H

The findings of this study suggest that few airports provide meetings facilities as a serious commercial venture. It may be that, as owners of large property, space is available for meeting facilities at airports and could play an important role in serving the needs of the airport, its partners, and stakeholders such as government and the local community. Thus, while the local orientation means that competition with other airports is likely to be minimal, competition with local providers of meetings facilities is likely to be much greater.

Questions 14–18

The text has eight paragraphs, **A–H***.*

Which paragraph contains the following information?

Write the correct letter, **A–H***, in boxes 14–18 on your answer sheet.*

***N.B.** You may use any letter more than once.*

Test Tip There is only one correct answer for each question so some paragraphs may not be tested.

If you are told that 'you may use any letter more than once', it means that the answer to two (occasionally three) questions may be found in the same paragraph.

14 evidence that a significant number of airports provide meeting facilities

15 a statement regarding the fact that no further developments are possible in some areas of airport trade

16 reference to the low level of income that meeting facilities produce for airports

17 mention of the impact of budget airlines on airport income

18 examples of airport premises that might be used for business purposes

Study Tip 14 In this question, you are looking for 'evidence', which is likely to be in the form of data. Which paragraphs contain data? Which of these paragraphs provides data about the number of airports with meeting facilities?

Study Tip 16 The important word is 'income'. Which paragraph discusses the 'low level' generated by meeting facilities?

Study Tip 18 You need to find examples so think about the sorts of things these might be.

Questions 19–22

Complete the sentences below.

Choose ***NO MORE THAN TWO WORDS*** *from the text for each answer. Write your answers in boxes 19–22 on your answer sheet.*

19 The length of time passengers spend shopping at airports has been affected by updated ....

20 Airports with a wide range of recreational facilities can become a .... for people rather than a means to travel.

21 Both passengers and .... may feel encouraged to use and develop a sense of loyalty towards airports that market their business services.

22 Airports that supply meeting facilities may need to develop a .... over other venues.

Test Tip Read through each sentence and underline words that will help you find the right place in the passage.

Questions 23–26

Complete the summary below.

Choose ***NO MORE THAN TWO WORDS*** *from the text for each answer.*

Write your answers in boxes 23–26 on your answer sheet.

Survey Findings

Despite financial constraints due to the **23** .... , a significant percentage of airports provide and wish to further support business meeting facilities. Also, just under 30% of the airports surveyed plan to provide these facilities within **24** ....

However, the main users of the facilities are **25** .... and as many as 16% of respondents to the survey stated that their users did not take any **26** .... at the airport.

Test Tip Re-read the summary with the gaps completed. Check that it makes sense and is a true reflection of what is stated in the passage.

Test Tip Use the title of the summary to find the right place in the passage. The summary may cover one paragraph or several paragraphs.

Read through the summary, underlining important words. The answers may not come in the same order in the passage as the questions.

Study Tip 24 Find a figure that is 'just under thirty per cent'.

Study Tip
25 Rephrase the first part of the sentence: 'Who are the main users of airport facilities?' Find the part of the passage that discusses this.

READING PASSAGE 3

*You should spend about 20 minutes on **Questions 27–40**, which are based on Reading Passage 3 below.*

IS PHOTOGRAPHY ART?

This may seem a pointless question today. Surrounded as we are by thousands of photographs, most of us take for granted that, in addition to supplying information and seducing customers, camera images also serve as decoration, afford spiritual enrichment, and provide significant insights into the passing scene. But in the decades following the discovery of photography, this question reflected the search for ways to fit the mechanical medium into the traditional schemes of artistic expression.

The much-publicized pronouncement by painter Paul Delaroche that the daguerreotype* signalled the end of painting is perplexing because this clever artist also forecast the usefulness of the medium for graphic artists in a letter written in 1839. Nevertheless, it is symptomatic of the swing between the outright rejection and qualified acceptance of the medium that was fairly typical of the artistic establishment. Discussion of the role of photography in art was especially spirited in France, where the internal policies of the time had created a large pool of artists, but it was also taken up by important voices in England. In both countries, public interest in this topic was a reflection of the belief that national stature and achievement in the arts were related.

From the maze of conflicting statements and heated articles on the subject, three main positions about the potential of camera art emerged. The simplest, entertained by many painters and a section of the public, was that photographs should not be considered 'art' because they were made with a mechanical device and by physical and chemical phenomena instead of by human hand and spirit; to some, camera images seemed to have more in common with fabric produced by machinery in a mill than with handmade creations fired by inspiration. The second widely held view, shared by painters, some photographers, and some critics, was that photographs would be useful to art but should not be considered equal in creativeness to drawing and painting. Lastly, by assuming that the process was comparable to other techniques such as etching and lithography, a fair number of individuals realized that camera images were or could be as significant as handmade works of art and that they might have a positive influence on the arts and on culture in general.

Artists reacted to photography in various ways. Many portrait painters – miniaturists in particular – who realized that photography represented the '**handwriting on the wall**' became involved with daguerreotyping or paper photography in an effort to save their careers; some incorporated it with painting, while others renounced painting altogether. Still other painters, the most prominent among them the French painter, Jean-Auguste-Dominique Ingres, began almost immediately to use photography to make a record of their own output and also to provide themselves with source material for poses and backgrounds, vigorously denying at the same time its influence on their vision or its claims as art.

The view that photographs might be worthwhile to artists was enunciated in considerable detail by Lacan and Francis Wey. The latter, an art and literary critic, who eventually recognised that camera images could be inspired as well as informative, suggested that they would lead to greater naturalness in the graphic depiction of anatomy, clothing, likeness, expression, and landscape. By studying photographs, true artists, he claimed, would be relieved of menial tasks and become free to devote themselves to the more important spiritual aspects of their work.

Wey left unstated what the incompetent artist might do as an alternative, but according to the influential French critic and poet Charles Baudelaire, writing in response to an exhibition of photography in 1859, lazy and untalented painters would become photographers. Fired by a belief in art as an imaginative embodiment of cultivated ideas and dreams, Baudelaire regarded photography as 'a very humble servant of art and science'; a medium largely unable to transcend 'external reality'. For this critic, photography was linked with 'the great industrial madness' of the time, which in his eyes exercised disastrous consequences on the spiritual qualities of life and art.

Eugene Delacroix was the most prominent of the French artists who welcomed photography as help-mate but recognized its limitations. Regretting that 'such a wonderful invention' had arrived so late in his lifetime, he still took lessons in daguerreotyping, and both commissioned and collected photographs. Delacroix's enthusiasm for the medium can be sensed in a journal entry noting that if photographs were used as they should be, an artist might 'raise himself to heights that we do not yet know'.

The question of whether the photograph was document or art aroused interest in England also. The most important statement on this matter was an unsigned article that concluded that while photography had a role to play, it should not be 'constrained' into 'competition' with art; a more stringent viewpoint led critic Philip Gilbert Hamerton to dismiss camera images as 'narrow in range, emphatic in assertion, telling one truth for ten falsehoods'.

These writers reflected the opposition of a section of the cultural elite in England and France to the 'cheapening of art' which the growing acceptance and purchase of camera pictures by the middle class represented. Technology made photographic images a common sight in the shop windows of Regent Street and Piccadilly in London and the commercial boulevards of Paris. In London, for example, there were at the time some 130 commercial establishments where portraits, landscapes, and photographic reproductions of works of art could be bought. This appeal to the middle class convinced the elite that photographs would foster a desire for realism instead of idealism, even though some critics recognized that the work of individual photographers might display an uplifting style and substance that was consistent with the defining characteristics of art.

* *the name given to the first commercially successful photographic images*

Questions 27–30

Choose the correct letter, ***A****,* ***B****,* ***C*** *or* ***D****.*

Write your answers in boxes 27–30 on your answer sheet.

27 What is the writer's main point in the first paragraph?

A Photography is used for many different purposes.
B Photographers and artists have the same principal aims.
C Photography has not always been a readily accepted art form.
D Photographers today are more creative than those of the past.

28 What public view about artists was shared by the French and the English?

A that only artists could reflect a culture's true values
B that only artists were qualified to judge photography
C that artists could lose work as a result of photography
D that artistic success raised a country's international profile

29 What does the writer mean in line 59 by 'the handwriting on the wall'?

A an example of poor talent
B a message that cannot be trusted
C an advertisement for something new
D a signal that something bad will happen

30 What was the result of the widespread availability of photographs to the middle classes?

A The most educated worried about its impact on public taste.
B It helped artists appreciate the merits of photography.
C Improvements were made in photographic methods.
D It led to a reduction in the price of photographs.

Test Tip Read the questions and underline words that will help you find the right part of the passage.

Study Tip 27 Read the first paragraph carefully and underline the main idea. Which of the options expresses this?

Study Tip 29 The phrase in inverted commas is in bold in the passage. Read around it to find out what it means.

Questions 31–34

Complete the summary of Paragraph 3 using the list of words, ***A–G,*** *below.*

Write your answers in boxes 31–34 on your answer sheet.

A	inventive	**C**	beneficial	**E**	mixed	**G**	inferior
B	similar	**D**	next	**F**	justified		

Test Tip Read the instructions carefully. Sometimes you are told which paragraph to read. You can also use the title of the summary to find the right place.

Camera art

In the early days of photography, opinions on its future were **31** .... , but three clear views emerged. A large number of artists and ordinary people saw photographs as **32** .... to paintings because of the way they were produced. Another popular view was that photographs could have a role to play in the art world, despite the photographer being less **33** .... Finally, a smaller number of people suspected that the impact of photography on art and society could be **34** ....

Study Tip
31 'opinions' and 'views' in the first sentence have a similar meaning. Which word at the start of Paragraph 3 also has this meaning? Which of the options expresses the views when photography began?

Questions 35–40

Look at the following statements and the list of people, ***A–E,*** *below.*

Match each statement with the correct person.

Write the correct letter, ***A–E****, in boxes 35–40 on your answer sheet.*

35 He claimed that photography would make paintings more realistic.

36 He highlighted the limitations and deceptions of the camera.

37 He documented his production of artwork by photographing his works.

38 He noted the potential for photography to enrich artistic talent.

39 He based some of the scenes in his paintings on photographs.

40 He felt photography was part of the trend towards greater mechanisation.

Test Tip If there are more statements than names, you will have to use one of the names twice.

A	Jean-Auguste-Dominique Ingres	**C**	Charles Baudelaire
		D	Eugene Delacroix
B	Francis Wey	**E**	Philip Gilbert Hamerton

WRITING

WRITING TASK 1

You should spend about 20 minutes on this task.

The chart below gives information on the percentage of British people giving money to charity by age range for the years 1990 and 2010.

Summarise the information by selecting and reporting the main features and make comparisons where relevant.

Write at least 150 words.

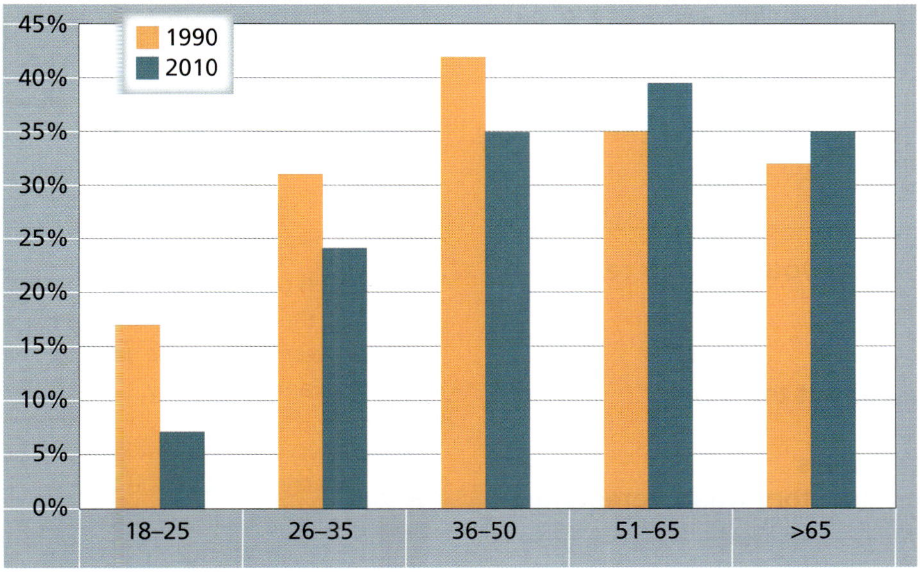

Study Tip Identify the main features of the chart: Which age-group donated most money to charity in each year? Which age-group donated the least? How does the generosity of the age-groups compare across the years?

Include an overview: How does the overall pattern in 2010 differ from the pattern in 1990?

Test Tip Begin with an introduction.

Highlight and compare the main features. Make your overview clear.

Use a range of relevant vocabulary and try to vary your sentence types. Link your ideas together so that your answer flows smoothly.

WRITING TASK 2

You should spend about 40 minutes on this task.

Some people work for the same organisation all their working life. Others think that it is better to work for different organisations.

Discuss both these views and give your own opinion.

Give reasons for your answer and include any relevant examples from your own knowledge or experience.

Write at least 250 words.

Test Tip Task 2 is worth twice as many marks as Task 1 so you are advised to spend twice as long writing your answer.

Write 250 words or more, and use your own words.

SPEAKING

PART 1

School days

- Tell me something about your secondary school.
- Which subject did you find most difficult at school? [Why?]
- Do you ever need that subject now? [Why? / Why not?]
- What did you enjoy about being a school student?

Buildings

- Are there any famous buildings in your home town? [What are they?]
- In what type of building do most people in your home town live?
- Should buildings be attractive to look at? [Why? / Why not?]
- What is the most unusual building you have ever seen? [Why?]

PART 2

Candidate task card:

Describe an interesting story that you heard or read about in the news.

You should say:
when you heard or read about the story
what the story was about
why the story was in the news
and explain why you thought the story was interesting.

Test Tip In Part 2, the examiner will ask you some more questions on familiar topics.

Listen carefully to the questions. Use the correct tense for each answer and include some relevant vocabulary.

Study Tip Use the one-minute preparation time to think about your topic and what you will say; make notes on each point. (Choose a story that you can easily talk about.)

Test Tip In Part 3, introduce your topic, link your ideas and aim to speak for two minutes.

Speak clearly and at a natural speed so that the examiner can understand you. Use stress and intonation to highlight important information and feelings.

PART 3

Reading newspapers

- When do people like to read the newspaper?
- How important is it for people to have a choice of newspaper?
- What does a 'good' newspaper contain?

The future of newspapers

- Why do some people choose to read the news on the Internet rather than in a newspaper?
- How is Internet news different from the news you read in the newspaper?
- Will Internet news ever replace newspapers? [Why? / Why not?]

Test 2

LISTENING

SECTION 1 *Questions 1–10*

Questions 1–6

Complete the notes below.

*Write **NO MORE THAN TWO WORDS AND/OR A NUMBER** for each answer.*

Short Story Competition	
Entry Details	
Example	
Cost of entry:	..........£5..........
Length of story:	approximately **1** ....
	Story must include: a **2** ....
Minimum age:	**3** ....
Last entry date:	1st **4** ....
Web address:	www. **5** .... .com
Don't:	**6** .... the story to the organisers

Questions 7–10

Complete the sentences below.

*Write **NO MORE THAN TWO WORDS** for each answer.*

Judging and Prize Details

The competition is judged by **7** ....

The top five stories will be available **8** ....

The top story will be chosen by the **9** ....

The first prize is a place at a writers' workshop in **10** ....

SECTION 2 *Questions 11–20*

Questions 11–17

Answer the questions below.

Write ***NO MORE THAN THREE WORDS*** *for each answer.*

Sea Life Centre – information

11 What was the Sea Life Centre previously called? ....

12 What is the newest attraction called? ....

13 When is the main feeding time? ....

14 What can you do with a VIP ticket? ....

15 What special event will the Sea Life Centre arrange for you? ....

16 Where will the petition for animal conservation be sent to? ....

17 What can you use to test what you have learnt? ....

Questions 18–20

What does the guide say about each attraction?

Choose ***THREE*** *answers from the box and write the correct letter,* ***A–E,*** *next to Questions 18–20.*

A	Aquarium
B	Crocodile Cave
C	Penguin Park
D	Seal Centre
E	Turtle Town

18 must not miss ....

19 temporarily closed ....

20 large queues ....

SECTION 3 *Questions 21–30*

Questions 21–22

*Choose **TWO** letters, **A–E**.*

*Which **TWO** subjects did Martina like best before going to university?*

A	Art	**B**	English	**C**	French
D	History	**E**	Science		

Questions 23–26

Complete the summary below.

*Write **NO MORE THAN TWO WORDS** for each answer.*

George's experience of university

George is studying Mechanical Engineering which involves several disciplines. He is finding **23** .... the most difficult. At the moment, his course is mainly **24** .... He will soon have an assignment which involves a study of **25** .... He thinks there are too many **26** .... and would like less of them.

Questions 27–30

*Choose the correct letter, **A**, **B** or **C**.*

27 Martina thinks the students at her university are

A sociable.
B intelligent.
C energetic.

28 George hopes that his tutor will help him

A lose his shyness.
B settle into university.
C get to know his subject better.

29 What does Martina know about her first assignment?

A the topic
B the length
C the deadline

30 George would like to live

A in a hall of residence.
B in a flat on his own.
C with a host family.

SECTION 4 *Questions 31–40*

Complete the notes below.

Write ***NO MORE THAN TWO WORDS*** *for each answer.*

Preparing and Giving a Presentation

Initial thoughts

Most important consideration: your audience

Three points to bear in mind:

- what they need to know
- how **31** .... they will be
- how big the audience will be

Structure

Start with information that makes the audience **32** ....

End with **33** ....

Design

The presentation needs to be **34** ....

Vary content by using a mix of words and **35** ....

Presenting

Look at the audience, be enthusiastic and energetic

Voice – vary speed and **36** ....

Occasionally add **37** .... for greater impact

Do not use **38** .... (e.g. *appears*, *seems*)

Questions and Interruptions

When asked a question, first of all you should **39** ....

Minimise interruptions by **40** .... them

READING

READING PASSAGE 1

*You should spend about 20 minutes on **Questions 1–13**, which are based on Reading Passage 1 below.*

The Flavor of Pleasure

When it comes to celebrating the flavor of food, our mouth gets all the credit. But in truth, it is the nose that knows.

No matter how much we talk about tasting our favorite flavors, relishing them really depends on a combined input from our senses that we experience through mouth, tongue and nose. The taste, texture, and feel of food are what we tend to focus on, but most important are the slight puffs of air as we chew our food – what scientists call 'retronasal smell'.

Certainly, our mouths and tongues have taste buds, which are receptors for the five basic flavors: sweet, salty, sour, bitter, and umami, or what is more commonly referred to as savory. But our tongues are inaccurate instruments as far as flavor is concerned. They evolved to recognise only a few basic tastes in order to quickly identify toxins, which in nature are often quite bitter or acidly sour.

All the complexity, nuance, and pleasure of flavor come from the sense of smell operating in the back of the nose. It is there that a kind of alchemy occurs when we breathe up and out the passing whiffs of our chewed food. Unlike a hound's skull with its extra long nose, which evolved specifically to detect external smells, our noses have evolved to detect internal scents. Primates specialise in savoring the many millions of flavor combinations that they can create for their mouths.

Taste without retronasal smell is not much help in recognising flavor. Smell has been the most poorly understood of our senses, and only recently has neuroscience, led by Yale University's Gordon Shepherd, begun to shed light on its workings. Shepherd has come up with the term 'neurogastronomy' to link the disciplines of food science, neurology, psychology, and anthropology with the savory elements of eating, one of the most enjoyed of human experiences.

In many ways, he is discovering that smell is rather like face recognition. The visual system detects patterns of light and dark and, building on experience, the brain creates a spatial map. It uses this to interpret the interrelationship of the patterns and draw conclusions that allow us to identify people and places. In the same way, we use patterns and ratios to detect both new and familiar flavors. As we eat, specialised receptors in the back of the nose detect the air molecules in our meals. From signals sent by the receptors, the brain understands smells as complex spatial patterns. Using these, as well as input from the other senses, it constructs the idea of specific flavors.

This ability to appreciate specific aromas turns out to be central to the pleasure we get from food, much as our ability to recognise individuals is central to the pleasures of social life. The process is so embedded in our brains that our sense of smell is critical to our enjoyment of life at large. Recent studies show that people who lose the ability to smell become socially insecure, and their overall level of happiness plummets.

Working out the role of smell in flavor interests food scientists, psychologists, and cooks alike. The relatively new discipline of molecular gastronomy, especially, relies on understanding the mechanics of aroma to manipulate flavor for maximum impact. In this discipline, chefs use their knowledge of the chemical changes that take place during cooking to produce eating pleasures that go beyond the 'ordinary'.

However, whereas molecular gastronomy is concerned primarily with the food or 'smell' molecules, neurogastronomy is more focused on the receptor molecules and the brain's spatial images for smell. Smell stimuli form what Shepherd terms 'odor objects', stored as memories, and these have a direct link with our emotions. The brain creates images of unfamiliar smells by relating them to other more familiar smells. Go back in history and this was part of our survival repertoire; like most animals, we drew on our sense of smell, when visual information was scarce, to single out prey.

Thus the brain's flavor-recognition system is a highly complex perceptual mechanism that puts all five senses to work in various combinations. Visual and sound cues contribute, such as crunching, as does touch, including the texture and feel of food on our lips and in our mouths. Then there are the taste receptors, and finally, the smell, activated when we inhale. The engagement of our emotions can be readily illustrated when we picture some of the wide-ranging facial expressions that are elicited by various foods – many of them hard-wired into our brains at birth. Consider the response to the sharpness of a lemon and compare that with the face that is welcoming the smooth wonder of chocolate.

The flavor-sensing system, ever receptive to new combinations, helps to keep our brains active and flexible. It also has the power to shape our desires and ultimately our bodies. On the horizon we have the positive application of neurogastronomy: manipulating flavor to curb our appetites.

Questions 1–5

Complete the sentences below.

Choose ***NO MORE THAN TWO WORDS*** *from the text for each answer.*

Write your answers in boxes 1–5 on your answer sheet.

1 According to scientists, the term .... characterises the most critical factor in appreciating flavour.

2 'Savoury' is a better-known word for ....

3 The tongue was originally developed to recognise the unpleasant taste of ....

4 Human nasal cavities recognise .... much better than external ones.

5 Gordon Shepherd uses the word 'neurogastronomy' to draw together a number of .... related to the enjoyment of eating.

Questions 6–9

Complete the notes below.

Choose ***NO MORE THAN TWO WORDS*** *from the text for each answer.*

Write your answers in boxes 6–9 on your answer sheet.

Face recognition	patterns of dark and light are used to put together a **6**	→	the brain identifies faces	facial recognition is key to our enjoyment of **7** ....
Smell	receptors recognise the **8** .... in food	→	the brain identifies certain **9**	smell is key to our enjoyment of food

Questions 10–13

Answer the questions below.

Choose ***NO MORE THAN ONE WORD*** *from the text for each answer.*

Write your answers in boxes 10–13 on your answer sheet.

10 In what form does the brain store 'odor objects'?

11 When seeing was difficult, what did we use our sense of smell to find?

12 Which food item illustrates how flavour and positive emotion are linked?

13 What could be controlled in the future through flavour manipulation?

READING PASSAGE 2

*You should spend about 20 minutes on **Questions 14–26**, which are based on Reading Passage 2 on the following pages.*

Questions 14–19

The text on the following pages has six paragraphs, **A–F**.

Choose the correct heading for each paragraph from the list of headings (i–ix) below.

*Write the correct number, **i–ix**, in boxes 14–19 on your answer sheet.*

List of Headings

i	Tackling the issue using a different approach
ii	A significant improvement on last time
iii	How robots can save human lives
iv	Examples of robots at work
v	Not what it seemed to be
vi	Why timescales are impossible to predict
vii	The reason why robots rarely move
viii	Following the pattern of an earlier development
ix	The ethical issues of robotics

14 Paragraph A

15 Paragraph B

16 Paragraph C

17 Paragraph D

18 Paragraph E

19 Paragraph F

Dawn of the robots

They're already here – driving cars, vacuuming carpets and feeding hospital patients. They may not be walking, talking, human-like sentient beings, but they are clever… and a little creepy.

A At first sight it looked like a typical suburban road accident. A Land Rover approached a Chevy Tahoe estate car that had stopped at a kerb; the Land Rover pulled out and tried to pass the Tahoe just as it started off again. There was a crack of fenders and the sound of paintwork being scraped, the kind of minor mishap that occurs on roads thousands of times every day. Normally drivers get out, gesticulate, exchange insurance details and then drive off. But not on this occasion. No one got out of the cars for the simple reason that they had no humans inside them; the Tahoe and Land Rover were being controlled by computers competing in November's DARPA (the U.S. Defence Advanced Research Projects Agency) Urban Challenge.

B The idea that machines could perform to such standards is startling. Driving is a complex task that takes humans a long time to perfect. Yet here, each car had its on-board computer loaded with a digital map and route plans, and was instructed to negotiate busy roads; differentiate between pedestrians and stationary objects; determine whether other vehicles were parked or moving off; and handle various parking manoeuvres, which robots turn out to be unexpectedly adept at. Even more striking was the fact that the collision between the robot Land Rover, built by researchers at the Massachusetts Institute of Technology, and the Tahoe, fitted out by Cornell University Artificial Intelligence (AI) experts, was the only scrape in the entire competition. Yet only three years earlier, at DARPA's previous driverless car race, every robot competitor – directed to navigate across a stretch of open desert – either crashed or seized up before getting near the finishing line.

C It is a remarkable transition that has clear implications for the car of the future. More importantly, it demonstrates how robotics sciences and Artificial Intelligence have progressed in the past few years – a point stressed by Bill Gates, the Microsoft boss who is a convert to these causes. 'The robotics industry is developing in much the same way the computer business did 30 years ago,' he argues. As he points out, electronics companies make toys that mimic pets and children with increasing sophistication. 'I can envision a future in which robotic devices will become a nearly ubiquitous part of our day-to-day lives,' says Gates. 'We may be on the verge of a new era, when the PC will get up off the desktop and allow us to see, hear, touch and manipulate objects in places where we are not physically present.'

D What is the potential for robots and computers in the near future? 'The fact is we still have a way to go before real robots catch up with their science fiction counterparts,' Gates says. So what are the stumbling blocks? One key difficulty is getting robots to know their place. This has nothing to do with class or etiquette, but concerns the simple issue of positioning. Humans orient themselves with other objects in a room very easily. Robots find the task almost impossible. 'Even something as simple as telling the difference between an open door and a window can be tricky for a robot,' says Gates. This has, until recently, reduced robots to fairly static and cumbersome roles.

E For a long time, researchers tried to get round the problem by attempting to re-create the visual processing that goes on in the human cortex. However, that challenge has proved to be singularly exacting and complex. So scientists have turned to simpler alternatives: 'We have become far more pragmatic in our work,' says Nello Cristianini, Professor of Artificial Intelligence at the University of Bristol in England and associate editor of the *Journal of Artificial Intelligence Research*. 'We are no longer trying to re-create human functions. Instead, we are looking for simpler solutions with basic electronic sensors, for example.' This approach is exemplified by vacuuming robots such as the Electrolux Trilobite. The Trilobite scuttles around homes emitting ultrasound signals to create maps of rooms, which are remembered for future cleaning. Technology like this is now changing the face of robotics, says philosopher Ron Chrisley, director of the Centre for Research in Cognitive Science at the University of Sussex in England.

F Last year, a new Hong Kong restaurant, Robot Kitchen, opened with a couple of sensor-laden humanoid machines directing customers to their seats. Each possesses a touch-screen on which orders can be keyed in. The robot then returns with the correct dishes. In Japan, University of Tokyo researchers recently unveiled a kitchen 'android' that could wash dishes, pour tea and make a few limited meals. The ultimate aim is to provide robot home helpers for the sick and the elderly, a key concern in a country like Japan where 22 per cent of the population is 65 or older. Over US$1 billion a year is spent on research into robots that will be able to care for the elderly. 'Robots first learn basic competence – how to move around a house without bumping into things. Then we can think about teaching them how to interact with humans,' Chrisley said. Machines such as these take researchers into the field of socialised robotics: how to make robots act in a way that does not scare or offend individuals. 'We need to study how robots should approach people, how they should appear. That is going to be a key area for future research,' adds Chrisley.

Questions 20–23

Look at the following statements (Questions 20–23) and the list of people below.

Match each statement with the correct person, ***A, B*** *or* ***C****.*

Write the correct letter in boxes 20–23 on your answer sheet.

NB *You may use any letter more than once.*

A Bill Gates
B Nello Cristianini
C Ron Chrisley

20 An important concern for scientists is to ensure that robots do not seem frightening.

21 We have stopped trying to enable robots to perceive objects as humans do.

22 It will take considerable time for modern robots to match the ones we have created in films and books.

23 We need to enable robots to move freely before we think about trying to communicate with them.

Questions 24–26

Complete the notes below.

Choose ***NO MORE THAN THREE WORDS*** *from the text for each answer.*

Write your answers in boxes 24–26 on your answer sheet.

Robot features

DARPA race cars:	**24** .... provides maps and plans for route
Electrolux Trilobite:	builds an image of a room by sending out **25** ....
Robot Kitchen humanoids:	have a **26** .... to take orders

READING PASSAGE 3

You should spend about 20 minutes on ***Questions 27–40****, which are based on Reading Passage 3 below.*

It's your choice! – Or is it really?

As we move from the industrial age to the information age, societal demands on our mental capabilities are no less taxing …

We are constantly required to process a wide range of information to make decisions. Sometimes, these decisions are trivial, such as what marmalade to buy. At other times, the stakes are higher, such as deciding which symptoms to report to the doctor. However, the fact that we are accustomed to processing large amounts of information does not mean that we are better at it (Chabris & Simons, 2009). Our sensory and cognitive systems have systematic ways of failing of which we are often, perhaps blissfully, unaware.

Imagine that you are taking a walk in your local city park when a tourist approaches you asking for directions. During the conversation, two men carrying a door pass between the two of you. If the person asking for directions had changed places with one of the people carrying the door, would you notice? Research suggests that you might not. Harvard psychologists Simons and Levi (1998) conducted a field study using this exact set-up and found that the change in identity went unnoticed by 7 (46.6%) of the 15 participants. This phenomenon has been termed 'change blindness' and refers to the difficulty that observers have in noticing changes to visual scenes (e.g. the person swap), when the changes are accompanied by some other visual disturbance (e.g. the passing of the door).

Over the past decade, the change blindness phenomenon has been replicated many times. Especially noteworthy is an experiment by Davies and Hine (2007) who studied whether change blindness affects eyewitness identification. Specifically, participants were presented with a video enactment of a burglary. In the video, a man entered a house, walking through the different rooms and putting valuables into a knapsack. However, the identity of the burglar changed after the first half of the film while the initial burglar was out of sight. Out of the 80 participants, 49 (61%) did not notice the change of the burglar's identity, suggesting that change blindness may have serious implications for criminal proceedings.

To most of us, it seems bizarre that people could miss such obvious changes while they are paying active attention. However, to catch those changes, attention must be targeted to the changing feature. In the study described above, participants were likely not to have been expecting the change to happen, and so their attention may have been focused on the valuables the burglar was stealing, rather than the burglar.

Drawing from change blindness research, scientists have come to the conclusion that we perceive the world in much less detail than previously thought (Johansson, Hall, & Sikström, 2008). Rather than monitoring all of the visual details that surround us, we seem to focus our attention only on those features that are currently meaningful or important, ignoring those that are irrelevant to our current needs and goals. Thus at any given time, our representation of the world surrounding us is crude and incomplete, making it possible for changes or manipulations to go undetected (Chabris & Simons, 2010).

Given the difficulty people have in noticing changes to visual stimuli, one may wonder what would happen if these changes concerned the decisions people make. To examine choice blindness, Hall and colleagues (2010) invited supermarket customers to sample two different kinds of jams and teas. After participants had tasted or smelled both samples, they indicated which one they preferred. Subsequently, they were purportedly given another sample of their preferred choice. On half of the trials, however, these were samples of the non-chosen jam or tea. As expected, only about one-third of the participants detected this manipulation. Based on these findings, Hall and colleagues proposed that choice blindness is a phenomenon that occurs not only for choices involving visual material, but also for choices involving gustatory and olfactory information.

Recently, the phenomenon has also been replicated for choices involving auditory stimuli (Sauerland, Sagana, & Otgaar, 2012). Specifically, participants had to listen to three pairs of voices and decide for each pair which voice they found more sympathetic or more criminal. The voice was then presented again; however, the outcome was manipulated for the second voice pair and participants were presented with the non-chosen voice. Replicating the findings by Hall and colleagues, only 29% of the participants detected this change.

Merckelbach, Jelicic, and Pieters (2011) investigated choice blindness for intensity ratings of one's own psychological symptoms. Their participants had to rate the frequency with which they experienced 90 common symptoms (e.g. anxiety, lack of concentration, stress, headaches etc.) on a 5-point scale. Prior to a follow-up interview, the researchers inflated ratings for two symptoms by two points. For example, when participants had rated their feelings of shyness, as 2 (i.e. *occasionally*), it was changed to 4 (i.e. *all the time*). This time, more than half (57%) of the 28 participants were blind to the symptom rating escalation and accepted it as their own symptom intensity rating. This demonstrates that blindness is not limited to recent preference selections, but can also occur for intensity and frequency.

Together, these studies suggest that choice blindness can occur in a wide variety of situations and can have serious implications for medical and judicial outcomes. Future research is needed to determine how, in those situations, choice blindness can be avoided.

Questions 27–31

Do the following statements agree with the claims of the writer in the text?

In boxes 27–31 on your answer sheet, write

YES	*if the statement agrees with the claims of the writer*
NO	*if the statement contradicts the claims of the writer*
NOT GIVEN	*if it is impossible to say what the writer thinks about this*

27 Doctors make decisions according to the symptoms that a patient describes.

28 Our ability to deal with a lot of input material has improved over time.

29 We tend to know when we have made an error of judgement.

30 A legal trial could be significantly affected by change blindness.

31 Scientists have concluded that we try to take in as much detail as possible from our surroundings.

Questions 32–36

Complete the table below.

Choose ***NO MORE THAN TWO WORDS*** *from the text for each answer.*

Write your answers in boxes 32–36 on your answer sheet.

Experiments in change blindness				
Researchers	**Purpose of experiment**	**Situation for participants**	**Focus of participants' attention**	**Percentage unaware of identity change**
Simons & Levi, 1998	to illustrate change blindness caused by a **32** …………………… , such as an object	giving **33** …………………… to a stranger	the movement of **34** ……………………	46.6%
Davies & Hine, 2007	to assess the impact of change blindness on **35** …………………… by eyewitnesses	watching a burglary	the collection of **36** ……………………	61%

Questions 37–38

*Choose **TWO** letters, **A–E**.*

*Which **TWO** statements are true for both the supermarket and voice experiments?*

Write your answers in boxes 37–38 on your answer sheet.

A The researchers focused on non-visual material.

B The participants were asked to explain their preferences.

C Some of the choices made by participants were altered.

D The participants were influenced by each other's choices.

E Percentage results were surprisingly low.

Questions 39–40

*Choose **TWO** letters, **A–E**.*

*Which **TWO** statements are true for the psychology experiment conducted by Merckelbach, Jelicic, and Pieters?*

Write your answers in boxes 39–40 on your answer sheet.

A The participants had to select their two most common symptoms.

B The participants gave each symptom a 1–5 rating.

C Shyness proved to be the most highly rated symptom.

D The participants changed their minds about some of their ratings.

E The researchers focused on the strength and regularity of symptoms.

WRITING

WRITING TASK 1

You should spend about 20 minutes on this task.

> ***The graph and table below show the average monthly temperatures and the average number of hours of sunshine per year in three major cities.***
>
> ***Summarise the information by selecting and reporting the main features and make comparisons where relevant.***

Write at least 150 words.

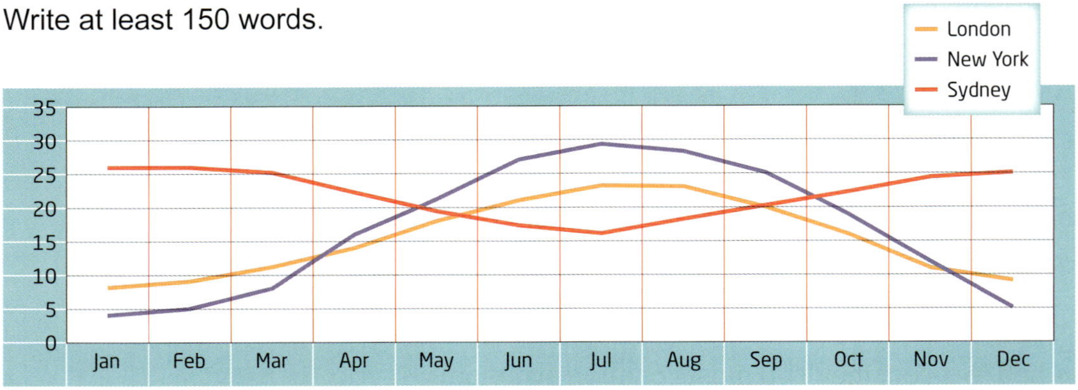

Total annual hours of sunshine for London, New York and Sydney

London	1,180
New York	2,535
Sydney	2,473

WRITING TASK 2

You should spend about 40 minutes on this task.

> ***One of the consequences of improved medical care is that people are living longer and life expectancy is increasing.***
>
> ***Do you think the advantages of this development outweigh the disadvantages?***

Give reasons for your answer and include any relevant examples from your own knowledge or experience.

Write at least 250 words.

SPEAKING

PART 1

Home town

- Is your home town a good place to live? [Why? / Why not?]
- What sort of jobs do people do in your home town?
- In which part of your home town do most people live?
- Where did you play in your home town when you were a child?

Films

- How often do you go to the cinema?
- Do you prefer to watch a film at the cinema or at home? [Why?]
- Which film from your childhood do you remember most? [Why?]
- What's your favourite film now? [Why?]

PART 2

Candidate task card:

Describe an interesting place that you have visited as a tourist.

You should say:
where this place is
why you went there
what you did there
and explain why you thought this place was so interesting.

PART 3

Places that tourists visit

- What areas of a town or city do tourists often like to visit?
- How important is it for local governments to look after popular tourist attractions?
- Should people pay to visit attractions such as museums and galleries? [Why? / Why not?]

Being a tourist

- How should tourists behave when they are in a different country?
- What can local people do to help tourists enjoy their visit?
- What can tourists learn from visiting new places?

Test 3

LISTENING

SECTION 1 *Questions 1–10*

Questions 1–5

Complete the form below.

Write ***NO MORE THAN TWO WORDS AND/OR A NUMBER*** *for each answer.*

SARAH'S HEALTH & FITNESS CLUB MEMBERSHIP FORM	
Example	
First name:	......Harry......
Last name:	**1** ....
Date of Birth:	Day: *11th*; Month: *December*; Year: **2** ....
Type of Membership:	**3** ....
Activities:	*Badminton* and **4** ....
Payment details:	Total: £450
	To be paid **5** ....

Questions 6–10

Answer the questions below.

Write ***NO MORE THAN TWO WORDS*** *for each answer.*

Lifestyle questionnaire	
What exercise do you do regularly?	**6** ....
Do you have any injuries?	*has a* **7** ....
What is your goal or target?	*a better* **8** ....
What is your occupation?	*a* **9** ....
How did you hear about the club?	**10** ....

SECTION 2 *Questions 11–20*

Questions 11–14

*Choose the correct letter, **A**, **B** or **C**.*

11 The next event at the hotel will be a

A trade fair.
B wedding.
C party.

12 The number of guests will be

A less than 50.
B from 50 to 100.
C more than 100.

13 Guests will start arriving at

A 7.15.
B 7.30.
C 7.45.

14 The entertainment will be a

A live band.
B comedian.
C magician.

Questions 15–17

Who will be responsible for the following jobs as the guests arrive?

*Choose **THREE** answers from the box and write the correct letter, **A–E**, next to Questions 15–17.*

A	Susan
B	Ahmed
C	Gary
D	Olav
E	Monica

15 offer drinks to guests ....

16 take guests' coats and hats ....

17 show guests where to go ....

Questions 18–20

Complete the sentences below.

*Write **NO MORE THAN THREE WORDS** for each answer.*

General instructions

In order to get the guests to move to the restaurant the hotel manager will **18** ....

Seating plans will be placed on each table and also in the **19** ....

There will be a total of three **20** ....

SECTION 3 *Questions 21–30*

Questions 21–25

Complete the flow-chart below.

Write ***NO MORE THAN TWO WORDS*** *for each answer.*

Paper Production and Recycling

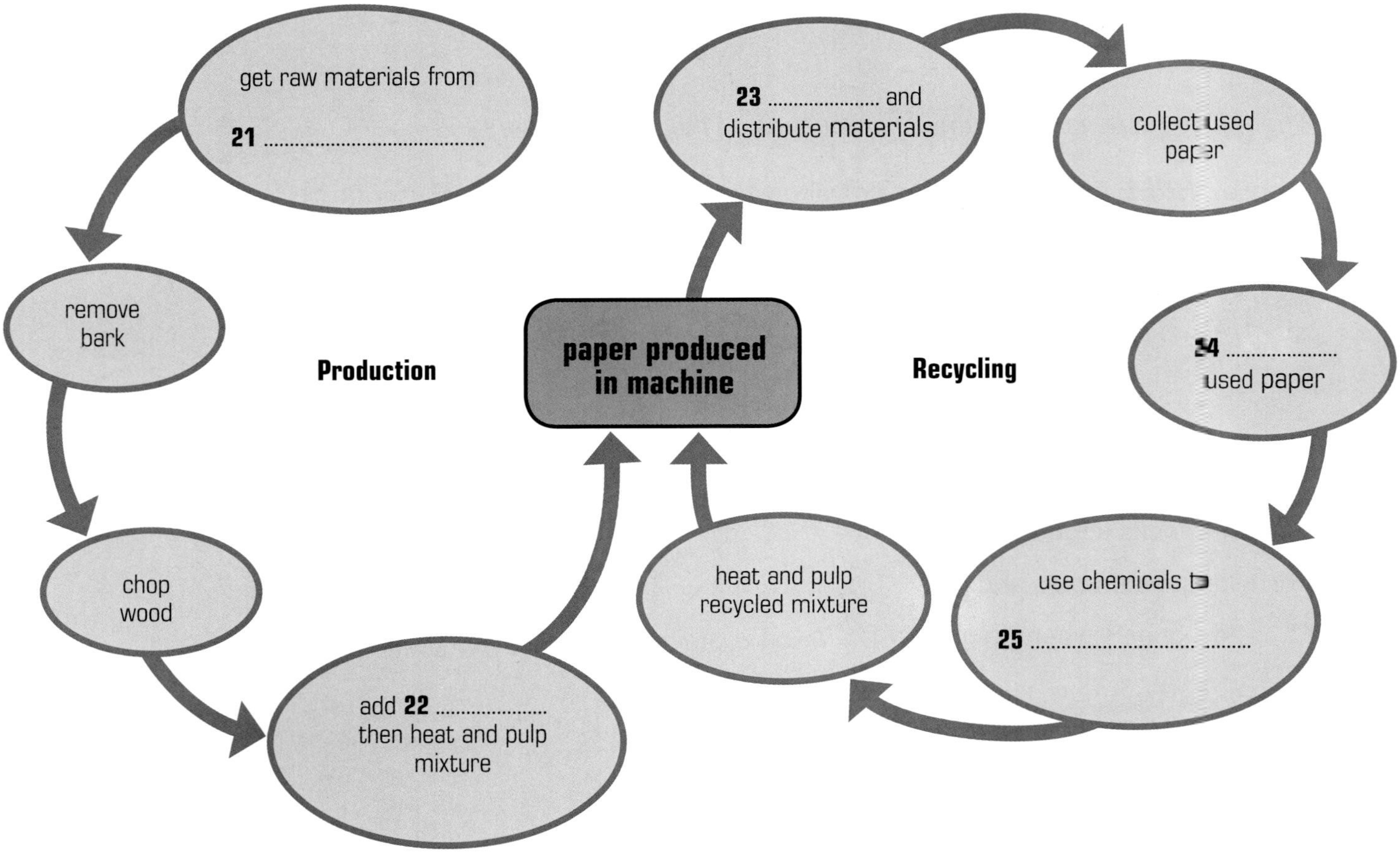

Questions 26–30

Answer the questions below.

Write **NO MORE THAN TWO WORDS** *for each answer.*

26 What part of the assignment is Alan going to start working on? ....

27 Where will Melanie get more information on used paper collection? ....

28 What will they add to the assignment to make it more interesting? ....

29 What do they agree to complete by the end of the month? ....

30 Who will they ask to review their work? ....

SECTION 4 *Questions 31–40*

Questions 31–38

Complete the notes below.

Write **ONE WORD AND/OR A NUMBER** *for each answer.*

HAIR

Facts about hair

- main purposes – warmth and **31** ....
- main component *keratin* – makes fingernails **32** ....
- full head of hair can support a large weight – equal to two **33** ....
- average number of strands of hair – **34** .... for an adult
- large amount of money spent on **35** .... for hair in the UK

Structure of hair

Three main parts:

a) bulb – like a **36** .... over end of hair follicle

b) root – contains glands that supply **37** .... to hair strand

c) shaft – not **38** ....

Questions 39–40

Complete the summary below.

Write **ONE WORD ONLY** *for each answer.*

Health and Hair

Changes in diet will take longer to affect your hair than your **39** .... Vitamins C, D and E are all important for healthy hair and **40** .... are one of the best sources of Vitamin C.

READING

READING PASSAGE 1

*You should spend about 20 minutes on **Questions 1–13**, which are based on Reading Passage 1 below.*

SECRETS OF THE SWARM

Insects, birds and fish tend to be the creatures that humans feel furthest from. Unlike many mammals they do not engage in human-like behaviour. The way they swarm or flock together does not usually get good press coverage either: marching like worker ants might be a common simile for city commuters, but it's a damning, not positive, image. Yet a new school of scientific theory suggests that these swarms might have a lot to teach us.

American author Peter Miller explains, 'I used to think that individual ants knew where they were going, and what they were supposed to do when they got there. But Deborah Gordon, a biologist at Stanford University, showed me that nothing an ant does makes any sense except in terms of the whole colony. Which makes you wonder if, as individuals, we don't serve a similar function for the companies where we work or the communities where we live.' Ants are not intelligent by themselves. Yet as a colony, they make wise decisions. And as Gordon discovered during her research, there's no one ant making decisions or giving orders.

Take food collecting, for example. No ant decides, 'There's lots of food around today; lots of ants should go out to collect it.' Instead, some forager ants go out, and as soon as they find food, they pick it up and come back to the nest. At the entrance, they brush past reserve foragers, sending a 'go out' signal. The faster the foragers come back, the more food there is and the faster other foragers go out, until gradually the amount of food being brought back diminishes. An organic calculation has been made to answer the question, 'How many foragers does the colony need today?' And if something goes wrong – a hungry lizard prowling around for an ant snack, for instance – then a rush of ants returning without food sends waiting reserves a 'Don't go out' signal.

But could such decentralised control work in a human organisation? Miller visited a Texas gas company that has successfully applied formulas based on ant colony behaviour to 'optimise its factories and route its trucks'. He explains, 'If ant colonies had worked out a reliable way to identify the best routes between their nest and food sources, the company managers figured, why not take advantage of that knowledge?' So they came up with a computer model, based on the self-organising principles of an ant colony. Data is fed into the model about deliveries needing to be made the next day, as well as things like weather conditions, and it produces a simulation determining the best route for the delivery lorries to take.

Miller explains that he first really understood the impact that swarm behaviour could have on humans when he read a study of honeybees by Tom Seeley, a biologist at Cornell University. The honeybees choose as a group which new nest to move to. First, scouts fly off to investigate multiple sites. When they return they do a 'waggle dance' for their spot, and other scouts will then fly off and investigate it. Many bees go out, but none tries to compare all sites. Each reports back on just one. The more they liked their nest, the more vigorous and lengthy their waggle dance and the more bees will choose to visit it. Gradually the volume of bees builds up towards one site; it's a system that ensures that support for the best site snowballs and the decision is made in the most democratic way.

Humans, too, can make clever decisions through diversity of knowledge and a little friendly competition. 'The best example of shared decision-making that I witnessed during my research was a town meeting I attended in Vermont, where citizens met face-to-face to debate their annual budget,' explains Miller. 'For group decision-making to work well, you need a way to sort through the various options they propose; and you need a mechanism to narrow down these options.' Citizens in Vermont control their municipal affairs by putting forward proposals, or backing up others' suggestions, until a consensus is reached through a vote. As with the bees, the broad sampling of options before a decision is made will usually result in a compromise acceptable to all. The 'wisdom of the crowd' makes clever decisions for the good of the group – and leaves citizens feeling represented and respected.

The Internet is also an area where we are increasingly exhibiting swarm behaviour, without any physical contact. Miller compares a wiki website, for example, to a termite mound. Indirect collaboration is the key principle behind information-sharing web sites, just as it underlies the complex constructions that termites build. Termites do not have an architect's blueprint or a grand construction scheme. They simply sense changes in their environment, as for example when the mound's wall has been damaged, altering the circulation of air. They go to the site of the change and drop a grain of soil. When the next termite finds that grain, they drop theirs too. Slowly, without any kind of direct decision-making, a new wall is built. A termite mound, in this way, is rather like a wiki website. Rather than meeting up and talking about what we want to post online, we just add to what someone – maybe a stranger on the other side of the world – already wrote. This indirect knowledge and skill-sharing is now finding its way into the corridors of power.

Questions 1–6

Do the following statements agree with the information in the text?

In boxes 1–6 on your answer sheet, write

TRUE	*if the statement agrees with the information*
FALSE	*if the statement contradicts the information*
NOT GIVEN	*if there is no information on this*

1 Commuters are often compared favourably with worker ants.

2 Some ants within a colony have leadership roles.

3 Forager ants tell each other how far away the food source is.

4 Forager ants are able to react quickly to a dangerous situation.

5 Termite mounds can be damaged by the wind.

6 Termites repair their mounds without directly communicating with each other.

Questions 7–9

Complete each sentence with the correct ending, ***A–F****, below.*

Write the correct letter, ***A–F****, in boxes 7–9 on your answer sheet.*

7 Managers working for a Texas gas company

8 Citizens in an annual Vermont meeting

9 Some Internet users

A provide support for each other's ideas in order to reach the best outcome.

B use detailed comments to create large and complicated systems.

C use decision-making strategies based on insect communities to improve their service.

D communicate with each other to decide who the leader will be.

E contribute independently to the ideas of others they do not know.

F repair structures they have built without directly communicating with each other.

Questions 10–13

Complete the flow-chart below.

Choose ***NO MORE THAN TWO WORDS*** *from the text for each answer.*

Write your answers in boxes 10–13 on your answer sheet.

How honeybees choose a new nest

Honeybee **10** .... explore possible nest sites

↓

they perform what is known as a **11** .... on their return

↓

other bees go out and report back

↓

enthusiasm and **12** .... increase for one particular site

↓

a final choice is reached using a **13** .... process

READING PASSAGE 2

*You should spend about 20 minutes on **Questions 14–26**, which are based on Reading Passage 2 on the following pages.*

Questions 14–18

The text on the following pages has five paragraphs, **A–E**.

Choose the correct heading for each paragraph from the list of headings below.

*Write the correct number, **i–viii**, in boxes 14–18 on your answer sheet.*

List of Headings

i	A joint business project
ii	Other engineering achievements
iii	Examining the overall benefits
iv	A building like no other
v	Some benefits of traditional methods
vi	A change of direction
vii	Examples of similar global brands
viii	From factory to building site

14 Paragraph A

15 Paragraph B

16 Paragraph C

17 Paragraph D

18 Paragraph E

High Speed, High Rise

A Chinese entrepreneur has figured out a way to manufacture 30-story, earthquake-proof skyscrapers that snap together in just 15 days.

A Zhang Yue is founder and chairman of Broad Sustainable Building (otherwise known as 'Broad') who, on 1 January, 2012, released a time-lapse video of its 30-story achievement. It shows construction workers buzzing around like gnats while a clock in the corner of the screen marks the time. In just 360 hours, a 100-metre-tall tower called the T30 rises from an empty site to overlook Hunan's Xiang River. At the end of the video, the camera spirals around the building overhead as the Broad logo appears on the screen: a lowercase b that wraps around itself in an imitation of the @ symbol. The company is in the process of franchising its technology to partners in India, Brazil, and Russia. What it is selling is the world's first standardized skyscraper and with it, Zhang aims to turn Broad into the McDonald's of the sustainable building industry. When asked why he decided to start a construction company, Zhang replies, 'It's not a construction company. It's a structural revolution.'

B So far, Broad has built 16 structures in China, plus another in Cancun. They are fabricated at two factories in Hunan, roughly an hour's drive from Broad Town, the sprawling headquarters. The floors and ceilings of the skyscrapers are built in sections, each measuring 15.6 by 3.9 meters with a depth of 45 centimeters. Pipes and ducts for electricity, water and waste are threaded through each floor module while it is still in the factory. The client's choice of flooring is also pre-installed on top. Standardized truckloads carry two modules each to the site with the necessary columns, bolts and tools to connect them stacked on top of each other. Once they arrive at the location, each section is lifted by crane directly to the top of the building, which is assembled like toy Lego bricks. Workers use the materials on the module to quickly connect the pipes and wires. The unique column design has diagonal bracing at each end and tabs that bolt into the floors above and below. In the final step, heavily insulated exterior walls and windows are slotted in by crane. The result is far from pretty but the method is surprisingly safe – and phenomenally fast.

C Zhang attributes his success to his creativity and to his outsider perspective on technology. He started out as an art student in the 1980s, but in 1988, Zhang left the art world to found Broad. The company started out as a maker of non-pressurized boilers. His senior vice-president, Juliet Jiang, says, 'He made his fortune on boilers. He could have kept doing this business, but … he saw the need for nonelectric air-conditioning.' Towards the end of the decade, China's economy was expanding past the capacity of the nation's electricity grid, she explains. Power shortages were becoming a serious obstacle to growth. Large air-conditioning (AC) units fueled by natural gas could help companies ease their electricity load, reduce overheads, and enjoy more reliable climate control into the bargain. Today, Broad has units operating in more than 70 countries, in some of the largest buildings and airports on the planet.

D For two decades, Zhang's AC business boomed. But a couple of events conspired to change his course. The first was that Zhang became an environmentalist. The second was the earthquake that hit China's Sichuan Province in 2008, causing the collapse of poorly constructed buildings. Initially, he says, he tried to convince developers to refit existing buildings to make them both more stable and more sustainable, but he had little success. So Zhang drafted his own engineers and started researching how to build cheap, environmentally friendly structures that could also withstand an earthquake. Within six months of starting his research, Zhang had given up on traditional methods. He was frustrated by the cost of hiring designers and specialists for each new structure. The best way to cut costs, he decided, was to take building to the factory. But to create a factory-built skyscraper, Broad had to abandon the principles by which skyscrapers are typically designed. The whole load-bearing structure had to be different. To reduce the overall weight of the building, it used less concrete in the floors; that in turn enabled it to cut down on structural steel.

E Around the world, prefabricated and modular buildings are gaining in popularity. But modular and prefabricated buildings elsewhere are, for the most part, low-rise. Broad is alone in applying these methods to skyscrapers. For Zhang, the environmental savings alone justify the effort. According to Broad's numbers, a traditional high-rise will produce about 3,000 tons of construction waste, while a Broad building will produce only 25 tons. Traditional buildings also require 5,000 tons of water onsite to build, while Broad buildings use none. The building process is also less dangerous. Elevator systems – the base, rails, and machine room – can be installed at the factory, eliminating the risk of injury. And instead of shipping an elevator car to the site in pieces, Broad orders a finished car and drops it into the shaft by crane. In the future, elevator manufacturers are hoping to preinstall the doors, completely eliminating any chance that a worker might fall. 'Traditional construction is chaotic,' he says. 'We took construction and moved it into the factory.' According to Zhang, his buildings will help solve the many problems of the construction industry and what's more, they will be quicker and cheaper to build.

Questions 19–22

Label the diagram below.

Choose ***ONE WORD ONLY*** *from the text for each answer.*

Write your answers in boxes 19–22 on your answer sheet.

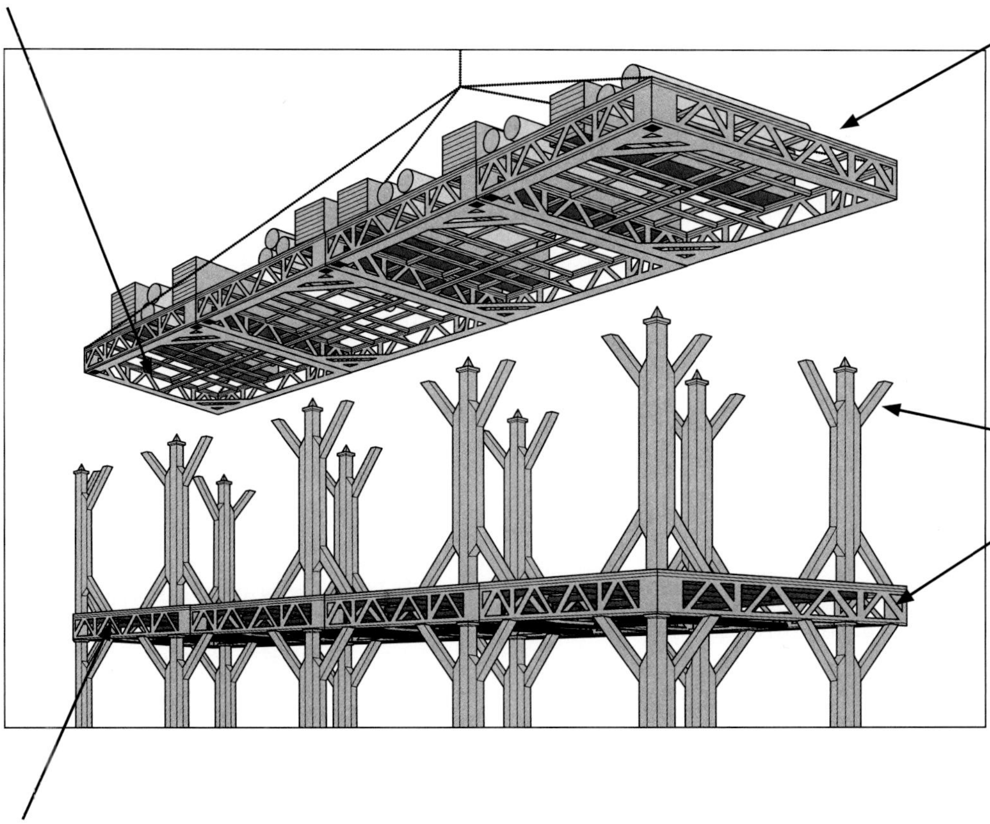

Questions 23–26

Complete the sentences below.

Choose ***NO MORE THAN TWO WORDS*** *from the text for each answer.*

Write your answers in boxes 23–26 on your answer sheet.

23 Zhang refers to his business as a ....

24 The first products Broad manufactured were ....

25 In the late eighties, ... were holding back industrial progress in China.

26 In addition to power and cost benefits, Broad's AC units improve ....

READING PASSAGE 3

*You should spend about 20 minutes on **Questions 27–40**, which are based on Reading Passage 3 below.*

When conversations flow

We spend a large part of our daily life talking with other people and, consequently, we are very accustomed to the art of conversing. But why do we feel comfortable in conversations that have flow, but get nervous and distressed when a conversation is interrupted by unexpected silences? To answer this question we will first look at some of the effects of conversational flow. Then we will explain how flow can serve different social needs.

The positive consequences of conversational flow show some similarities with the effects of 'processing fluency'. Research has shown that processing fluency – the ease with which people process information – influences people's judgments across a broad range of social dimensions. For instance, people feel that when something is easily processed, it is more true or accurate. Moreover, they have more confidence in their judgments regarding information that came to them fluently, and they like things that are easy to process more than things that are difficult to process. Research indicates that a speaker is judged to be more knowledgeable when they answer questions instantly; responding with disfluent speech markers such as 'uh' or 'um' or simply remaining silent for a moment too long can destroy that positive image.

One of the social needs addressed by conversational flow is the human need for 'synchrony' – to be 'in sync' or in harmony with one another. Many studies have shown how people attempt to synchronize with their partners, by coordinating their behavior. This interpersonal coordination underlies a wide array of human activities, ranging from more complicated ones like ballroom dancing to simply walking or talking with friends.

In conversations, interpersonal coordination is found when people adjust the duration of their utterances and their speech rate to one another so that they can enable turn-taking to occur, without talking over each other or experiencing awkward silences. Since people are very well-trained in having conversations, they are often able to take turns within milliseconds, resulting in a conversational flow of smoothly meshed behaviors. A lack of flow is characterized by interruptions, simultaneous speech or mutual silences. Avoiding these features is important for defining and maintaining interpersonal relationships.

The need to belong has been identified as one of the most basic of human motivations and plays a role in many human behaviors. That conversational flow is related to belonging may be most easily illustrated by the consequences of flow disruptions. What happens when the positive experience of flow is disrupted by, for instance, a brief silence? We all know that silences can be pretty awkward, and research shows that even short disruptions in conversational flow can lead to a sharp rise in distress levels. In movies, silences are often used to signal non-compliance or confrontation (Piazza, 2006). Some researchers even argue that 'silencing someone' is one of the most serious forms of exclusion. Group membership is of elementary importance to our wellbeing and because humans are very sensitive to signals of exclusion, a silence is generally taken as a sign of rejection. In this way, a lack of flow in a conversation may signal that our relationship is not as solid as we thought it was.

Another aspect of synchrony is that people often try to validate their opinions to those of others. That is, people like to see others as having similar ideas or worldviews as they have themselves, because this informs people that they are correct and their worldviews are justified. One way in which people can justify their worldviews is by assuming that, as long as their conversations run smoothly, their interaction partners probably agree with them. This idea was tested by researchers using video observations. Participants imagined being one out of three people in a video clip who had either a fluent conversation or a conversation in which flow was disrupted by a brief silence. Except for the silence, the videos were identical. After watching the video, participants were asked to what extent the people in the video agreed with each other. Participants who watched the fluent conversation rated agreement to be higher than participants watching the conversation that was disrupted by a silence, even though participants were not consciously aware of the disruption. It appears that the subjective feeling of being out of sync informs people of possible disagreements, regardless of the content of the conversation.

Because people are generally so well-trained in having smooth conversations, any disruption of this flow indicates that something is wrong, either interpersonally or within the group as a whole. Consequently, people who do not talk very easily may be incorrectly understood as being less agreeable than those who have no difficulty keeping up a conversation. On a societal level, one could even imagine that a lack of conversational flow may hamper the integration of immigrants who have not completely mastered the language of their new country yet. In a similar sense, the ever-increasing number of online conversations may be disrupted by misinterpretations and anxiety that are produced by insuperable delays in the Internet connection. Keeping in mind the effects of conversational flow for feelings of belonging and validation may help one to be prepared to avoid such misunderstandings in future conversations.

Questions 27–32

Do the following statements agree with the claims of the writer in the text?

In boxes 27–32 on your answer sheet, write

YES	*if the statement agrees with the claims of the writer*
NO	*if the statement contradicts the claims of the writer*
NOT GIVEN	*if it is impossible to say what the writer thinks about this*

27 Conversation occupies much of our time.

28 People assess information according to how readily they can understand it.

29 A quick response to a question is thought to show a lack of knowledge.

30 Video observations have often been used to assess conversational flow.

31 People who talk less often have clearer ideas than those who talk a lot.

32 Delays in online chat fail to have the same negative effect as disruptions that occur in natural conversation.

Questions 33–40

Complete the summary below.

Choose **NO MORE THAN TWO WORDS** *from the text for each answer.*

Write your answers in boxes 33–40 on your answer sheet.

Synchrony

There is a human desire to co-ordinate **33** .... in an effort to be 'in harmony'. This co-ordination can be seen in conversations when speakers alter the speed and extent of their speech in order to facilitate **34** .... This is often achieved within milliseconds: only tiny pauses take place when a conversation flows; when it doesn't, there are **35** .... and silences, or people talk at the same time.

Our desire to **36** .... is also an important element of conversation flow. According to research, our **37** .... increase even if silences are brief. Humans have a basic need to be part of a group, and they experience a sense of **38** .... if silences exclude them.

People also attempt to co-ordinate their opinions in conversation. In an experiment, participants' judgement of the overall **39** .... among speakers was tested using videos of a fluent and a slightly disrupted conversation. The results showed that the **40** .... of the speakers' discussion was less important than the perceived synchrony of the speakers.

WRITING

WRITING TASK 1

You should spend about 20 minutes on this task.

> ***The diagrams below show the changes that have taken place at West Park Secondary School since its construction in 1950.***
>
> ***Summarise the information by selecting and reporting the main features and make comparisons where relevant.***

Write at least 150 words.

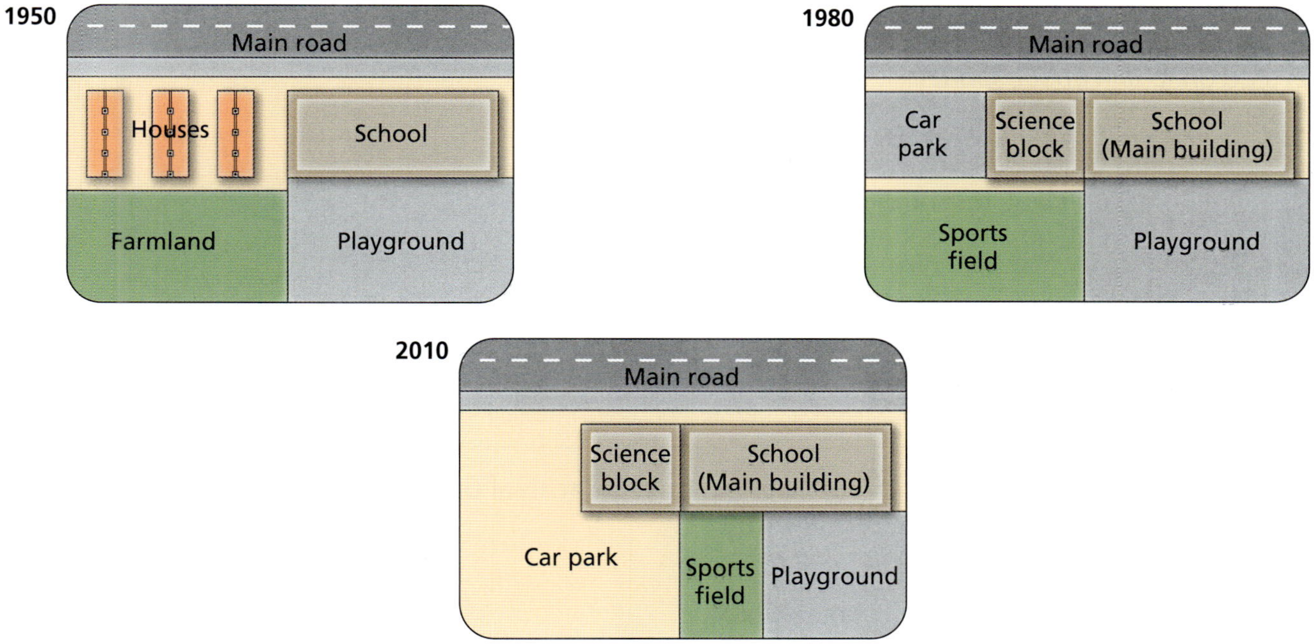

WRITING TASK 2

You should spend about 40 minutes on this task.

> ***Car ownership has increased so rapidly over the past thirty years that many cities in the world are now 'one big traffic jam'.***
>
> ***How true do you think this statement is?***
>
> ***What measures can governments take to discourage people from using their cars?***

Give reasons for your answer and include any relevant examples from your own knowledge or experience.

Write at least 250 words.

SPEAKING

PART 1

Let's talk about what you do. Do you work or are you a student?

Work	**Study**
• Why did you choose your job? • What are your working hours? • Tell me something about the people who work with you. • What don't you like about your job?	• Why did you choose your subject(s)? • When do you prefer to study on your own? [Why?] • Tell me something about the other students on your course. • What don't you like about your studies?

Let's go on to talk about sport.

- What sports are popular in your country?
- Did you learn any sports at school? [Why? / Why not?]
- How often do you watch sport? [Why not?]
- Do you participate in any sports at the moment? [Which ones?]

PART 2

Candidate task card:

Describe a special event (e.g. a festival, carnival or other celebration) that takes place in your country.

You should say:
when the event takes place
why it takes place
what people do
and explain why the event is special.

PART 3

Celebrations for families and friends

- What sort of occasions do families and friends like to celebrate?
- How important are celebrations in people's lives? [Why? / Why not?]
- Should people have time off work for important celebrations? [Why? / Why not?]

National celebrations

- Why do many people enjoy participating in national celebrations?
- Have national celebrations become more or less important over time? [Why?]
- What sort of things do you think countries will celebrate in the future?

Test 4

LISTENING

SECTION 1 *Questions 1–10*

Questions 1–6

Complete the table below.

Write ***NO MORE THAN ONE WORD AND/OR A NUMBER*** *for each answer.*

Community Centre Evening Classes				
Class	**Where**	**When**	**What to bring**	**Cost**
Painting with watercolours	*Example* in the ......hall......	at **1** .... pm on Tuesdays	water jar and set of **2**	£45 – four classes
Maori language	the small room at the **3** .... of the building	starts in **4**	small recorder	£40 – five classes
Digital photography	room 9	6 pm Wednesday evenings	the **5** .... for the camera	**6** £...................... – eight classes

Questions 7–10

Complete the sentences below.

Write ***ONE WORD ONLY*** *for each answer.*

7 The watercolours class suits people who are ....

8 To find out about the Maori language class, contact Jason ....

9 For the photography class, check the .... for the camera.

10 There is a trip to a local .... in the final week of the photography class.

SECTION 2 ***Questions 11–20***

Questions 11 and 12

Choose ***TWO*** *letters,* ***A–E****.*

Which ***TWO*** *tasks will the volunteers in Group A be responsible for?*

A widening pathways

B planting trees

C picking up rubbish

D putting up signs

E building fences

Questions 13 and 14

Choose ***TWO*** *letters,* ***A–E****.*

Which ***TWO*** *items should volunteers in Group A bring with them?*

A food and water

B boots

C gloves

D raincoats

E their own tools

Questions 15–20

Label the plan below.

*Write the correct letter, **A–I**, next to Questions 15–20.*

15 Vegetable beds ....
16 Bee hives ....
17 Seating ....
18 Adventure playground ....
19 Sand area ....
20 Pond ....

Hadley Park Community Gardens Project

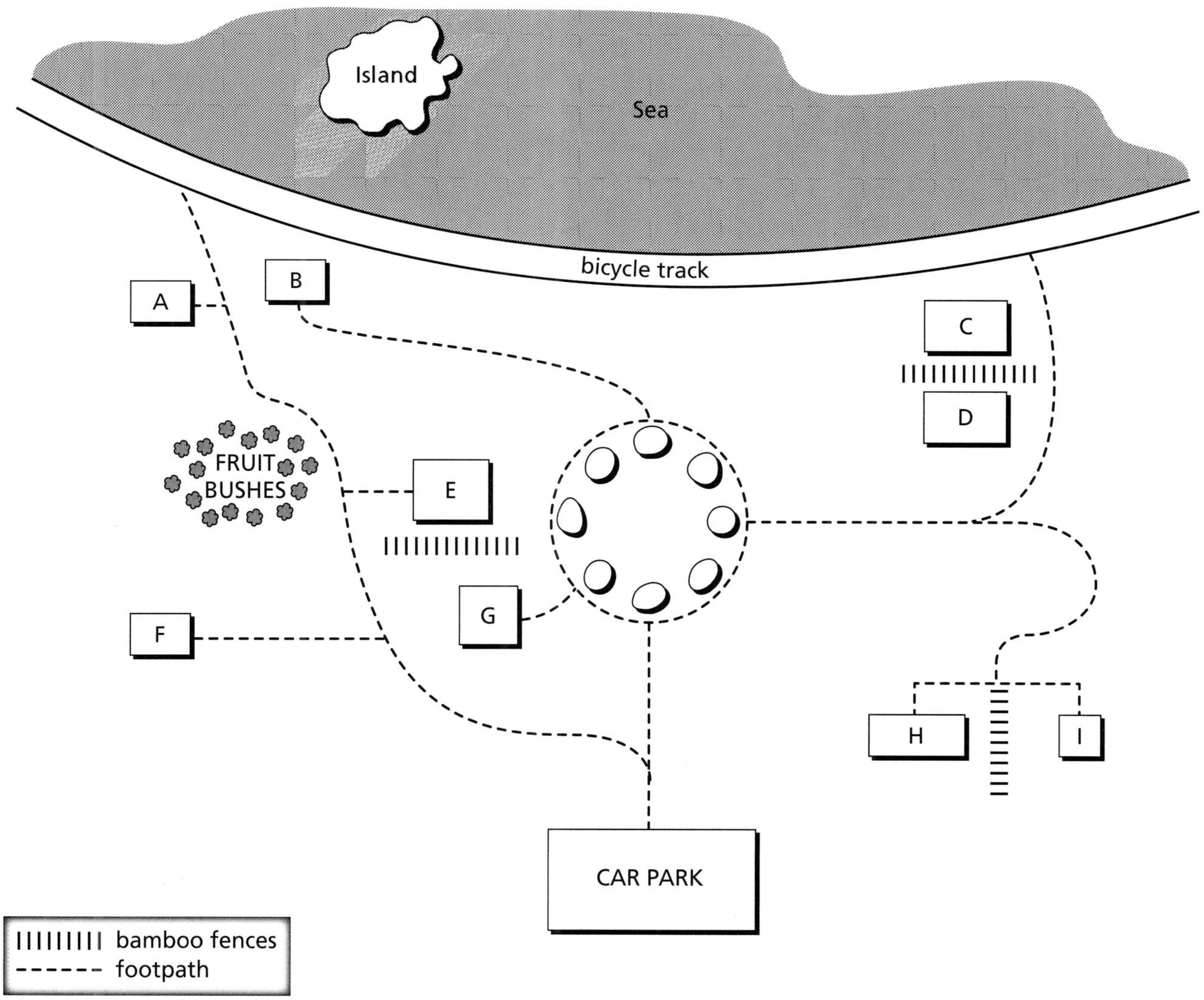

SECTION 3 *Questions 21–30*

Questions 21–25

*Choose the correct letter, **A**, **B** or **C**.*

Food Waste

21 What point does Robert make about the 2013 study in Britain?

A It focused more on packaging than wasted food.
B It proved that households produced more waste than restaurants.
C It included liquid waste as well as solid waste.

22 The speakers agree that food waste reports should emphasise the connection between carbon dioxide emissions and

A food production.
B transport of food to landfill sites.
C distribution of food products.

23 Television programmes now tend to focus on

A the nutritional value of food products.
B the origin of food products.
C the chemicals found in food products.

24 For Anna, the most significant point about food waste is

A the moral aspect.
B the environmental impact.
C the economic effect.

25 Anna and Robert decide to begin their presentation by

A handing out a questionnaire.
B providing statistical evidence.
C showing images of wasted food.

Questions 26–30

What advantage do the speakers identify for each of the following projects?

*Choose **FIVE** answers from the box and write the correct letter, **A–G**, next to Questions 26–30.*

Advantages

A It should save time.
B It will create new jobs.
C It will benefit local communities.
D It will make money.
E It will encourage personal responsibility.
F It will be easy to advertise.
G It will involve very little cost.

Projects

26 edible patch ....
27 ripeness sensor ....
28 waste tracking technology ....
29 smartphone application ....
30 food waste composting ....

SECTION 4 *Questions 31–40*

Complete the notes below.

Write **ONE WORD** *for each answer.*

Kite-making by the Maori people of New Zealand

Making and appearance of the kites

- The priests who made the kites had rules for size and scale
- **31** .... was not allowed during a kite's preparation

Kites:

- often represented a bird, a god, or a **32** ....
- had frames that were decorated with grasses and **33** ....
- had a line of noisy **34** .... attached to them.
- could be triangular, rectangular or **35** .... shaped.
- had patterns made from clay mixed with **36** .... oil.
- sometimes had human-head masks with **37** .... and a tattoo.

Purpose and function of kites:

- a way of sending **38** .... to the gods
- a way of telling other villages that a **39** .... was necessary
- a means of **40** .... if enemies were coming.

READING

READING PASSAGE 1

*You should spend about 20 minutes on **Questions 1–13**, which are based on Reading Passage 1 below.*

South Pole Adventurer

In the race to the South Pole, there was a Japanese team attempting to be first, led by heroic explorer Nobu Shirase

FOR a few weeks in January 1912, Antarctica was full of explorers. Norwegian Roald Amundsen had reached the South Pole on 14 December and was speeding back to the coast. On 17 January, Robert Scott and the men of the British Antarctic expedition had arrived at the pole to find they had been beaten to it. Just then, a third man arrived; Japanese explorer Nobu Shirase. However, his part in one of the greatest adventure stories of the 20th century is hardly known outside his own country, even by fellow explorers. Yet as Scott was nearing the pole and with the rest of the world still unaware of Amundsen's triumph, Shirase and his team sailed into Antarctica's Bay of Whales in the smallest ship ever to try its luck in these dangerous waters.

Since boyhood Shirase had dreamed of becoming a polar explorer. Like Amundsen, he initially set his sights on the North Pole. But after the American Robert Peary claimed to have reached it in 1909, both men hastily altered their plans. Instead they would aim for the last big prize: the South Pole. In January 1910, Shirase put his plans before Japanese government officials, promising to raise the flag at the South Pole within three years. For many of them, the question wasn't could he do it but why would it be worth doing? 15 years earlier the International Geographical Congress had said that as the last unknown continent the Antarctic offered the chance to add to knowledge in almost every branch of science. So, like the British, Shirase presented his expedition as a search for knowledge: he would bring back fossils, make meteorological measurements and explore unknown parts of the continent.

The response from the government was cool, however, and Shirase struggled to raise funds. Fortunately, a few months later, Japan's former prime minister Shigenobu Okuma came to Shirase's rescue. With Okuma's backing, Shirase got together just enough money to buy and equip a small ship. He eventually acquired a scientist, too, called Terutaro Takeda. At the end of November 1910, his ship the *Kainan Maru* finally left Tokyo with 27 men and 28 Siberian dogs on board. Before leaving, Shirase confidently outlined his plans to the media. He would sail to New Zealand, then reach Antarctica in February, during the southern summer, and then proceed to the pole the following spring. This was not to be, however. Bad weather delayed the expedition and they didn't reach New Zealand until 8 February; Amundsen and Scott had already been in Antarctica for a month, preparing for winter.

In New Zealand local reporters were astonished: the ship was half the size of Amundsen's ship. True, it was reinforced with iron plate and extra wood, but the ship had only the feeblest engine to help force its way through ice. Few doubted Shirase's courage, but most reckoned the expedition to be ill-prepared as the Japanese had only lightweight sledges for transport across the ice, made of bamboo and wood.

But Shirase's biggest challenge was time. Antarctica is only accessible by sea for a few weeks in summer and expeditions usually aimed to arrive in January or February. 'Even with their determination and daring, our Japanese friends are running it rather fine,' wrote local reporters. Nevertheless, on 11 February the *Kainan Maru* left New Zealand and sailed straight into the worst weather the captain had ever seen. Then, on 6 March, they approached the coastline of Antarctica's Ross Sea, looking for a place to land. The ice began to close in, threatening to trap them for the winter, an experience no one was likely to survive. With a remarkable piece of seamanship, the captain steered the ship out of the ice and turned north. They would have to wait out the winter in a warmer climate.

A year later than planned, Shirase and six men finally reached Antarctica. Catching up with Scott or Amundsen was out of the question and he had said he would stick to science this time. Yet Shirase still felt the pull of the pole and eventually decided he would head southward to experience the thrills and hardships of polar exploration he had always dreamed of. With provisions for 20 days, he and four men would see how far they could get.

Shirase set off on 20 January 1912 with Takeda and two dog handlers, leaving two men at the edge of the ice shelf to make meteorological measurements. For a week they struggled through one blizzard after another, holing up in their tents during the worst of the weather. The temperature fell to –25°C, and frostbite claimed some of the dogs. On 26 January, Shirase estimated there were enough provisions to continue for two more days. Two days later, he announced it was time to turn back. Takeda calculated they had reached 80° 5 south and had travelled 250 kilometres. The men hoisted the Japanese flag.

On 3 February, all the men were heading home. The ship reached Tokyo in June 1912 - and Shirase was greeted like a hero despite the fact that he never reached the pole. Nor did he contribute much to science - but then nor did Amundsen, whose only interest was in being first to the pole. Yet Shirase's expedition was heroic. They travelled beyond 80° south, one of only four teams to have gone so far south at the time. Furthermore, they did it all without the advantages of the other teams and with no previous experience.

Questions 1–8

Do the following statements agree with the information given in Reading Passage 1?

In boxes 1–8 on your answer sheet, write

TRUE	*if the statement agrees with the information*
FALSE	*if the statement contradicts the information*
NOT GIVEN	*if there is no information on this*

1 Shirase's trip to the South Pole is well-known to other explorers.

2 Since Shirase arrived in Antarctica, smaller ships have also made the journey.

3 Shirase's original ambition was to travel to the North Pole.

4 Some Japanese officials thought Shirase's intention to travel to the South Pole was pointless.

5 The British team announced their decision to carry out scientific research in Antarctica before Shirase.

6 Shirase found it easy to raise the money he needed for his trip to the South Pole.

7 A previous prime minister of Japan persuaded a scientist to go with Shirase.

8 The weather that slowed down Shirase's progress to New Zealand was unusually bad for the season.

Questions 9–13

Choose the correct letter, ***A****,* ***B****,* ***C*** *or* ***D****.*

Write your answers in boxes 9–13 on your answer sheet.

9 When reporters in New Zealand met Shirase, they were
- **A** concerned about the quality of his equipment.
- **B** impressed with the design of his ship.
- **C** certain he was unaware of the dangers ahead.
- **D** surprised by the bravery he demonstrated.

10 What are we told about the captain of the *Kainan Maru* in the fifth paragraph?
- **A** He had given Shirase some poor advice.
- **B** His skill at sailing saved the boat and crew.
- **C** He refused to listen to the warnings of others.
- **D** He was originally confident they could reach Antarctica.

11 After Shirase finally reached Antarctica he realised that
- **A** he was unsure of the direction he should follow.
- **B** he would have to give up on fulfilling his personal ambition.
- **C** he might not have enough food to get to the South Pole.
- **D** he still wanted to compete in the race against the other teams.

12 What is the writer doing in the seventh paragraph?
- **A** criticising a decision concerning scientific research.
- **B** explaining why a particular mistake had occurred.
- **C** describing the conditions that the expedition faced.
- **D** rejecting the idea that Shirase was poorly prepared.

13 What is the writer's main point in the final paragraph?
- **A** Considering the problems Shirase had to deal with, his achievement was incredible.
- **B** In Japan, the reaction to Shirase's adventure in Antarctica came as a surprise to him.
- **C** It was obvious that Amundsen would receive more attention as an explorer than Shirase.
- **D** Shirase had achieved more on the Antarctic expedition than even he had expected.

READING PASSAGE 2

*You should spend about 20 minutes on **Questions 14–26**, which are based on Reading Passage 2 below.*

The rise of the agribots

The use of robots and automation in the farming industry

The next time you stand at the supermarket checkout, spare a thought for the farmers who helped fill your shopping basket as life is hard for them right now. This, in turn, inevitably means bigger grocery bills for consumers, and greater hardship for the millions in countries where food shortages are a matter of life and death. Worse, studies suggest that the world will need twice as much food by 2050. Yet while farmers must squeeze more out of the land, they must also address the necessity of reducing their impact on the soil, waterways and atmosphere. All this means rethinking how agriculture is practiced, and taking automation to a whole new level. On the new model farms of the future, precision will be key. Why dose a whole field with chemicals if you can spray only where they are needed? Each plant could get exactly the right amount of everything, no more or less, an approach that could slash chemical use and improve yields in one move. But this is easier said than done; the largest farms in Europe and the U.S. can cover thousands of acres. That's why automation is key to precision farming. Specifically, say agricultural engineers, precision farming needs robot farmers.

One day, we might see fields with 'agribots' (agricultural robots) that can identify individual seedlings and encourage them along with drops of fertilizer. Other machines would distinguish problem weeds from crops and eliminate them with shots from high-power lasers or a microdot of pesticide. These machines will also be able to identify and harvest all kinds of vegetables. More than a century of mechanization has already turned farming into an industrial-scale activity in much of the world, with farms that grow cereals being the most heavily automated. But a variety of other crops, including oranges and tomatoes destined to become processed foods, are also picked mechanically, albeit to a slightly lesser extent. Yet the next wave of autonomous farm machinery is already at work. You probably haven't even noticed, for these robots are disguised as tractors. Many are self-steering, use GPS to cross a field, and can even 'talk' to their implements – a plough or sprayer, for example. And the implements can talk back, telling the tractor that it's going too fast or needs to move to the left. This kind of communication is also being developed in other farm vehicles. A new system allows a combine harvester, say, to send a call over to a tractor-trailer so the driver can unload the grain as and when necessary.

However, when fully autonomous systems take to the field, they'll look nothing like tractors. With their enormous size and weight, today's farm machines have significant downsides: they compact the soil, reducing porosity and killing beneficial life, meaning crops don't grow so well. Simon Blackmore, who researches agricultural technology at Harper Adams University College in England believes that fleets of lightweight autonomous robots have the potential to solve this problem and that replacing brute force with precision is key. 'A seed only needs one cubic centimeter of soil to grow. If we cultivate just that we only put tiny amounts of energy in and the plants still grow nicely.' There is another reason why automation may be the way forward according to Eldert van Henten, a robotics researcher at Wageningen University in the Netherlands. 'While the population is growing and needs to be fed, a rapidly shrinking number of people are willing to work in agriculture,' he points out. Other researchers such as Linda Calvin, an economist at the U.S. Department of Agriculture, and Philip Martin at the University of California, Davis, have studied trends in mechanization to predict how US farms might fare. Calvin and Martin have observed how rising employment costs have led to the adoption of labour-saving farm technology in the past, citing the raisin industry as an example. In 2000, a bumper harvest crashed prices and, with profits squeezed, farmers looked for a solution. With labour one of their biggest costs – 42 percent of production expenses on U.S. farms, on average – they started using a mechanical harvester adapted from a machine used by wine makers. By 2007, almost half of California's raisins were mechanically harvested and a labour force once numbering 50,000 had shrunk to 30,000.

As well as having an impact on the job market, the widespread adoption of agribots might bring changes at the supermarket. Lewis Holloway, who studies agriculture at the University of Hull, UK, says that robotic milking is likely to influence the genetics of dairy herds as farmers opt for 'robot-friendly' cows, with udder shape, and even attitudes, suited to automated milking. Similarly, he says, it's conceivable that agribots could influence what fruit or vegetable varieties get to the shops, since farmers may prefer to grow those with, say, leaf shapes that are easier for their robots to discriminate from weeds. Almost inevitably, these machines will eventually alter the landscape, too. The real tipping point for robot agriculture will come when farms are being designed with agribots in mind, says Salah Sukkarieh, a robotics researcher at the Australian Center for Field Robotics, Sydney. This could mean a return to smaller fields, with crops planted in grids rather than rows and fruit trees pruned into two-dimensional shapes to make harvesting easier. This alien terrain tended by robots is still a while away, he says 'but it will happen.'

Questions 14–17

Do the following statements agree with the claims of the writer in Reading Passage 2?

In boxes 14–17 on your answer sheet, write

YES	*if the statement agrees with the claims of the writer*
NO	*if the statement contradicts the claims of the writer*
NOT GIVEN	*if it is impossible to say what the writer thinks about this*

14 Governments should do more to ensure that food is generally affordable.

15 Farmers need to reduce the harm they do to the environment.

16 In the future, farmers are likely to increase their dependency on chemicals.

17 Farms in Europe and the US may find it hard to adapt to precision farming.

Questions 18–21

Complete the sentences below.

Choose ***ONE WORD ONLY*** *from the passage for each answer.*

Write your answers in boxes 18–21 on your answer sheet.

18 In the future, agribots will provide .... to young plants.

19 Some machines will use chemicals or .... to get rid of unwanted plants.

20 It is the production of .... which currently uses most machinery on farms.

21 .... between machines such as tractors is making farming more efficient.

Questions 22–26

Look at the following researchers (Questions 22–26) and the list of statements below.

Match each researcher with the correct statement, ***A–H****.*

Write the correct letter, ***A–H****, in boxes 22–26 on your answer sheet.*

22 Simon Blackmore

23 Eldert van Henten

24 Linda Calvin and Philip Martin

25 Lewis Holloway

26 Salah Sukkarieh

List of Findings

A The use of automation might impact on the development of particular animal and plant species.

B We need to consider the effect on employment that increased automation will have.

C We need machines of the future to be exact, not more powerful.

D As farming becomes more automated the appearance of farmland will change.

E New machinery may require more investment than certain farmers can afford.

F There is a shortage of employees in the farming industry.

G There are limits to the environmental benefits of automation.

H Economic factors are often the driving force behind the development of machinery.

READING PASSAGE 3

*You should spend about 20 minutes on **Questions 27–40**, which are based on Reading Passage 3 below.*

Homer's Literary Legacy

Why was the work of Homer, famous author of ancient Greece, so full of clichés?

A Until the last tick of history's clock, cultural transmission meant oral transmission and poetry, passed from mouth to ear, was the principal medium of moving information across space and from one generation to the next. Oral poetry was not simply a way of telling lovely or important stories, or of flexing the imagination. It was, argues the classicist Eric Havelock, a "massive repository of useful knowledge, a sort of encyclopedia of ethics, politics, history and technology which the effective citizen was required to learn as the core of his educational equipment". The great oral works transmitted a shared cultural heritage, held in common not on bookshelves, but in brains. In India, an entire class of priests was charged with memorizing the Vedas with perfect fidelity. In pre-Islamic Arabia, people known as Rawis were often attached to poets as official memorizers. The Buddha's teachings were passed down in an unbroken chain of oral tradition for four centuries until they were committed to writing in Sri Lanka in the first century B.C.

B The most famous of the Western tradition's oral works, and the first to have been systematically studied, were Homer's *Odyssey* and *Iliad*. These two poems – possibly the first to have been written down in the Greek alphabet – had long been held up as literary archetypes. However, even as they were celebrated as the models to which all literature should aspire, Homer's masterworks had also long been the source of scholarly unease. The earliest modern critics sensed that they were somehow qualitatively different from everything that came after – even a little strange. For one thing, both poems were oddly repetitive in the way they referred to characters. Odysseus was always "clever Odysseus". Dawn was always "rosy-fingered". Why would someone write that? Sometimes the epithets seemed completely off-key. Why call the murderer of Agamemnon "blameless Aegisthos"? Why refer to "swift-footed Achilles" even when he was sitting down? Or to "laughing Aphrodite" even when she was in tears? In terms of both structure and theme, the *Odyssey* and *Iliad* were also oddly formulaic, to the point of predictability. The same narrative units – gathering armies, heroic shields, challenges between rivals – pop up again and again, only with different characters and different circumstances. In the context of such finely spun, deliberate masterpieces, these quirks* seemed hard to explain.

C At the heart of the unease about these earliest works of literature were two fundamental questions: first, how could Greek literature have been born ex nihilo* with two masterpieces? Surely a few less perfect stories must have come before, and yet these two were among the first on record. And second, who exactly was their author? Or was it authors? There were no historical records of Homer, and no trustworthy biography of the man exists beyond a few self-referential hints embedded in the texts themselves.

D Jean-Jacques Rousseau was one of the first modern critics to suggest that Homer might not have been an author in the contemporary sense of a single person who sat down and wrote a story and then published it for others to read. In his 1781 Essay on the Origin of Languages, the Swiss philosopher suggested that the *Odyssey* and *Iliad* might have been "written only in men's memories. Somewhat later they were laboriously collected in writing" – though that was about as far as his enquiry into the matter went.

E In 1795, the German philologist Friedrich August Wolf argued for the first time that not only were Homer's works not written down by Homer, but they weren't even by Homer. They were, rather, a loose collection of songs transmitted by generations of Greek bards*, and only redacted* in their present form at some later date. In 1920, an eighteen-year-old scholar named Milman Parry took up the question of Homeric authorship as his Master's thesis at the University of California, Berkeley. He suggested that the reason Homer's epics seemed unlike other literature was because they were unlike other literature. Parry had discovered what Wood and Wolf had missed: the evidence that the poems had been transmitted orally was right there in the text itself. All those stylistic quirks, including the formulaic and recurring plot elements and the bizarrely repetitive epithets – "clever Odysseus" and "gray-eyed Athena" – that had always perplexed readers were actually like thumbprints left by a potter: material evidence of how the poems had been crafted. They were mnemonic* aids that helped the bard(s) fit the meter and pattern of the line, and remember the essence of the poems.

F The greatest author of antiquity was actually, Parry argued, just "one of a long tradition of oral poets that ... composed wholly without the aid of writing". Parry realised that if you were setting out to create memorable poems, the *Odyssey* and the *Iliad* were exactly the kind of poems you'd create. It's said that clichés* are the worst sin a writer can commit, but to an oral bard, they were essential. The very reason that clichés so easily seep into our speech and writing – their insidious memorability – is exactly why they played such an important role in oral storytelling. The principles that the oral bards discovered as they sharpened their stories through telling and retelling were the same mnemonic principles that psychologists rediscovered when they began conducting their first scientific experiments on memory around the turn of the twentieth century. Words that rhyme are much more memorable than words that don't, and concrete nouns are easier to remember than abstract ones. Finding patterns and structure in information is how our brains extract meaning from the world, and putting words to music and rhyme is a way of adding extra levels of pattern and structure to language.

Glossary

quirk: behaviour or a habit which seems to be unique to one person
ex nihilo: a Latin phrase used to express the idea of 'creation out of nothing'
bard: a person who composed and recited long, heroic poems
redacted: published
mnemonic: a sentence or short poem used for helping someone to remember something
cliché: a phrase or idea that is unoriginal because people use it very frequently

Questions 27–32

Reading Passage 3 has six paragraphs, **A–F**.

Which paragraph contains the following information?

*Write the correct letter, **A–F**, in boxes 27–32 on your answer sheet.*

***NB** You may use any letter more than once.*

27 the claim that the *Odyssey* and *Iliad* were not poems in their original form.

28 a theory involving the reinterpretation of the term 'author'

29 references to the fact that little is known about Homer's life

30 a comparison between the construction of Homer's poems and another art form

31 examples of the kinds of people employed to recall language

32 doubts regarding Homer's apparently inappropriate descriptions

Questions 33 and 34

*Choose **TWO** letters, **A–E**.*

Write the correct letters in boxes 33 and 34 on your answer sheet.

*Which **TWO** of these points are made by the writer of the text about the* Odyssey *and the* Iliad*?*

A They are sometimes historically inaccurate.

B It is uncertain which century they were written in.

C Their content is very similar.

D Later writers referred to them as ideal examples of writing.

E There are stylistic differences between them.

Questions 35 and 36

Choose ***TWO*** *letters,* ***A–E****.*

Write the correct letters in boxes 35 and 36 on your answer sheet.

Which ***TWO*** *of the following theories does the writer of the text refer to?*

A Homer wrote his work during a period of captivity.

B Neither the *Odyssey* nor the *Iliad* were written by Homer.

C Homer created the *Odyssey* and *Iliad* without writing them down.

D Homer may have suffered from a failing memory in later life.

E The oral and written versions of Homer's work may not be identical.

Questions 37–40

Complete the summary below.

Choose ***ONE WORD ONLY*** *from the passage for each answer.*

Write your answers in boxes 37–40 on your answer sheet.

The importance of the spoken word and how words are remembered

Spoken poetry was once the means by which each **37** .... of a particular culture or community could pass on its knowledge. Indeed, it has been suggested that it was the duty of a **38** .... to know poetry so they would be informed about subjects such as politics and history.

Psychologists now know that when people are trying to remember information, they may find it difficult to remember words that express **39** .... ideas. It is easier to remember words which sound similar or go together with **40** ....

WRITING

WRITING TASK 1

You should spend about 20 minutes on this task.

The chart below gives information about Southland's main exports in 2000, *20.., and future projections for 2025.

Summarise the information by selecting and reporting the main features, and make comparisons where relevant.

Write at least 150 words.

Southland's main exports in 2000 and *20.., and future projections for 2025

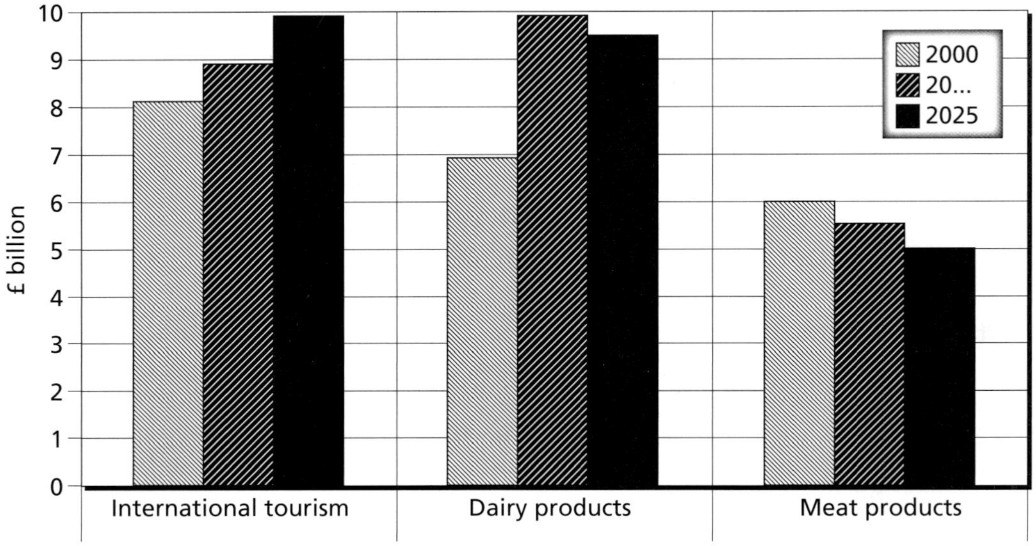

*(***20..** : for test purposes, use and refer to the current year)*

WRITING TASK 2

You should spend about 40 minutes on this task.

In some countries an increasing number of people are suffering from health problems as a result of eating too much fast food. It is therefore necessary for governments to impose a higher tax on this kind of food.

To what extent do you agree or disagree with this opinion?

Give reasons for your answer and include any relevant examples from your own knowledge or experience.

Write at least 250 words.

SPEAKING

PART 1

Home town or city

- What kind of place is your town/city?
- What's the most interesting part of your town/city?
- Has your town/city changed in any way in your life time? [How?]
- Would you say your town/city is a good place for young people to live? [Why? / Why not?]

Shopping

- What kind of things do you prefer shopping for?
- In what kind of places do you like to go shopping? [Why?]
- What effect has online shopping had in your country?
- What would you recommend that tourists buy from your country? [Why?]

PART 2

Candidate task card:

Describe a popular teacher that you know.

You should say:
what this teacher looks like
what sort of person this teacher is
what this teacher helped you to learn
and explain why this teacher is popular.

You will have to talk about the topic for one to two minutes.

You have one minute to think about what you are going to say.

You can make some notes to help you if you wish.

PART 3

Education in school

- What can schools do to help students prepare for the next stage in their lives?
- What advice would you give to someone who doesn't like school?
- What can schools teach children that they can't learn from their parents?

Education after school

- In general, what opportunities are available to students after they leave school?
- How do you think school life differs from university life?
- How important do you think it is for individuals to carry on learning after they have finished school and university?

Test 5

LISTENING

SECTION 1 *Questions 1–10*

Complete the form below.

*Write **ONE WORD AND/OR A NUMBER** for each answer.*

City Transport Lost Property Enquiry

Example

Main item lost: ......suitcase......

Description of main item: black with thin **1** .... stripes

Other items:	a set of **2** .... keys
	some documents
	a **3** .... in a box
	a blue **4** ....

Journey details

Date and time:	2.00–2.30 pm on **5** ....
Basic route:	caller travelled from the **6** .... to Highbury
Mode of travel:	caller thinks she left the suitcase in a **7** ....

Personal details

Name:	Lisa **8** ....
Address:	15A **9** .... Rd, Highbury
Phone number:	**10** ....

SECTION 2 *Questions 11–20*

Questions 11–15

Label the map below.

Write the correct letter, ***A–H****, next to Questions 11–15.*

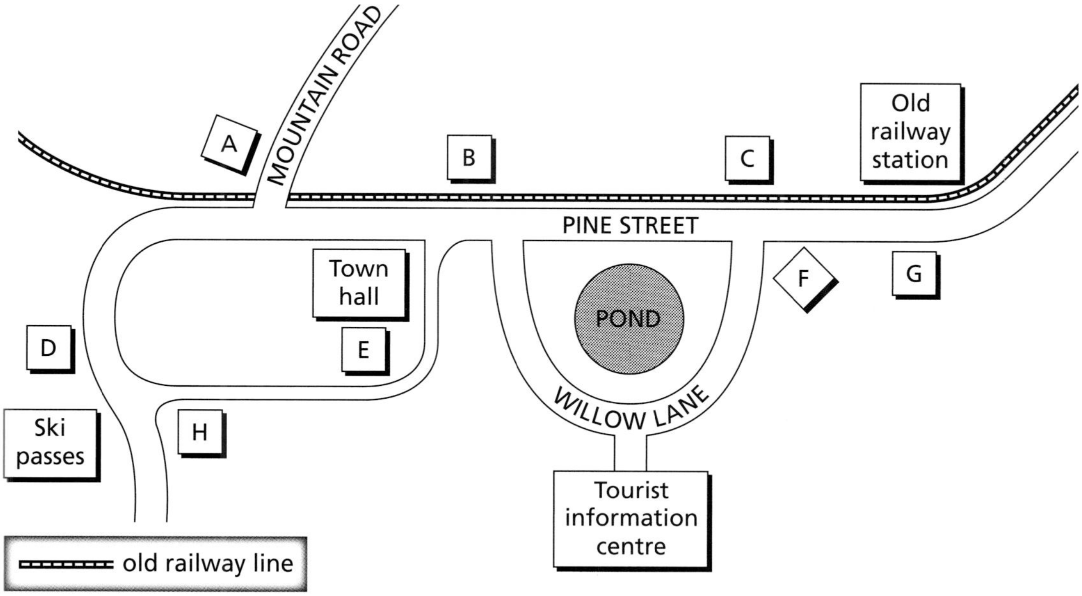

11 *supermarket* ....

12 *climbing supplies store* ....

13 *museum* ....

14 *bike hire* ....

15 *café* ....

Questions 16–20

What comment does the speaker make about each of the following tracks?

*Write the correct letter, **A**, **B** or **C**, next to Questions 16–20.*

A	It is possible to get lost here.
B	It only offers basic accommodation.
C	It requires physical strength.

Track

16 North Point

17 Silver River

18 Valley Crossing

19 Stonebridge

20 Henderson Ridge

SECTION 3 *Questions 21–30*

Questions 21–25

Choose the correct letter, ***A****,* ***B*** *or* ***C****.*

21 Why has James chosen to do a case study on the company *Furniture Rossi*?

A It has enjoyed global success.
B It is still in a developmental phase.
C It is an example of a foreign company being rebranded for Australia.

22 According to James, why did Luca Rossi start a furniture company?

A Furniture-making was already a family occupation.
B Rossi saw a need for hand-crafted furniture.
C The work Rossi had done previously was unrewarding.

23 What gave *Furniture Rossi* a competitive advantage over other furniture companies?

A its staff
B its lower prices
C its locally sourced products

24 What does the tutor recommend James does when writing the second draft of his case study?

A provide more detailed references
B check for written accuracy
C add his own views

25 What do the tutor and James agree was wrong with James' last presentation?

A It was too short.
B It focused too much on statistics.
C There was not enough interaction with the audience.

Questions 26–30

Complete the flow-chart below.

*Choose **FIVE** answers from the list below and write the correct letter, **A–G**, next to Questions 26–30.*

A website

B locations

C designs

D TV advertising campaigns

E quality

F values

G software programs

History of *Furniture Rossi*

The product **26** .... led to a wider customer base.
↓
Greater customer demand meant other **27** .... were needed.
↓
Better **28** .... increased overall profitability.
↓
Changes to the **29** .... were brought on by customer complaints.
↓
Furniture Rossi wants to make people more aware of its **30** ....

SECTION 4 *Questions 31–40*

Questions 31–36

Complete the notes below.

*Write **ONE WORD ONLY** for each answer.*

Rock art

Why rock art is important to researchers

It provides evidence about

- evolution
- **31** ....

Global similarities in rock art

- humans often had large **32** ....
- animals were common, but a **33** .... was always drawn from the side or from above.
- unlikely that contact through **34** .... resulted in similar artistic styles

Why our ancestors produced rock art

Research suggests rock art was produced

- firstly for reasons of **35** ....
- later for social, spiritual and **36** .... reasons.

Questions 37–40

Answer the questions below.

*Write **ONE WORD ONLY** for each answer.*

*What **TWO** images drawn by Aboriginal people show their contact with Europeans?*

- **37** ....
- **38** ....

Which human activities does the lecturer say are the main threats to Aboriginal rock art?

- **39** ....
- vandalism
- **40** ....

READING

READING PASSAGE 1

*You should spend about 20 minutes on **Questions 1–13**, which are based on Reading Passage 1 on the following pages.*

Questions 1–7

*Reading Passage 1 has seven paragraphs, **A–G**.*

Choose the correct heading for each paragraph from the list of headings below.

*Write the correct number, **i–x**, in boxes 1–7 on your answer sheet.*

List of Headings

- **i** How deforestation harms isolated trees
- **ii** How other plants can cause harm
- **iii** Which big trees support the most diverse species
- **iv** Impact of big tree loss on the wider environment
- **v** Measures to prevent further decline in big tree populations
- **vi** How wildlife benefits from big trees
- **vii** Risk from pests and infection
- **viii** Ways in which industry uses big tree products
- **ix** How higher temperatures slow the rate of tree growth
- **x** Factors that enable trees to grow to significant heights

1 Paragraph **A** ....

2 Paragraph **B** ....

3 Paragraph **C** ....

4 Paragraph **D** ....

5 Paragraph **E** ....

6 Paragraph **F** ....

7 Paragraph **G** ....

Trees in trouble

What is causing the decline of the world's giant forests?

A Big trees are incredibly important ecologically. For a start, they sustain countless other species. They provide shelter for many animals, and their trunks and branches can become gardens, hung with green ferns, orchids and bromeliads, coated with mosses and draped with vines. With their tall canopies* basking in the sun, they capture vast amounts of energy. This allows them to produce massive crops of fruit, flowers and foliage that sustain much of the animal life in the forest.

B Only a small number of tree species have the genetic capacity to grow really big. The mightiest are native to North America, but big trees grow all over the globe, from the tropics to the boreal forests of the high latitudes. To achieve giant stature, a tree needs three things: the right place to establish its seedling, good growing conditions and lots of time with low adult mortality*. Disrupt any of these, and you can lose your biggest trees.

C In some parts of the world, populations of big trees are dwindling because their seedlings cannot survive or grow. In southern India, for instance, an aggressive non-native shrub, *Lantana camara,* is invading the floor of many forests. Lantana grows so thickly that young trees often fail to take root. With no young trees to replace them, it is only a matter of time before most of the big trees disappear. Across much of northern Australia, gamba grass from Africa is overrunning native savannah woodlands. The grass grows up to four metres tall and burns fiercely, creating super-hot fires that cause catastrophic tree mortality.

D Without the right growing conditions trees cannot get really big, and there is some evidence to suggest tree growth could slow in a warmer world, particularly in environments that are already warm. Having worked for decades at La Selva Biological Station in Puerto Viejo de Sarapiqui, Costa Rica, David and Deborah Clark and colleagues have shown that tree growth there declines markedly in warmer years. "During the day, their photosynthesis* shuts down when it gets too warm, and at night they consume more energy because their metabolic rate increases, much as a reptile's would when it gets warmer," explains David Clark. With less energy produced in warmer years and more being consumed just to survive, there is even less energy available for growth.

E The Clarks' hypothesis, if correct, means tropical forests would shrink over time. The largest, oldest trees would progressively die off and tend not to be replaced. According to the Clarks, this might trigger a destabilisation of the climate; as older trees die, forests would release some of their stored carbon into the atmosphere, prompting a vicious cycle of further warming, forest shrinkage and carbon emissions.

F Big trees face threats from elsewhere. The most serious is increasing mortality, especially of mature trees. Across much of the planet, forests of slow-growing ancient trees have been cleared for human use. In western North America, most have been replaced by monocultures of fast-growing conifers. Siberia's forests are being logged at an incredible rate. Logging in tropical forests is selective but the timber cutters usually prioritise the biggest and oldest trees. In the Amazon, my colleagues and I found the mortality rate for the biggest trees had tripled in small patches of rainforest surrounded by pasture land. This happens for two reasons. First, as they grow taller, big trees become thicker and less flexible: when winds blow across the surrounding cleared land, there is nothing to stop their acceleration. When they hit the trees, the impact can snap them in half. Second, rainforest fragments dry out when surrounded by dry, hot pastures and the resulting drought can have devastating consequences: one four-year study has shown that death rates will double for smaller trees but will increase 4.5 times for bigger trees.

G Particular enemies to large trees are insects and disease. Across vast areas of western North America, increasingly mild winters are causing massive outbreaks of bark beetle. These tiny creatures can kill entire forests as they tunnel their way through the inside of trees. In both North America and Europe, fungus-causing diseases such as Dutch elm disease have killed off millions of stately trees that once gave beauty to forests and cities. As a result of human activity, such enemies reach even the remotest corners of the world, threatening to make the ancient giants a thing of the past.

Glossary

a canopy: leaves and branches that form a cover high above the ground

mortality: the number of deaths within a particular group

photosynthesis: a process used by plants to convert the light energy from the sun into chemical energy that can be used as food

Questions 8–13

Complete the sentences below.

Choose ***NO MORE THAN TWO WORDS*** *from the passage for each answer.*

Write your answers in boxes 8–13.

8 The biggest trees in the world can be found in ....

9 Some trees in northern Australia die because of .... made worse by gamba grass.

10 The Clarks believe that the release of .... from dead trees could lead to the death of more trees.

11 Strong .... are capable of damaging tall trees in the Amazon.

12 .... has a worse impact on tall trees than smaller ones.

13 In western Northern America, a species of .... has destroyed many trees.

READING PASSAGE 2

*You should spend about 20 minutes on **Questions 14–26**, which are based on Reading Passage 2 below.*

Whale Strandings

Why do whales leave the ocean and become stuck on beaches?

When the last stranded whale of a group eventually dies, the story does not end there. A team of researchers begins to investigate, collecting skin samples for instance, recording anything that could help them answer the crucial question: why? Theories abound, some more convincing than others. In recent years, navy sonar has been accused of causing certain whales to strand. It is known that noise pollution from offshore industry, shipping and sonar can impair underwater communication, but can it really drive whales onto our beaches?

In 1998, researchers at the Pelagos Cetacean Research Institute, a Greek non-profit scientific group, linked whale strandings with low-frequency sonar tests being carried out by the North Atlantic Treaty Organisation (NATO). They recorded the stranding of 12 Cuvier's beaked whales over 38.2 kilometres of coastline. NATO later admitted it had been testing new sonar technology in the same area at the time as the strandings had occurred. 'Mass' whale strandings involve four or more animals. Typically they all wash ashore together, but in mass atypical strandings (such as the one in Greece), the whales don't strand as a group; they are scattered over a larger area.

For humans, hearing a sudden loud noise might prove frightening, but it does not induce mass fatality. For whales, on the other hand, there is a theory on how sonar can kill. The noise can surprise the animal, causing it to swim too quickly to the surface. The result is decompression sickness, a hazard human divers know all too well. If a diver ascends too quickly from a high-pressure underwater environment to a lower-pressure one, gases dissolved in blood and tissue expand and form bubbles. The bubbles block the flow of blood to vital organs, and can ultimately lead to death.

Plausible as this seems, it is still a theory and based on our more comprehensive knowledge of land-based animals. For this reason, some scientists are wary. Whale expert Karen Evans is one such scientist. Another is Rosemary Gales, a leading expert on whale strandings. She says sonar technology cannot always be blamed for mass strandings. "It's a case-by-case situation. Whales have been stranding for a very long time – pre-sonar." And when 80% of all Australian whale strandings occur around Tasmania, Gales and her team must continue in the search for answers.

When animals beach next to each other at the same time, the most common cause has nothing to do with humans at all. "They're highly social creatures," says Gales. "When they mass strand – it's complete panic and chaos. If one of the group strands and sounds the alarm, others will try to swim to its aid, and become stuck themselves."

Activities such as sonar testing can hint at *when* a stranding may occur, but if conservationists are to reduce the number of strandings, or improve rescue operations, they need information on *where* strandings are likely to occur as well. With this in mind, Ralph James, physicist at the University of Western Australia in Perth, thinks he may have discovered why whales turn up only on some beaches. In 1986 he went to Augusta, Western Australia, where more than 100 false killer whales had beached. "I found out from chatting to the locals that whales had been stranding there for decades. So I asked myself, what is it about this beach?" From this question that James pondered over 20 years ago, grew the university's Whale Stranding Analysis Project.

Data has since revealed that all mass strandings around Australia occur on gently sloping sandy beaches, some with inclines of less than 0.5%. For whale species that depend on an echolocation system to navigate, this kind of beach spells disaster. Usually, as they swim, they make clicking noises, and the resulting sound waves are reflected in an echo and travel back to them. However, these just fade out on shallow beaches, so the whale doesn't hear an echo and it crashes onto the shore.

But that is not all. Physics, it appears, can help with the *when* as well as the *where*. The ocean is full of bubbles. Larger ones rise quickly to the surface and disappear, whilst smaller ones – called microbubbles – can last for days. It is these that absorb whale 'clicks'. "Rough weather generates more bubbles than usual," James adds. So, during and after a storm, echolocating whales are essentially swimming blind.

Last year was a bad one for strandings in Australia. Can we predict if this – or any other year – will be any better? Some scientists believe we can. They have found trends which could be used to forecast 'bad years' for strandings in the future. In 2005, a survey by Klaus Vanselow and Klaus Ricklefs of sperm whale strandings in the North Sea even found a correlation between these and the sunspot cycle, and suggested that changes in the Earth's magnetic field might be involved. But others are sceptical. "Their study was interesting … but the analyses they used were flawed on a number of levels," says Evans. In the same year, she co-authored a study on Australian strandings that uncovered a completely different trend. "We analysed data from 1920 to 2002 … and observed a clear periodicity in the number of whales stranded each year that coincides with a major climatic cycle." To put it more simply, she says, in the years when strong westerly and southerly winds bring cool water rich in nutrients closer to the Australia coast, there is an increase in the number of fish. The whales follow.

So what causes mass strandings? "It's probably many different components," says James. And he is probably right. But the point is we now know what many of those components are.

Questions 14–17

Choose **NO MORE THAN TWO WORDS** *from the passage for each answer.*

Write your answers in boxes 14–17 on your answer sheet.

14 What do researchers often take from the bodies of whales?

15 What do some industries and shipping create that is harmful to whales?

16 In which geographical region do most whale strandings in Australia happen?

17 Which kind of whale was the subject of a study in the North Sea?

Questions 18–21

Label the diagram below.

Choose **NO MORE THAN TWO WORDS** *from the passage for each answer.*

Write your answers in boxes 18–21 on your answer sheet.

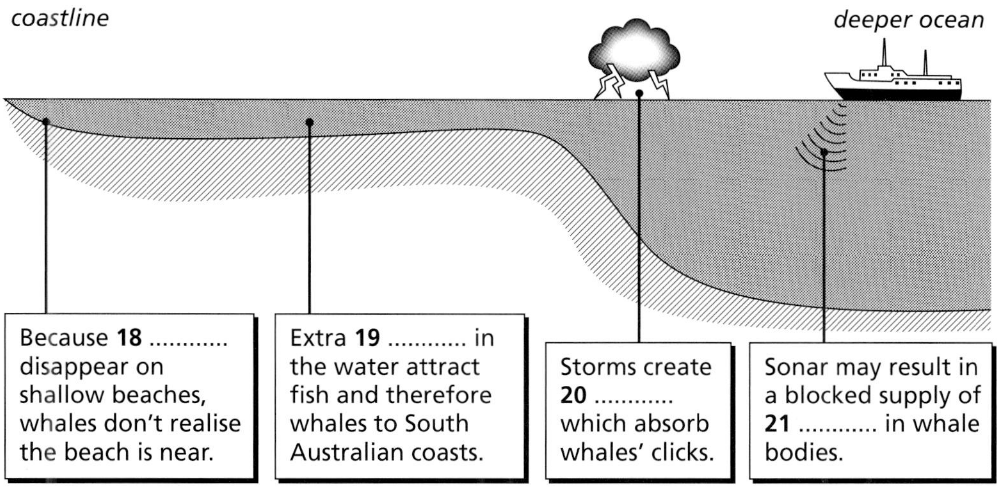

Questions 22–26

Do the following statements agree with the information given in Reading Passage 2?

In boxes 22–26 on your answer sheet, write

TRUE	*if the statement agrees with the information*
FALSE	*if the statement contradicts the information*
NOT GIVEN	*if there is no information on this*

22 The aim of the research by the Pelagos Institute in 1998 was to prove that navy sonar was responsible for whale strandings.

23 The whales stranded in Greece were found at different points along the coast.

24 Rosemary Gales has questioned the research techniques used by the Greek scientists.

25 According to Gales, whales are likely to try to help another whale in trouble.

26 There is now agreement amongst scientists that changes in the Earth's magnetic fields contribute to whale strandings.

READING PASSAGE 3

*You should spend about 20 minutes on **Questions 27–40**, which are based on Reading Passage 3 below.*

Science in Space

How will NASA transform the International Space Station from a building site into a cutting-edge research laboratory?

A premier, world-class laboratory in low Earth orbit. That was how the National Aeronautics and Space Administration agency (NASA) sold the International Space Station (ISS) to the US Congress in 2001. Today no one can doubt the agency's technological ambition. The most complex engineering project ever attempted has created an enormous set of interlinked modules that orbits the planet at more than 27,000 kilometres per hour. It might be travelling fast but, say critics, as a lab it is going nowhere. So far, it has gone through $150 billion.

So where should its future priorities lie? This question was addressed at the recent 1st annual ISS research and development conference in Colorado. Among the presenters was Satoshi Iwase of Aichi Medical University in Japan who has spent several years developing an experiment that could help solve one of the key problems that humans will face in space: keeping our bodies healthy in weightlessness. One thing that physiologists have learned is that without gravity our bodies begin to lose strength, leaving astronauts with weakened bones, muscles and cardiovascular systems. To counter these effects on a long-duration mission to, say, Mars, astronauts will almost certainly need to create their own artificial gravity. This is where Iwase comes in. He leads a team designing a centrifuge for humans. In their preliminary design, an astronaut is strapped into the seat of a machine that resembles an exercise bike. Pedalling provides a workout for the astronaut's muscles and cardiovascular system, but it also causes the seat to rotate vertically around a central axis so the rider experiences artificial gravity while exercising.

The centrifuge project highlights the station's potential as a research lab. Similar machines have flown in space aboard NASA's shuttles, but they couldn't be tested for long enough to prove whether they were effective. It's been calculated that to properly assess a centrifuge's impact on human physiology, astronauts would have to ride it for 30 minutes a day for at least two months. 'The only way to test this is in weightlessness, and the only time we have to do that is on the space station,' says Laurence Young, a space medicine expert at the Massachusetts Institute of Technology.

There are certainly plenty of ideas for other experiments: but many projects have yet to fly. Even if the centrifuge project gets the green light, it will have to wait another five years before the station's crew can take a spin. Lengthy delays like this are one of the key challenges for NASA, according to an April 2011 report from the US National Academy of Sciences. Its authors said they were 'deeply concerned' about the state of NASA's science research, and made a number of recommendations. Besides suggesting that the agency reduces the time between approving experiments and sending them into space, it also recommended setting clearer research priorities.

NASA has already begun to take action, hiring management consultants ProOrbis to develop a plan to cut through the bureaucracy. And Congress also directed NASA to hire an independent organisation, the Centre for the Advancement of Science in Space (CASIS), to help manage the station's US lab facilities. One of CASIS's roles is to convince public and private investors that science on the station is worth the spend because judged solely by the number of papers published, the ISS certainly seems poor value: research on the station has generated about 3,100 papers since 1998. The Hubble Space Telescope, meanwhile, has produced more than 11,300 papers in just over 20 years, yet it cost less than one-tenth of the price of the space station.

Yet Mark Uhran, assistant associate administrator for the ISS, refutes the criticism that the station hasn't done any useful research. He points to progress made on a salmonella vaccine, for example. To get the ISS research back on track, CASIS has examined more than 100 previous microgravity experiments to identify promising research themes. From this, it has opted to focus on life science and medical research, and recently called for proposals for experiments on muscle wasting, osteoporosis and the immune system. The organisation also maintains that the ISS should be used to develop products with commercial application and to test those that are either close to or already on the market. Investment from outside organisations is vital, says Uhran, and a balance between academic and commercial research will help attract this.

The station needs to attract cutting-edge research, yet many scientists seem to have little idea what goes on aboard it. Jeanne DiFrancesco at ProOrbis conducted more than 200 interviews with people from organisations with potential interests in low gravity studies. Some were aware of the ISS but they didn't know what's going on up there, she says. 'Others know there's science, but they don't know what kind.'

According to Alan Stern, planetary scientist, the biggest public relations boost for the ISS may come from the privately funded space flight industry. Companies like *SpaceX* could help NASA and its partners when it comes to resupplying the ISS, as it suggests it can reduce launch costs by two-thirds. Virgin Atlantic's *SpaceShipTwo* or *Zero2Infinity*'s high-altitude balloon could also boost the space station's fortunes. They might not come close to the ISS's orbit, yet Stern believes they will revolutionise the way we, the public, see space. Soon everyone will be dreaming of interplanetary travel again, he predicts. More importantly, scientists are already queuing for seats on these low-gravity space-flight services so they can collect data during a few minutes of weightlessness. This demand for low-cost space flight could eventually lead to a service running on a more frequent basis, giving researchers the chance to test their ideas before submitting a proposal for experiments on the ISS. Getting flight experience should help them win a slot on the station, says Stern.

Questions 27–30

Choose the correct letter, ***A***, ***B***, ***C*** *or* ***D***.

Write the correct letter in boxes 27–30 on your answer sheet.

27 What does the writer state about the ISS in the first paragraph?

A Its manufacture has remained within the proposed budget.
B It is a great example of technological achievement.
C There are doubts about the speed it has attained.
D NASA should have described its purpose more accurately.

28 What are we told about Satoshi Iwase's experimental machine?

A It is based on conventional exercise equipment.
B It was originally commissioned by NASA.
C It is designed only to work in low-gravity environments.
D It has benefits that Iwase did not anticipate.

29 The writer refers to the Hubble Space Telescope in order to

A show why investment in space technology has decreased.
B highlight the need to promote the ISS in a positive way.
C explain which kind of projects are more likely to receive funding.
D justify the time required for a space project to produce results.

30 In the sixth paragraph, we are told that CASIS has

A rejected certain applications for experiments on the ISS.
B expressed concern about testing products used for profit.
C questioned the benefits of some of the projects currently on the ISS.
D invited researchers to suggest certain health-based projects.

Questions 31–35

Look at the following opinions (Questions 31–35) and the list of people below.

Match each opinion with the correct person, ***A, B, C*** *or* ***D****.*

Write the correct letter, ***A****,* ***B****,* ***C*** *or* ***D****, in boxes 31–35 on your answer sheet.*

NB *You may use any letter more than once.*

31 The ISS should be available for business-related ventures.

32 There is general ignorance about what kinds of projects are possible on the ISS.

33 The process of getting accepted projects onto the ISS should be speeded up.

34 Some achievements of the ISS are underrated.

35 To properly assess new space technology, there has to be an absence of gravity.

List of people

A Laurence Young
B Authors of the US National Academy of Sciences report
C Mark Uhran
D Jeanne DiFrancesco

Questions 36–39

*Complete the summary using the lists of words, **A–H**, below.*

*Write the correct letter, **A–H**, in boxes 36–39 on your answer sheet.*

The influence of commercial space flight on the ISS

According to Alan Stern, private space companies could affect the future of the ISS. He believes they could change its image; firstly because sending food and equipment there would be more **36** ………………… if a commercial craft were used, and secondly, because commercial flights might make the whole idea of space exploration seem **37** ………………… to ordinary people. Another point is that as the demand for space flights increases, there is a chance of them becoming more **38** ………………… . And by working on a commercial flight first, scientists would be more **39** ………………… if an ISS position came up.

A safe	**B** competitive	**C** flexible	**D** real
E rapid	**F** regular	**G** suitable	**H** economical

Question 40

*Choose the correct letter, **A**, **B**, **C** or **D**.*

Write the correct letter in box 40 on your answer sheet.

40 The writer's purpose in writing this article is to

A promote the advantages of space flight in general.
B illustrate how the ISS could become more effective.
C criticise the ISS for its narrow-minded attitude.
D contrast useful and worthless space projects.

WRITING

WRITING TASK 1

You should spend about 20 minutes on this task.

> ***The pie charts below show the online shopping sales for retail sectors in New Zealand in 2003 and 2013.***
>
> ***Summarise the information by selecting and reporting the main features, and make comparisons where relevant.***

Write at least 150 words.

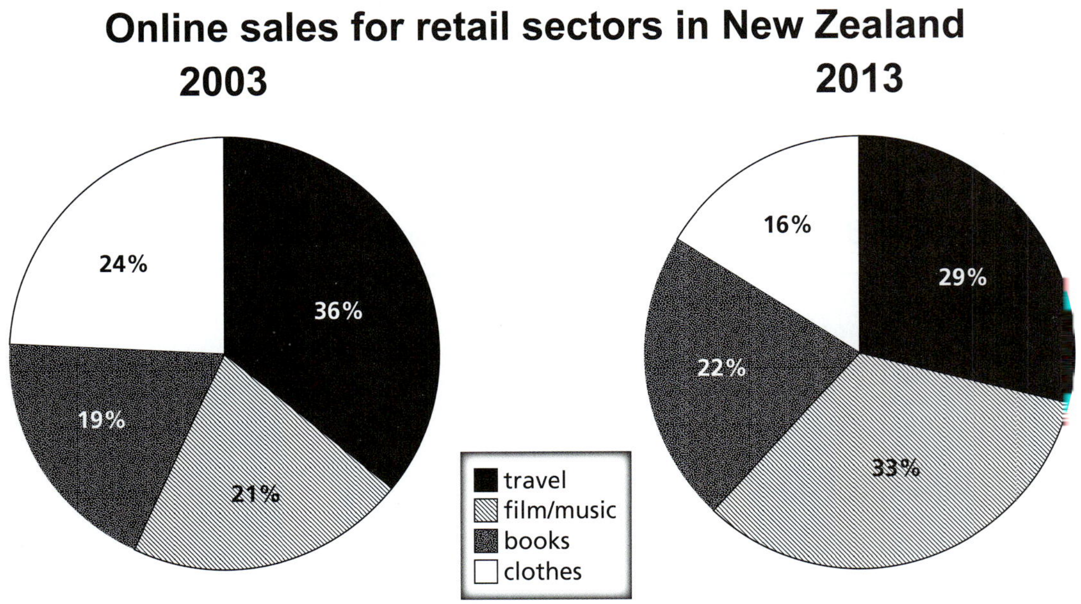

WRITING TASK 2

You should spend about 40 minutes on this task.

> ***Nowadays technology is increasingly being used to monitor what people are saying and doing (for example, through cellphone tracking and security cameras). In many cases, the people being monitored are unaware that this is happening.***
>
> ***Do you think the advantages of this development outweigh the disadvantages?***

Give reasons for your answer and include any relevant examples from your own knowledge or experience.

You should write at least 250 words.

SPEAKING

PART 1

Your life

Let's talk about what you do. Do you work or are you a student? [Examiner chooses appropriate questions.]

Work

- What job do you do?
- What skills do you need for your job?
- What do you particularly like about your job?

Study

- What subject are you studying?
- Why did you want to study that subject?
- How long have you been studying (English/nursing/accountancy, etc.)?

Television

- How often do you watch television?
- What kinds of television programmes are most popular in your country?
- Is there anything you would like to change about television in your country? [Why? / Why not?]

PART 2

Candidate task card:

Describe a restaurant you enjoyed going to.

You should say:
where the restaurant was
who you went with
what type of food you ate in this restaurant
and explain why you thought the restaurant was good.

You will have to talk about the topic for one to two minutes.

You have one minute to think about what you are going to say.

You can make some notes to help you if you wish.

PART 3

Food and society

- Do you think that people eat healthier food than they did in the past? [Why? / Why not?]
- How important do you think it is for families to eat meals together?
- What effects has modern technology had on the food we eat?

Restaurants

- Why do people go to restaurants when they want to celebrate important occasions?
- Do you think that food prepared at home is always better than in restaurants?
- Which are more popular in your country: fast food restaurants or traditional restaurants? [Why?]

Test 6

LISTENING

SECTION 1 *Questions 1–10*

Complete the notes below.

Write ***ONE WORD AND/OR A NUMBER*** *for each answer.*

ACCOMMODATION FORM: RENTAL PROPERTIES	
Example	*Answer*
Name:	Jane ....Ryder..........
Contact phone number:	**1** (0044) ....
Email address:	**2** richard@.......................... co.uk
Occupation:	a local **3** ....
Type of accommodation:	a 2-bedroom apartment wanted (must have its own **4** ....)
	no **5** .... required (family bringing theirs)
	a **6** .... in the kitchen is preferable
Preferred location:	near a **7** ....
Maximum rent:	**8** .... per month
Other requests:	the accommodation has to be **9** .... in the daytime
How did you first hear about us?	through a **10** ....

SECTION 2 *Questions 11–20*

Questions 11–15

Complete the sentences below.

Write ***NO MORE THAN TWO WORDS*** *for each answer.*

The police officer suggests neighbours give each other their **11** ....

Neighbours should discuss what to do if there's any kind of **12** ....

It's a good idea to leave on the **13** ....

Think carefully about where you put any **14** ....

It's a good idea to buy good-quality **15** ....

Questions 16–20

Which crime prevention measure is proposed for each area affected by crime?

Choose ***FIVE*** *answers from the box and write the correct letter,* ***A–G****, next to Questions 16–20.*

Proposed crime prevention measures

A install more lighting
B have more police officers on patrol
C remove surrounding vegetation
D contact local police
E fix damage quickly
F change road design
G use security cameras

Areas affected by crime

16 skate park ....
17 local primary schools ....
18 Abbotsford Street ....
19 shops on Victoria Street ....
20 supermarket car park ....

SECTION 3 *Questions 21–30*

Questions 21–26

*Choose the correct letter, **A**, **B** or **C**.*

Presentation on the problems and potential of biofuels

21 Mike suggests they begin their presentation by

A explaining what kind of harm is caused by fossil fuels.
B pointing out that biofuels were in use before fossil fuels.
C ensuring students know the difference between fossil fuels and biofuels.

22 Karina doesn't want to discuss the production of ethanol because

A other students will already be familiar with the process.
B there will not be time to cover more important information.
C they may not provide an accurate description.

23 Which source of biofuel do the students agree is least environmentally friendly?

A sugar cane
B corn
C canola

24 What is the main problem facing the development of the biofuel industry in the USA?

A inadequate infrastructure for transporting ethanol
B not enough farmers growing biofuel crops
C little government support of biofuel development

25 Karina doubts that sugar cane production in Brazil will

A lead to the loss of wildlife habitats.
B create a large number of jobs in the biofuel sector.
C continue to provide enough energy for the country's needs.

26 Karina and Mike conclude that in order to increase the use of biofuels

A the price of fossil fuels must go up.
B more machinery must be adapted to use them.
C production methods must be more energy-efficient.

Questions 27–30

Answer the questions below.

*Write **NO MORE THAN TWO WORDS** for each answer.*

*What **TWO** biofuel-related problems do Mike and Karina decide to focus on in the last section of their presentation?*

- **27** ....
- **28** ....

Which two sources of biofuel do Mike and Karina say are being tried out?

- **29** ....
- algae
- **30** ....

SECTION 4 *Questions 31–40*

Questions 31–34

Complete the summary below.

Write ***ONE WORD ONLY*** *for each answer.*

The 'weak-tie' theory: how friends-of-friends influence us

In 1973, Mark Granovetter claimed that the influence of 'weak-ties' can affect the behaviour of populations in the fields of information science, politics and **31** .... Although friends-of-friends may be unlike us, they have similar enough **32** .... to have a beneficial effect on our lives. An example of this influence is when we hear about **33** .... because information about them is provided by weak-ties. Since Granovetter proposed his theory, other studies have shown that weak-tie networks also benefit our **34** ....

Questions 35 and 36

*Choose **TWO** letters, **A–E**.*

*Which does the speaker believe are **TWO** real benefits of online social networking?*

A people can gain higher self-esteem

B people can access useful medical information

C people can form relationships more quickly

D people can improve academic performance

E people can be reliably informed about current affairs

Questions 37 and 38

*Choose **TWO** letters, **A–E**.*

*Which **TWO** problems related to online social networking will increase, according to the speaker?*

A criminal activity

B poorer grades at school

C a decline in physical fitness

D less work done by employees

E loss of career prospects

Questions 39 and 40

*Choose **TWO** letters, **A–E**.*

*Which **TWO** claims are made by Robin Dunbar about social networking sites?*

A They are not helpful for developing certain social skills.

B They cannot fully reveal a person's real character.

C They are not a good starting point for building new relationships.

D They do not encourage people to widen their social circle.

E They will not retain their popularity with the young generation.

READING

READING PASSAGE 1

*You should spend about 20 minutes on **Questions 1–13**, which are based on Reading Passage 1 on the following page.*

Questions 1–6

*Reading Passage 1 has six paragraphs, **A–F**.*

Choose the correct heading for each paragraph from the list of headings below.

*Write the correct number, **i–ix**, in boxes 1–6 on your answer sheet.*

List of Headings

i	A business-model approach to education
ii	The reforms that improved education in Finland
iii	Educational challenges of the future
iv	Ways in which equality is maintained in the Finnish education system
v	The benefits of the introduction of testing
vi	An approach that helped a young learner
vii	Statistical proof of education success
viii	Support for families working and living in Finland
ix	The impact of the education system on Finland's economy

1 Paragraph **A** ....

2 Paragraph **B** ....

3 Paragraph **C** ....

4 Paragraph **D** ....

5 Paragraph **E** ....

6 Paragraph **F** ....

Why Are Finland's Schools Successful?

The country's achievements in education have other nations doing their homework

A At Kirkkojarvi Comprehensive School in Espoo, a suburb west of Helsinki, Kari Louhivuori, the school's principal, decided to try something extreme by Finnish standards. One of his sixth-grade students, a recent immigrant, was falling behind, resisting his teacher's best efforts. So he decided to hold the boy back a year. Standards in the country have vastly improved in reading, math and science literacy over the past decade, in large part because its teachers are trusted to do whatever it takes to turn young lives around. 'I took Besart on that year as my private student,' explains Louhivuori. When he was not studying science, geography and math, Besart was seated next to Louhivuori's desk, taking books from a tall stack, slowly reading one, then another, then devouring them by the dozens. By the end of the year, he had conquered his adopted country's vowel-rich language and arrived at the realization that he could, in fact, *learn*.

B This tale of a single rescued child hints at some of the reasons for Finland's amazing record of education success. The transformation of its education system began some 40 years ago but teachers had little idea it had been so successful until 2000. In this year, the first results from the Programme for International Student Assessment (PISA), a standardized test given to 15-year-olds in more than 40 global venues, revealed Finnish youth to be the best at reading in the world. Three years later, they led in math. By 2006, Finland was first out of the 57 nations that participate in science. In the latest PISA scores, the nation came second in science, third in reading and sixth in math among nearly half a million students worldwide.

C In the United States, government officials have attempted to improve standards by introducing marketplace competition into public schools. In recent years, a group of Wall Street financiers and philanthropists such as Bill Gates have put money behind private-sector ideas, such as charter schools, which have doubled in number in the past decade. President Obama, too, apparently thought competition was the answer. One policy invited states to compete for federal dollars using tests and other methods to measure teachers, a philosophy that would not be welcome in Finland. 'I think, in fact, teachers would tear off their shirts,' said Timo Heikkinen, a Helsinki principal with 24 years of teaching experience. 'If you only measure the statistics, you miss the human aspect.'

D There are no compulsory standardized tests in Finland, apart from one exam at the end of students' senior year in high school. There is no competition between students, schools or regions. Finland's schools are publicly funded. The people in the government agencies running them, from national officials to local authorities, are educators rather than business people or politicians. Every school has the same national goals and draws from the same pool of university-trained educators. The result is that a Finnish child has a good chance of getting the same quality education no matter whether he or she lives in a rural village or a university town.

E It's almost unheard of for a child to show up hungry to school. Finland provides three years of maternity leave and subsidized day care to parents, and preschool for all five-year-olds, where the emphasis is on socializing. In addition, the state subsidizes parents, paying them around 150 euros per month for every child until he or she turns 17. Schools provide food, counseling and taxi service if needed. Health care is even free for students taking degree courses.

F Finland's schools were not always a wonder. For the first half of the twentieth century, only the privileged got a quality education. But In 1963, the Finnish Parliament made the bold decision to choose public education as the best means of driving the economy forward and out of recession. Public schools were organized into one system of comprehensive schools for ages 7 through 16. Teachers from all over the nation contributed to a national curriculum that provided guidelines, not prescriptions, for them to refer to. Besides Finnish and Swedish (the country's second official language), children started learning a third language (English is a favorite) usually beginning at age nine. The equal distribution of equipment was next, meaning that all teachers had their fair share of teaching resources to aid learning. As the comprehensive schools improved, so did the upper secondary schools (grades 10 through 12). The second critical decision came in 1979, when it was required that every teacher gain a fifth-year Master's degree in theory and practice, paid for by the state. From then on, teachers were effectively granted equal status with doctors and lawyers. Applicants began flooding teaching programs, not because the salaries were so high but because autonomous decision-making and respect made the job desirable. And as Louhivuori explains, 'We have our own motivation to succeed because we love the work.'

Questions 7–13

Complete the notes below.

Choose ***NO MORE THAN TWO WORDS AND/OR A NUMBER*** *from the passage for each answer.*

Write your answers in boxes 7–13 on your answer sheet.

The school system in Finland

PISA tests

- In the most recent tests, Finland's top subject was **7** ....

History

1963:

- A new school system was needed to improve Finland's **8** ....
- Schools followed **9** .... that were created partly by teachers.
- Young pupils had to study an additional **10** ....
- All teachers were given the same **11** .... to use.

1979:

- Teachers had to get a **12** .... but they did not have to pay for this.
- Applicants were attracted to the **13** .... that teaching received.

READING PASSAGE 2

*You should spend about 20 minutes on **Questions 14–26**, which are based on Reading Passage 2 on the following pages.*

Questions 14–18

Reading Passage 2 has six paragraphs, **A–F**.

Which paragraphs contain the following information?

*Write the correct letter, **A–F**, in boxes 14–18 on your answer sheet.*

***NB** You may use any letter more than once.*

14 descriptions of naturally occurring events that make the past hard to trace

15 an account of the discovery of a particular animal which had died out

16 the reason why a variety of animals all died in the same small area

17 the suggestion that a procedure to uncover fossilised secrets was inappropriate

18 examples of the kinds of animals that did not die out as a result of hunting

Questions 19 and 20

*Choose **TWO** letters, **A–E**.*

Write the correct letters in boxes 19 and 20 on your answer sheet.

*Which **TWO** of these possible reasons for Australian megafauna extinction are mentioned in the text?*

A human activity

B disease

C loss of habitat

D a drop in temperature

E the introduction of new animal species

Questions 21 and 22

*Choose **TWO** letters, **A–E**.*

Write the correct letters in boxes 21 and 22 on your answer sheet.

The list below shows possible forms of proof for humans having contact with Australian megafauna.

*Which **TWO** possible forms of proof does the writer say have been found in Australia?*

A bone injury caused by a man-made object

B bones near to early types of weapon

C man-made holes designed for trapping animals

D preserved images of megafauna species

E animal remains at camp fires

Questions 23–26

Do the following statements agree with the claims of the writer in Reading Passage 2?

In boxes 23–26 on your answer sheet, write

YES	*if the statement agrees with the claims of the writer*
NO	*if the statement contradicts the claims of the writer*
NOT GIVEN	*if it is impossible to say what the writer thinks about this*

23 Extinct megafauna should receive more attention than the extinction of the dinosaurs.

24 There are problems with Paul Martin's 'blitzkrieg' hypothesis for the Americas.

25 The Aborigines should have found a more effective way to protest about Flannery's book.

26 There is sufficient evidence to support Tim Flannery's ideas about megafauna extinction.

Australia's Lost Giants

What happened to Australia's megafauna, the giant animals that once existed across this enormous continent?

A In 1969, a fossil hunter named Rod Wells came to Naracoorte in South Australia to explore what was then known as Victoria Cave. Wells clawed through narrow passages, and eventually into a huge chamber. Its floor of red soil was littered with strange objects. It took Wells a moment to realize what he was looking at; the bones of thousands of creatures that must have fallen through holes in the ground above and become trapped. Some of the oldest belonged to mammals far larger than any found today in Australia. They were the ancient Australian megafauna – huge animals of the Pleistocene epoch. In boneyards across the continent, scientists have found the fossils of a giant snake, a huge flightless bird, and a seven foot kangaroo, to name but a few. Given how much ink has been spilled on the extinction of the dinosaurs, it's a wonder that even more hasn't been devoted to megafauna. Prehistoric humans never threw spears at *Tyrannosaurus rex* but really did hunt mammoths and mastodons.

B The disappearance of megafauna in America – mammoths, saber-toothed cats, giant sloths, among others – happened relatively soon after the arrival of human beings, about 13,000 years ago. In the 1960s, paleoecologist Paul Martin developed what became known as the *blitzkrieg hypothesis.* Modern humans, Martin said, created havoc as they spread through the Americas, wielding spears to annihilate animals that had never faced a technological predator. But this period of extinction wasn't comprehensive. North America kept its deer, black bears and a small type of bison, and South America its jaguars and llamas.

C What happened to Australia's large animals is baffling. For years scientists blamed the extinctions on climate change. Indeed, Australia has been drying out for over a million years, and the megafauna were faced with a continent where vegetation began to disappear. Australian paleontologist Tim Flannery suggests that people, who arrived on the continent around 50,000 years ago, used fire to hunt, which led to deforestation. Here's what's certain, Flannery says. Something dramatic happened to Australia's dominant land creatures – somewhere around 46,000 years ago, strikingly soon after the invasion of a tool-wielding, highly intelligent predator.

In Flannery's 1994 book called *The Future Eaters,* he sets out his thesis that human beings are a new kind of animal on the planet, and are in general, one prone to ruining ecosystems. Flannery's book proved highly controversial. Some viewed it as critical of the Aborigines, who pride themselves on living in harmony with nature. The more basic problem with Flannery's thesis is that there is no direct evidence that they killed any Australian megafauna. It would be helpful if someone uncovered a *Diprotodon* skeleton with a spear point embedded in a rib – or perhaps *Thylacoleo* bones next to the charcoal of a human campfire. Such kill sites have been found in the Americas but not in Australia.

D The debate about megafauna pivots to a great degree on the techniques for dating old bones and the sediments in which they are buried. If scientists can show that the megafauna died out fairly quickly and that this extinction event happened within a few hundred, or even a couple thousand years, of the arrival of people, that's a strong case – even if a purely circumstantial one – that the one thing was the direct result of the other. As it happens, there is one place where there may be such evidence: Cuddie Springs in New South Wales. Today the person most vocal about the site is archeologist Judith Field. In 1991, she discovered megafauna bones directly adjacent to stone tools – a headline-making find. She says there are two layers showing the association, one about 30,000 years old, the other 35,000 years old. If that dating is accurate, it would mean humans and megafauna coexisted in Australia for something like 20,000 years. "What Cuddie Springs demonstrates is that you have an extended overlap of humans and megafauna," Field says. Nonsense, say her critics. They say the fossils have been moved from their original resting places and redeposited in younger sediments.

E Another famous boneyard in the same region is a place called Wellington Caves, where *Diprotodon*, the largest known marsupial*, was first discovered. Scientist Mike Augee says that: "This is a sacred site in Australian paleontology." Here's why: In 1830 a local official named George Rankin lowered himself into the cave on a rope tied to a protrusion in the cave wall. The protrusion turned out to be a bone. A surveyor named Thomas Mitchell arrived later that year, explored the caves in the area, and shipped fossils off to Richard Owen, the British paleontologist who later gained fame for revealing the existence of dinosaurs. Owen recognized that the Wellington cave bones belonged to an extinct marsupial. Later, between 1909 and 1915 sediments in Mammoth Cave that contained fossils were hauled out and examined in a chaotic manner that no scientist today would approve. Still, one bone in particular has drawn extensive attention: a femur with a cut in it, possibly left there by a sharp tool.

F Unfortunately, the Earth preserves its history haphazardly. Bones disintegrate, the land erodes, the climate changes, forests come and go, rivers change their course – and history, if not destroyed, is steadily concealed. By necessity, narratives are constructed from limited data. Australia's first people expressed themselves in rock art. Paleontologist Peter Murray has studied a rock painting in far northern Australia that shows what looks very much like a megafauna marsupial known as *Palorchestes.* In Western Australia another site shows what appears to be a hunter with either a marsupial lion or a Tasmanian tiger – a major distinction, since the marsupial lion went extinct and the much smaller Tasmanian tiger survived into the more recent historical era. But as Murray says, "Every step of the way involves interpretation. The data doesn't just speak for itself."

Glossary

marsupial: an animal which carries its young in a pouch e.g. kangaroos and koalas

READING PASSAGE 3

*You should spend about 20 minutes on **Questions 31–40**, which are based on Reading Passage 3 below.*

The Swiffer

For a fascinating tale about creativity, look at a cleaning product called the *Swiffer* and how it came about, urges writer Jonah Lehrer. In the story of the *Swiffer*, he argues, we have the key elements in producing breakthrough ideas: frustration, moments of insight and sheer hard work. The story starts with a multinational company which had invented products for keeping homes spotless, and couldn't come up with better ways to clean floors, so it hired designers to watch how people cleaned. Frustrated after hundreds of hours of observation, they one day noticed a woman do with a paper towel what people do all the time: wipe something up and throw it away. An idea popped into lead designer Harry West's head: the solution to their problem was a floor mop with a disposable cleaning surface. Mountains of prototypes and years of teamwork later, they unveiled the *Swiffer*, which quickly became a commercial success.

Lehrer, the author of *Imagine*, a new book that seeks to explain how creativity works, says this study of the imagination started from a desire to understand what happens in the brain at the moment of sudden insight. 'But the book definitely spiraled out of control,' Lehrer says. 'When you talk to creative people, they'll tell you about the 'eureka'* moment, but when you press them they also talk about the hard work that comes afterwards, so I realised I needed to write about that, too. And then I realised I couldn't just look at creativity from the perspective of the brain, because it's also about the culture and context, about the group and the team and the way we collaborate.'

When it comes to the mysterious process by which inspiration comes into your head as if from nowhere, Lehrer says modern neuroscience has produced a 'first draft' explanation of what is happening in the brain. He writes of how burnt-out American singer Bob Dylan decided to walk away from his musical career in 1965 and escape to a cabin in the woods, only to be overcome by a desire to write. Apparently '*Like a Rolling Stone*' suddenly flowed from his pen. 'It's like a ghost is writing a song,' Dylan has reportedly said. 'It gives you the song and it goes away.' But it's no ghost, according to Lehrer.

Instead, the right hemisphere of the brain is assembling connections between past influences and making something entirely new. Neuroscientists have roughly charted this process by mapping the brains of people doing word puzzles solved by making sense of remotely connecting information. For instance, subjects are given three words – such as 'age', 'mile' and 'sand' – and asked to come up with a single word that can precede or follow each of them to form a compound word. (It happens to be 'stone'.) Using brain-imaging equipment, researchers discovered that when people get the answer in an apparent flash of insight, a small fold of tissue called the anterior superior temporal gyrus suddenly lights up just beforehand. This stays silent when the word puzzle is solved through careful analysis. Lehrer says that this area of the brain lights up only after we've hit the wall on a problem. Then the brain starts hunting through the 'filing cabinets of the right hemisphere' to make the connections that produce the right answer.

Studies have demonstrated it's possible to predict a moment of insight up to eight seconds before it arrives. The predictive signal is a steady rhythm of alpha waves emanating from the brain's right hemisphere, which are closely associated with relaxing activities. 'When our minds are at ease – when those alpha waves are rippling through the brain – we're more likely to direct the spotlight of attention towards that stream of remote associations emanating from the right hemisphere,' Lehrer writes. 'In contrast, when we are diligently focused, our attention tends to be towards the details of the problems we are trying to solve.' In other words, then we are less likely to make those vital associations. So, heading out for a walk or lying down are important phases of the creative process, and smart companies know this. Some now have a policy of encouraging staff to take time out during the day and spend time on things that at first glance are unproductive (like playing a PC game), but day-dreaming has been shown to be positively correlated with problem-solving. However, to be more imaginative, says Lehrer, it's also crucial to collaborate with people from a wide range of backgrounds because if colleagues are too socially intimate, creativity is stifled.

Creativity, it seems, thrives on serendipity. American entrepreneur Steve Jobs believed so. Lehrer describes how at Pixar Animation, Jobs designed the entire workplace to maximise the chance of strangers bumping into each other, striking up conversations and learning from one another. He also points to a study of 766 business graduates who had gone on to own their own companies. Those with the greatest diversity of acquaintances enjoyed far more success. Lehrer says he has taken all this on board, and despite his inherent shyness, when he's sitting next to strangers on a plane or at a conference, forces himself to initiate conversations. As for predictions that the rise of the Internet would make the need for shared working space obsolete, Lehrer says research shows the opposite has occurred; when people meet face-to-face, the level of creativity increases. This is why the kind of place we live in is so important to innovation. According to theoretical physicist Geoffrey West, when corporate institutions get bigger, they often become less receptive to change. Cities, however, allow our ingenuity to grow by pulling huge numbers of different people together, who then exchange ideas. Working from the comfort of our homes may be convenient, therefore, but it seems we need the company of others to achieve our finest 'eureka' moments.

Glossary

Eureka: In ancient Greek, the meaning was 'I have found!'. Now it can be used when people suddenly find the solution to a difficult problem and want to celebrate.

Questions 27–30

*Choose the correct letter, **A**, **B**, **C** or **D**.*

Write the correct letter in boxes 27–30 on your answer sheet.

27 What are we told about the product called a 'Swiffer'?

A Its designers had little experience working with household objects.
B Once the idea for it was conceived, it did not take long to develop.
C It achieved profits beyond the manufacturer's expectations.
D Its design was inspired by a common housework habit.

28 When Jonah Lehrer began writing his book,

A he had not intended to focus on creativity.
B he ended up revising his plans for the content.
C he was working in a highly creative environment.
D he was driven by his own experience of the 'eureka' moment.

29 Lehrer refers to the singer Bob Dylan in order to

A illustrate how ideas seem spontaneous.
B exemplify ways in which we might limit our inventiveness.
C contrast different approaches to stimulating the imagination.
D propose particular approaches to regaining lost creativity.

30 What did neuroscientists discover from the word puzzle experiment?

A Memories are easier to retrieve when they are more meaningful.
B An analytical approach to problem-solving is not necessarily effective.
C One part of the brain only becomes active when a connection is made suddenly.
D Creative people tend to take a more instinctive approach to solving language problems.

Questions 31–34

Complete each sentence with the correct ending, ***A–G****, below.*

Write the correct letter, ***A–G****, in boxes 31–34 on your answer sheet.*

31 Scientists know a moment of insight is coming

32 Mental connections are much harder to make

33 Some companies require their employees to stop working

34 A team will function more successfully

A	when people are not too familiar with one another.
B	because there is greater activity in the right side of the brain.
C	if people are concentrating on the specifics of a problem.
D	so they can increase the possibility of finding answers.
E	when people lack the experience required for problem-solving.
F	when the brain shows strong signs of distraction.
G	when both hemispheres of the brain show activity.

Questions 35–39

Complete the notes below.

Choose **ONE WORD ONLY** *from the passage for each answer.*

Write your answers in boxes 35–39 on your answer sheet.

How other people influence our creativity

- Steve Jobs
  - made changes to the **35** .... to encourage interaction at Pixar.
- Lehrer
  - company owners must have a wide range of **36** .... to do well.
  - it's important to start **37** .... with new people
  - the **38** .... has not replaced the need for physical contact.
- Geoffrey West
  - living in **39** .... encourages creativity.

Question 40

Choose the correct letter, ***A****,* ***B****,* ***C*** *or* ***D****.*

Write the correct letter in box 40 on your answer sheet.

40 Which of the following is the most suitable title for Reading Passage 3?

A Understanding what drives our moments of inspiration
B Challenging traditional theories of human creativity
C Creative solutions for enhancing professional relationships
D How the future is shaped by innovative ideas and inspired people

WRITING

WRITING TASK 1

You should spend about 20 minutes on this task.

> ***The chart below shows the changes that took place in three different areas of crime in Newport city centre from 2003–2012.***
>
> ***Summarise the information by selecting and reporting the main features, and make comparisons where relevant.***

Write at least 150 words.

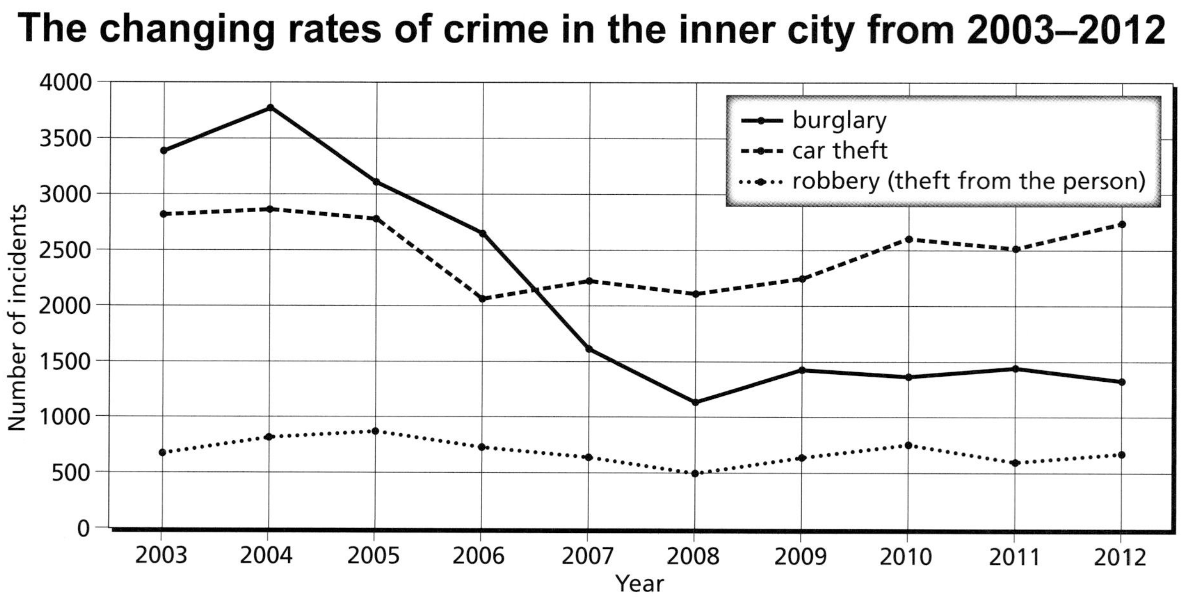

WRITING TASK 2

You should spend about 40 minutes on this task.

> ***In the past, when students did a university degree, they tended to study in their own country.***
>
> ***Nowadays, they have more opportunity to study abroad.***
>
> ***What are the advantages and disadvantages of this development?***
>
> ***You should use your own ideas, knowledge and experience and support your arguments with examples and relevant evidence.***

Give reasons for your answer and include any relevant examples from your own knowledge or experience.

Write at least 250 words.

SPEAKING

PART 1

Your country

- Do most people live in houses or apartments in your country?
- What do people usually do in their free time in your country?
- What do you enjoy most about living in your country?
- Would you say that your country is a good place to visit? [Why?]

Food

- What is your favourite meal?
- Do you prefer to eat out or eat at home? [Why?]
- Are there any traditional meals that you would recommend? [Why?]
- How have people's eating habits changed in your country?

PART 2

Candidate task card:

Describe a television programme that you watch.

You should say:
which kind of television programme it is
what usually happens in the television programme
why you enjoy watching the television programme
and explain why you would recommend the television programme to other people.

You will have to talk about the topic for one to two minutes.

You have one minute to think about what you are going to say.

You can make some notes to help you if you wish.

PART 3

The role of advertising on television

- How do you feel about the amount of advertising on television?
- In what ways has television advertising changed in the last ten years?
- To what extent are people influenced by the advertising they see on television?

The effect of films on society

- Why do people still enjoy going to the cinema to watch a film?
- What sort of influence can films have on people?
- Should film-makers be responsible for the impact their films can have on people?

Test 7

LISTENING

SECTION 1 *Questions 1–10*

Questions 1–6

Complete the table below.

Write ***NO MORE THAN ONE WORD AND/OR A NUMBER*** *for each answer.*

Hostel accommodation in Darwin		
Name	**Price per person (dormitory rooms)**	**Comments and reviews**
Example ....Top........... **End Backpackers**	$19	• parking available • staff are **1** .... • nice pool • air-conditioning is too **2** ....
Gum Tree Lodge	**3** $	• good quiet location • pool and gardens • **4** .... in the dormitories
Kangaroo Lodge	$22	• downtown location • reception at the lodge is always open • no lockers in the rooms • the **5** .... are very clean • seems to be a **6** .... every night

Questions 7–10

Complete the notes below.

Write ***ONE WORD ONLY*** *for each answer.*

Kangaroo Lodge

Address: on **7** .... Lane

General information about hostel accommodation

- sheets are provided
- can hire a **8** ....
- **9** .... is included
- a shared **10** .... is available

SECTION 2 *Questions 11–20*

Questions 11–16

*Choose the correct letter, **A**, **B** or **C**.*

Anglia Sculpture Park

11 The land where the Sculpture Park is located was previously

A completely covered by forest.
B the site of a private house.
C occupied by a factory.

12 What is unusual about the Anglia Sculpture Park?

A Artists have made sculptures especially for it.
B Some of its sculptures were donated by the artists.
C It only shows contemporary sculptures.

13 What is the theme of Joe Tremain's 'burnt' sculptures?

A the contrast between nature and urban life
B the effect of man on the environment
C the violence of nature

14 The path by the Lower Lake

A is rather wet in some places.
B has recently been repaired.
C is difficult to walk on.

15 What does the speaker say about the Visitor Centre?

A It is being enlarged at present.
B It has received an international award.
C It was designed by a Canadian architect.

16 Today, visitors can buy snacks and sandwiches

A at the kiosk.
B in the Terrace Room.
C at the Lower Lake Café.

Questions 17–20

Label the map below.

*Write the correct letter, **A–F**, next to Questions 17–20.*

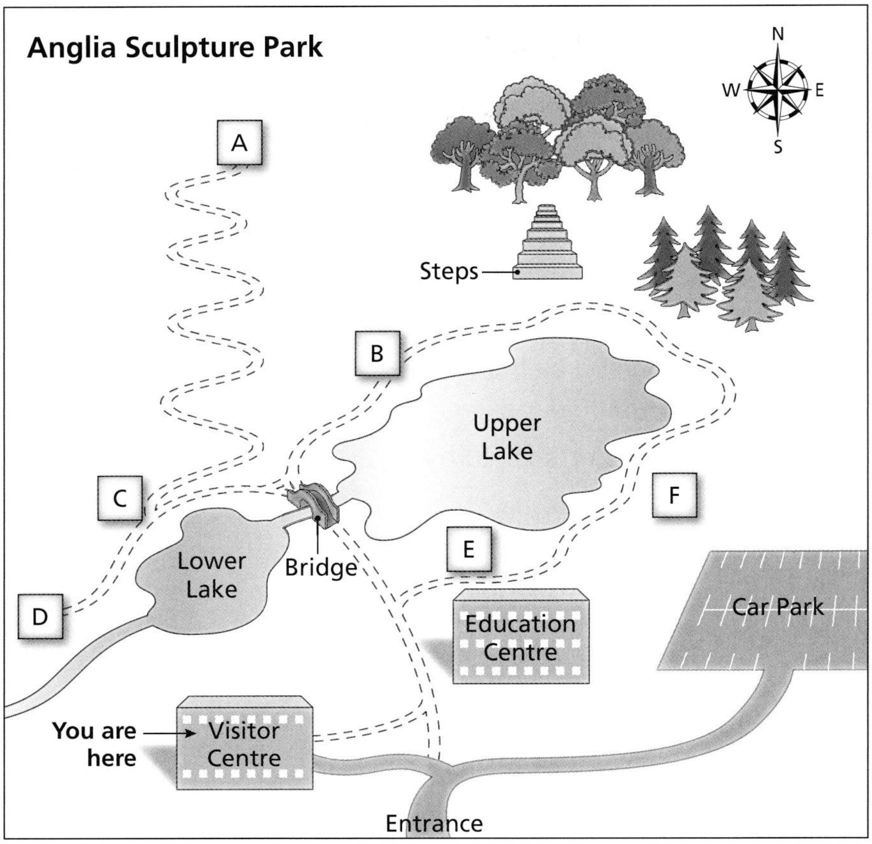

17 Joe Tremain sculptures

18 Giorgio Catalucci bird sculptures

19 Garden Gallery

20 Long House

SECTION 3 *Questions 21–30*

Questions 21–26

*Choose the correct letter, **A**, **B** or **C**.*

Marketing report

21 Why did Leo choose instant coffee as the topic for his marketing report?

A He found plenty of material on the topic.
B He had some practical experience in the area.
C He had an idea of a brand he wanted to target.

22 Leo discovered that in Australia, recent technological developments

A are producing less healthy types of instant coffee.
B are reducing the demand for instant coffee.
C are improving the quality of instant coffee.

23 What do the speakers agree about Leo's table of coffee products?

A It needs more explanation in the text.
B It is factually inaccurate in some places.
C It would be best to put this in the appendix.

24 What do they decide about the description of Shaffers coffee as a market follower?

A Leo needs to define his terms.
B Leo needs to provide more evidence.
C Leo needs to put it in a different section.

25 What does Anna say about originality in someone's first marketing report?

A Clear analysis of data can be considered original.
B Graphs and diagrams should be original, not copied.
C Reports should contain some original data collected by the student.

26 What difference between his school assignments and this report has surprised Leo?

A not knowing the criteria for getting a good mark
B being required to produce work without assistance
C having to do a great deal of research

Questions 27–30

Complete the notes below.

Write ***ONE WORD ONLY*** *for each answer.*

Notes on specific sections of marketing report

Executive summary

- Give a brief overview including the **27** ....

Problems

- Link each problem to a **28** .... which explains it

Implementation

- Practical solutions to problems
- Include details such as participants, **29** .... and sequence
- Section is often poorly done because of lack of **30** ....

Conclusion

- Don't use new material here

SECTION 4 *Questions 31–40*

Complete the notes below.

*Write **ONE WORD ONLY** for each answer.*

History of Fireworks in Europe

13th–16th centuries

- Fireworks were introduced from China.
- Their use was mainly to do with:
  - war
  - **31** .... (in plays and festivals)

17th century

- Various features of **32** .... were shown in fireworks displays.
- Scientists were interested in using ideas from fireworks displays:
  - to make human **33** .... possible
  - to show the formation of **34** ....
- **London:**
  - Scientists were distrustful at first
  - Later, they investigated **35** .... uses of fireworks (e.g. for sailors)
- **St Petersburg:**
  - Fireworks were seen as a method of **36** .... for people
- **Paris:**
  - Displays emphasised the power of the **37** ....
  - Scientists aimed to provide **38** ....

18th century

- Italian fireworks specialists became influential.
- Servandoni's fireworks display followed the same pattern as an **39** ....
- The appeal of fireworks extended to the middle classes.
- Some displays demonstrated new scientific discoveries such as **40** ....

READING

READING PASSAGE 1

*You should spend about 20 minutes on **Questions 1–13**, which are based on Reading Passage 1 below.*

The Hidden Histories of Exploration Exhibition

A We have all heard tales of lone, heroic explorers, but what about the local individuals who guided and protected European explorers in many different parts of the globe? Or the go-betweens – including interpreters and traders – who translated the needs and demands of explorers into a language that locals could understand? Such questions have received surprisingly little attention in standard histories, where European explorers are usually the heroes, sometimes the villains. *The Hidden Histories of Exploration* exhibition at Britain's Royal Geographical Society in London sets out to present an alternative view, in which exploration is a fundamentally collective experience of work, involving many different people. Many of the most famous examples of explorers said to have been 'lone travellers' – say, Mungo Park or David Livingstone in Africa – were anything but 'alone' on their travels. They depended on local support of various kinds – for food, shelter, protection, information, guidance and solace – as well as on other resources from elsewhere.

B The Royal Geographical Society (RGS) seeks to record this story in its Hidden Histories project, using its astonishingly rich collections. The storage of geographical information was one of the main rationales for the foundation of the RGS in 1830, and the Society's collections now contain more than two million individual items, including books, manuscripts, maps, photographs, art-works, artefacts and film – a rich storehouse of material reflecting the wide geographical extent of British interest across the globe. In addition to their remarkable scope and range, these collections contain a striking visual record of exploration: the impulse to collect the world is reflected in a large and diverse image archive. For the researcher, this archive can yield many surprises: materials gathered for one purpose – say, maps relating to an international boundary dispute or photographs taken on a scientific expedition – may today be put to quite different uses.

C In their published narratives, European explorers rarely portrayed themselves as vulnerable or dependent on others, despite the fact that without this support they were quite literally lost. Archival research confirms that Europeans were not merely dependent on the work of porters, soldiers, translators, cooks, pilots, guides, hunters and collectors: they also relied on local expertise. Such assistance was essential in identifying potential dangers – poisonous species, unpredictable rivers, uncharted territories – which could mean the difference between life and death. The assistants themselves were usually in a strong bargaining position. In the Amazon, for example, access to entire regions would depend on the willingness of local crew members and other assistants to enter areas inhabited by relatively powerful Amerindian groups. In an account of his journey across South America, published in 1836, William Smyth thus complained of frequent 'desertion' by his helpers: 'without them it was impossible to get on'.

D Those providing local support and information to explorers were themselves often not 'locals'. For example, the history of African exploration in the nineteenth century is dominated by the use of Zanzibar as a recruiting station for porters, soldiers and guides who would then travel thousands of miles across the continent. In some accounts, the leading African members of expedition parties – the 'officers' or 'foremen' – are identified, and their portraits published alongside those of European explorers.

E The information provided by locals and intermediaries was of potential importance to geographical science. How was this evidence judged? The formal procedures of scientific evaluation provided one framework. Alongside these were more 'common sense' notions of veracity and reliability, religiously-inspired judgments about the authenticity of testimony, and the routine procedures for cross-checking empirical observations developed in many professions.

F Given explorers' need for local information and support, it was in their interests to develop effective working partnerships with knowledgeable intermediaries who could act as brokers in their dealings with local inhabitants. Many of these people acquired far more experience of exploration than most Europeans could hope to attain. Some managed large groups of men and women, piloted the explorers' river craft, or undertook mapping work. The tradition was continued with the Everest expeditions in the 1920s and 1930s, which regularly employed the Tibetan interpreter Karma Paul. In Europe, exploration was increasingly thought of as a career; the same might be said of the non-Europeans on whom their expeditions depended.

G These individuals often forged close working relationships with European explorers. Such partnerships depended on mutual respect, though they were not always easy or intimate, as is particularly clear from the history of the Everest expeditions depicted in the Hidden Histories exhibition. The entire back wall is covered by an enlarged version of a single sheet of photographs of Sherpas taken during the 1936 Everest expedition. The document is a powerful reminder of the manpower on which European mountaineering expeditions depended, and also of the importance of local knowledge and assistance. Transformed from archive to wall display, it tells a powerful story through the medium of individual portraits – including Karma Paul, veteran of previous expeditions, and the young Tensing Norgay, 17 years before his successful 1953 ascent. This was a highly charged and transitional moment as the contribution of the Sherpas, depicted here with identity tags round their necks, was beginning to be much more widely recognised. These touching portraits encourage us to see them as agents rather than simply colonial subjects or paid employees. Here is a living history, which looks beyond what we already know about exploration: a larger history in which we come to recognise the contribution of everyone involved.

Questions 1–7

Do the following statements agree with the information given in Reading Passage 1?

In boxes 1–7 on your answer sheet, write

TRUE	*if the statement agrees with the information*
FALSE	*if the statement contradicts the information*
NOT GIVEN	*if there is no information on this*

1 The Hidden Histories of Exploration exhibition aims to show the wide range of people involved in expeditions.

2 The common belief about how Park and Livingstone travelled is accurate.

3 The RGS has organised a number of exhibitions since it was founded.

4 Some of the records in the RGS archives are more useful than others.

5 Materials owned by the RGS can be used in ways that were not originally intended.

6 In their publications, European explorers often describe their dependence on their helpers.

7 Local helpers refused to accompany William Smyth during parts of his journey.

Questions 8–13

Reading Passage 1 has seven paragraphs, **A–G**.

Which paragraph contains the following information?

*Write the correct letter, **A–G**, in boxes 8–13 on your answer sheet.*

8 reference to the distances that some non-European helpers travelled

9 description of a wide range of different types of documents

10 belief about the effect of an exhibition on people seeing it

11 examples of risks explorers might have been unaware of without local help

12 reference to various approaches to assessing data from local helpers

13 reference to people whose long-term occupation was to organise local assistance for European explorers

READING PASSAGE 2

You should spend about 20 minutes on ***Questions 14–26****, which are based on Reading Passage 2 below.*

Fatal Attraction

Evolutionist Charles Darwin first marvelled at flesh-eating plants in the mid-19th century. Today, biologists, using 21st-century tools to study cells and DNA, are beginning to understand how these plants hunt, eat and digest – and how such bizarre adaptations arose in the first place.

A The leaves of the Venus flytrap plant are covered in hairs. When an insect brushes against them, this triggers a tiny electric charge, which travels down tunnels in the leaf and opens up pores in the leaf's cell membranes. Water surges from the cells on the inside of the leaf to those on the outside, causing the leaf to rapidly flip in shape from convex to concave, like a soft contact lens. As the leaves flip, they snap together, trapping the insect in their sharp-toothed jaws.

B The bladderwort has an equally sophisticated way of setting its underwater trap. It pumps water out of tiny bag-like bladders, making a vacuum inside. When small creatures swim past, they bend the hairs on the bladder, causing a flap to open. The low pressure sucks water in, carrying the animal along with it. In one five-hundredth of a second, the door swings shut again. The Drosera sundew, meanwhile, has a thick, sweet liquid oozing from its leaves, which first attracts insects, then holds them fast before the leaves snap shut. Pitcher plants use yet another strategy, growing long tube-shaped leaves to imprison their prey. Raffles' pitcher plant, from the jungles of Borneo, produces nectar that both lures insects and forms a slick surface on which they can't get a grip. Insects that land on the rim of the pitcher slide on the liquid and tumble in.

C Many carnivorous plants secrete enzymes to penetrate the hard exoskeleton of insects so they can absorb nutrients from inside their prey. But the purple pitcher plant, which lives in bogs and infertile sandy soils in North America, enlists other organisms to process its food. It is home to an intricate food web of mosquito larvae, midges and bacteria, many of which can survive only in this unique habitat. These animals shred the prey that fall into the pitcher, and the smaller organisms feed on the debris. Finally, the plant absorbs the nutrients released.

D While such plants clearly thrive on being carnivorous, the benefits of eating flesh are not the ones you might expect. Carnivorous animals such as ourselves use the carbon in protein and the fat in meat to build muscles and store energy. Carnivorous plants instead draw nitrogen, phosphorus, and other critical nutrients from their prey in order to build light-harvesting enzymes. Eating animals, in other words, lets carnivorous plants do what all plants do: carry out photosynthesis, that is, grow by harnessing energy directly from the sun.

E Carnivorous plants are, in fact, very inefficient at converting sunlight into tissue. This is because of all the energy they expend to make the equipment to catch animals – the enzymes, the pumps, and so on. A pitcher or a flytrap cannot carry out much photosynthesis because, unlike plants with ordinary leaves, they do not have flat solar panels that can grab lots of sunlight. There are, however, some special conditions in which the benefits of being carnivorous do outweigh the costs. The poor soil of bogs, for example, offers little nitrogen and phosphorus, so carnivorous plants enjoy an advantage over plants that obtain these nutrients by more conventional means. Bogs are also flooded with sunshine, so even an inefficient carnivorous plant can photosynthesise enough light to survive.

F Evolution has repeatedly made this trade-off. By comparing the DNA of carnivorous plants with other species, scientists have found that they evolved independently on at least six separate occasions. Some carnivorous plants that look nearly identical turn out to be only distantly related. The two kinds of pitcher plants – the tropical genus Nepenthes and the North American Sarracenia – have, surprisingly, evolved from different ancestors, although both grow deep pitcher-shaped leaves and employ the same strategy for capturing prey.

G In several cases, scientists can see how complex carnivorous plants evolved from simpler ones. Venus flytraps, for example, share an ancestor with Portuguese sundews, which only catch prey passively, via 'flypaper' glands on their stems. They share a more recent ancestor with Drosera sundews, which can also curl their leaves over their prey. Venus flytraps appear to have evolved an even more elaborate version of this kind of trap, complete with jaw-like leaves.

H Unfortunately, the adaptations that enable carnivorous plants to thrive in marginal habitats also make them exquisitely sensitive. Agricultural run-off and pollution from power plants are adding extra nitrogen to many bogs in North America. Carnivorous plants are so finely tuned to low levels of nitrogen that this extra fertilizer is overloading their systems, and they eventually burn themselves out and die.

I Humans also threaten carnivorous plants in other ways. The black market trade in exotic carnivorous plants is so vigorous now that botanists are keeping the location of some rare species a secret. But even if the poaching of carnivorous plants can be halted, they will continue to suffer from other assaults. In the pine savannah of North Carolina, the increasing suppression of fires is allowing other plants to grow too quickly and outcompete the flytraps in their native environment. Good news, perhaps, for flies. But a loss for all who, like Darwin, delight in the sheer inventiveness of evolution.

Questions 14–18

Complete the notes below.

Choose **NO MORE THAN TWO WORDS** *from the passage for each answer.*

Write your answers in boxes 14–18 on your answer sheet.

How a Venus flytrap traps an insect

- insect touches **14** .... on leaf of plant
- small **15** .... passes through leaf
- **16** .... in cell membrane open
- outside cells of leaves fill with **17** ....
- leaves change so that they have a **18** .... shape and snap shut

Questions 19–22

Look at the following statements (Questions 19–22) and the list of plants.

Match each statement with the correct plant, ***A, B, C, D*** *or* ***E.***

Write the correct letter, ***A, B, C, D*** *or* ***E,*** *in boxes 19–22 on your answer sheet.*

19 It uses other creatures to help it digest insects.

20 It produces a slippery substance to make insects fall inside it.

21 It creates an empty space into which insects are sucked.

22 It produces a sticky substance which traps insects on its surface.

List of plants

A Venus flytrap
B bladderwort
C Drosera sundew
D Raffles' pitcher plant
E purple pitcher plant

Questions 23–26

Reading Passage 2 has nine paragraphs, **A–I**.

Which paragraph contains the following information?

Write the correct letter, ***A–I****, in boxes 23–26 on your answer sheet.*

23 a mention of a disadvantage of the leaf shape of some carnivorous plants

24 an example of an effort made to protect carnivorous plants

25 unexpected information about the origins of certain carnivorous plants

26 an example of environmental changes that shorten the life cycles of carnivorous plants

READING PASSAGE 3

*You should spend about 20 minutes on **Questions 27–40**, which are based on Reading Passage 3 on the following pages.*

Questions 27–32

Reading Passage 3 has seven paragraphs, **A–G**.

Choose the correct heading for paragraphs B–G from the list of headings below.

*Write the correct number, **i–x**, in boxes 27–32 on your answer sheet.*

List of Headings

i	A shift in our fact-finding habits
ii	How to be popular
iii	More personal information being known
iv	The origins of online social networks
v	The link between knowledge and influence
vi	Information that could change how you live
vii	The emotional benefits of online networking
viii	A change in how we view our online friendships
ix	The future of networking
x	Doubts about the value of online socialising

27 Paragraph **B**

28 Paragraph **C**

29 Paragraph **D**

30 Paragraph **E**

31 Paragraph **F**

32 Paragraph **G**

WANT TO BE FRIENDS?

Could the benefits of online social networking be too good to miss out on?

A For many hundreds of thousands of people worldwide, online networking has become enmeshed in our daily lives. However, it is a decades-old insight from a study of traditional social networks that best illuminates one of the most important aspects of today's online networking. In 1973 sociologist Mark Granovetter showed how the loose acquaintances, or 'weak ties', in our social network exert a disproportionate influence over our behaviour and choices. Granovetter's research showed that a significant percentage of people get their jobs as a result of recommendations or advice provided by a weak tie. Today our number of weak-tie contacts has exploded via online social networking. 'You couldn't maintain all of those weak ties on your own,' says Jennifer Golbeck of the University of Maryland. 'Online sites, such as Facebook, give you a way of cataloguing them.' The result? It's now significantly easier for the schoolfriend you haven't seen in years to pass you a tip that alters your behaviour, from recommendation of a low-cholesterol breakfast cereal to a party invite where you meet your future wife or husband.

B The explosion of weak ties could have profound consequences for our social structures too, according to Judith Donath of the Berkman Center for Internet and Society at Harvard University. 'We're already seeing changes,' she says. For example, many people now turn to their online social networks ahead of sources such as newspapers and television for trusted and relevant news or information. What they hear could well be inaccurate, but the change is happening nonetheless. If these huge 'supernets' – some of them numbering up to 5,000 people – continue to thrive and grow, they could fundamentally change the way we share information and transform our notions of relationships.

C But are these vast networks really that relevant to us on a personal level? Robin Dunbar, an evolutionary anthropologist at the University of Oxford, believes that our primate brains place a cap on the number of genuine social relationships we can actually cope with: roughly 150. According to Dunbar, online social networking appears to be very good for 'servicing' relationships, but not for establishing them. He argues that our evolutionary roots mean we still depend heavily on physical and face-to-face contact to be able to create ties.

D Nonetheless, there is evidence that online networking can transform our daily interactions. In an experiment at Cornell University, psychologist Jeff Hancock asked participants to try to encourage other participants to like them via instant messaging conversation. Beforehand, some members of the trial were allowed to view the Facebook profile of the person they were trying to win over. He found that those with Facebook access asked questions to which they already knew the answers or raised things they had in common, and as result were much more successful in their social relationships. Hancock concluded that people who use these sites to keep updated on the activities of their acquaintances are more likely to be liked in subsequent social interactions.

E Online social networking may also have tangible effects on our well-being. Nicole Ellison of Michigan State University found that the frequency of networking site use correlates with greater self-esteem. Support and affirmation from the weak ties could be the explanation, says Ellison. 'Asking your close friends for help or advice is nothing new, but we are seeing a lowering of barriers among acquaintances,' she says. People are readily sharing personal feelings and experiences to a wider circle than they might once have done. Sandy Pentland at the Massachusetts Institute of Technology agrees. 'The ability to broadcast to our social group means we need never feel alone,' he says. 'The things that befall us are often due to a lack of social support. There's more of a safety net now.'

F Henry Holzman, also at MIT, who studies the interface between online social networking and the real world, points out that increased visibility also means our various social spheres – family, work, friends – are merging, and so we will have to prepare for new societal norms. 'We'll have to learn how to live a more transparent life,' he says. 'We may have to give up some ability to show very limited glimpses of ourselves to others.'

G Another way that online networking appears to be changing our social structures is through dominance. In one repeated experiment, Michael Kearns of the University of Pennsylvania asked 30 volunteers to quickly reach consensus in an online game over a choice between two colours. Each person was offered a cash reward if they succeeded in persuading the group to pick one or other colour. All participants could see the colour chosen by some of the other people, but certain participants had an extra advantage: the ability to see more of the participants' chosen colours than others. Every time Kearns found that those who could see the choices of more participants (in other words, were better connected) persuaded the group to pick their colour, even when they had to persuade the vast majority to give up their financial incentive. While Kearns warns that the setting was artificial, he says it's possible that greater persuasive power could lie with well-connected individuals in the everyday online world too.

Questions 33–36

Look at the following findings (Questions 33–36) and the list of researchers below.

Match each finding with the correct researcher, ***A–F****.*

Write the correct letter, ***A–F****, in boxes 33–36 on your answer sheet.*

33 People who network widely may be more able to exert pressure on others.

34 We have become more willing to confide in an extensive number of people.

35 There is a limit to how many meaningful relationships we can maintain.

36 There is a social advantage in knowing about the lives of our online contacts.

List of researchers

A	Mark Granovetter	**D**	Jeff Hancock
B	Judith Donath	**E**	Nicole Ellison
C	Robin Dunbar	**F**	Michael Kearns

Questions 37–40

For Questions 37–40, choose ***TWO*** *answers,* ***A–E****.*

Write your answers in boxes 37–40 on your answer sheet.

37–38

Which ***TWO*** *of these advantages of online social networking are mentioned in Reading Passage 3?*

A Social networking sites can be accessed on any day and at any time.

B Online socialising is an efficient way of keeping in touch with a lot of people.

C It is very easy to establish new friendships online.

D Online social networking can solve problems in real-world relationships.

E It can be reassuring to be part of an online social network.

39–40

Which ***TWO*** *of these disadvantages of online social networking are mentioned in Reading Passage 3?*

A Information from online social contacts may be unreliable.

B We may become jealous of people who seem to have a wide circle of friends.

C We may lose the ability to relate to people face-to-face.

D It is easy to waste a lot of time on social networking sites.

E Using social networking sites may result in a lack of privacy.

WRITING

WRITING TASK 1

You should spend about 20 minutes on this task.

The maps below show the village of Stokeford in 1930 and in 2010.

Summarise the information by selecting and reporting the main features, and make comparisons where relevant.

Write at least 150 words.

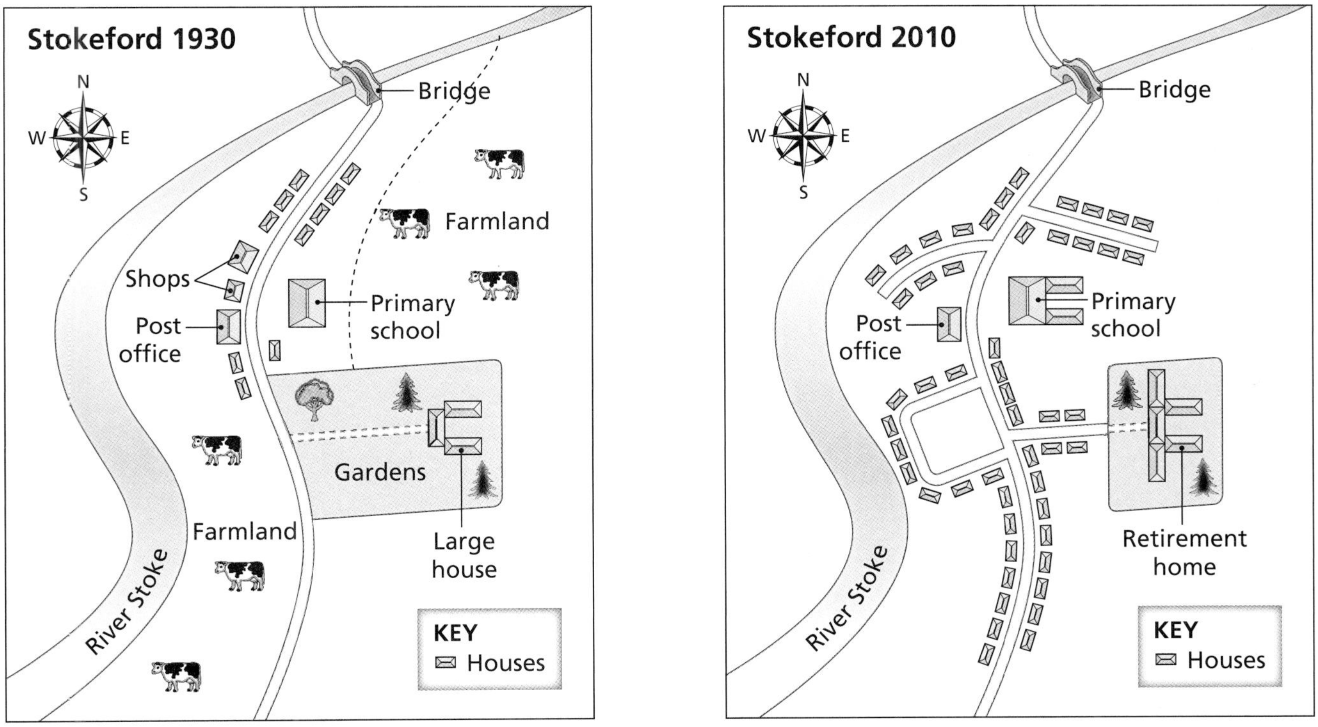

WRITING TASK 2

You should spend about 40 minutes on this task.

The continued rise in the world's population is the greatest problem faced by humanity at the present time.

What are the causes of this continued rise?

Do you agree that it is the greatest problem faced by humanity?

Give reasons for your answer and include any relevant examples from your own knowledge or experience.

Write at least 250 words.

SPEAKING

PART 1 (4–5 MINUTES)

Introduction

- Let's talk about where you live …
- What do you like most about your home town?
- Is your home town a popular place for tourists to visit? [Why? / Why not?]
- Has your home town changed much in recent years? [Why? / Why not?]

Writing

Now let's talk about writing.
- What different types of writing do you do, for example letters, emails, reports or essays?
- Do you prefer writing with a pen or using a computer? [Why?]
- Do you write more now or less than you did a few years ago? [Why?]
- Do you like to write stories or poems? [Why? / Why not?]

Music

Let's talk about music.
- How often do you listen to music? [Why?]
- Do you prefer to buy CDs or download music from the Internet? [Why?]
- Have you always liked the same kind of music? [Why? / Why not?]
- Is there a musical instrument you would like to learn to play? [Why? / Why not?]

PART 2

Candidate task card:

Describe a time when you helped someone.

You should say:
who you helped and why
how you helped this person
what the result was
and explain how you felt about helping this person.

PART 3

- **Helping neighbours**
  – (describe) practical things people can do to help their neighbours
  – (explain) why neighbours should help each other
  – (consider) whether people in small towns help each other more than people in cities

- **Jobs that involve helping people**
  – (identify) jobs that focus on helping other people
  – (outline) the qualities that people need to do jobs that involve helping others
  – (comment on) whether salaries for jobs that involve helping people are generally too low

- **Attitudes towards helping other people**
  – (account for) some people not wanting to help other people
  – (agree/disagree) governments have a responsibility to help people
  – (consider) whether some people deserve help more than others

General Training Reading and Writing Test

READING

SECTION 1 *Questions 1–14*

Read the text below and answer ***Questions 1–8****.*

Some places to visit

A Beautiful **Kingsley House** was built in the 18th century, and all the rooms are decorated and furnished in the style of the time. They include the dining room, study and dressing room, which contains a display of 18th-century ladies' clothing. Our volunteer guides in each room bring the house to life with stories of the past.

B The **Africa Museum** was founded 50 years ago, and to commemorate the event, we have chosen 50 treasures from the permanent collection and put them together to tell the fascinating story of that continent. This exhibition continues until the end of the year. The Folk Art Gallery opens to the public next month, exhibiting traditional paintings and other objects from all over Africa.

C From the outside, **17 Mansfield Street** may not look particularly exciting, but come inside, and you'll find yourself in a historic building that started life as a theatre, before becoming a bank and then a restaurant, which is still in operation. On Sundays and Mondays, when the restaurant is closed, a guide is available to show you round the building and its fascinating architectural features.

D The **Industrial Heritage Centre** tells the fascinating story of a local family firm. Mr John Carroll started his engineering business in this building exactly 150 years ago. The firm closed in 1969, but the factory has been re-created, with machines like those that Mr Carroll was familiar with. See what working life could be like in the 19th century, a life far removed from the elegance of the wealthy.

E The **Fashion Museum** has only just opened. It is home to an outstanding collection of more than 30,000 objects worn by men, women and children, dating from the 17th century to the present day. You'll see how people used to dress! As well as the permanent exhibits, you can currently see *Dressing the Stars*, which displays original costumes worn by the stars of many popular films.

F Having spent the best part of two years being refurbished, the **Mason Museum** has recently opened its doors again. It provides a magnificent setting for its art collection and for the beautiful 18th-century furniture for which the Mason is famous. Open Mondays to Fridays 10–4, and weekends 10–6.

Questions 1–8

The text above has six descriptions of places to visit in the same city, **A–F**.

Which description mentions the following information?

*Write the correct letter, **A–F**, in boxes 1–8 on your answer sheet.*

***NB** You may use any letter more than once.*

1 clothes that well-known people have worn

2 a display that cannot be seen yet

3 people who talk in an entertaining way

4 the museum having just reopened

5 a building that has changed its function several times

6 furniture of the same kind that was used when the building was new

7 being open for tours on certain days of the week

8 a special event to mark an anniversary

Read the text below and answer Questions 9–14.

LearnWithUs courses

LearnWithUs courses are a great way to learn, because they're so flexible. All our courses are taken online using a computer, so you can work through the course at your own speed, and go back to any session whenever you want to. For some courses there are workbooks, in addition to the computer course, to provide extra written practice.

We offer hundreds of courses in a whole range of subjects from reading, writing and maths to business and management. Many of these are specially designed for people whose first language isn't English.

Step one: have a chat with a friendly member of staff in one of our 1,500 LearnWithUs centres around the country. They can advise you on the most suitable course. They'll also work out whether you qualify for funding, so that you won't have to pay the full fee for the course.

You might want to try a taster lesson first. This is a single computer session in any subject of your choice, and it will show you what learning with LearnWithUs is like.

When you've made your final decision, step two is to register on your course. Once you've done this, a staff member will show you how to get started, whether you're using a computer at home, at work or at a LearnWithUs centre.

That's all you need to do! When you start your course, you can contact your LearnWithUs centre by phone (we're open during normal office hours) or email if you need help.

Questions 9–14

Do the following statements agree with the information given in the text above?

In boxes 9–14 on your answer sheet, write

TRUE	*if the statement agrees with the information*
FALSE	*if the statement contradicts the information*
NOT GIVEN	*if there is no information on this*

9 You can work through parts of a course more than once.

10 The number of courses offered by LearnWithUs has increased enormously.

11 Many staff members have worked through a LearnWithUs course themselves.

12 You may have to pay to take a LearnWithUs course.

13 Everybody takes the same taster lesson.

14 LearnWithUs centres are open seven days a week.

SECTION 2 *Questions 15–27*

*Read the text below and answer **Questions 15–20**.*

The benefits of having a business mentor

Introduction

If you're starting your own business, you probably need a mentor. This is a business person who volunteers to give their time to help somebody else with their work – particularly somebody who is new to business. They have a wealth of experience they are willing to share, perhaps from setting up and running their own company. The mentor's role is to support, develop, stimulate and challenge. However, business mentors won't solve your problems for you or tell you what to do: they will talk things over with you, rather than acting as consultants. Many people setting up their first business have found that a mentor can have a very positive effect on its success.

Why business mentoring is important

If you have a gap in your knowledge or experience, then mentoring could work very well for you. For example, you may have a great concept for a business but need a bit of assistance to turn it into a successful venture.

A mentor can provide you with a number of benefits, such as:

- guidance on developing and improving your business
- help with decisions – particularly difficult ones
- ideas for new products or services, or for working practices that will improve your efficiency
- tips for your business that are gained from practical experience
- access to a network of contacts with other business people

A business mentor can also help you to:

- develop key business skills
- improve your problem-solving abilities
- build confidence
- work on your personal development

Face-to-face business mentoring

If you decide that face-to-face business mentoring is right for you, mentor and mentee should decide in advance on the nature of the relationship.

You will need to agree on the degree of involvement that suits you both. Some mentors and mentees work extremely closely, keeping in touch with each other most weeks or even most days. In the majority of cases, however, a mentor will provide help every few weeks or months. In either case, they might meet, speak on the phone, or exchange emails.

You should also agree on a level of structure to suit you both. Mentoring can be a very formal process with regular meetings which follow a specific agenda and work towards a specific set of goals. It can also be quite a casual arrangement, where the mentee calls on the mentor as and when problems or questions arise.

Questions 15–20

Complete the notes below.

Choose **ONE WORD ONLY** *from the text for each answer.*

Write your answers in boxes 15–20 on your answer sheet.

How can a mentor help somebody setting up a business?

A mentor **15** .... to help a new business person.

Mentors have a different role from **16** ....

A mentor can:

- help you turn your idea into a successful business
- assist when you need to make **17** ....
- suggest how your business can increase its **18** ....
- introduce you to a business network
- help you to develop your skills, abilities and provide you with more

  19 ....

To be agreed:

- how much **20** .... the mentor should have
- how much structure the mentoring process should have

Read the text below and answer ***Questions 21–27****.*

A Planning Process for Middle-Sized Projects

Any business project – such as reducing energy costs, or improving efficiency – needs to be planned, and time spent planning will save far more time later on. The typical stages in this planning process are explained below.

- Your first task is to spot what needs to be done. Examine your firm's current position, perhaps making a formal analysis of its strengths and weaknesses. Then think about how you might improve that position: what opportunities are there for achieving this?
- The next step is to decide precisely what the aim of your plan is. This is best expressed in a simple single sentence, to ensure that it is clear and sharp in your mind. Doing this helps you to avoid wasting effort on irrelevant side issues.
- Next you should work out how to do it. It is tempting just to grasp the first idea that comes to mind, but it is better to consider a wide range of options: this way, you may come up with less obvious but better solutions.
- Once you have explored the options available to you, the selection of which option to use is the next step. If you have the time and resources, you might decide to evaluate all options, carrying out some planning, such as costing, for each. Normally you will not have this luxury.
- You already have a broad idea of what your project will consist of. Now is the time to work out the full details, identifying the most efficient and effective method of carrying it out, including answering the questions of 'who', 'what' and 'when'.
- The next stage is to review your plan and decide whether it will work satisfactorily. This evaluation enables you to change to another option that might be more successful, or to accept that no plan is needed.
- Once you have finished your plan and decided that it will work satisfactorily, it is time for implementation. Your plan will cover how this is to be done.
- Once you have achieved a plan, you can close the project. At this point it is often worth assessing the project to see whether there are any lessons that you can learn.

Questions 21–27

Complete the flow-chart below.

*Choose **ONE WORD ONLY** from the text for each answer.*

Write your answers in boxes 21–27 on your answer sheet.

Suggested stages in a planning process

Start by identifying opportunities for making improvements to current situation.

↓

Decide and define the plan's exact **21** ....

↓

Identify and consider a **22** .... of possible solutions.

↓

Make a **23** .... from possible solutions.

↓

Plan all the **24** .... of every aspect of the project.

↓

Carry out an **25** .... of your plan before any action is taken.

↓

Carry out the **26** .... of your completed plan.

↓

Identify whether the project has provided any **27** .... for you.

SECTION 3 *Questions 28–40*

Read the text below and answer ***Questions 28–40****.*

The Penny Black

It might not have looked very impressive, but the Penny Black, now 170 years old, was the first stamp to be created and it launched the modern postal system in Britain.

Before 1840 and the arrival of the Penny Black, you had to be rich and patient to use the Royal Mail. Delivery was charged according to the miles travelled and the number of sheets of paper used; a 2-page letter sent from Edinburgh to London, for example, would have cost 2 shillings, or more than £7 in today's money. And when the top-hatted letter carrier came to deliver it, it was the recipient who had to pay for the postage. Letter writers employed various ruses to reduce the cost, doing everything possible to cram more words onto a page. Nobody bothered with heavy envelopes; instead, letters would be folded and sealed with wax. You then had to find a post office – there were no pillar boxes – and hope your addressee didn't live in one of the several rural areas which were not served by the system. If you were lucky, your letter would arrive (it could take days) without being read or censored.

The state of mail had been causing concern throughout the 1830s, but it was Rowland Hill, an inventor, teacher and social reformer from Kidderminster, who proposed a workable plan for change. Worried that a dysfunctional, costly service would stifle communication just as Britain was in the swing of its second industrial revolution, he believed reform would ease the distribution of ideas and stimulate trade and business, delivering the same promise as the new railways.

Hill's proposal for the penny post, which meant any letter weighing less than half an ounce (14 grams) could be sent anywhere in Britain for about 30p in today's money, was so radical that the Postmaster General, Lord Lichfield, said, 'Of all the wild and visionary schemes which I ever heard of, it is the most extravagant.' Lord Lichfield spoke for an establishment not convinced of the need for poor people to post anything. But merchants and reformers backed Hill. Soon the government told him to make his scheme work. And that meant inventing a new type of currency.

Hill quickly settled on 'a bit of paper covered at the back with a glutinous wash which the user might, by applying a little moisture, attach to the back of a letter'. Stamps would be printed in sheets of 240 that could be cut using scissors or a knife. Perforations would not arrive until 1854. The idea stuck, and in August 1839 the Treasury launched a design competition open to 'all artists, men of science and the public in general'. The new stamp would need to be resistant to forgery, and so it was a submission by one Mr Cheverton that Hill used as the basis for one of the most striking designs in history. Cheverton, who worked as a sculptor and an engineer, determined that a portrait of Queen Victoria, engraved for a commemorative coin when she was a 15-year-old princess, was detailed enough to make copying difficult, and recognisable enough to make fakes easy to spot. The words 'Postage' and 'One Penny' were added alongside flourishes and ornamental stars. Nobody thought to add the word 'Britain', as it was assumed that the stamps would solely be put to domestic use.

With the introduction of the new postal system, the Penny Black was an instant hit, and printers struggled to meet demand. By the end of 1840, more than 160 million letters had been sent – more than double the previous year. It created more work for the post office, whose reform continued with the introduction of red letter boxes, new branches and more frequent deliveries, even to the remotest address, but its lasting impact on society was more remarkable.

Hill and his supporters rightly predicted that cheaper post would improve the 'diffusion of knowledge'. Suddenly, someone in Scotland could be reached by someone in London within a day or two. And as literacy improved, sections of society that had been disenfranchised found a voice.

Tristram Hunt, an historian, values the 'flourishing of correspondence' that followed the arrival of stamps. 'While I was writing my biography of Friedrich Engels I could read the letters he and Marx sent between Manchester and London,' he says. 'They wrote to each other three times a day, pinging ideas back and forth so that you can almost follow a real-time correspondence.'

The penny post also changed the nature of the letter. Weight-saving tricks such as cross-writing began to die out, while the arrival of envelopes built confidence among correspondents that mail would not be stolen or read. And so people wrote more private things – politically or commercially sensitive information or love letters. 'In the early days of the penny post, there was still concern about theft,' Hunt says. 'Engels would still send Marx money by ripping up five-pound notes and sending the pieces in different letters.' But the probity of the postal system became a great thing and it came to be expected that your mail would not be tampered with.

For all its brilliance, the Penny Black was technically a failure. At first, post offices used red ink to cancel stamps so that they could not be used again. But the ink could be removed. When in 1842, it was determined that black ink would be more robust, the colour of the Penny Black became a sort of browny red, but Hill's brainchild had made its mark.

Questions 28–30

Choose the correct letter, ***A****,* ***B****,* ***C*** *or* ***D****.*

Write the correct letter in boxes 28–30 on your answer sheet.

28 One of the characteristics of the postal service before the 1840s was that

A postmen were employed by various organisations.
B letters were restricted to a certain length.
C distance affected the price of postage.
D the price of delivery kept going up.

29 Letter writers in the 1830s

A were not responsible for the cost of delivery.
B tried to fit more than one letter into an envelope.
C could only send letters to people living in cities.
D knew all letters were automatically read by postal staff.

30 What does the text say about Hill in the 1830s?

A He was the first person to express concern about the postal system.
B He considered it would be more efficient for mail to be delivered by rail.
C He felt that postal service reform was necessary for commercial development.
D His plan received support from all the important figures of the day.

Questions 31–34

Look at the following statements (Questions 31–34) and the list of people below.

*Match each statement with the correct person, **A**, **B**, **C** or **D**.*

*Write the correct letter, **A**, **B**, **C** or **D**, in boxes 31–34 on your answer sheet.*

***NB** You may use any letter more than once.*

31 His inspiration came from a particular picture.

32 He claimed that the postal system would lead to the spread of information.

33 He organised the creation of the first stamp.

34 He expressed doubts about the plans to change the postal service.

List of People

A Rowland Hill

B Lord Lichfield

C Cheverton

D Tristram Hunt

Questions 35–40

Complete the notes below.

Choose **NO MORE THAN TWO WORDS** *from the passage for each answer.*

Write your answers in boxes 35–40 on your answer sheet.

The Penny Black

- Design came about as a result of a competition organised by the **35** ....
- Based on an engraving of Queen Victoria featured on a **36** ....
- Apart from the Queen's face, the stamp had just three words and pictures of **37** .... as decoration
- No mention of **38** .... , as plan was for stamps to be for domestic use only
- The **39** .... , which was applied to indicate that the stamp had been used, proved to be ineffective
- In 1842, the **40** .... of the stamp was changed

WRITING

TASK 1

You should spend about 20 minutes on this task.

> ***Your local hospital has advertised for people to do unpaid work helping at the hospital. You would like to do some work at the hospital in your free time.***
>
> ***Write a letter to the hospital. In your letter***
> - ***explain why you would like to do unpaid work at the hospital***
> - ***say what type of unpaid work you would be able to do***
> - ***give details of when you would be available for this work***

Write at least 150 words.

You do **NOT** need to write any addresses.

Begin your letter as follows:

Dear Sir or Madam,

TASK 2

You should spend about 40 minutes on this task.

> ***It is sometimes said that people should be encouraged to get married before they are 30, as this is best both for the individual and for society.***
>
> ***Do you agree or disagree?***

Give reasons for your answer and include any relevant examples from your own knowledge or experience.

Write at least 250 words.

Test 8

LISTENING

SECTION 1 *Questions 1–10*

Complete the notes below.

Write ***NO MORE THAN TWO WORDS AND/OR A NUMBER*** *for each answer.*

Hilary Lodge Retirement Home

Example

The name of the ....manager.... is Cathy

Activities programme involving volunteers

Monday evenings: computer training

- Training needed in how to produce **1** ....

Tuesday afternoons: singing

- The home has a **2** .... and someone to play it

Thursday mornings: growing **3** ....

- The home doesn't have many **4** .... for gardening

Once a month: meeting for volunteers and staff

Interview

- Go in on **5** .... , any time
- Interview with assistant called **6** ....
- Address of home: 73 **7** .... Road

'Open house' days

- Agreed to help on **8** ....
- Will show visitors where to **9** ....
- Possibility of talking to a **10** .... reporter

SECTION 2 *Questions 11–20*

Questions 11–15

Label the plan below.

*Write the correct letter, **A–H**, next to Questions 11–15.*

Plan of Learning Resource Centre (Ground Floor)

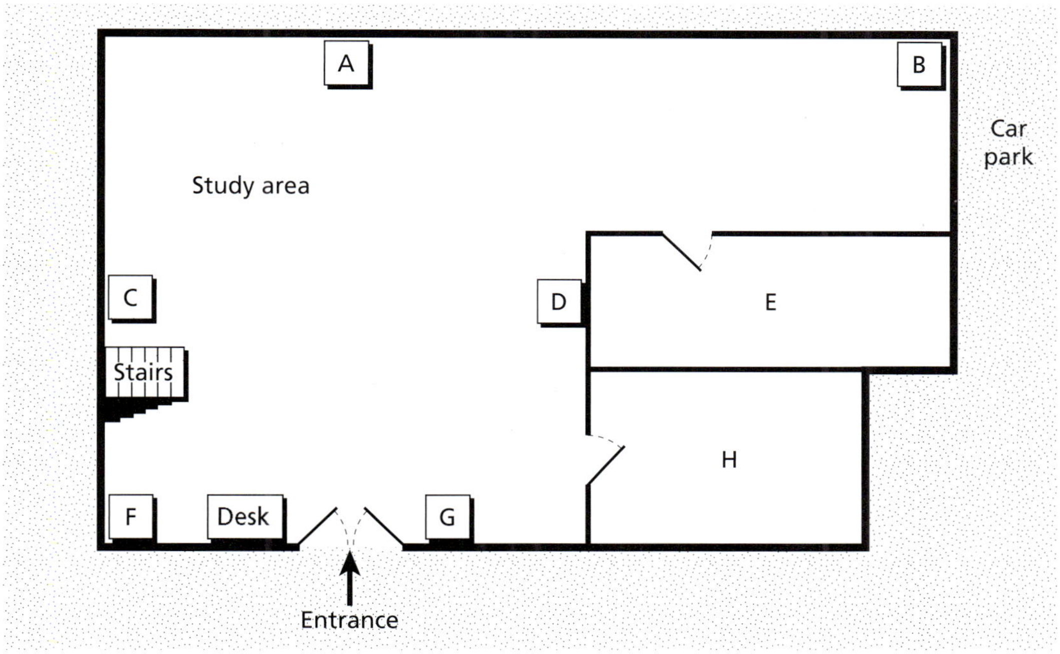

11 Newspapers ....

12 Computers ....

13 Photocopier ....

14 Café ....

15 Sports books ....

Questions 16–20

Complete the table below.

*Write **ONE WORD ONLY** for each answer.*

New staff responsibilities

Name	New responsibility
Jenny Reed	Buying **16** .... for the Centre
Phil Penshurst	Help with writing **17** .... for courses
Tom Salisbury	Information on topics related to the **18** ....
Saeed Aktar	Finding a **19** ....
Shilpa Desai	Help with **20** ....

SECTION 3 *Questions 21–30*

Questions 21–27

What helped Stewart with each of the following stages in making his training film for museum employees?

Choose ***SEVEN*** *answers from the box and write the correct letter,* ***A–I****, next to Questions 21–27.*

What helped Stewart	
A	advice from friends
B	information on a website
C	being allowed extra time
D	meeting a professional film maker
E	good weather conditions
F	getting a better computer
G	support of a manager
H	help from a family member
I	work on a previous assignment

Stages in making the training film for museum employees

21 finding a location ....

22 deciding on equipment ....

23 writing the script ....

24 casting ....

25 filming ....

26 editing ....

27 designing the DVD cover ....

Questions 28–30

Complete the notes below.

Write ***ONE WORD ONLY*** *for each answer.*

Stewart's work placement: benefits to the Central Museum Association

- his understanding of the Association's **28** ....
- the reduction in expense
- increased co-operation between **29** ....
- continuous **30** .... which led to a better product
- ideas for distribution of the film

SECTION 4 *Questions 31–40*

Complete the notes below.

*Write **ONE WORD ONLY** for each answer.*

New Caledonian crows and the use of tools

Examples of animals using tools

- some chimpanzees use stones to break nuts
- Betty (New Caledonian crow) made a

  31 .... out of wire to move a bucket of food
- Barney (New Caledonian crow) used sticks to find food

New Zealand and Oxford experiment

- three stages: crows needed to move a **32** .... in order to reach a short stick; then use the short stick to reach a long stick; then use the long stick to reach food

Oxford research

- crows used sticks to investigate whether there was any **33** .... from an object
- research was inspired by seeing crows using tools on a piece of cloth to investigate a spider design
- Barney used a stick to investigate a snake made of **34** ....
- Pierre used a stick to investigate a **35** ....
- Corbeau used a stick to investigate a metal toad
- the crows only used sticks for the first contact

Conclusions of above research

- ability to plan provides interesting evidence of the birds' cognition
- unclear whether this is evidence of the birds' **36** ....

Exeter and Oxford research in New Caledonia

- scientists have attached very small cameras to birds' **37** ....
- food in the form of beetle larvae provides plenty of **38** .... for the birds
- larvae's specific **39** .... composition can be identified in birds that feed on them
- scientists will analyse what the birds include in their **40** ....

READING

READING PASSAGE 1

*You should spend about 20 minutes on **Questions 1–13**, which are based on Reading Passage 1 below.*

The Phoenicians: an almost forgotten people

The Phoenicians inhabited the region of modern Lebanon and Syria from about 3000 BC. They became the greatest traders of the pre-classical world, and were the first people to establish a large colonial network. Both of these activities were based on seafaring, an ability the Phoenicians developed from the example of their maritime predecessors, the Minoans of Crete.

An Egyptian narrative of about 1080 BC, the *Story of Wen-Amen*, provides an insight into the scale of their trading activity. One of the characters is Wereket-El, a Phoenician merchant living at Tanis in Egypt's Nile delta. As many as 50 ships carry out his business, plying back and forth between the Nile and the Phoenician port of Sidon.

The most prosperous period for Phoenicia was the 10th century BC, when the surrounding region was stable. Hiram, the king of the Phoenician city of Tyre, was an ally and business partner of Solomon, King of Israel. For Solomon's temple in Jerusalem, Hiram provided craftsmen with particular skills that were needed for this major construction project. He also supplied materials – particularly timber, including cedar from the forests of Lebanon. And the two kings went into trade in partnership. They sent out Phoenician vessels on long expeditions (of up to three years for the return trip) to bring back gold, sandalwood, ivory, monkeys and peacocks from Ophir. This is an unidentified place, probably on the east coast of Africa or the west coast of India.

Phoenicia was famous for its luxury goods. The cedar wood was not only exported as top-quality timber for architecture and shipbuilding. It was also carved by the Phoenicians, and the same skill was adapted to even more precious work in ivory. The rare and expensive dye for cloth, Tyrian purple, complemented another famous local product, fine linen. The metalworkers of the region, particularly those working in gold, were famous. Tyre and Sidon were also known for their glass.

These were the main products which the Phoenicians exported. In addition, as traders and middlemen, they took a commission on a much greater range of precious goods that they transported from elsewhere.

The extensive trade of Phoenicia required much book-keeping and correspondence, and it was in the field of writing that the Phoenicians made their most lasting contribution to world history. The scripts in use in the world up to the second millennium BC (in Egypt, Mesopotamia or China) all required the writer to learn a large number of separate characters – each of them expressing either a whole word or an element of its meaning. By contrast, the Phoenicians, in about 1500 BC, developed an entirely new approach to writing. The marks made (with a pointed tool called a stylus, on damp clay) now attempted to capture the sound of a word. This required an alphabet of individual letters.

The trading and seafaring skills of the Phoenicians resulted in a network of colonies, spreading westwards through the Mediterranean. The first was probably Citium, in Cyprus, established in the 9th century BC. But the main expansion came from the 8th century BC onwards, when pressure from Assyria to the east disrupted the patterns of trade on the Phoenician coast.

Trading colonies were developed on the string of islands in the centre of the Mediterranean – Crete, Sicily, Malta, Sardinia, Ibiza – and also on the coast of north Africa. The African colonies clustered in particular around the great promontory which, with Sicily opposite, forms the narrowest channel on the main Mediterranean sea route. This is the site of Carthage.

Carthage was the largest of the towns founded by the Phoenicians on the north African coast, and it rapidly assumed a leading position among the neighbouring colonies. The traditional date of its founding is 814 BC, but archaeological evidence suggests that it was probably settled a little over a century later.

The subsequent spread and growth of Phoenician colonies in the western Mediterranean, and even out to the Atlantic coasts of Africa and Spain, was as much the achievement of Carthage as of the original Phoenician trading cities such as Tyre and Sidon. But no doubt links were maintained with the homeland, and new colonists continued to travel west.

From the 8th century BC, many of the coastal cities of Phoenicia came under the control of a succession of imperial powers, each of them defeated and replaced in the region by the next: first the Assyrians, then the Babylonians, Persians and Macedonian Greeks.

In 64 BC, the area of Phoenicia became part of the Roman province of Syria. The Phoenicians as an identifiable people then faded from history, merging into the populations of modern Lebanon and northern Syria.

Questions 1–8

Complete the sentences below.

Choose **ONE WORD ONLY** *from the passage for each answer.*

Write your answers in boxes 1–8 on your answer sheet.

The Phoenicians' trading activities

The Phoenicians' skill at **1** .... helped them to trade.

In an ancient story, a **2** .... from Phoenicia, who lived in Egypt, owned 50 ships.

A king of Israel built a **3** .... using supplies from Phoenicia.

Phoenicia supplied Solomon with skilled **4** ....

The main material that Phoenicia sent to Israel was **5** ....

The kings of Phoenicia and Israel formed a business **6** .... in order to carry out trade.

Phoenicians carved **7** .... , as well as cedar.

The Phoenicians also earned a **8** .... for shipping goods.

Questions 9–13

Do the following statements agree with the information given in Reading Passage 1?

In boxes 9–13 on your answer sheet, write

TRUE *if the statement agrees with the information*
FALSE *if the statement contradicts the information*
NOT GIVEN *if there is no information on this*

9 Problems with Assyria led to the establishment of a number of Phoenician colonies.

10 Carthage was an enemy town which the Phoenicians won in battle.

11 Phoenicians reached the Atlantic ocean.

12 Parts of Phoenicia were conquered by a series of empires.

13 The Phoenicians welcomed Roman control of the area.

READING PASSAGE 2

You should spend about 20 minutes on ***Questions 14–26****, which are based on Reading Passage 2 on the following pages.*

Questions 14–19

Reading Passage 2 has six paragraphs, **A–F**.

Choose the correct heading for each paragraph from the list of headings below.

Write the correct number, ***i–viii****, in boxes 14–19 on your answer sheet.*

List of Headings

i	The power within each studio
ii	The movie industry adapts to innovation
iii	Contrasts between cinema and other media of the time
iv	The value of studying Hollywood's Golden Age
v	Distinguishing themselves from the rest of the market
vi	A double attack on film studios' power
vii	Gaining control of the industry
viii	The top movies of Hollywood's Golden Age

14 Paragraph **A** ....

15 Paragraph **B** ....

16 Paragraph **C** ....

17 Paragraph **D** ....

18 Paragraph **E** ....

19 Paragraph **F** ....

The Hollywood Film Industry

A This chapter examines the 'Golden Age' of the Hollywood film studio system and explores how a particular kind of filmmaking developed during this period in US film history. It also focuses on the two key elements which influenced the emergence of the classic Hollywood studio system: the advent of sound and the business ideal of vertical integration. In addition to its historical interest, inspecting the growth of the studio system may offer clues regarding the kinds of struggles that accompany the growth of any new medium. It might, in fact, be intriguing to examine which changes occurred during the growth of the Hollywood studio, and compare those changes to contemporary struggles in which production companies are trying to define and control emerging industries, such as online film and interactive television.

B The shift of the industry away from 'silent' films began during the late 1920s. Warner Bros.' 1927 film *The Jazz Singer* was the first to feature synchronized speech, and with it came a period of turmoil for the industry. Studios now had proof that 'talkie' films would make them money, but the financial investment this kind of filmmaking would require, from new camera equipment to new projection facilities, made the studios hesitant to invest at first. In the end, the power of cinematic sound to both move audiences and enhance the story persuaded studios that talkies were worth investing in. Overall, the use of sound in film was well-received by audiences, but there were still many technical factors to consider. Although full integration of sound into movies was complete by 1930, it would take somewhat longer for them to regain their stylistic elegance and dexterity. The camera now had to be encased in a big, clumsy, unmoveable soundproof box. In addition, actors struggled, having to direct their speech to awkwardly-hidden microphones in huge plants, telephones or even costumes.

C Vertical integration is the other key component in the rise of the Hollywood studio system. The major studios realized they could increase their profits by handling each stage of a film's life: production (making the film), distribution (getting the film out to people) and exhibition (owning the theaters in major cities where films were shown first). Five studios, 'The Big Five', worked to achieve vertical integration through the late 1940s, owning vast real estate on which to construct elaborate sets. In addition, these studios set the exact terms of films' release dates and patterns. Warner Bros., Paramount, 20th Century Fox, MGM and RKO formed this exclusive club. 'The Little Three' studios – Universal, Columbia and United Artists – also made pictures, but each lacked one of the crucial elements of vertical integration. Together these eight companies operated as a mature oligopoly, essentially running the entire market.

D During the Golden Age, the studios were remarkably consistent and stable enterprises, due in large part to long-term management heads – the infamous 'movie moguls' who ruled their kingdoms with iron fists. At MGM, Warner Bros. and Columbia, the same men ran their studios for decades. The rise of the studio system also hinges on the treatment of stars, who were constructed and exploited to suit a studio's image and schedule. Actors were bound up in seven-year contracts to a single studio, and the studio boss generally held all the options. Stars could be loaned out to other production companies at any time. Studio bosses could also force bad roles on actors, and manipulate every single detail of stars' images with their mammoth in-house publicity departments. Some have compared the Hollywood studio system to a factory, and it is useful to remember that studios were out to make money first and art second.

E On the other hand, studios also had to cultivate flexibility, in addition to consistent factory output. Studio heads realized that they couldn't make virtually the same film over and over again with the same cast of stars and still expect to keep turning a profit. They also had to create product differentiation. Examining how each production company tried to differentiate itself has led to loose characterizations of individual studios' styles. MGM tended to put out a lot of all-star productions while Paramount excelled in comedy and Warner Bros. developed a reputation for gritty social realism. 20th Century Fox forged the musical and a great deal of prestige biographies, while Universal specialized in classic horror movies.

F In 1948, struggling independent movie producers and exhibitors finally triumphed in their battle against the big studios' monopolistic behavior. In the United States versus Paramount federal decree of that year, the studios were ordered to give up their theaters in what is commonly referred to as 'divestiture' – opening the market to smaller producers. This, coupled with the advent of television in the 1950s, seriously compromised the studio system's influence and profits. Hence, 1930 and 1948 are generally considered bookends to Hollywood's Golden Age.

Questions 20–23

Do the following statements agree with the information given in Reading Passage 2?

In boxes 20–23 on your answer sheet, write

TRUE	*if the statement agrees with the information*
FALSE	*if the statement contradicts the information*
NOT GIVEN	*if there is no information on this*

20 After *The Jazz Singer* came out, other studios immediately began making movies with synchronized sound.

21 There were some drawbacks to recording movie actors' voices in the early 1930s.

22 There was intense competition between actors for contracts with the leading studios.

23 Studios had total control over how their actors were perceived by the public.

Questions 24–26

Complete the summary below.

Choose ***NO MORE THAN TWO WORDS*** *from the passage for each answer.*

Write your answers in boxes 24–26 on your answer sheet.

THE HOLLYWOOD STUDIOS

Throughout its Golden Age, the Hollywood movie industry was controlled by a handful of studios. Using a system known as **24** .... , the biggest studios not only made movies, but handled their distribution and then finally showed them in their own theaters. These studios were often run by autocratic bosses – men known as **25** .... , who often remained at the head of organisations for decades. However, the domination of the industry by the leading studios came to an end in 1948, when they were forced to open the market to smaller producers – a process known as **26** ....

READING PASSAGE 3

*You should spend about 20 minutes on **Questions 27–40**, which are based on Reading Passage 3 below.*

Left or right?

An overview of some research into lateralisation: the dominance of one side of the body over the other

A Creatures across the animal kingdom have a preference for one foot, eye or even antenna. The cause of this trait, called lateralisation, is fairly simple: one side of the brain, which generally controls the opposite side of the body, is more dominant than the other when processing certain tasks. This does, on some occasions, let the animal down: such as when a toad fails to escape from a snake approaching from the right, just because its right eye is worse at spotting danger than its left. So why would animals evolve a characteristic that seems to endanger them?

B For many years it was assumed that lateralisation was a uniquely human trait, but this notion rapidly fell apart as researchers started uncovering evidence of lateralisation in all sorts of animals. For example, in the 1970s, Lesley Rogers, now at the University of New England in Australia, was studying memory and learning in chicks. She had been injecting a chemical into chicks' brains to stop them learning how to spot grains of food among distracting pebbles, and was surprised to observe that the chemical only worked when applied to the left hemisphere of the brain. That strongly suggested that the right side of the chick's brain played little or no role in the learning of such behaviours. Similar evidence appeared in songbirds and rats around the same time, and since then, researchers have built up an impressive catalogue of animal lateralisation.

C In some animals, lateralisation is simply a preference for a single paw or foot, while in others it appears in more general patterns of behaviour. The left side of most vertebrate brains, for example, seems to process and control feeding. Since the left hemisphere processes input from the right side of the body, that means animals as diverse as fish, toads and birds are more likely to attack prey or food items viewed with their right eye. Even humpback whales prefer to use the right side of their jaws to scrape sand eels from the ocean floor.

D Genetics plays a part in determining lateralisation, but environmental factors have an impact too. Rogers found that a chick's lateralisation depends on whether it is exposed to light before hatching from its egg – if it is kept in the dark during this period, neither hemisphere becomes dominant. In 2004, Rogers used this observation to test the advantages of brain bias in chicks faced with the challenge of multitasking. She hatched chicks with either strong or weak lateralisation, then presented the two groups with food hidden among small pebbles and the threatening shape of a fake predator flying overhead. As predicted, the birds incubated in the light looked for food mainly with their right eye, while using the other to check out the predator. The weakly-lateralised chicks, meanwhile, had difficulty performing these two activities simultaneously.

E Similar results probably hold true for many other animals. In 2006, Angelo Bisazza at the University of Padua set out to observe the differences in feeding behaviour between strongly-lateralised and weakly-lateralised fish. He found that strongly-lateralised individuals were able to feed twice as fast as weakly-lateralised ones when there was a threat of a predator looming above them. Assigning different jobs to different brain halves may be especially advantageous for animals such as birds or fish, whose eyes are placed on the sides of their heads. This enables them to process input from each side separately, with different tasks in mind.

F And what of those animals who favour a specific side for almost all tasks? In 2009, Maria Magat and Culum Brown at Macquarie University in Australia wanted to see if there was general cognitive advantage in lateralisation. To investigate, they turned to parrots, which can be either strongly right- or left-footed, or ambidextrous (without dominance). The parrots were given the intellectually demanding task of pulling a snack on a string up to their beaks, using a co-ordinated combination of claws and beak. The results showed that the parrots with the strongest foot preferences worked out the puzzle far more quickly than their ambidextrous peers.

G A further puzzle is why are there always a few exceptions, like left-handed humans, who are wired differently from the majority of the population? Giorgio Vallortigara and Stefano Ghirlanda of Stockholm University seem to have found the answer via mathematical models. These have shown that a group of fish is likely to survive a shark attack with the fewest casualties if the majority turn together in one direction while a very small proportion of the group escape in the direction that the predator is not expecting.

H This imbalance of lateralisation within populations may also have advantages for individuals. Whereas most co-operative interactions require participants to react similarly, there are some situations – such as aggressive interactions – where it can benefit an individual to launch an attack from an unexpected quarter. Perhaps this can partly explain the existence of left-handers in human societies. It has been suggested that when it comes to hand-to-hand fighting, left-handers may have the advantage over the right-handed majority. Where survival depends on the element of surprise, it may indeed pay to be different.

Questions 27–30

Complete each sentence with the correct ending, ***A–F****, below.*

Write the correct letter, ***A–F****, in boxes 27–30 on your answer sheet.*

27 In the 1970s, Lesley Rogers discovered that

28 Angelo Bisazza's experiments revealed that

29 Magat and Brown's studies show that

30 Vallortigara and Ghirlanda's research findings suggest that

A lateralisation is more common in some species than in others.

B it benefits a population if some members have a different lateralisation than the majority.

C lateralisation helps animals do two things at the same time.

D lateralisation is not confined to human beings.

E the greater an animal's lateralisation, the better it is at problem-solving.

F strong lateralisation may sometimes put groups of animals in danger.

Questions 31–35

Complete the summary below.

Choose ***ONE WORD ONLY*** *from the passage for each answer.*

Write your answers in boxes 31–35 on your answer sheet.

Lesley Rogers' 2004 Experiment

Lateralisation is determined by both genetic and **31** .... influences. Rogers found that chicks whose eggs are given **32** .... during the incubation period tend to have a stronger lateralisation. Her 2004 experiment set out to prove that these chicks were better at **33** .... than weakly lateralised chicks. As expected, the strongly lateralised birds in the experiment were more able to locate **34** .... using their right eye, while using their left eye to monitor an imitation **35** .... located above them.

Questions 36–40

*Reading Passage 3 has eight paragraphs, **A–H**.*

Which paragraph contains the following information?

*Write the correct letter, **A–H**, in boxes 36–40 on your answer sheet.*

***NB** You may use any letter more than once.*

36 description of a study which supports another scientist's findings

37 the suggestion that a person could gain from having an opposing lateralisation to most of the population

38 reference to the large amount of knowledge of animal lateralisation that has accumulated

39 research findings that were among the first to contradict a previous belief

40 a suggestion that lateralisation would seem to disadvantage animals

WRITING

WRITING TASK 1

You should spend about 20 minutes on this task.

The chart below shows the annual number of rentals and sales (in various formats) of films from a particular store between 2002 and 2011.

Summarise the information by selecting and reporting the main features, and make comparisons where relevant.

Write at least 150 words.

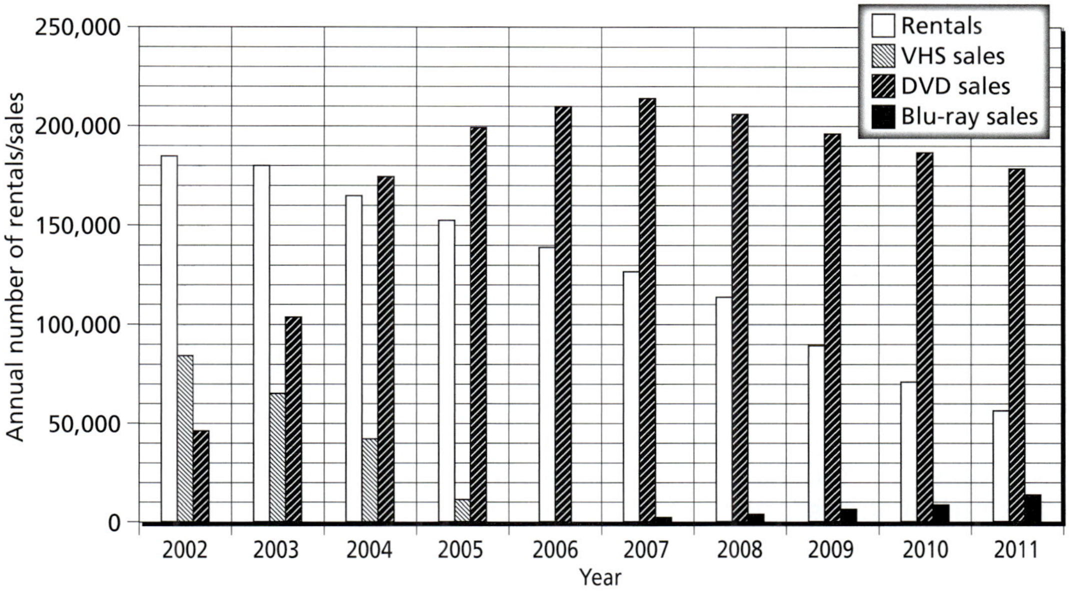

WRITING TASK 2

You should spend about 40 minutes on this task.

Some people get into debt by buying things they don't need and can't afford.

What are the reasons for this behaviour?

What action can be taken to prevent people from having this problem?

Give reasons for your answer and include any relevant examples from your own knowledge or experience.

Write at least 250 words.

SPEAKING

PART 1

Films/Movies

- When was the last time you went to the cinema?
- How popular are cinemas where you live? [Why?]
- What sorts of films/movies do you enjoy most? [Why?]
- Where do you prefer to watch films/movies, at the cinema or at home? [Why?]

Special days

- What are the most important festivals in your culture? [Why?]
- How do people celebrate New Year in your culture? [Why?]
- Which festival did you enjoy celebrating most when you were a child? [Why?]
- Which festival in another country would you like to go to? [Why?]

PART 2

Candidate task card:

Describe a shopping centre/mall that you have visited or that you know about.

You should say:
where the shopping centre/mall is
how people travel to the shopping centre/mall
what kinds of shops it has
and explain whether you think it is a good place to go shopping.

You will have to talk about the topic for one to two minutes.

You have one minute to think about what you are going to say.

You can make some notes to help you if you wish.

PART 3

Different types of shop

- Where do people in your country buy food?
- Is it better to buy clothes in small shops?
- What are the advantages of internet shopping?

Customer service in shops

- What is good customer service?
- Why do some shops provide better customer service than other shops?
- How important is customer service to the success of a shop?

Shopping and society

- Why is shopping such a popular activity?
- What are the advantages to society of a highly developed shopping centre?
- Is society becoming increasingly materialistic?

General Training Reading and Writing Test

READING

SECTION 1 *Questions 1–14*

Read the text below and answer ***Questions 1–7****.*

Interesting Day Courses in your Area

A **Photographing Wildlife**
This workshop includes an introduction in the classroom, two photography sessions with specially arranged access to the zoo enclosures so that you can take natural-looking close-ups of the most exotic species, and the opportunity to review and discuss your images as a group.

B **Drawing For Fun**
You will learn some basic techniques using soft pencils and charcoal. These and different types of paper are provided. Just bring yourself and a willingness to 'have a go'. This is a start-up day so people who have already attended courses should not apply.

C **Find Your Voice**
You may feel you can't sing or you may be an established singer who wants to improve or gain confidence. You will be shown how to sing in tune, how to breathe correctly and how to project your voice. You may attend this course more than once and each time have a wonderful experience. Everyone can sing and it's great fun.

D **Focus On Landscapes**
This course is designed for students who are familiar with painting in watercolours, but are having difficulty with some techniques. We will discuss choice of materials, colour mixing and any other areas that may be raised.

The day will start with a demonstration, followed by an opportunity to sketch outdoors. After a light lunch cooked in the studio, there will be a further practical session.

E **Taking Happy Pictures**
The main objective is to introduce you to the skills required to take good photographs of people at special events, such as parties or weddings.

We will discuss camera settings, dealing with varied light or bad weather, and how to get a good atmosphere. Lunch is provided at a nearby hotel, followed by a practical session inside the studio.

F **The Music Takeaway**
Get some friends, family or colleagues together for your own music course in a venue of your choice, which could be your front room, basement or workplace. We send two guitar tutors to lead a one-day session for you in the style of music you prefer, such as rock, country, funk or blues.

Questions 1–7

Look at the six advertisements, ***A–F****, on page 319.*

For which course are the following statements true?

Write the correct letter, ***A–F****, in boxes 1–7 on your answer sheet.*

NB *You may use any letter more than once.*

1 Participants can decide where the course is held.

2 Different ability levels are welcome.

3 All the necessary materials are supplied.

4 Participants will be able to go where the public are not normally allowed.

5 It is possible to repeat this course.

6 You can select what to study from a range of options.

7 The course will provide advice on how to overcome difficult conditions.

Read the text below and answer ***Questions 8–14****.*

Learn to Skydive

Accelerated Freefall (AFF) is an intensive skydiving course and you can experience freefall on your very first jump. We offer the AFF Level 1 course as a unique introduction to the world of parachuting and skydiving. It's great as a one-off freefall experience. However, the full eight-level Accelerated Freefall course is the best way to learn to skydive and attain your licence as a qualified parachutist, which allows you to jump at skydiving centres across the world.

The AFF Level 1 course begins with an intensive day of ground training. During the day, you will learn how your parachute equipment works and how to check and fit it, how to exit the aircraft, how to maintain the correct body position in the air, monitor your altitude and deploy your parachute and how to deal with emergencies. The day will finish with a written test. The training can be both mentally and physically tiring so you should stay overnight if you wish to do your first jump the next day. For safety reasons we require you to return and jump in less than a month after your training in order to complete the Level 1 course.

When you come to do your jump you will receive refresher training before you board the aircraft. You will exit the aircraft with two AFF Level 1 instructors. They will provide in-air coaching as they fall alongside you, holding onto your harness. You will experience about one minute of freefall and deploy your own parachute, then fly and navigate for around five minutes before landing on the dropzone. Following this, you will meet your instructors to debrief the jump and collect your certificate. Shortly after you arrive home, you will receive an email link to the instructors' footage of your skydive to post online.

There are some restrictions for solo skydiving. The maximum acceptable weight is 95 kg fully clothed and a reasonable level of fitness is required. As far as age is concerned, the minimum is 16 and a parental signature of consent is required for students of 16–17 on three forms. Adults over 45 wishing to skydive must bring a completed Declaration of Fitness form signed and stamped by their doctor. Acceptance rests with the head instructor.

Questions 8–14

Do the following statements agree with the information given in the text on page 321?

In boxes 8–14 on your answer sheet, write

TRUE	*if the statement agrees with the information*
FALSE	*if the statement contradicts the information*
NOT GIVEN	*if there is no information on this*

8 After doing the AFF Level 1 course, people can skydive in different countries.

9 The AFF Level 1 course takes more than one day to complete.

10 Students must do their first jump within a certain period.

11 Training continues after the student jumps out of the plane.

12 During a first jump, an instructor will open the student's parachute.

13 Instructors usually film the first jumps that the students make.

14 Students will be divided into age groups when taking the course.

SECTION 2 *Questions 15–27*

Read the text below and answer ***Questions 15–20****.*

Mistakes when applying for a job

There are many mistakes that people make when writing their résumé (CV) or completing a job application. Here are some of the most common and most serious.

The biggest problem is perhaps listing the duties for which you were responsible in a past position: all this tells your potential employers is what you were supposed to do. They do not necessarily know the specific skills you used in executing them, nor do they know what results you achieved – both of which are essential. In short, they won't know if you were the best, the worst, or just average in your position.

The more concrete information you can include, the better. As far as possible, provide measurements of what you accomplished. If any innovations you introduced saved the organization money, how much did they save? If you found a way of increasing productivity, by what percentage did you increase it?

Writing what you are trying to achieve in life – your objective – is a waste of space. It tells the employer what you are interested in. Do you really think that employers care what you want? No, they are interested in what *they* want! Instead, use that space for a career summary. A good one is brief – three to four sentences long. A good one will make the person reviewing your application want to read further.

Many résumés list 'hard' job-specific skills, almost to the exclusion of transferable, or 'soft', skills. However, your ability to negotiate effectively, for example, can be just as important as your technical skills.

All information you give should be relevant, so carefully consider the job for which you are applying. If you are applying for a job that is somewhat different than your current job, it is up to you to draw a connection for the résumé reviewer, so that they will understand how your skills will fit in their organization. The person who reviews your paperwork will not be a mind reader.

If you are modest about the skills you can offer, or the results you have achieved, a résumé reader may take what you write literally, and be left with a low opinion of your ability: you need to say exactly how good you are. On the other hand, of course, never stretch the truth or lie.

Questions 15–20

Complete the sentences below.

*Choose **ONE WORD ONLY** from the text for each answer.*

Write your answers in boxes 15–20 on your answer sheet.

15 It is a mistake to specify your .... in past positions.

16 Do not include a description of your .... in life.

17 Include soft skills such as an ability to .... successfully.

18 Think hard about the position so you can ensure that the information in your application is ....

19 Make the .... between your abilities and the job you are applying for clear.

20 Do not be too .... about what you can do.

*Read the text below and answer **Questions 21–27**.*

HEALTH AND SAFETY CERTIFICATE FOR THE CONSTRUCTION INDUSTRY
(H&S Certificate)

Who should register for this course?
The H&S Certificate is aimed at people who work as supervisors within the construction industry (whether or not that is part of their job title), who are required to ensure that activities under their control are undertaken safely.

Course duration
Option 1 – Conversion Course (for those who have a PHS Certificate – see below): 10 days, either one day a week or two weeks full-time

Option 2 – Full Course (for all others): 15 days, either one day a week or three weeks full-time

For both options, the written exam and practical assessment take half a day.

About the course
The course provides thorough preparation for the H&S Certificate, which is an award in health and safety specifically designed for the construction industry. It combines theory with practice, ensuring that those who gain the certificate are capable of managing health and safety throughout each stage of the construction process, from planning and design to use and finally demolition.

You may already be one step towards gaining an H&S Certificate
The PHS (Principles of Health and Safety) Certificate can be taken separately or as part of the H&S Certificate. If you gained this qualification no more than five years before entering for the H&S Certificate, it will be recognised as contributing to your Certificate without the need to repeat that unit of the course.

Course content
The H&S Certificate is divided into three units. Unit 1 covers the principles of health and safety (and is identical to the PHS Certificate), Unit 2 covers the identification and control of hazards, and Unit 3 deals with practical applications of health and safety.

How is the course assessed?
Candidates take written examinations for Units 1 and 2. Unit 3 is assessed by a practical examination testing the ability to identify health and safety issues in a construction workplace. Unit 3 needs to be taken within 14 days of a written examination.

A full certificate is issued on successful completion of all three units.

Funding
Candidates from non-EU countries may be eligible for a small number of grants. These cover the cost of tuition, but not examination fees. For details, please contact the Registrar.

Enquiries
For further information please contact our administration office.

Questions 21–27

Answer the questions below.

Choose ***ONE WORD ONLY AND/OR A NUMBER*** *from the text for each answer.*

Write your answers in boxes 21–27 on your answer sheet.

21 Which position is the Certificate intended for?

22 How many days must a student without a PHS Certificate study?

23 What is the last stage of the construction process that is covered by the course?

24 For how long does a PHS Certificate count towards the H&S Certificate?

25 What do students learn to identify and deal with in Unit 2?

26 What type of examination is used for Unit 3?

27 What will a grant pay for?

SECTION 3 Questions 28–40

Questions 28–34

The text on pages 328 and 329 has seven sections, **A–G**.

Choose the correct heading for each section from the list of headings below.

*Write the correct number, **i–x**, in boxes 28–34 on your answer sheet.*

List of Headings

i	The instructions for old dances survive
ii	Inspired by foreign examples
iii	Found in a number of countries and districts
iv	An enthusiastic response from certain people
v	Spectators join in the dancing
vi	How the street event came about
vii	From the height of popularity to a fall from fashion
viii	A surprise public entertainment
ix	Young people invent their own clog dances
x	Clog dancing isn't so easy

28 Section A ....

29 Section B ....

30 Section C ....

31 Section D ....

32 Section E ....

33 Section F ....

34 Section G ....

Clog dancing's big street revival

A The streets of Newcastle, in the north-east of England, have begun to echo with a sound that has not been heard for about a century. A sharp, rhythmic knocking can be heard among the Saturday crowds in one of the city's busiest intersections. It sounds a little like dozens of horses galloping along the street, but there are none in sight. In fact, it's the noise of a hundred people dancing in wooden shoes, or clogs.

The shoppers are about to be ambushed by the UK's biggest clog dance event. The hundred volunteers have been coached to perform a mass routine. For ten minutes, the dancers bring the city centre to a standstill. There are people clogging on oil drums and between the tables of pavement cafés. A screaming, five-man team cuts through the onlookers and begins leaping over swords that look highly dangerous. Then, as swiftly as they appeared, the cloggers melt back into the crowd, leaving the slightly stunned spectators to go about their business.

B This strange manifestation is the brainchild of conductor Charles Hazlewood, whose conversion to clog dancing came through an encounter with a folk band, *The Unthanks*. 'Rachel and Becky Unthank came to develop some ideas in my studio,' Hazlewood says. 'Suddenly, they got up and began to mark out the rhythm with their feet – it was an extraordinary blur of shuffles, clicks and clacks that was an entirely new music for me. I thought, "Whatever this is, I want more of it".'

Hazlewood was inspired to travel to Newcastle to make a television programme, *Come Clog Dancing*, in which he and a hundred other people learn to clog in a fortnight. Yet when he first went out recruiting, local people seemed unaware of their heritage. 'We went out on to the streets, looking for volunteers, but nobody seemed to know anything about clog dancing; or if they did, they thought it originated in the Netherlands.'

C The roots of clog dancing go back several hundred years, and lie in traditional dances of the Dutch, Native Americans and African-Americans, in which the dancer strikes the ground with their heel or toes, to produce a rhythm that's audible to everyone around. In England, clogging is believed to have first developed in the mid-19th century in the cotton mills of Lancashire, in the north-west, where workers created a dance that imitated the sound of the machinery. The style quickly spread and developed a number of regional variations. In Northumberland, it became a recreation for miners, who danced solo or to the accompaniment of a fiddle.

'The Northumberland style is very distinct from Lancashire clogging,' says Laura Connolly, a virtuoso dancer who worked with Hazlewood on the programme. 'Northumbrian dancing is quite neat and precise with almost no upper-body movement, whereas the Lancastrian style is more flamboyant.'

D Whatever the region, clogging remains very much a minority pursuit. Yet at the turn of the 20th century, clogging was a fully-fledged youth craze. Two famous comic film actors, Stan Laurel and Charlie Chaplin, both began their careers as cloggers. But the dance almost completely died out with the passing of the industrial age. 'People danced in clogs because they were cheap, hardwearing and easily repaired,' Connolly says. 'Yet eventually clogs became associated with poverty and people were almost ashamed to wear them.'

E Fortunately, the key steps of the dances were preserved and handed down in a series of little blue books, often named after their inventors. 'It means that we still know what Mrs Willis's Rag or Ivy Sands's Hornpipe were like,' Connolly says. 'It's my dream that one day there'll be a little blue book called Laura Connolly's Jig.'

F Her biggest challenge to date was to teach Hazlewood and 100 other beginners a routine sufficiently accomplished to perform on television, from scratch, in less than two weeks. 'I started people off with something simple,' she says. 'It's a basic shuffle that most people can pick up.' Once Hazlewood had absorbed the basics, Connolly encouraged him to develop a short solo featuring more complex steps – though he nearly came to grief attempting a tricky manoeuvre known as Charlie Chaplin Clicks, so named as it was the signature move of Chaplin's film character the Little Tramp.

'To be honest, I never quite got those right,' Hazlewood says with a laugh. 'We came up with a slightly easier version, which Laura thought we should call Charlie Hazlewood Clicks. The thing about clogs is that they're all surface: there's no grip and they're slightly curved so you stand in a slightly peculiar way. The potential to fall over is enormous.'

On the day, Hazlewood managed to pull off a decent solo, clicks and all. 'I wasn't convinced, until the moment I did it, that I was going to get it right,' he admits. 'But in the end, clog dancing is not so very different from conducting. Both require you to communicate a beat – only I had to learn how to express it with my feet, rather than my hands. But it's a good feeling.'

G 'People forget that clogging was originally a street dance,' Connolly says. 'It was competitive, it was popular, and now young people are beginning to rediscover it for themselves. As soon as we finished in Newcastle, I had kids coming up to me saying, "Clog dancing's cool – I want to do that!"'

Questions 35–37

Complete the summary below.

Choose ***NO MORE THAN TWO WORDS*** *from the text for each answer.*

Write your answers in boxes 35–37 on your answer sheet.

A clog dancing event in Newcastle

First the city's shoppers hear a sound that seems to be created by a large number of **35** .... , and then over a hundred people wearing clogs appear and dance. Most dance on the pavement, some on oil drums. One group uses **36** .... as part of its dance. The event was organised by Charles Hazlewood, a **37** .... He was introduced to clog dancing by a folk band working with him in his studio.

Questions 38–40

Complete the notes below.

Choose ***ONE WORD ONLY*** *from the text for each answer.*

Write your answers in boxes 38–40 on your answer sheet.

The origins of clog dancing

- Originated in the Netherlands and North America
- In England, probably invented by factory workers copying the noise made by the **38** .... in mills
- In Northumberland, was danced by **39** ....
- Very popular in the early 20th century
- Lost popularity when clogs were thought to indicate **40** ....

WRITING

TASK 1

You should spend about 20 minutes on this task.

> ***You have been doing some voluntary work to help your local community. However, now you are unable to continue doing this work.***
>
> ***Write a letter to the manager of the organisation where you have been working. In your letter***
>
> - ***describe the work you have been doing***
> - ***explain why you can no longer do this work***
> - ***recommend another person who is interested in the work***

Write at least 150 words.

You do **NOT** need to write any addresses.

Begin your letter as follows:

Dear ....,

TASK 2

You should spend about 40 minutes on this task.

> ***Many people like to wear fashionable clothes.***
>
> ***Why do you think this is the case?***
>
> ***Is this a good thing or a bad thing?***

Give reasons for your answer and include any relevant examples from your own knowledge or experience.

Write at least 250 words.

Recording scripts

Listening skills

1 Getting ready to listen

1 Understanding the context

▶ 2

1 You will hear a telephone conversation between a man and his daughter Susie about a birthday party they need to organise.
2 You will hear a woman speaking on the radio about buying presents for people of different ages.
3 You will hear two biology students explaining their research ideas to their university lecturer.
4 You will hear an ecology student giving a presentation about a recent field trip to Canada.

2 Using the correct spelling

▶ 3

1 I'm not sure, but I think it starts with an F.
2 No, I'm pretty sure it's double L.
3 Is that M for Mary?
4 Sorry, was that last letter a T or a C?
5 Do you know if it's spelt with a C-H or S-H?

▶ 4

1

A: And can I have your name, please?
B: Yes, it's Andrew Browne.
A: Is that spelt the same as the colour?
B: Yes, but with an E at the end.

2

A: And what's your address, in case we need to post any information out to you?
B: Oh, OK, I live at 63, Beeton Road. That's B-double E-T-O-N.
A: Sorry, was that last letter N or M?
B: N for November.

3

A: Do you have a website I can go to?
B: Yes, just go to www.kickers.com
A: Is that K-I-C-K-E-R-S?
B: That's right, all one word and all lower case.

4

A: Where shall we meet then? Somewhere in the city?
B: That's a good idea. What about at that hotel on the corner of Queen Street and Mary Street? What's it called?
A: Oh, it's the Rose Hotel, like the flower.
B: Yes, that's the one, I'll see you there at seven.
A: Uhuh.

5

A: Right, and can I get your car registration number? Have you got a normal one or is it one of those specially made ones that's a word or a name?
B: No, I haven't got the money for a personalised plate. It's just three letters and three numbers. It's H-L-P 528.

3 Writing numbers

▶ 5

a 3rd
b $10.50
c 6th
d 70
e 19
f 15
g 62
h £110
i 31st
j 27th

▶ 6

1

A: I hope you've enjoyed your stay with us.
B: Yes, it was lovely, but I had to pay £95, which seems a bit expensive. Last time I stayed here, I only paid £80.
A: Yes, I'm sorry, madam. We had to increase our prices considerably this year. But that is actually a discounted price as you're a regular guest. It would normally be £105.
B: Oh!

2

Now, on Thursday, there will be a special class, which will be given by a wonderful local artist. As this isn't included in your fees, you will need to pay for this on the day. We've kept the costs low. It's only $10 for our regular students here. If you want to bring along anyone else who hasn't studied with us before, the cost for them is $15. We charge them an extra $5 for the use of equipment, which old students have already paid for.

3

A: Can you tell me how big the garage is? I just want to make sure our cars will fit.
B: Let me have a look. How big are your cars?
A: Mine's about 1.5 metres wide and my wife's is almost the same.
B: Hmm, I don't think it's wide enough, I'm afraid. It says here that it's 3.5 metres across, and you need at least a metre between the cars to be able to open the doors.
A: You're right. What about the height? Mine's a van I use for work and I carry a lot of equipment on top.
B: Let me see. It's two and a half metres. Would that be tall enough?
A: Oh, not for my big ladders, no. I'd like three metres at least.

4

A: I'm thinking of taking my children to the Gold Coast in the holidays. Can you tell me how much it would cost on the bus? I don't want to drive all that way.
B: Right, you'd qualify for a family ticket, which is the cheapest way to do it. It'll be $55 altogether, normally a child's fare is $25 and an adult is $45.
A: Oh, that's a good deal!

5

A: I'm trying to organise a party and I wondered if your hotel had a room we could use?
B: We do have several function rooms, what date did you have in mind for the party? I'll just warn you we're already fully booked for most of June, the first available date I have is 14th July.
A: Oh, that's not a problem. It's for my dad's birthday, which isn't until 1st August.
B: That's a Tuesday.
A: Yes, so I'd like to hold it at the end of July, on the Saturday before.
B: So, that's the 29th?
A: Yes, that's right.

▶ 7

1 We had a good response to our survey and we found that, while 80% of our students drink coffee, only 15% drink tea, with the rest preferring water.
2 Over 800,000 people in the US are estimated to have tried skiing. This may seem a large number but it represents just over 0.26% of the total population of 300 million. So, per capita, it is surprisingly small.
3 It's estimated that India is home to between 38,000 and 53,000 wild elephants, while Africa has between 470,000 and 690,000. Exact figures are difficult to determine.
4 An elephant can weigh between 2.5 and 5 tonnes. This is comparable to the tongue of the blue whale, which alone can weigh 2.7 tonnes. In fact, a blue whale can weigh 15 times more than an elephant, and can grow to about 10 times the size of a standard bus.

2 Following a conversation

1 Identifying the speakers

▶ 8

1

A: Good morning, Harrisons Travel Agency, how can I help you?
B: Oh, good morning, I'm thinking of going on a skiing trip. Can you tell me about any good offers on at the moment?

2

A: Welcome to the York Hotel, are you checking in?
B: Yes, that's right. My name's Bob Clarke. I've got a booking.
A: Great. I'll just get a few personal details from you.

3

A: Well, I don't think I have any more questions. Is there anything you'd like to ask me about the job?
B: Yes, I was wondering if it involves a lot of travel, and what the working hours are.

▶ 9

1

A: This one's a good deal. It costs £150 and airfares are included in that price. Once you land, you still need to get to the ski slopes. It's a two-hour journey.
B: Yes, I know, I have a friend there who's going to meet me and we'll travel together.
A: Oh, that's fine, I usually organise a coach ticket for my customers, because a taxi is far too expensive. But a lift from a local is even better. What about skiing equipment?
B: I've already got all of that, but I would like to arrange insurance if that's possible.
A: Yes, of course. And it's a very good idea for a holiday like that.

2

A: And it says here you'll be staying with us for two nights, is that right?
B: Actually, my plans have changed since I made the booking and I was hoping I'd be able to stay for one extra night, if it's possible.
A: I'll just have a look and try to make sure you don't have to change rooms on the third night. Yes, that's fine, and in fact you'll get a 25% discount as well.
B: Oh, great. Do you have a gym or a sports centre in the hotel? And I need access to your business centre as well.
A: Yes, we have all of those. Now, your room is up on the tenth floor, and the elevators are right behind you. You'll actually be on the same floor as the business centre, and it's clearly signposted. The gym is down on this level and so is the restaurant. You need to go there in the morning for breakfast.

3

A: Now, according to your CV, you've lived and worked in a few different countries, haven't you?
B: That's right. I was born here in England and my family emigrated to Australia when I was very young.
A: But your longest employment so far was in America, if I'm not mistaken?
B: That's right. I moved there once I'd graduated and worked for five years before coming back to England in January.
A: Right. And you've worked briefly in accounts but in sales, mostly ... Is that the area you are still interested in working in? We have a very strong sales department.
B: Actually, I'm hoping to move into the area of marketing. I've always been interested in it, and it was my major at university.
A: I see. Well, with your references I'm sure we can discuss it.

2 Identifying function

▶ 10

1 What about getting her a new bike?
2 That's right. We arrive on 22nd July.
3 That sounds great. Let's do that.
4 I don't think I'd enjoy that one.
5 You said you'd prefer to have the party outside, is that right?

6 Actually, it's just gone up to $250.
7 Now, what about accommodation? Where would you like to stay?

▶ 11

Section 1

A: Hi Sam, we'd better start planning the party, it's in less than two weeks, isn't it?
B: Yeah, I guess it is. There isn't much to do, is there?
A: Well, we need to sort out food, for a start.
B: Why don't we just order some pizzas?
A: But we always do that. Let's do something a bit different. Besides, it's pretty expensive.
B: What about a barbecue then, or we could just do hot dogs.
A: Hmm, too much preparation involved. There are a lot coming, you know.
B: Sandwiches then? That's easy enough.
A: Sandwiches? That's a good idea. Hmm, hang on, that would be even more preparation than the barbecue! Better go back to the original idea, I suppose.
B: Pizzas it is, then!
A: Now, we also need to think about music, and invitations.
B: Well, we don't need to buy invitations, I think we should just do them on the computer and keep costs down.
A: Good idea. And what about music?
B: We can just use the same stuff we had last time. It's fine.
A: OK, well, if we don't let people know soon there won't be anyone there. So let's make that our priority. Have you got your laptop?
B: Yeah, told you there wasn't much to do.

Section 3

A: Hi Julie, have you got time to plan our project?
B: Sure, I've got a few minutes. We need to choose a topic based on the theme of pollution, don't we?
A: That's right. Have you got any preferences?
B: Well, I did a huge assignment on water pollution last year so we could just do that?
A: Actually, the tutor did make a point of saying not to use last year's materials. So we'd better not.
B: It's probably a bit out of date now anyway. Also, it focused specifically on industry and I think we're supposed to take a broad view.
A: That's right. We could look at something totally different, like the effects of fumes on air quality.
B: Hmm, good idea. And we could make sure we include all of the sources, like traffic and factories.
A: So, what else do we need to do? Shall we go to the library and look for resources?
B: Actually, I think we'd be better off looking online. The good resources in the library are often all out at this time of the year. Anyway, before we notify the tutor which topic we've chosen, I think we need to ask the others what they're doing.
A: You're right. We need to make sure we're not all doing the same thing. Let's ask them this afternoon in the tutorial.
B: Great idea.

3 Understanding categories

▶ 12

A: Hi, I'm interested in buying a ticket for the small business expo next week, but I'm not sure it will be useful for me.
B: Well, this year we wanted to focus on computer skills. So, as well as representatives from 400 small businesses, we've invited over 250 specialists in that area.
A: Oh, that should be interesting.

3 Recognising paraphrase

1 Identifying distractors

▶ 13

1

A: Right, so, you need to book some flights, is that right?
B: Yes, for me and my family. We're going to Scotland for my sister's wedding.
A: Oh, lovely! When's the wedding?
B: It's on 21st July.
A: That should be wonderful, but I assume you'll want to fly in earlier? What about the 20th or even the 19th?
B: It will have to be the 18th, I've actually got to attend a special dinner on the 19th.

2

Welcome aboard, everyone! I hope you'll enjoy your stay with us and get a lovely glimpse of country life. We're going to a wonderful market on Tuesday morning, I'm sure you'll love that with all the local farm produce on sale. Then on the Wednesday you'll get to see where all that lovely produce comes from as John Smith, a local farmer, has invited us to see him at work. On Thursday, you'll have a day to relax before we leave on Friday.

3

A: So, what topic are we going to choose for our project? It's due in three weeks.
B: I know, it's not a lot of time. I was going to suggest we do one on the environment.
A: But that's so broad a topic. We should try to narrow it down. What about recycling?
B: That's a good idea, there's a lot of information and I think the other groups are concentrating on pollution. So this would be nice and different.

4

We encountered quite a few problems during our research. Firstly, the weather was horrendous and made our work conditions very difficult indeed. Luckily, we had the right equipment to deal with that, and could carry on regardless. Unfortunately though, in spite of having so many volunteers, we did run out of funds halfway through the project. So, we were forced to postpone the second half of our trip.

2 Recognising paraphrase

▶ 14

1

A: We really need to organise our trip, you know.
B: I know, I was thinking the same. We need to arrange accommodation and flights.
A: And we'll need transport while we're there – we could hire a car?
B: My dad said we could borrow his.
A: Well, that's one less thing to worry about.
B: I'm a bit worried that hotels will all get booked up.
A: OK, let's sort that out straight away.
B: Yes, then I can contact the travel agent and book our flights in the morning.
A: Great.

2

I just wanted to tell you about some of the recent changes we've made to the garden at the back of the complex, which we all have access to. As you know, there are some attractive and well-established plants in there and we didn't want to take any of these out. But many of these are struggling in the harsh sun, which falls directly on that area. To solve this we're going to plant trees along the western edge of the garden, just near the pond. This should also become a very pleasant place to sit and watch the ducks in the water.

3

A: It's nearly there. I think we've found plenty of information.
B: Yes, lots, in fact do you think we need to reduce any of it?
A: Not at all, in fact I was thinking we could try and include some of those nice graphics you found.
B: OK, it would certainly make it look a bit more interesting.

4

Studying ice cores in the South Pole can tell us a lot about the past climate, which, in turn, can help us understand how today's climate is changing. My particular area of study is snow. While we scientists understand the process of how snow is created, very little is known about how snow interacts with the atmosphere and influences our weather patterns. One of the things we're trying to do is to link what we already know about meteorology and clouds and determine the impact that snow has on that.

3 Selecting from a list

▶ 15

In today's show I'm going to be looking at what's new in technology this week. And I'd like to start by looking at the much-awaited OP56 mobile phone from technology giants Optiware. It has some amazing features. The first thing you notice is how much slimmer and lighter it is compared to the heavier older models. It's incredible considering that they have actually increased the screen size on this one, though it still fits neatly into your pocket. They've also improved the camera and you'll find you can take much better quality photos on this model. This has an impact on the battery though, as it takes a lot of power and I found it didn't run for very long before needing to be recharged. Despite all its amazing features, it's extremely easy to use, but I do have to say that it is overpriced, and will be beyond the budget of most people shopping for a new phone.

4 Places and directions

1 Describing a place

▶ 16

1

A: Excuse me, can you tell me where the gift shop is?
B: Yes, you need to go into the shopping centre, the entrance is over there on your left.
A: Yes, I see it.
B: Well, you go in there, then go straight ahead. The shop you want is opposite the toilets. Next to the lifts.
A: Thanks very much!

2

Welcome to the resort! I'll just tell you about some of our facilities. We've got a lovely little pond, where guests are welcome to sit and have a picnic. You'll see it as you come in the entrance. In the middle of the resort, you'll see a circular courtyard, it has some lovely cool places to sit as well. You can see our famous fig tree from there, it's enormous! To the right of the courtyard, you'll find a small shop where you can pick up things like postcards and stamps. It's just behind the tree.

3

A: Hello, Professor Jones, would you be able to help me with my assignment?
B: Of course. Are you having problems with choosing a good location for the new bridge?
A: Yes. I was thinking of putting it right in the middle as the river is at its narrowest there.
B: Well, that would save costs.
A: Exactly, but I realised that it would create costs in other areas as it would mean some important buildings being knocked down. So I think it would be better if it's at the eastern end of the motorway.
B: That's a good idea, it would be a lot more useful than if it was at the western end.

4

The Traviston Frog is different to many other species of frog. It is very small and so, unlike other species, it is unable to live in the area of a pond, though it does need to live in fairly close proximity to water so that it can feed. Rather than choosing the safety of a tree, which would be too tall and may actually increase the threat from predators, it elects to live in a tiny burrow surrounded by bushes.

2 Following directions

▶ 17

A: Can you tell me how to get to the supermarket?
B: Sure, let me have a think. We're in Bridge Street now and it's in Queens Road.

A: Oh, the only street I know is Riverside Street, I know my hotel's on the corner there.
B: That's right. You need to go up Bridge Street as far as the traffic lights, then turn right. That's Riverside Street.
A: I see.
B: Then you walk along there to the next set of traffic lights and you'll be at Queens Road. You turn left there and it's the second shop on your left.
A: Thanks very much!

3 Labelling a map

▶ 18

Morning everyone, thanks for coming. Now, from next week there'll be a rota for all of you to help out at the information stand here at Brookside Market. So, I just wanted to give you a briefing about what you can find where. The information booth is to the right of the entrance and I've given you all a plan to mark important places on. One of the most common enquiries is where can I pay for my parking? People are amazed when we tell them that it's free now. We used to charge for it and there was a ticket booth to the left of the entrance, but now that it's been turned into a small stage, we hold cookery demonstrations there. Local chefs come in and show people how to prepare dishes. It's really popular and you get a nice view of the fountain there. We have over 50 stalls at the markets, selling everything from fresh fruit and vegetables to locally made crafts. Which unfortunately means people won't find things like books or anything second-hand. We have a famous baker at the market and many people get here really early just to buy his produce. His stall is located at the back of the markets next to the barbecue. We sell burgers and sausages there but a lot of people like to bring their own lunch to eat and they're welcome to go to the special area near the tree in the middle of the markets where they can do just that. It's handy for the toilets too. The markets are located next to a circus school that holds classes for children at the weekend, so we often get a lot of family groups in. There's a playground on the right-hand side that's popular with them, and just in front of that is where the farmers bring along chickens, rabbits and lambs for the children to pet. That's always a very popular feature so you'll definitely be asked about that. Just let people know there is a small fee if the children want to feed them. Well, that's everything for now …

5 Listening for actions and processes

1 Understanding mechanical parts

▶ 19

A
At the bottom of the system, there is a storage tank, which can hold up to 500 litres of rainwater. The water stored in the tank can be used for general gardening and cleaning.

B
A small spring in the centre causes the toy inside to bounce out with a twisting movement. The spring coils back down easily enough so that the toy can fit back into the box.

C
The water passes through the pipe and, as it travels along, it carries the weeds with it.

D
The water in the pool was becoming quite polluted so a pump was used to pump the water out of the pool and force it through a filter.

E
There is a very fine grille at different points along the pipe. These filter out any large rocks or stones. So the water is very finely strained by the time it reaches the dam.

F
There is a wheel on the side, which is attached to a small motor that turns the wheel. As it spins, a long chain passes around the outside of it and …

▶ 20

Hello, I've come along to tell you about an invention of mine called the Party Popper Machine. Here is a diagram of the machine and I'll just explain how it works. It's basically a set of interconnected cogs and wheels that rotate in turn and cause a party popper to pop! The process begins with what I like to call the party starter! It's located on the top of the base at the front. I was very fond of wind-up toys when I was young, but sadly I couldn't find a way to attach a winder to this contraption, but I think this big round button looks nice and dramatic and my children fight over getting to push it! The button activates a small motor that's housed directly under the box at the front. It generates enough power to get everything going but not so much that it overheats and needs a cooling fan! The legs elevate the base and help with that. The base also has another use as it can also hold up to 10 spare party poppers! So you never need to worry about running out. Once the motor is running, it turns the spiky wheel that is attached to the loaded party popper. I call this the detonator! As it turns, the string of the party popper slowly wraps around it and is pulled tighter and tighter until it explodes! So much fun!

2 Describing an action or process

▶ 21

A The thermometer on the end of the device allows us to measure changes in temperature.
B I had to use my calculator to work out the final figure and calculate how much profit we'd made.
C We put the animals on to the scales to weigh them, and recorded their weight at the beginning and end of the experiment.
D We attached a speedometer so that we could measure our speed and adjust it if necessary.

3 Describing a process

▶ 22

Here's how to wrap a present. First, gather together all of the things you need: wrapping paper, sticky tape, scissors, some ribbon and, of course, a present. Then, place your present on the opened wrapping paper and cut a suitable amount using the scissors. Next, wrap the paper around the present and stick it down with sticky tape. Then, neatly fold up each of the ends of the paper and stick them down. Finally, tie the ribbon around your present. It's now ready to present!

6 Attitude and opinion

1 Identifying attitudes and opinions

▶ 23

1 Well, I agree up to a point.
2 I think that's a really valid point.
3 Well, I'm not so sure about that.
4 I think you're absolutely right.
5 Hmm, that's a bit hard to believe.
6 I think that's highly unlikely.
7 That seems doubtful to me.
8 I have to admit I don't like the sound of that at all.

▶ 24

A: So what did you think about the research?
B: I thought it was well thought out, although it did take three years to produce any results.
A: Yes, but that's to be expected given the age of the participants. I mean, they had to chart their progress over several years.
B: I suppose so.
A: But didn't you think the results were astonishing? I know I did.
B: Yeah, me too. It's amazing to think that watching TV can have such a clearly demonstrated effect on children's obesity problems. It's quite alarming really.
A: I agree.
B: People were generally unimpressed by the findings though, which is typical when there's a suggestion that we change our behaviour.

2 Persuading and suggesting

▶ 25

A: Right, let's organise our presentation on the new science equipment, shall we?
B: Yes, I'm a bit worried it's overly long – we only have 10 minutes.
A: Why don't we go through each section then.
B: OK, what about the introduction? I think that's OK.
A: Hmm. It's not very exciting.
B: I don't think we should cut any of it though.
A: Of course, and we can still do it the same way, but maybe we should bring along some actual equipment?
B: Great idea, that would help grab their attention. Now, next we look at the benefits of this technology. We've got plenty about that.
A: I agree. In fact, some of the ones we've chosen are pretty obvious, I think, perhaps we could leave some out?
B: Agreed. And that would save some time.
A: Yes, now, when it comes to the negatives, I'd like to propose something a little different.
B: I like that section, it's always enjoyable hearing about technology going wrong!
A: Well, we've got a few thought-provoking quotes from people who've encountered specific problems. And we were planning on just reading them out but I think we should video them and play the recording instead.
B: Oh, that would be better. And if we use a variety of media, I think we'll get a higher mark.
A: Yes. That's what I was thinking,
B: OK, let's give it a try. Now, what about the conclusion? Should we include something else? It's pretty short at the moment.
A: Yes, but I think that's OK. There's not much more to say, really. We've already verified all our sources, so I don't think there's anything else left to do.
B: Well, I think I'll do an Internet search anyway, just to be sure we haven't missed anything.
A: OK, it would be good to be able to state that we have included all the very latest information.
B: Absolutely.

3 Reaching a decision

▶ 26

Section 1

A: How are we going to get to the airport on Monday? Shall we get a taxi?
B: It would be nice and convenient but the fare is so expensive.
A: That's true. Well, if you want to save money, we could always take the bus.
B: It might be cheaper but the bus doesn't start running until 7 o'clock and we need to be at the airport by 6. I'll ask my sister if she can give us a lift.
A: That would be great if she could drive us.
B: Yes. I'm sure she won't mind.

Section 3

A: So, what else have we got to do?
B: Well, we've gathered enough information. I don't think we need to find out any more.
A: You're right. Should we go and see Professor Smith, then? We could ask his advice.
B: Well, he could check it for us and make sure we've done enough. But I'd rather do that after we've put it all together. At the moment, we only have a lot of handwritten notes. I don't want to show him that.
A: OK. Let's divide the material up and each put it on to a disc so that we can print off a nicely presented copy.

7 Following a lecture or talk

1 Identifying main ideas

▶ 27

Good morning, everyone. My name is Paul and I'm a palaeontologist. Now, when most people hear that, they immediately get an image of an old professor studying dried-up dinosaur bones or else they think of a great adventurer from the movies! Well, I'm neither. But I would like to talk to you today about how I came to be a palaeontologist and the reason I believe it is an important job. All my life, my main interest has been the environment. So, I actually started out as an ecology student. As a part of my degree course, I had to do a compulsory unit on extinction and a lecturer visiting from another university gave us a talk on Australia's extinct animals. One of the animals he talked about was called the Diprotodon. It's an ancestor of the modern Australian wombat. He described this enormous animal crossing ancient lakes, getting stuck in the mud and becoming part of the fossil record, which is what we call the preserved remains of animals and plants that we find. And I was fascinated. So fascinated that I immediately changed courses.

But palaeontology isn't all easy going. The very first field trip I went on was pretty awful and we didn't find anything! We went to an outback fossil site and we were digging in extreme conditions. I've learned since then that that's pretty standard for work like this. But to make matters worse, after five days, I'd found nothing. I was getting really disheartened and I was starting to regret my decision, when on the last day of the trip, I was digging into the bank of an ancient dried-up riverbed and I found a funny-looking piece of rock. Inside it was a tooth from a giant kangaroo. Finding that one fossil made me realise that this was a field I really wanted to continue working in.

2 Understanding how ideas are connected

▶ 28

1

A: I don't really understand why you contacted Professor Higgins. He has nothing to do with our faculty.

B: Well, we wanted to understand what impact an invention like this would have on the environment. And that's his area of expertise.

2

A: First of all we put video cameras in the animals' cages ...

B: Yes, and then we put various tools inside the cages and let the animals back in.

A: We video-recorded them over seven days and nights to see what they would do with the tools.

3

After gathering all of our data, we looked at the results. We realised that the number of frogs in this area had actually increased over the last 10 years rather than declined.

4

A: So, what does that all show?

B: Well, I think we can deduce from this that any development in this area should be halted until the animals have all been safely removed.

▶ 29

What I appreciate most about my work is the fact that I can turn the fossils I find into information we can actually use. So, how do we extract that information? Well, first we need to run the fossil through a special machine. That gives me a date for the fossil. From then on, I begin to work out what type of animal it was, what it ate and how it interacted with the landscape.

Earlier this year, I was lucky enough to be awarded a grant from a government-funding body. Palaeontology isn't only about the past. It can help with current issues too. For example, I plan to use these funds to excavate new areas and try to find out how ancient creatures evolved during their own period of climate change, just as animals today have to.

In another project, I'm going to study fossil collections that are housed in museums around Australia. I'm doing that to try to find out when Australia's mega-fauna became extinct – that is, all the giant mammals, lizards and birds. That will help us to finally find out what caused these extinctions. Was it nature or was it humans?

3 Understanding an explanation

▶ 30

1

We've recently been doing some research involving mice. We were trying to find out what causes the cells in our body to age. Is it linked to diet or exercise? What we found was that if we allowed the mice no exercise, their cells deteriorated fairly rapidly, giving them a prematurely old body. The mice that did exercise, showed less change in their cell structure and so seemed younger.

2

We've known for decades that pigeons can navigate using the Earth's magnetic field as a sort of compass. What we don't know is how this works. In our research, we discovered that the pigeon's brain receives a signal from its middle ear that the brain then processes to determine both their direction and the strength of the magnetic field. Previously, it had been thought that it was the bird's beak that held the answer. But this has since been proven false.

8 Contrasting ideas

1 Signposting words

▶ 31

1 OK, let's move on to the late 19th century, when a great deal of changes were taking place.
2 Now, first of all, I wanted to give you some background information.
3 So, let's have a look at some possible reasons for this.
4 And finally, I'd like to talk about some future projects.
5 So, what conclusions did we reach?
6 I'll begin by explaining what this machine can do.

2 Comparing and contrasting ideas

▶ 32

In my talk today, I'm going to be looking at plants that have had an impact on our world and our history. Let's start with the potato. It was originally one of the staple foods of Central and South America and when Spanish explorers travelled to the Americas some time in the 16th century the potato found its way into Europe. This had several important consequences. In particular, it almost totally altered people's diet in many European countries. The potato is also believed to have been responsible for the start of a new trend – that of migrating to

America. So you could say that the humble potato actually allowed many people to change their lives.

However, there were also problems associated with this crop. Largely in Ireland, where the poor were very much reliant on the success of the crops. Sadly, a disease in the crop spread rapidly across the country and led to widespread potato crop failures in the mid-1800s. This meant that millions died from starvation as a result.

Let's move on to look at another plant from the same part of the world, the tobacco plant. This originated in the Americas and had an enormous influence on the way North America developed in the 1800s. It's famed for being the original cash crop there and for funding a great deal of the development that occurred during this time.

On the downside, the success of this crop resulted in a greater demand for slaves to work the crops and this eventually led to war breaking out between the Northern States and those in the South.

Now, the next plant I'd like to mention is one known and used all around the world. Tea. It originated in China and in terms of its historical significance, it played a large part in the US independence from Great Britain. This came about because the British government declared that the colonies had to pay a tax on the produce brought into America. It was because of the protest against these taxes that the American Revolution came about.

The final plant I'll look at today is the White Mulberry. Again it originated in China and had an enormous influence on development in this part of the world, in particular in establishing trade between the East and the West. Sadly, the increase in trade brought with it the spread of disease and weapons.

3 Using notes to follow a talk

▶ 33

In today's lecture, I'm going to talk about the part that plants have played in our history, something most of us probably never give any thought to. Flowers began changing the way the world looked almost as soon as they appeared on Earth about 130 million years ago. That's relatively recent in geologic time – if all Earth's history were compressed into an hour, flowering plants would exist for only the last 90 seconds. Without those flowering plants, it's likely we wouldn't be here. They are fundamental to our existence, forming a vital part of our food supplies.

If we look further on in time, to the year 2737 BC, we arrive at the discovery of tea by a Chinese emperor, when a leaf fell into a cup of hot water. This discovery eventually played a very important part in the history of China, the USA and the UK. For Britain, where demand for tea was high, there were financial implications when a Chinese emperor declared that it could only be bought with silver, which they were then forced to find overseas.

A second influential plant emerged around 202 BC in the form of the White Mulberry. It became extremely sought after and it remained so until 220 AD because white mulberries provide food for the worm that creates silk. This luxurious material was responsible for establishing extremely valuable trade routes. And it was along these same routes that different religions made their way around the world. But, unfortunately, they also caused the spread of previously unknown diseases, as well as weapons of war such as gunpowder.

Finally, moving into more recent history, we come to the 16th century and the potato. It originated in Central America but it was the Spanish who introduced it to the European diet. There, it quickly became popular because not only did it cost little to grow, but it was also a food source that was rich in vitamins. So much so that its arrival has been credited with ridding Britain of a disease known as scurvy. However, it is perhaps more famous now for the potato famines of the mid-1800s in Ireland. The Irish people were so dependent on the crop that its widespread failure over this period caused the deaths of over a million people and the emigration of a further million to mainland Britain, Canada and the US.

Speaking skills

▶ 34

1 it **2** look **3** fool **4** bad **5** workman **6** far **7** bird **8** sport **9** uncle **10** stars **11** heart **12** near **13** chased **14** cruel **15** coin **16** could **17** fair **18** bike **19** can't **20** day **21** breeze **22** defend **23** bland **24** sort **25** close **26** shave **27** air **28** vet

▶ 35

1 it / eat
2 look / luck
3 full / fool
4 bad / bed
5 workmen / workman
6 fur / far
7 board / bird
8 spot / sport
9 ankle / uncle
10 stairs / stars
11 heart / hot
12 knee / near
13 chest / chased
14 crawl / cruel
15 con / coin
16 could / code
17 fur / fair
18 back / bike
19 can't / count
20 day / they
21 breathe / breeze
22 depend / defend
23 bland / brand
24 sort / thought
25 close (adj) / close (v)
26 save / shave
27 hair / air
28 bet / vet

▶ 36

based	arrived	hoped
played	acted	wanted
laughed	chased	poured
changed	increased	decided
waited	learned	washed

▶ 37

contact	depend	expert
respect	develop	difficult
equal	environment	expensive
practice	technique	

▶ 38

Over the years, I've interviewed hundreds of candidates for jobs at many different levels. The point of every job interview is to make sure a candidate has the skills necessary to do the work. Hiring the wrong person can be an expensive mistake. But, apart from references, how can you determine if the candidate actually knows what he says he knows? A very effective way to sort out the good candidates from the bad is by asking 'How did you do that?' and 'Why did you do that?' at appropriate stages in the interview.

Practice Tests

Practice Test 1

Listening Section 1

▶ 39

A: Good morning – Dave Smith speaking.
B: Hi – could I speak to the organiser of the Preston Park Run?
A: Yes that's me.
B: Great – um – I was talking to some friends of mine about the run and they suggested I contact you to get some more details.
A: Sure – what would you like to know?
B: Well – they said it takes place every Saturday, is that right?
A: Yes it does.
B: OK – great!
A: Do you know where the park is?
B: Oh yes – I've been there before. But it's quite big and I'm not sure where to go.
A: Well there's a circular track that goes right around the park. The run starts at the café, goes past the tennis courts then twice around the lake and finishes back where it started.
B: OK and what time is the run?
A: Well the actual run begins at 9 am but the runners start arriving at about 8.45.
B: OK – so I need to get up early Saturday morning then. And how long is the run?
A: Well it used to be three kilometres but most people wanted to do a bit more than that so we lengthened it to five kilometres – we now go round the lake twice and that adds an extra two kilometres.
B: Right – not sure I've ever run that far so I'd better start doing a bit of training.
A: That's a good idea. But it's not a race, it's really just for fun and the best thing would be to take it easy the first few times you do it and then see if you can gradually improve your time.
B: Is the run timed then? How do I know how well I've done?
A: When you cross the finish line you'll be given a bar code and you take this to one of the run volunteers, who will scan it. Then you can get your time online when you go home.
B: Oh – I see. You collect all the results.
A: Exactly.
B: I see – that's great. So how do I register?
A: Well there are several ways. I could take your details over the phone but it's much easier if you do it using the website.
B: OK – good. Um, I think that's probably all I need to know for now. Oh yes – does it cost anything to register or do you collect money each week?
A: Well it doesn't cost anything to register but we do charge for the run. In fact we have just increased the charge to £1.50. It used to be a pound but because we were making a bit of a loss we have had to increase it by 50p.
B: OK thanks. I think I have enough information on taking part in the run.

[pause]

B: Um – you mentioned volunteers. I have a friend who is interested in helping out. Can you give me some details so I can pass them on to her?
A: Sure – well you need to ask your friend to contact Pete Maughan. He manages all the volunteers.
B: OK – I didn't quite catch his surname – was it Morn – M–O–R–N?
A: No – just a bit more complicated – it's M–A–U–G–H–A–N.
B: Right – thanks. And could you give me his phone number?
A: Yes – just a moment. It's here somewhere – let me just find it. Ah I've two numbers for him. I think the one that begins 0–1–2–7–3 is an old one so use this one: it's 0–1–4–double 4–7–3–2–9–double zero.
B: OK – got that. Can you tell me anything about the volunteering? Like what kind of activities it involves?
A: Sure – well we need volunteers for basic stuff like setting up the course. We have to do that before all the runners arrive.
B: OK – so that's a really early start!
A: Yes that's right. But if your friend would prefer to arrive a bit later she can also help with guiding the runners so they don't go the wrong way.
B: I see. I believe you do a report on some of the races.
A: Yes that's right. In fact we do a weekly report on each race and we always try to illustrate it.
B: OK – well my friend really likes taking photographs. She's just bought a new camera.
A: Actually that would be great. I don't know whether Pete has anyone to take photographs this week.
B: Oh, I'll let her know.
A: OK good. Could you ask your friend to phone Pete and let him know?
B: Yes I will.
A: OK thanks. Goodbye.
B: Goodbye.

Listening Section 2

▶ 40

Thank you for calling the phoneline for the Pacton-on-Sea bus tour. This is a recorded message lasting approximately four minutes and it provides general information on the town bus tour.

Pacton-on-Sea is a beautiful west coast town and has attracted tourists for many years. One of the best ways of getting to know the town is to take the bus tour, which provides a wonderful viewing experience from one of our open-top buses. The tour is a round-trip of the town and there are a total of 4 stops where passengers can get on and off the bus. A lot of people start at the first stop which is at the train station as this is where many tourists arrive in the town. The next stop after the station is the aquarium which is famous for its dolphin show and which has recently expanded to include sharks. This is well worth a visit and is very reasonably priced. Leaving the aquarium, the bus tour goes along the coast road and after a few kilometres comes to the Old Fishing Village where you can get off to stroll along the waterfront. There are some original buildings here but most of the area has been modernised and is now used as a harbour for all kinds of sea craft including yachts and some amazing power boats. The tour then heads off to the last stop and this is where most of the shops are. So for those of you keen to do a bit of shopping this is the place for you. Our advice is to go to this part of the town in the morning when it is relatively quiet. It does get very busy in the afternoons, especially at the height of the season. This area of the town includes an ancient water fountain where many people like to have their photograph taken – so do look out for this.

[pause]

Now some details of the costs and timings. A family ticket, which includes two adults and up to three children, costs £30. An adult ticket costs £15, children under the age of fifteen are £5 and student tickets are £10 as long as you have a student card. All tickets are valid for 24 hours, which means that you can get on and off the bus as many times as you like within a 24-hour period. So you could, for example, start the tour in the afternoon and complete it the following morning. The first bus of the day leaves the station at 10 am and the last one of the day leaves at 6 pm. Buses leave every thirty minutes and each tour takes a total of fifty minutes. There are many attractions at each of the stops, so wherever you get off the bus there will be plenty to do. The bus tour tickets do not include entrance to any of these attractions apart from the museum which is located near the aquarium. Some buses have local guides, who will point out places of interest and will provide information on the town. However, we cannot guarantee that every bus will have a guide and so we also have an audio commentary that has been specially recorded for the bus tour by the tourist office. Headphones are available on the bus and these are easy to operate. There is no extra charge for these – just plug in, select the required language and adjust the volume.

Due to the winter months being rather cold and wet in Pacton-on-Sea, the bus tours only operate from March to September. The weather is usually warm and sunny during these months so remember to bring some sun protection, especially on hot days. And of course, it does occasionally rain here in the summer so if the weather looks bad, remember to bring some rainwear. The bus tours are available no matter what the weather.

At the height of the summer the tours can get very busy so you are advised to book. You can book tickets online, over the phone and also at the station and at any of the other tour stops. When booking over the phone you can collect your tickets at any of the stops at the start of your tour. When you do it online you can print your e-ticket which you must remember to bring with you.

Thank you for calling the Pacton-on-Sea phoneline and we look forward to seeing you soon on one of our tour buses.

Listening Section 3

▶ 41

Randhir: Hello – I'm Randhir Ghotra from the technologies department.

Dave: Ah yes. Good. I'm Dave Hadley. Thanks for coming to see me.

Randhir: That's OK. I believe you want us to do some work for you?

Dave: Yes that's right. Um, I'm responsible for student admissions to the college and I use a computer system to help process student enrolments and to do the timetabling. But it really doesn't suit the way we work these days. It's over ten years old and although it was fine when it was first introduced, it is just not good enough now.

Randhir: OK – what problems are you experiencing?

Dave: Well, 20 years ago, the college was quite small and we didn't have the numbers of students or tutors that we have now.

Randhir: So the system can't handle the increasing volumes …

Dave: Well, there's a lot more data now and it sometimes seems the system has crashed but, in fact, it just takes ages to go from one screen to the next.

Randhir: Right. Is that the only problem?

Dave: Well that's the main one, but there are others. In the past, doing the timetabling was quite simple but now we have a lot more courses and what's made it complicated is that many of them have options.

Randhir: Right – but the system should allow you to include those.

Dave: Well no, it doesn't. It was supposed to – and a few years ago we did ask someone from the technologies department to fix it, but they never seemed to have the time.

Randhir: Hmm … are there any other issues with the system?

Dave: Well – I've been given extra responsibilities and so I have even less time to do the timetabling. If there was anything you could do, Randhir, to make the process more efficient, that would be really helpful.

Randhir: Well it sounds like you could do with an assistant but that's obviously not possible, so what about having an online system that students can use to do their scheduling?

Dave: How would that work?

Randhir: Well – it may mean less choice for students but we could create a fixed schedule of all the courses and options and they could then view what was available …

Dave: … and work it out for themselves – that sounds great.

Randhir: OK, so … um … we'll need to decide whether

or not to improve the existing system or to build a completely new system.

Dave: Well I'd much prefer to have a new system. Quite frankly, I've had enough of the old one.

Randhir: OK – that'll probably take longer although it may save you money in the long run. When were you hoping to have this in place?

Dave: Well it's January now and the new intake of students will be in September. We need to start processing admissions – in the next few weeks really.

Randhir: Well it will take more than a few weeks, I'm afraid. As an initial estimate I think we'll be looking at April or May to improve the existing system but for a new system it would take at least nine months. That would be October at the earliest.

[pause]

Dave: What are the next steps if we are to have a new system?

Randhir: Well, the first question is – do you have support from your senior management?

Dave: Yes, I've already discussed it with them and they're also keen to get this work done.

Randhir: OK, because I was going to say, that's the first thing you need to do and without that we can't go ahead.

Dave: Yes, I've done that.

Randhir: That's good.

Dave: Actually, they mentioned that there's probably a form I need to complete to formally start the project.

Randhir: Yes – that's the next thing you need to do. I'll send you an email with a link so you can fill it in online. It's called a 'project request form'.

Dave: OK, great. And then what happens?

Randhir: Well, I have a list of things but I think the third thing you should do is see Samir. He's our analyst who will look at the system and identify what needs to be done.

Dave: OK – can you send me his contact details and I'll set up a meeting with him.

Randhir: OK that's good, so we should soon be able to get a team together to start the work. Some members of our team work in different locations so it's not easy to have face-to-face meetings.

Dave: That's OK – I'm used to having conference calls providing they are not late at night.

Randhir: Right – so I'll send you details of the team and if you could set up a call that would be great.

Dave: OK, I'll do that.

Randhir: Thanks.

Listening Section 4

42

Hi everyone – today I'm going to be talking about the origins of ceramics. So, first of all, let's start off with – what is a ceramic? Well, generally speaking, ceramics are what you get when you apply heat to certain inorganic, non-metallic solids and then allow them to cool. And examples of ceramics are everyday things like earthenware pots, crockery, glassware and even concrete.

So how did it all begin? Well it all started around 29,000 years ago when humans discovered that if you dig up some soft clay from the ground, mould it into a shape and then heat it up to a very high temperature, when it cools the clay has been transformed into something hard and rigid. And so – what did those first humans do with their discovery? Well – they created figurines which were small statues and which depicted animals or gods or any shape that the clay could be moulded into. And all this activity was centred around southern Europe where there is also evidence of ceramics that were created much later.

The early humans also found a practical use for their discovery, such as storing things like grain – although there were drawbacks. The pots were porous so that, although they could carry water in them, it wasn't possible to store it over a long period. And also, they were quite brittle and shattered very easily if they were dropped.

But despite these problems, it was many thousands of years before there were any improvements. In China at around 200 BC, they discovered that by adding minerals to the clay they could improve both the appearance and the strength of the ceramics. But it took nearly a thousand years before they perfected the process to produce high-quality ceramics known as porcelain. And once they had perfected the process, they kept it a secret – for another thousand years! Compared to the first ceramics, porcelain was lighter, finer, harder and whiter and became an important commodity in China's trading with the rest of the world for hundreds of years. In fact, it became so valuable that it was known as white gold and spies were sent to China to discover what they did to the clay to produce such high-quality merchandise.

It wasn't until the eighteenth century that the secret began to unravel. A German alchemist called Johann Friedrich Bottger was asked by the king to make gold out of lead. Unfortunately, Bottger failed to achieve this and soon gave up, but in order to please the king he attempted to make high-quality porcelain. And after many years of experimentation, he discovered that by adding quartz and a material called china stone to very high-quality clay he managed to get the same results that the Chinese had been achieving for the last 1,000 years.

We'll now look at another ceramic which is made from mixing sand with minerals and heating to over 600 degrees Celsius. When this mixture cools the result is of course glass. The main difference between ceramics made from clay and glass is that clay is made up of crystalline plates which become locked together in the cooling process whereas glass cools too quickly for crystals to form. Apart from that, the process of heating up naturally occurring materials to transform them is the same.

The origins of glass date back to 3500 BC but it wasn't until the Roman Empire, 2,000 years ago, that the art of glass-blowing and the practical uses of glass became more widespread. One of the more innovative uses was to use it in windows as, up until then, they had just been holes in walls. It must have been very draughty in those days!

The Romans were also responsible for inventing concrete. And although the origins are uncertain, experts think that this is largely due to the high level of volcanic activity in the area. The Romans observed that, when volcanic ash mixes with water and then cools, it gets extremely hard and almost impossible to break up. The chemical reaction that follows is very complex and continues for many years, and the concrete just keeps getting harder. Evidence of this is the numerous Roman remains that are still standing, many of which are almost completely intact.

One of the most important facts about concrete for the Romans was that it can be created underwater. As the Roman Empire grew, the Romans needed to take control of the seas and for this they needed to build harbours capable of holding a fleet of ships. Pouring concrete mixture into the sea immediately started the hardening process and rather than just dissolving in the mass of water, the substance was tough and long-lasting. This strange characteristic of concrete made a significant contribution to the success of the Roman Empire.

Practice Test 2

Listening Section 1

▶ 43

A: Good morning. Dave speaking.
B: Oh hi. I'm phoning about a short story competition. Um, I saw an advert in a magazine and I was just calling to get some details.
A: Yes – certainly. I'm the competition organiser so I should be able to help. What kind of details are you looking for?
B: Well – erm – does it cost anything to enter?
A: Yes – there's an entry fee of five pounds.
B: OK – that should be fine.

[pause]

B: It's a short story competition – so how many words is that?
A: Well – we want to give people a reasonable amount of freedom but the guidelines are around 3,000 words.
B: Oh – that sounds quite a lot.
A: Well – it's not as much as it used to be. We did have a limit of 5,000 words but some people thought that was too many so this year we've reduced it.
B: Right – and does the story need to be about anything in particular?
A: No – you can write about any topic you like. But the main point of the competition is that it has to have a surprise ending.
B: Oh – I see. That sounds interesting. I don't think I've ever written a story like that before.
A: Yes – it's something we've introduced for this year's competition.
B: Right. Um – I'm eighteen. Is there any age limit?
A: Yes – you need to be sixteen or over, so if you're eighteen that's fine.
B: Great. So you have the competition once a year. Is that right?
A: Yes – we start advertising in January and the competition takes up a lot of the year. We give people a few months to write their story and then it takes quite a long time to judge all the entries and to announce the winners.
B: I see. So when is the closing date for the competition? It's already April – I hope I'm not too late.
A: No you've still got plenty of time. You need to submit your entry by the 1st of August. After then it will be too late, although you can always enter next year's competition!
B: OK good. So how do I enter?
A: Well we have a website and the best way to enter is to complete the entry form online. We also have more details of the competition on the site. Shall I give you the web address?
B: Yes please.
A: OK – it's www dot C – O – M – P – 4 – S –S dot com. And that's the number four not the word four.
B: OK – thanks. I've got that. So – I can complete the entry form online but how do I send the story? Do I print it out and send it to you?
A: Well you may want to print the story out so you can review it but don't post it to us. When you've finished your story you will need to email it to us. The email address is on the website I gave you.
B: OK – that's fine. *[pause]* Um can you tell me a bit about how the competition is judged and what the prizes are?
A: Yes of course. Well, once we have all the entries I send them to all the judges. Our competition is quite popular so we are lucky to be able to use famous authors who are very interested in the competition.
B: That's fantastic. It's great to know that someone famous will be reading my story!
A: Yes that's right. It takes them quite a while to read through the entries but eventually they decide on the top five stories.
B: I see – and what happens then?
A: Well, they will be published online so everyone can read them. They will not be in any order at this point. They will just be the five stories that the judges think are the best.
B: And do all the top five stories get prizes?
A: No – it's just the top story and the runner-up.
B: So how is the top story decided?
A: Well once the top five stories are available, it will be the public who will vote for their favourite story.
B: Right – I see. So I need to get all my friends to vote for me then!
A: Er, yes – that's a good idea.
B: And what is the prize?
A: Well, the runner-up gets a prize of £300, but the winner gets a trip to Spain to attend a workshop for writers.
B: Wow – that's brilliant! I'd better get writing straight away.
A: Yes – good luck!
B: Thanks.

Listening Section 2

▶ 44

OK – so hi everybody and welcome to the Sea Life Centre. Before you start on your tour I'd just like to give you some information about things to look out for as you go. Well first of all, I guess some of you may have been here before and may be surprised to see the name has changed. We are not called World of Water any more – since the beginning of this summer we've been renamed, and we've also made a few other changes. However, the main attractions like the aquarium, the crocodiles, the penguins and so on are still here. But we have a new restaurant and picnic area and the latest thing that we have – and it was only finished last week – is the splash ride. This is an exciting new area of the centre and is pretty scary and of course you do get a bit wet so make sure you're not wearing your best clothes!

As I said, the main attractions are still here and the most popular thing that everyone wants to see is feeding time, especially for the crocodiles and the seals. We used to have the main feeding time in the afternoon at around 3 pm but we found that some of the animals got a bit hungry waiting until then and so we now have it at noon. They seem much happier with the new time – although it's a bit difficult to know what they're thinking!

Now – I'd like to mention something new that we've introduced this year that we're very excited about. It's called a VIP ticket. The VIP ticket costs an extra £2 per person and you will be amazed at what it allows you to do. With this you'll be allowed to feed the sharks. Now I know that for some people this might be quite a frightening thing to do, but it *is* perfectly safe. For those of you who are a bit unsure, we do have a video you can watch to see what happens. It's a great experience and your friends will be very impressed!

Speaking of friends, I'd just like to remind you that the Sea Life Centre will be more than happy to organise a birthday party for you and your family and friends. If you need more details you can speak to me afterwards and there are also forms at the entrance that you can fill in.

I'd also like to bring your attention to the good work that the Sea Life Centre is doing in support of animal conservation. I am sure you're all aware of the worrying situation with a large number of species facing extinction. Here at the Sea Life Centre we're taking action by asking as many people as possible to sign a petition. Once we have over 5,000 signatures we are planning to send it to the government in the hope that more people will begin to take it seriously.

Right – well there's obviously a lot going on at the Centre, and a lot of things to discover. At all the attractions there is helpful information so please read as much as you can and, if you want to see what you've remembered, please do the quiz after your visit. There are no prizes of course, but I'm sure you'll be surprised by how much you've learnt.

[pause]

So before I leave you all to start your tour, I've just got a few tips. There are a large number of attractions and you may not have time to see them all. Of course, there are the old favourites like the Aquarium and the Crocodile Cave but if you don't have time to see everything make sure you visit Turtle Town, which is beyond the Aquarium and the Seal Centre. This is very special and has a large number of endangered species, and as it's at the far corner of the Sea Life Centre it often gets overlooked. I also have to apologise for the Penguin Park. This has needed some urgent work to be done and so will not be open for the next week. We are very sorry about this but I'm sure you'll find the Seal Centre which is directly opposite it will keep you entertained just as much – if not more!

We're also very busy today as you may have noticed on your way in. Everyone starts here at the Aquarium but as it's so big, there's no waiting to get in. But today we're expecting a lot of people to want to see the Crocodile Cave as a couple of eggs have hatched out. So expect delays there and, if you like, move on to the Seal Centre first and then go back when things are quieter, towards the end of the day.

So I'll leave you now but if you have any questions I won't be far away and have a great time at the Sea Life Centre!

Listening Section 3

45

Martina: Oh hi George, how's it going?

George: Hi Martina, it's going well. How about you? How's university life?

Martina: Well it's great – apart from the studying of course.

George: Yeah – me too! What are you studying? I seem to remember that you were going to do Art. That was your best subject, wasn't it?

Martina: No – not really – I just liked the teacher. He was French and had an amazing accent. My favourite subject was History but I couldn't see what career that would give me.

George: Ah, right. So what did you choose?

Martina: Well I found it really difficult to decide. I was really good at Science but I must admit I never really enjoyed studying it. So, in the end I decided to opt for English which was my second favourite subject and I thought it would be more useful to me than studying anything else. So – that's what I'm doing. Um – how are you finding university?

George: Well – it's a bit of a challenge I suppose.

Martina: Are you finding it difficult?

George: Well, some of it. I'm doing Mechanical Engineering which is really interesting but it covers quite a lot of areas like materials science, machine design, physics and of course mechanics – and they're all fine. But it's maths that I'm struggling with. It's a lot harder than it was at school.

Martina: I can believe it. It all sounds very difficult to me. But then I never was very good at mechanical things. I suppose it must involve some practical work?

George: Well – not at the moment. Currently, it's nearly all theory, so it's a bit heavy-going.

Martina: I guess you need to start with that so that you can get a grasp of the concepts and learn a few facts before you start putting it into practice. It must be a lot different to the course that I'm taking.

George: Yes – but in a few weeks we'll be having a lot more practical experience. In fact, I've got a great assignment this term working on jet engines which means I'll be going on a few field trips to a nearby airport.

Martina: Oh – that's great. It sounds like you're going to be very busy.

George: Yes I'm not sure how I'm going to cope with the work. We have a lot of lectures – and that's fine. The lecturers are very knowledgeable and I learn a lot from them. But we also have a lot of seminars and I find with so many people expressing their views it can get quite frustrating. It would be better if we didn't have so many of those.

Martina: Yes – it's the same for me. *[pause]* Um – how are the students at your place?

George: Well I haven't really met anyone yet. They all seem a bit quiet.

Martina: Perhaps they're working hard – they don't appear to be very studious here, but they are very friendly. I must say I've been doing a lot of sitting around and chatting over the last week or so.

George: Well, that's good. The only person I've spoken to really is my tutor. He's very approachable and seems to understand how difficult it can be starting university.

Martina: It's good to have someone you can talk to. And he may help you meet other students.

George: Actually that doesn't bother me. I'm bound to get to know some people sooner or later. It's more a question of finding out what I need to do, where to go and so on. I hope he can help me with that.

Martina: Oh I would have thought so. Well we certainly have a lot of work ahead of us. It seems like a long time, doesn't it – studying for three years.

George: Yes it does – but I'm sure it'll go quickly. You know I'm really dreading the first assessment.

Martina: Yes – for the course I'm doing we have to hand our first one in at the end of next month.

George: Really – so have you got the topic yet?

Martina: No – but we'll get it soon. I'm not sure how much we have to write yet – not too much, I hope!

George: I know what you mean. And it's hard to study especially where I am now.

Martina: Oh – where are you living?

George: I'm living in a hall of residence. I thought that would be a good idea as there'd be a lot of people around but I'm finding it a bit noisy. I can see that I'm going to have problems when I really need to get down to some work.

Martina: So I guess you need to be somewhere on your own then?

George: Yes – well I do like to have some people around me, so I'd prefer to live with a family somewhere in a house not too far from the university.

Martina: Well good luck with that.

George: Yes thanks – and good luck to you as well. I have to dash now. I've another lecture in ten minutes. Bye for now.

Martina: Bye.

Listening Section 4

46

Hello everyone. You've all been given an assignment for your Sociology course which will involve giving a presentation to the rest of the group. And so, today, I'm going to be giving you a few tips on how to prepare your presentations. This should help you with your current assignment – but a lot of the principles I'll be putting across will be general principles which will, of course, help you with all your future presentations.

So first of all, the most important thing to consider is your audience and in this instance, your audience are the other students in your group. There are three points to bear in mind. Firstly, you need to ask yourself what they need to know; secondly, it's useful to consider whether they'll be supportive or not; and thirdly – will it be a small group, say three or four, a moderate gathering of twenty or so people (as for your current assignment) or will there be hundreds of people? *[pause]* Having said all that, what I'm about to tell you will apply equally to any audience.

So – how do you structure your presentation? Right at the beginning, you should tell them something that forces them to pay attention. This could be something surprising or even shocking but it needs to be relevant! After that, you need a list of items or topics showing them what you'll be covering – rather like an agenda – and then the main part of the presentation will follow. This main part will be the detailed information you'll be presenting and could include facts, statistics, personal experiences, etc. After this you should summarise what you've presented and close with what I call 'next steps'. For this assignment, you could simply point the group to other Sociology reference material. In other cases, you may want to suggest some actions that people can take.

Now – what about the design of the slides for your laptop? Well the important thing here is to be consistent. You need to have the same type of font and use the same colour and size for the same elements. For example, all headers need to look the same, all bullet points need to be presented in the same way. And don't just stick to words. Bring the presentation to life by adding graphics. These could be in several forms such as pictures, flow-charts, diagrams, histograms and so on.

And so – let's move on now to presenting. You have your presentation prepared and you're ready to start. Well – it's important to give a good impression from the start. So take three deep breaths, look at the audience, no matter how frightening they may be, and be enthusiastic and energetic. As you go through the presentation remember to provide some variety in the way you speak. So, for example, you can talk fairly rapidly for information that may be familiar, but then slow down for more unfamiliar sections. And change your tone as you speak – don't keep it at the same level all the way through. As I mentioned, look at your audience. Er, a good tip is to pick people out and look at them for around five seconds. Not looking at the audience gives the impression that you're either not interested in them or terrified of them. Looking too long at one particular person may make them feel rather uncomfortable. There may be points in your presentation that you want your audience to really absorb and in order to make important points stand out you may consider adding silence right after these. It will give people time to reflect on what you've just said. Also – you may be presenting complicated ideas or technical details but try to keep everything as simple as possible. Use simple words and as few as possible. And be clear. If you say something like 'this appears to be', it implies uncertainty. So using weak verbs such as 'appears', 'seems', 'could be', etc. needs to be avoided.

I'll just finish off with a few thoughts on questions and interruptions from the audience. You may choose to invite questions from the audience as you go or ask them to wait until the end. Either way, questions should be encouraged as it provides you with some feedback on how interested the audience is and how well they're understanding you. When a question is asked you need to provide an answer that is as accurate as possible. So initially, my tip is to repeat it. This will ensure you have heard it correctly and will give you a few seconds to gather your thoughts.

Interruptions, on the other hand, can be unwelcome and you may get them for a variety of reasons. It's likely, however, that there's something in your presentation that's unclear or confusing. So my advice is to reduce problems by reading through your presentation beforehand and predicting potential points which could cause interruptions. You may then want to change that part of your presentation or, at least, you will be prepared if someone does interrupt you.

Now, do *you* have any questions ...

Practice Test 3

Listening Section 1

▶ 47

A: Hi – can I help you?
B: Hello – yes, um, is your club taking on new members at the moment?
A: Oh yes – we're always interested in taking on new members. Just give me a moment and I'll get an application form. Right – here we are. So – let's start with your name.
B: It's Harry.
A: OK – and your surname?
B: It's Symonds.
A: Is that like Simon with an 's'?
B: No, um, it's S–Y–M–O–N–D–S. Most people find it rather difficult to spell.
A: I see – it has a silent D. I guess a lot of people miss that. *[pause]* Now let me see – can you tell me when you were born?
B: Yes certainly – the 11th of December.
A: Thanks – and the year?
B: 1996.
A: OK good. Now – are you thinking of becoming a full-time member?
B: Er, probably not. What kind of memberships do you have?
A: Well, we also have off-peak membership which is between 9 and 12 in the morning and 2 and 5 in the afternoon ... and then we do have a weekend membership.
B: So a weekend membership is just Saturday and Sunday?
A: Yes, that's right.
B: OK – well *that's* not going to work for me. It looks like I'll have to be full-time. I'm afraid off-peak membership won't do as I'm not free at those times and I don't just want to be restricted to weekends.
A: OK. I'll make a note of that. *[pause]* Right – we have several facilities at the club including a gym, a swimming pool, tennis and squash courts. What activities are you planning on doing?
B: Well, do you have badminton?
A: Yes we do.
B: And table tennis?
A: I'm afraid not – well not at the moment anyway.
B: Oh – OK. Well I'm also very keen on swimming so I'm glad you have a pool. I'll certainly be doing a lot of that.
A: OK – I've got that. Will you be using the gym?
B: No – I'm not interested in that.
A: OK. So just let me work out what the cost will be ... Yes – that comes to £450 for the year. You can choose to pay annually for the full year or monthly. It's up to you.
B: Oh, I'd prefer to pay regularly in small amounts, rather than have a large amount to pay in one go, if that's OK?
A: Sure – that's fine. Right, I've got the most important details for now.
[pause]
A: So – I'd just like to ask you a few questions about your lifestyle if that's OK with you?
B: Yes that's fine.
A: Um, do you do any regular exercise at the moment?
B: Yes I do a bit.
A: Good – and what do you do?
B: Well every few days I go jogging.
A: Yes – that's good. How long do you go for?
B: Well it varies. I guess it depends on how energetic I'm feeling.
A: Yes of course. Every little bit helps. Um, do you have any injuries at the moment?
B: Well, I did break a bone in my foot playing football a long time ago but that's all healed up now. But, in the last few days I've realised I have a bad ankle. I think I must have injured it last week and it's a bit sore now. But apart from that I'm fine.
A: Right – I guess you might need to rest it for a few days to let it recover.
B: Yes I will.
A: So – let me just ask you what you want to achieve by joining the club. Do you have any targets or goals?
B: Well I suppose my main aim is to build up my fitness level. Is that the kind of thing you mean?
A: Yes – that's fine. All the activities you're going to be doing should certainly help you with that.
B: OK.
A: And could you tell me what you do for a living?
B: Well – I was a student up until recently.
A: OK – so what are you doing at the moment?
B: Well – I'm a charity worker.
A: Oh that's fine. I'll write that down. OK – nearly done. One last question – can I ask how you heard about the club? Did you see it advertised or did you go to our website for example?
B: Well I've been looking for a health club for a while and I asked my friends for suggestions but they weren't much help. And then I was listening to the radio and your club was mentioned, so I thought – I'll go along and see what it's like.
A: Great – well we look forward to having you as a member.

Listening Section 2

▶ 48

Good morning everyone. I hope you're all feeling OK after the activities of the last week or so. I know you've all been working very hard recently and we've been exceptionally busy, especially with the wedding last weekend and the trade fair straight after that. And now we have only three days to prepare for the birthday party this weekend. The events recently have gone extremely well and the hotel is beginning to get a very good reputation, so we need to keep it up. At the moment, we don't have exact numbers of guests and though we usually only cater for groups of less than fifty, we will have quite a few more than that. So – as I said – not sure of numbers but of course we won't go over the maximum of 100. But it's likely that we will need all of you to work this weekend so if any of you can't, please let me know as soon as possible.

Right – so what time will the event start? Well the invitation says guests should arrive between 7.30 and 7.45 but our experience is that there are always a few who like to arrive early so we'll expect the first people at 7.15. As the numbers are quite large, this will certainly be the case. Food will be served at around 8.30 and then, depending on how long the meal takes, the entertainment will start about two hours later. Now, for this, we were expecting a live band for the occasion which is always fun, but apparently this has been cancelled due to illness. So – the hosts know someone who is a comedian who will be replacing the band. We had hoped that the resident magician who worked here through the summer would be able to help out but they weren't keen on that idea.

[pause]

So I'd just like to go through who's doing what when the guests arrive and I think we'll make a few changes from the last party held here. If I remember correctly, it was Olav who co-ordinated the task of providing the guests with drinks or was it Ahmed? *(checking)* Um, I'm not sure – but Gary asked to do it this time – so that will be his job. There's been no decision yet on what the drinks are going to be but I hope they decide soon in case we need to order something special. Now – for receiving the guests' coats and hats, it's important we have someone experienced doing this as we don't want guests losing their belongings. And Monica, last time this was your responsibility. Susan, I know you wanted to do this but as the numbers are quite high for this event I won't make a change here. Right – now last time there was some confusion as to where guests were supposed to go once they had deposited their things and we had guests roaming around the whole hotel. So Ahmed and Olav – I believe you discussed the problems with Susan and thought she would be good at guiding guests after they had arrived – and I'm fine with that.

Right – and now for some general instructions. Once the guests have arrived they will be in and around the lounge area and then at around 8.30 we need to get them to move to the restaurant for their meal. This often proves difficult and can take a long time so I will ring a bell so that everyone knows it's time to eat! Hopefully this will speed things up a bit. Also – for this event there'll be a seating plan, so the guests won't be able to decide for themselves where to sit – they'll have to sit according to the plan. There'll be a plan on each table and I've been thinking about where to put the master plan so everyone can view it before they enter the restaurant. As they'll be spending quite a while in the lounge, I've decided to also put a plan there. This should speed up the start of the meal.

Once the meal starts, you'll all be very busy waiting on the tables and I'm sure I don't need to tell you to be good-humoured and polite to all the guests. The organiser of the event will be saying a few words and so will two of his colleagues. So when the speeches start all activity must stop in the restaurant so that the three people giving them can be heard. This shouldn't take long – and it should be towards the end of the meal. After that, the guests will move back to the lounge for the entertainment.

So – I think that's it. Any questions – come and see me later.

Listening Section 3

▶ 49

Alan: Hi Melanie – what did you think of the assignment that we got today? It looks interesting, doesn't it?

Melanie: Yes Alan, I've always been interested in recycling but there's a lot of research to do.

Alan: Yes – there are a lot of things I'm unsure of so it's going to be good working with you.

Melanie: OK – well why don't we start by making a flow-chart from the notes our tutor gave us?

Alan: Yes, um, so … on one side we could have the paper production cycle – here on the left – and on the other side the recycling.

Melanie: Good idea. Let's start at the top with the production. The first step in the process is to get the raw materials.

Alan: Yes – and they tend to come from pine forests.

Melanie: OK – and then the bark is removed from the outside of the tree and after that the wood is chopped up – that's the first three stages.

Alan: It sounds a bit complicated after that. Um, it says water is added and then the mixture is heated and made into pulp. This will be the thick paste that is used to make paper.

Melanie: Yes – you're right because after that they use a machine to make the paper and we can put that right in the centre of the flow-chart because it's also where the recycled paper joins the process.

Alan: Yes. So once the paper has been produced in the machine, what happens then?

Melanie: Well, I think we should write 'print' as the next step because this is when newspapers, magazines, etc. are produced. And we could also add that they have to be distributed to stores and people's homes.

Alan: Right, then the recycling bit starts. The old paper's collected and then it says it's taken somewhere so that someone or something can sort it. I imagine there are different kinds of paper – or things like paper clips that need to be removed.

Melanie: Yes. Let's have a step after that. Now, how did our tutor say they do this? Oh yes – it involves chemicals, so – how is your chemistry?

Alan: Well – not very good I'm afraid. But this is how they remove ink so – this is definitely going to need a bit of research.

Melanie: Right – the last step in the recycling section is similar to the last step in the production process with heating and pulping – before the cycle begins again.

[pause]

Alan So I think going through the processes helped. Now we need to decide how we're going to do this assignment.

Melanie: Yes. I guess what we need to do is take the processes and divide them up between us. But we could start thinking about an introduction.

Alan: Yes, OK … well I can start doing that. I think I have enough to go on already.

Melanie: Good. And there are a few areas where we need a lot more information. I think I'll start with something easy – let's say the paper collection. I could go to the resource centre to do some research.

Alan: Well I think a better idea would be to approach someone who's involved in the process. What about contacting the council?

Melanie: Oh – good idea. Yes – I'll do that instead. They're bound to have some information. And I know just the thing to add to our work to make it even more interesting.

Alan: And what's that?

Melanie: Well – in my last assignment, I added a few pictures and the feedback I got was that this wasn't 'academic' enough. So what might really bring it to life would be to include some data – provided we can find some.

Alan: Yes – that sounds excellent. Well – we certainly have a lot to do and not much time to do it in.

Melanie: You're right. I think we have about five weeks so I suggest we create a plan of work today. The end of the month is nearly three weeks away and then we have a few days' holiday.

Alan: Yes – so let's see if we can get the first draft done by then so we can take a short break.

Melanie: OK – then after the break we'll have just over a week to complete it. I wonder if we could get someone to review our work for us a few days before the deadline so we can make some final changes. What about your friend Henry?

Alan: Well – the best person would be our tutor. Henry's very good but he's taking a whole week's holiday and there won't be enough time when he returns.

Melanie: OK, then. That's fine.

Listening Section 4

50

Good morning and welcome to this lecture on hair which is a part of the human biology course. This lecture covers a number of facts about hair – its structure and what can affect the general health of hair.

So, first of all, what is hair and why do we have it? If we look back at our ancestors, we'll see that they had a lot more hair on their bodies than we do now. And there are – or were – two main reasons for having hair. One is to provide warmth … but as humans have worn clothes for many years, body hair has significantly reduced. The other is for protection – and again this isn't as significant as it was once, but hair does still benefit areas of the body such as the head and around the eyes.

Now hair, whatever it is for and wherever it is on the human body, is composed mainly of a protein called keratin. This, by the way, is also found in fingernails. In fact, it's keratin which makes them flexible and without it they would be very rigid. Another interesting fact about hair is that it is very strong – as strong as iron in fact. One single strand can support a weight of up to 100 grams. This may not sound all that much, but a full head of hair can support up to 12 tonnes, which is the equivalent of a couple of elephants, which is simply amazing – though I advise you not to put this to the test!

Humans lose up to 100 strands of hair a day, but we do have quite a lot of hair to start with. There's some variation depending on hair colour but for an average adult the strand count is 100,000, so losing 100 a day is not too bad. Although this is the average, people with red hair have around 80,000 strands, black or brown hair 100,000 and blondes have about 120,000.

So hair used to be important for the reasons I mentioned earlier but nowadays I'd say the main importance of hair is the fact that it is big business. Apart from the money involved in haircutting, shaving, trimming, etc., a fortune is spent just on hair products. In the UK alone, consumers spend over five billion pounds each year on these.

[pause]

So next, I'd like to just give you a quick overview of the structure of hair. As you can see, along the length of the hair, there are three main parts called the bulb, the root and the shaft. A single hair is fixed at one end below the skin in the bulb. The bulb acts rather like a cap – it encloses the end of the hair in the head. The next part of the hair is the root and this is the part of the hair which lies just beneath the skin and, in terms of hair production, is the most important. This can be considered the control centre for each strand of hair and is where the glands are found. These produce oil which flows along the length of the hair and the health of the root determines the overall health of the strand of hair. The last part is the shaft and this is the hair which is above the skin and is, of course, what we can see. Fortunately, this is not active and I say 'fortunately' because otherwise it would be very painful to have your hair cut!

And finally I'd just like to go over a few factors that impact on the overall health of hair. Like every other part of the body, our diet – that is what we eat – is extremely important to the condition of our hair. But whereas a change in your diet to, for example, eating unhealthy foods will soon be noticeable in your skin, changes to your hair will take a lot longer. A change in diet today could take several months to have an effect on your hair. And so – what is the key to healthy hair? Well – eating a balanced diet is the most important thing. There are a number of vitamins that are vital for good hair health, the main ones being vitamins C, D and E, and in a balanced diet all these vitamins should be readily available. If you need a boost of vitamin C, for example, one of the best things to eat are blueberries. For Vitamin D, the best examples are fish, mushrooms and eggs and for vitamin E, nuts and seeds.

Right so let's go on to …

Practice Test 4

Listening Section 1

▶ 51

Woman: Hello. Eastwood Community Centre.

Man: Oh, hello. My name's Andrew Dyson. I'm calling about the evening classes you offer.

Woman: OK, Mr Dyson, are there any classes in particular that you're interested in?

Man: Yes, you've got a class called 'Painting with watercolours', I believe.

Woman: That's right. It's a popular class so this term it'll be moving to the hall, so they've got more room.

Man: Right. I know it's on Tuesdays but what time exactly?

Woman: It was 6.30 last term, but let me just have a look at the details. OK, it'll be 7.30 this time, probably it suits more people.

Man: Well, it's my wife who's really interested and that'll be good for her because she's home from work by 7.15 – that'll give her just enough time to get there. Um, what does she need to bring?

Woman: OK, well paints are provided by the tutor, I know that. Um, the information says she'll need just a jar for water – and some pencils for drawing. There are also lots of aprons here, so she needn't worry what she's wearing. And the cost for four classes is £45, including paints, as I said.

Man: OK, now we're both quite keen on the Maori language class.

Woman: There are spaces on the next course, so you could join that.

Man: Oh, good. Which room will that be in?

Woman: When you come in through the entrance of the community centre building, you'll need to go straight up the stairs in front of you, all the way to the top. And it's the small room you'll find there.

Man: I see. All right, and let me just check when it's starting. I heard from someone that the July course has been delayed until August.

Woman: I'm afraid so. And we're halfway through the June course at the moment so there's not much point you taking that.

Man: I guess we'll have to wait, then.

Woman: Well, when you do come, the tutor recommends bringing a small recorder with you just so you can listen again later, and er, the cost for five classes is currently £40.

Man: OK, useful information to know. Um, there's one more class I'm interested in – that's the digital photography class.

Woman: Oh, I've taken that class myself. The tutor's very good. That'll be in room 9 and it's starting in two weeks' time – in the evening – every Wednesday at 6 o'clock.

Man: Um, obviously I need to bring the camera with me. I suppose it'd be useful to have the instructions that go with the camera, too.

Woman: I'd say so. Um, some people bring along a lot of accessories like extra lenses, but there's really no need for this class. It's mainly focusing on composition really, and getting the most out of the basic camera.

Man: That's exactly what I need. And how much does it cost?

Woman: Let's see. For four classes, it's £35, but if you take eight, it works out as £55, so you're making a bit of a saving – £15 that is.

Man: I see.

[pause]

Man: OK, now just another question for the watercolours class; I've just remembered that my wife asked me to find out about the level – who's it for?

Woman: OK, well you don't have to be very skilled or anything like that. It's designed for beginners, actually. People who might see art as a hobby rather than as a professional opportunity.

Man: That sounds like my wife. And er, who do I talk to if I want to find out some more about the Maori language classes?

Woman: Probably best to talk to the tutor directly. He'll be in the office in about half an hour. His name's Jason Kahui. That's K–A–H–U–I.

Man: Good – I'll give him a call.

Woman: Oh, if you do decide to come to the photography class, don't forget to look at your camera battery and make sure it's charged. I know it sounds obvious but I've seen a few people suddenly find the camera's stopped working right in the middle of class.

Man: Yes, I can imagine it'd be easy to forget that. Oh, that reminds me, in the final week of the photography course, is it right that there's a visit to a show in the local area? I work in the city, you see, so I might have to come home early for that one.

Woman: Yes. They'll decide the date once the class has started. Is there anything else I can …

Listening Section 2

▶ 52

Good morning – it's great to see so many people here. Thank you all very much for coming. Well, as you know, the community gardens at Hadley Park are really not looking as good as they should, quite bad really, and although the local council has a budget to deal with *some* of the problems, we do need volunteers for other tasks. If you don't mind, I'm going to divide you into two groups. So, everyone on this side of the room is Group A, and the rest of you are Group B. So, Group A, there are a couple of things we'd like you to help with. Um, first of all, don't worry about any litter or empty bottles you see lying about – one of the local schools has offered to help out with that as part of their own environmental project. The priority for you will be to give us a hand with the new wooden fencing – it needs constructing along parts of the bicycle track, as there are parts which have now fallen down or broken – as

I'm sure you've seen. You've probably also noticed that some of the pathways that come from the bicycle track are quite narrow – and there are plans to make them wider – but the council will be dealing with that later in the year, and they've also promised to produce some informational signs about the plants in the gardens. Hopefully they'll be up in a few weeks' time. The other thing we're doing is getting rid of some of the foreign species that are growing in the gardens and putting back some native plants and trees. So, you'll be doing some digging for us and getting those into the ground.

So, Group A, there's some items you'll need to bring along with you. I *was* going to say 'raincoats' but the forecast has changed so you can leave those at home. I'd definitely recommend a strong pair of boots, waterproof would be best; it's quite muddy at the moment, and your own gloves would also be advisable. Tools will be available – spades and hammers, that kind of thing. You just need to make sure they go back in the trucks. And, there's no need to worry about food and drink as we'll be supplying sandwiches and coffee – possibly some biscuits, even!

[pause]

OK, Group B, your turn. Does everyone have a copy of the plan? Great. OK, we'll all be meeting in the car park – that's on the bottom of the plan, see? Now, if you've been assigned to the vegetable beds, to get there, you go out of the car park and go up the footpath until you reach the circle of trees – there they are – in the middle of the plan, and you see that the footpath goes all the way around them. Well, on the left-hand side of that circular footpath, there's a short track which takes you directly to the vegetable beds. You can see a bamboo fence marked just above them. All right? OK, if you're helping out with the bee hives, pay attention. Look again at the circle of trees in the middle of the plan, and the footpath that goes around them. On the right side of that circle – you can see that the footpath goes off in an easterly direction – heading towards the right-hand side of the plan. And then, the path splits into two and you can either go up or down. You want the path that heads down and at the end of this, you see two areas divided by a bamboo fence – and as we're looking at the plan, the bee hives are on the right of the fence – the smaller section, I mean. Now don't worry – all the bees have been removed! You just need to transport the hives back to the car park. OK, for the seating, look at the circular footpath, at the top of it, there's a path that goes from there and takes you up to the seating area, alongside the bicycle track and with a good view of the island, I suppose. OK, if you're volunteering for the adventure playground area, let's start from the car park again and go up the footpath, but then you want the first left turn. Go up there, and then you see there's a short path that goes off to the right – go down there and that's the adventure playground area, above the bamboo fence. That fence does need repairing, I'm afraid. Right, what else? Oh yes, the sand area. We've got that circular footpath in the middle – find the track that goes east, towards the right-hand side of the plan, and where that track divides, you need the little path that goes up towards the bicycle track. The sand area is just above the bamboo fence there. And finally, the pond area. So, it's on the left-hand side of your plan – towards the top – just above the fruit bushes and to the left of the little path. OK, as I said already, hopefully we'll …

Listening Section 3

▶ 53

Anna: Hi, Robert.

Robert: Hi. Sorry I'm late. I was just printing off some pages about food waste in Britain.

Anna: Do you want to include *Britain* in the presentation? I thought we were concentrating on the USA?

Robert: Well, it is a *global* problem, so I thought we ought to provide some statistics that show that.

Anna: Fair enough. What did you find out?

Robert: Well, I was looking at a British study from 2013. It basically concluded that 12 billion pounds' worth of food and drink was thrown away each year – all of it ending up in landfill sites. Over eight million tons – and that wasn't including packaging.

Anna: An incredible amount.

Robert: Yes, and they were only looking at what households threw away, so there's no information about restaurants and the catering industry. But one thing the study *did* investigate was the amount of milk and soft drinks that were wasted, and I think it was probably quite unique in that respect.

Anna: Interesting. You know, in the other European reports I've read – there's one thing they have in common when they talk about carbon dioxide emissions.

Robert: I know what you are going to say. They never refer to the fuel that farms and factories require to *produce* the food, and the carbon dioxide *that* releases?

Anna: Exactly. We could really cut down on carbon emissions if less food was supplied in the first place. To my mind, the reports talk too much about the carbon dioxide produced by the trucks that deliver the fresh goods to the shops and take the waste away. They forget about one of the key causes of carbon dioxide.

Robert: Absolutely. If the reports are actually going to be useful to people, they need to be more comprehensive.

Anna: Who do you mean by 'people'?

Robert: Well, the government, industries … people making television programmes. Have you seen any documentaries about food waste?

Anna: Not that I remember.

Robert: My point exactly. These days they all seem to be focusing on where your meat, fruit and vegetables are sourced from. We're being encouraged to buy locally, not from overseas. That's probably a good thing but I'd still like to see something about waste.

Anna: Yes, it's the same with magazine articles – it's all about fat and sugar content and the kind of additives and colouring in food – but nothing about how it reaches your table and what happens after it ends up in the bin.

Robert: Well, we've only got 15 minutes for this presentation, so I think we'll have to limit what we say about the consequences of food waste. What do we want to concentrate on?

Anna: Well, I know some of the other presentations are looking at food and farming methods and what they do to the environment, so I think we'll avoid that. *And* the fact that in some countries, people can't afford the food grown on their own farms – that was covered last term.

Robert: OK. We don't want to repeat stuff.

Anna: What concerns me above all else is that in a recession governments should be encouraging business to find ways to cut costs. Apparently supermarkets in the USA lose about 11% of their fruit to waste. That's throwing money away.

Robert: All right – we'll focus on that problem. It should get the others' attention, anyway. Now, how do you want to begin the presentation? Let's not start with statistics, though, because that's what everybody does.

Anna: I agree. How about we give the other students a set of questions to answer – about what they suspect they waste every day?

Robert: I'm fine with that. Probably a better option than showing pictures of landfill sites. It'll be more personalised, that way.

Anna: All right, now let's start …

[pause]

Robert: OK, shall we now have a look at the projects that different researchers and organisations are working on?

Anna: For me, the project I really liked was the one at Tufts University – you know, where they've invented tiny edible patches to stick on fresh foods that show you what level of bacteria is present, and so whether you can still eat it.

Robert: It's a great idea as it tells you if you need to hurry up and eat the food before it goes off. The other good thing about the patches is that apparently they'll be cheap to manufacture.

Anna: Good. Then the other thing I thought was great was the Massachusetts Institute of Technology project.

Robert: I hadn't seen that.

Anna: Well, they've developed these sensors that can detect tiny amounts of ethylene. Ethylene is the natural plant hormone in fruit that makes them turn ripe, apparently. The researchers think that they can attach the sensors to cardboard boxes – and then supermarkets can scan the sensors with a portable device to see how ripe the fruit inside is. That's got to be a quicker way to check for ripeness than taking each box off the shelf and opening it.

Robert: Definitely. And I thought that Lean Path was worth mentioning, too. Their waste tracking technology means that caterers can see how much food is being wasted and why. That'll increase profits for them eventually.

Anna: Yes. And did you read about Zero PerCent? They've produced this smartphone application that allows restaurants to send donation alerts to food charities. The charities can then pick up the unwanted food and distribute it to people in need.

Robert: In the long run, that'll definitely benefit poorer families in the neighbourhood. No kid should go to school hungry.

Anna: I agree. And I read that quite a few local governments in the USA are thinking about introducing compulsory composting in their states – so you can't put *any* food waste into your rubbish bins, just the compost bin.

Robert: Well, I guess that means a bit more work for people. I mean, they have to separate the organic and inorganic waste themselves before they take it out to the compost bin, and you know how lazy some people are! But I guess if we *all* start composting, we'd be doing something positive about the problem of food waste *ourselves*, rather than relying on the government to sort it out. Having said that, not everyone has a garden so …

Listening Section 4

54

Well, good morning everyone. As you know, we've been looking at different kinds of art and craft that were practised by the Maori people of New Zealand – at least before the Europeans began to arrive in the 18th century. So, the focus of this lecture is kite making; how the kites were made, their appearance and the purposes they served.

Well, let's start with the way they were made. As with other Maori artistic traditions, kite-making involved certain rituals. So, firstly, only priests were allowed to fly and handle the largest, most sacred kites. There were rules, too, for the size and scale of the kites that the priests had to follow, and during the preparation of both small and large kites, food was strictly forbidden.

In terms of appearance, kites were frequently designed in the image of a native bird, or a Maori god, and sometimes, perhaps less often, a well-known hero. You can imagine that when Maori first arrived in the new country, in New Zealand, it may have taken some time to find suitable materials for their kites – but through trial and error no doubt, they found plants and trees that provided bark and even roots that they could use to make the frames and wings of their kites. And after the frame had been constructed, the kite then had to be decorated. For this the priests used long grasses, and these – when the kite was in the air – would stream along behind it. They also used a variety of feathers to add, um, colour to their creations. Well, all this meant it was easy to *see* a kite in the sky but you could also *hear* Maori kites. They could be quite noisy indeed, and this was because some priests liked to hang a long row of shells from the kite. You can imagine how they'd rattle and clatter in the wind – how they might completely capture your attention. As I said before, the most common image was probably a bird, and that's the same for other kite-making cultures, but the kites were designed in particular shapes – so there were kites that were triangular, rectangular and also shaped like a diamond. And some of them were so large, it would actually require several men to operate them. Um, some of the kites were also covered in patterns, and to make these patterns, the Maori used different pigments of red and black, and these were either made from a charcoal base or from red-brown clay which had been combined with oil obtained from a local species of shark.

Now, before I forget, if you have a chance, do visit the Auckland Museum because they have the last surviving 'birdman' kite on display. This is the kind of kite that has a wooden mask at the top of the frame – it's a mask of a human head – and you can clearly see it has a tattoo and also a set of teeth. Quite impressive – and a good example of Maori craftsmanship and symbolism.

Right, turning to the purpose and function of the kites, they certainly had multiple uses. Primarily, the flying of kites was a way of communicating with the gods and when the kites rose into the air, the Maori used them to deliver messages – perhaps requesting a good harvest, good fortune in war, a successful hunting expedition. So, these kites were incredibly valuable to a community – treasured objects that one generation would pass to the next. People would also fly kites for other reasons, for example, to attract the attention of a neighbouring village. This was done when a meeting was required between Maori elders – a convenient method, indeed. And finally, when it comes to war, there are traditional stories that describe how when a Maori warrior found himself surrounded by his enemies, a kite could actually provide the possibility of escape – the kites were powerful enough to take a man up into the air; and for this reason, they could also be used to lower him into enemy fortifications so that an attack could begin from the inside.

Well, I'm happy to say there seems to be a revival and growing interest in kite-making, and …

Practice Test 5

Listening Section 1

▶ 55

Staff member: Hello. City Transport Lost Property. How can I help you?

Woman: Oh, hello. Yes, I'm, er, calling about a suitcase I lost yesterday. I don't suppose I'll get it back but I thought I'd try.

Staff member: Well, some people do hand lost items in so you might be lucky. Let's put the details into the computer.

Woman: OK.

Staff member: Right, so, let's start with a description of the suitcase.

Woman: OK, well, it's small, and it's the type you can pull along on wheels.

Staff member: How about the colour?

Woman: Yes – it's black but not exactly plain black – it has some narrow stripes down it, sort of grey. Actually – no, they're *white* now I think about it.

Staff member: OK, I'll just add that information. Now were there any items inside it?

Woman: Yes. I had a big bunch of keys in there. Luckily my assistant manager has an identical set so she's going out this morning to get some copies made.

Staff member: So, they're for your office?

Woman: That's right. My house keys were in my pocket, thank goodness.

Staff member: Anything else?

Woman: Um, there were a lot of documents, but they're saved on my laptop anyway, so, er, they don't matter so much. But the thing I'm really worried about – I mean, I haven't even taken it out of the box yet – is a camera I just bought. That's really why I'm calling. I can't believe I've lost it already.

Staff member: I see. Well, let's hope we can find it for you. Was there anything else?

Woman: I don't think so.

Staff member: Any credit cards?

Woman: They were in my handbag. And I had my passport inside my jacket pocket.

Staff member: Money, clothing, any personal items?

Woman: Oh, let me think. I had an umbrella. It was black, no blue, but obviously that isn't as important as the other things.

Staff member: No, but it all helps us identify your property and get it back to you. Anyway, I just need to ask you for some basic details about your journey. So it was yesterday, was it?

Woman: That's right. In the afternoon – around 2 pm, maybe 2.30.

Staff member: OK. So that'd be May the 13th.

Woman: Yes. I was heading to Highbury. That's where I live.

Staff member: All right, and you mentioned a passport, I think. So you were coming from the airport, I presume.

Woman: Yes – and I was looking forward to getting home so much – and what with being tired and everything – I think that's why I just forgot about the case.

Staff member: And how were you travelling when you lost your property? I mean, what kind of transport were you using?

Woman: I thought about getting the train, but that would have meant a bus journey as well, and I couldn't be bothered so I decided to take a taxi eventually. That's where I must have left it.

Staff member: Well, that's good news in a way. It's more likely that a driver would have found it and handed it in.

Woman: I hope so.

Staff member: Well, I need your personal details now. Can I have your full name, please?

Woman: Yes. It's Lisa Docherty. I'll spell that for you. It's D–O–C–H–E–R–T–Y.

Staff member: Thank you. And next, if I could have your address – the best address to send you the property if we manage to locate it?

Woman: Sure. It's number 15A River Road – and that's Highbury, as I said.

Staff member: Thank you. Just a moment. There's just one final thing – that's your phone number.

Woman: I guess my mobile would be best. Er, hang on, I can never remember my own number. OK, I've got it. It's 07979605437.

Staff member: Very well. I think that's everything we need at this end. I'll have a look at the data on …

Listening Section 2

▶ 56

Welcome to everyone here. I hope you enjoy your stay in our village and enjoy the local scenery. I'll tell you a bit about the forest and mountain tracks in a minute, but first, I'll just give you an idea of where everything is in the village. So, we're here in the tourist information centre, and when you come out of the centre, you're on Willow Lane, just opposite the pond. If you want to get to the supermarket for your supplies of food and water, go right, that's the quickest way, and then turn right at the top of Willow Lane, and it's the second building you come to, opposite the old railway station. If you're planning on doing some serious climbing and you need some equipment, we do have an excellent climbing supplies store just five minutes' walk away. Turn left once you're outside the tourist information centre, take Willow Lane all the way up to Pine Street – you want to go left along here – then keep walking and go past Mountain Road on your right, until you come to the next turning on the left – head down there, and you'll come to the climbing supplies store. If you get to the small building that sells ski passes, you'll know you've gone too far. You also need to head to Pine Street for the museum – it's small but well worth a visit if you're interested in the history of the village and the old gold mining industry. So, when you reach Pine Street from here, you'll see the old railway line on the other side of the road – turn left into Pine Street, and keep going until you come to Mountain Road, and just up here, the museum will be on your left, just behind the railway line. Don't worry about crossing over the tracks. The trains stopped running through here in 1985. If you're planning on following one of the easier forest walks, you might like to hire a bicycle. To get to the hire shop, again you need to head to Pine Street. On the left-hand side of Pine Street, you'll see the Town Hall, go down the little road that you come to just before it, and you'll find the bike hire shop just behind the hall. They have a good range of bikes so I'm sure you'll find something that suits your needs. Last but not least, if you're hungry after a long day's trek I can recommend our local café. Again, when you leave the tourist information centre, turn right and follow Willow Lane until it joins Pine Street – and right opposite – on the far side of the railway tracks – is the café.

[pause]

OK, let me tell you a little bit about the different tracks we have here. All of them start at the end of Mountain Road – and you'll find a parking lot there where you can leave your vehicles. Let's start with North Point track. It's a gentle route through lowland forest – good for biking and probably the one for you if you have small children. There's a wooden hut where you can stay at the end of the track but be aware that it's really just an overnight shelter, and you'll need to take your own sleeping bags and cooking equipment. Another option is the Silver River track. As the name suggests, you'd be following the river for most of the way, and you get to see some of our beautiful native birds, but the track also goes through a densely forested area. Unfortunately, the signposting isn't very good in places and you do need good map-reading skills to avoid becoming disoriented, which happens to visitors a little too frequently, I'm afraid. Valley Crossing will take you through some stunning scenery but there are several points along the way where you'll need the level of fitness required to get over some pretty big rocks. Stonebridge is one of the shorter tracks, but very steep as it takes you up to the waterfall, and you do need to be in good condition to manage it. Lastly, the Henderson Ridge track will take you all the way to the summit of the mountain. Do bear in mind, though, that at this time of year the weather is very changeable and if the cloud suddenly descends, it's all too easy to wander off the track. It's best to check with us for a weather report on the morning you think you want to go. On the way to the summit, there's a hotel which provides comfortable rooms and quality meals, so it's worth climbing all …

Listening Section 3

57

Tutor: Well James, I've had a look over your case study and for a first draft, it looks promising.

James: I have to be honest, when you told us we had to write about a furniture company, it didn't sound like the kind of thing that would interest me, but since then, I've changed my mind.

Tutor: Why's that?

James: Well, as you know, *Furniture Rossi* is an Australian company, still comparatively small compared to some of the high street stores, but it's got plans to expand into foreign markets. So I chose it for that reason. It's going through a transition – it's a family-run business aiming to build a global brand.

Tutor: All right, and you've made that clear in your writing. One thing, though, that I think you've overlooked is why Luca Rossi started a furniture company here in Australia in the first place.

James: Well, he'd just got an arts degree, hadn't he? And people were trying to talk him into an academic profession but he wanted a practical job – something he thought would be more satisfying in the long run. His grandfather had been a craftsman. He'd made furniture in Italy and he'd passed this skill on to Luca's father, and well, Luca thought he'd like to continue the tradition.

Tutor: Yes, that was the motivation behind his decision. And what was it, do you think, that gave *Furniture Rossi* a competitive edge over other furniture companies?

James: I wouldn't think it was price. It's always been at the higher end of the market, but according to my research, it was to do with the attitude of the employees – they were really focused on giving good customer service.

Tutor: Yes, Luca Rossi insisted on that. Their promotional campaigns also emphasised the fact that the wood only came from Australian forests, but that was the case with their rivals, too, so it wouldn't have made them stand out. OK, we'll have a careful look at the *content* of your case study in a minute, but I just want to make a general comment first, before you start writing your second draft.

James: OK.

Tutor: Yes, what I'd like to see more of is your opinion, a bit more critical thinking, rather than the bare facts. But it's good to see you've been careful with your referencing, this time.

James: Thanks. And I read and re-read my work so I'm pretty sure there aren't any errors with the language.

Tutor: Yes, it's fine. Oh, but there's one other thing I could probably mention at this point.

James: Yes?

Tutor: Well, at the end of term, you'll also be giving a presentation – also on *Furniture Rossi*.

James: Yes, I haven't given it much thought yet.

Tutor: Understandably. But, while you're writing the case study, I'd recommend you think about what kind of information would be suitable to use in your presentation. Remember – the last time you gave a presentation on a company, you spent a considerable part of the time providing the audience with financial data, but they probably needed to hear more about company strategy.

James: Yes, I did concentrate rather too much on the figures. I'll make sure there's a balance this time.

Tutor: Good.

[pause]

Tutor: OK, so let's just think about the content of your case study – the history of *Furniture Rossi*. I see here in paragraph four you're talking about how Luca Rossi raised the capital for his new business venture – and then you're talking about the customer base growing much wider – but what was it that prompted this growth?

James: Well, that was to do with the quality of the furniture products that the company was selling. People loved that it was all hand-made and would last.

Tutor: And because demand from customers kept growing?

James: Well, then Rossi needed to take on more craftsmen so they could make sure the orders were ready on time, and then, he also had to set up two new warehouses to make distribution quicker.

Tutor: Yes. And from there, the company really grew. But think what happened next. They started looking at ways to increase their profits and called in a consultant. And what he saw immediately was that the infrastructure was completely outdated – they were paying three full-time admin staff just for data-entry. So he recommended they upgrade their software programs and that, in turn, cut operational costs and just speeded everything up.

James: I'm surprised they didn't get on to that earlier, but I suppose Luca Rossi was more interested in the design aspect, rather than the finance side of things.

Tutor: Yes, I imagine that's why he eventually turned the day-to-day running of the company over to his son. And in fact, it was the son, Marco, who persuaded his father to move on from traditional television advertising and go online instead.

James: I guess that's the best way to reach people.

Tutor: It can be, but initially, customers actually complained.

James: Why?

Tutor: Well, some users found it hard to navigate their way around the website – so they were getting frustrated and giving up. So then the company called in a professional to improve it.

James: I see. He must have done a good job. They've had a continuous three-year rise in revenue – so things must be going well.

Tutor: Indeed. And what of the future?

James: Well, I probably need to talk about this a bit more in the concluding paragraphs, don't I? Consumers are already aware of the quality of the furniture, that's for sure, but I think the company is aiming to publicise their values – the fact that they have respect for beauty, durability and functionality, and the environment. A lot of companies are already …

Listening Section 4

▶ 58

Hello everyone and welcome. As part of this series of lectures on the development of early humans, today we are looking at rock art: the paintings and drawings produced by prehistoric peoples as they spread across the continents. If you've been lucky enough to look at a piece of rock art close up, you'll know it's an experience that makes you wonder about the passage of time and our own history. But rock art also has a practical value for researchers and let's start by considering why that is. Firstly it provides vital information about the way that people evolved – information not always easily obtainable from excavated artefacts alone. Secondly, rock art tells us about migration: where people came from and where, perhaps, they went next. Rock art is found all over the world and this in itself is not surprising. But what is rather amazing, you might think, is how similar some images are, whether you're looking at a rock face in South Africa or standing inside a cave in Spain. Let me give you an example. When our ancestors drew humans, they would often draw them as stick figures, but if they drew a face, then the eyes were almost always very prominent – very open and wide. And of course, animals are very common in rock art, but one animal which is very interesting to researchers is the lizard, because whenever you see a prehistoric painting of one – it's depicted either in profile or looking down on it from above. And these drawings are produced by people of totally different cultural backgrounds. Amazing. But how can this be the case – that similar artistic styles exist in such distant locations? In the past archaeologists believed that trade must have brought people together, and that it gave them the opportunity to observe each other's culture, including art styles, but this didn't prove to be the case.

Recently researchers have come up with a new theory. They believe that the brains of our ancestors evolved to notice certain images before others and this was important – actually essential because in an environment full of constant danger, it was necessary for survival. So the need to quickly recognise things that could be helpful or harmful could have had a great influence on rock art and explain why some images are more common across cultures than others. Later on, there would have been other reasons why communities produced art – certainly for spiritual and social purposes and no doubt for political ones, too, as different tribes looked for allies and struggled against their enemies.

Well, as I said before, you can find rock art all over the world, but I'd like to focus now on the rock art of the Aboriginal people of Australia. The images that survive in this part of the world span at least 20,000 years. In fact, the Aborigines were still practising this art form in the late 18th century, when the Europeans began to arrive, and certain images point to the contact between them. For example, the Aborigines began to draw ships which they would have seen along the coast – it's hard for us to imagine what they must have thought when these first began to appear. Another image that is evidence of European arrival is that of horses; an animal that would have been very alien to the Australian landscape. Um, it isn't actually known how many sites there are across Australia where rock art can be found – but unfortunately we do know that much of the art is being lost to us. Erosion, of course, is one of the key reasons for its destruction, but human activity is also increasingly responsible. Since the 1960s, industry alone has destroyed around an estimated 10,000 pieces of art. At this rate, in 50 years, half of all Australian rock art could have disappeared for good. Vandalism is sadly another factor. And although most people, I believe, would wish to preserve this art, I'm afraid that tourism is another reason why the art is disappearing. In some cases, the art is damaged when …

Practice Test 6

Listening Section 1

59

Agent: Fairfield Rentals. Andrew Williams. How can I help you?

Woman: Oh hello. I'm calling from the UK – um, my family are moving to Canada early next year, and we're hoping to find somewhere to rent in Fairfield for the first six months while we settle in.

Agent: Right, I see. Well, let's get your details.

Woman: Yes, my name's Jane Ryder.

Agent: OK, Jane. And can I have a phone number – the best number to get you on?

Woman: Well, that'd probably be our home number – so 0044 for the UK, and then it's 208 613 2978.

Agent: Alright. And an email address, please, so we can send you out all the information and forms.

Woman: I think it's best if I give you my husband's email – he's sitting in front of a computer all day so he can print stuff off and get it back to you sooner than I could. It's richard@visiontech.co.uk. I'll just spell the company name for you. That's V–I–S–I–O–N–T–E–C–H.

Agent: Great. And we have a question here about occupation.

Woman: Richard's an IT specialist for an advertising company. They're transferring him to their Fairfield branch.

Agent: Actually, just *your* job for now, thanks.

Woman: Me? I'm a doctor at the hospital in our town.

Agent: OK, I'll put that down. Now, what kind of accommodation are you looking for? House, apartment?

Woman: An apartment, probably, as long as it has two bedrooms. There'll be me, my husband and our ten-year-old son.

Agent: And so with an apartment, you're less likely to get a garden.

Woman: That's OK.

Agent: But what about a garage – is that something you'll want the apartment to have?

Woman: Yes, that's definitely important.

Agent: OK, just a moment, I'll just make a note of that.

Woman: But – er before we go on – I should probably say now that what we don't need is any furniture – because we'll be shipping all that over, and I don't really want to pay for storage while we're waiting to buy a house.

Agent: Not a problem. I'll make a note of that.

Woman: Actually, though, just thinking about the kitchen, what can I expect from a rental property? I mean, what kind of equipment is provided?

Agent: Well, the normal thing is that you get a stove – I think that's a cooker in British English.

Woman: OK, good to know, but how about a fridge? We'll be selling ours before we come, so if possible, we'd like the apartment to have one for when we arrive.

Agent: I can certainly add that to the form. If there's any other whiteware that you need – like a dishwasher for example, there are plenty of stores here that'll arrange delivery on the same day as purchase.

Woman: Thanks. Hopefully we won't need to buy too many things.

Agent: Now, how about location? Have you done any research into the Fairfield area?

Woman: Not that much so far.

Agent: Well, you mentioned you have a boy – I imagine you'd like to be fairly close to a school.

Woman: Good idea. That would help. What's public transport like in Fairfield? Is it easy to get around?

Agent: The bus service is pretty comprehensive – there are plenty of local routes, services into the city and out of town.

Woman: OK, and for a two-bedroom apartment – what sort of rent should we expect to pay?

Agent: Well, looking at the properties we have at the moment, prices start from around £730 per month, and – depending on the area – can go up to £1,200.

Woman: That's too much. Something halfway would be better.

Agent: So, would your limit be, say, £950?

Woman: I'd say so, yes.

Agent: Can I ask if you smoke or if you have any pets?

Woman: No to both questions. But I do have one more request, please.

Agent: Yes?

Woman: Well, I've also been offered a job – at Victoria General Hospital – and I suspect I'll be working nights occasionally – so what I really need from any apartment is for it to be quiet – so I can catch up on sleep if necessary during the day.

Agent: Congratulations on the job offer. I'll add your request to the form. Well, what I'll do is compile a list of suitable properties for you and send them via email. Um, can I just ask – how did you hear about us? Obviously not from our commercials if you're living in the UK.

Woman: Actually, it was a friend of ours. He spent a few months in Fairfield a couple of years ago and he pointed us in the direction of your website.

Agent: Well, it's good to be recommended. So, what I'll do is …

Listening Section 2

60

Well, good afternoon. I'm Constable James McDonald, and as you may know, I'm the community police officer for the local area. That means that – as part of my job – I try to get out in the community as much as possible – talk to the people that live in this neighbourhood – people like yourselves – and make sure there's an effective level of communication between the public and the police – hence the reason for this meeting. There have been several burglaries in the area in the last few weeks and I'd like to talk about ways you can keep your home and property safe.

So, I'd suggest that a good way to start is by talking to your neighbours and exchanging contact details with them. This'll allow you to get in touch immediately if there's anything suspicious happening next door. Then, make sure you have a good discussion about the best course of action to take in case of emergency – make sure everyone is clear about what to do and who to call. If you plan ahead, this'll prevent uncertainty and even panic should anything happen later. Another thing that I would advise you to do is always leave your radio playing – even when you go out. And if you keep your curtains closed, burglars are less likely to try and break in because they can't be sure whether someone's home or not. Now, none of us want to be in the situation where we can't get into our own home, but do take time to think where the best and safest place is to leave your spare keys. Putting them under the door mat or anywhere near the front door is just asking for trouble. You'd be surprised how many people actually do this – and it makes life really easy for burglars. All these things will help keep your community safe and will cost you nothing. However, if you are going to spend some money, what I'd recommend more than anything else is that you invest in some well-made window locks for your house. This will give you peace of mind.

[pause]

OK, moving on. Unfortunately, there's been an increase in the number of minor crimes and anti-social behaviour in the general area and I want to talk about some specific prevention measures that are being proposed. First of all, the skate park. As you probably know, it's well used by younger people in our community but unfortunately we're getting more and more reports of broken glass – making it especially dangerous for younger children. One possible solution here is to get rid of some of the trees and bushes around the park – making it more visible to passersby and vehicles. If the vandals know they're being watched, this might act as a deterrent. As you will have heard, a couple of local primary schools have also been vandalised recently – despite the presence of security guards. The schools don't have the funds for video surveillance – so we need people in the neighbourhood to call their nearest police station and report any suspicious activity immediately. Please don't hesitate to do this. I expect most of you are familiar with the problems facing Abbotsford Street. It seems that no amount of warning signs or speed cameras will slow speeding drivers down. I'm happy to say, however, that the council have agreed to begin work over the next few months to put in a new roundabout. What else? Oh, yes. The newsagent and the gift shop on Victoria Street were both broken into last week, and although no money was taken, the properties have suffered some serious damage. Access was gained to these shops through the small alleyway at the back of the properties – it's dark and as you can imagine, no one saw the thief or thieves in action. So, we've been advising shop owners along there about what kind of video recording equipment they can have put in – we'll then be able to get evidence of any criminal activity on film. The supermarket car park is also on our list of problem areas. We've talked to the supermarket managers and council authorities and we've advised them to get graffiti cleaned off immediately and get the smashed lights replaced. If you don't deal with this sort of thing at once, there's a strong possibility that the activity will increase and spread, and then it becomes …

Listening Section 3

61

Karina: Hi, Mike. How's it going?

Mike: Actually, I was up last night with an assignment so – yeah, I'm tired, but I guess we'd better sort this presentation out.

Karina: Well, we've done enough background reading, but I think we need to organise exactly *what* we're going to say about biofuels during the presentation, and the order.

Mike: I thought we could start by asking our audience what car engines were first designed to run on – fossil fuels or biofuels.

Karina: Nice idea.

Mike: Yes, when most people think about cars and fuel, they think about all the carbon dioxide that's produced, but they don't realise that that wasn't always the case.

Karina: You're probably right. The earliest car engines ran on fuel made from corn and peanut oil, didn't they?

Mike: Yes. The manufacturers used the corn and peanut oil and turned them into a kind of very pure alcohol.

Karina: You mean ethanol?

Mike: Yes. In fact, most biofuels are still based on ethanol. Actually, I've got some notes here about the process of turning plant-matter *into* ethanol – the chemical reactions and the fermentation stages and …

Karina: It's interesting – the other students would appreciate it, but different biofuels use different processes and if we give a general description, there's a risk we'll get it wrong, and then the tutor might mark us down. I'd rather we focus on the environmental issues.

Mike: Fair enough. So, um – the main plants that are used for biofuel production now are sugar cane, corn …

Karina: And canola. Of all of them, canola is probably the least harmful because machines that use it don't produce as much carbon monoxide.

Mike: Sugar cane seems to be controversial. It doesn't require as much fertilizer as corn does to grow, but when they burn the sugar cane fields, that releases loads of greenhouse gases.

Karina: Yes, but some critics have suggested that the production of corn ethanol *uses up* more fossil fuel energy than the biofuel energy it eventually *produces*. For that reason, I'd say it was more harmful to the environment.

Mike: I see what you mean. You're probably right. It's interesting how everyone saw the biofuel industry as the answer to our energy problems, but in some ways, biofuels have created *new* problems.

Karina: Well, in the USA, I wouldn't say that farmers are having problems – the biofuel industry for them has turned out to be really profitable.

Mike: I think, though, that even in the USA, ethanol is still only used as an additive to gasoline, or petrol. The problem is that it still has to be transported by trucks or rail because they haven't built any pipelines to move it. Once they do, it'll be cheaper and the industry might move forward.

Karina: That'll have to happen one day. At least the government are in *favour* of biofuel development.

Mike: Yes. But Brazil's probably in the lead as far as biofuels are concerned – they've got to the point where they don't need to import any oil now.

Karina: Which is great, and the industry in Brazil employs a huge number of people, but is it sustainable? I mean, as the population grows, and there are more vehicles on the roads and there's more machinery, surely they can't depend so much on sugar cane? At some point, there has to be a limit on how much land can be used for sugar cane production – certainly if you want to preserve natural habitats and native wildlife.

Mike: I think that whatever problems Brazil's facing now – the same will be true for any country – you have to weigh up the pros and cons.

Karina: Well, we probably won't see an increase in biofuel use – I mean, they won't replace fossil fuels until we can find ways to produce them cheaply and quickly and with less cost to the environment.

Mike: … making sure they require minimal energy to produce.

Karina: Exactly. And in a way that means they have to cost less than fossil fuels – certainly when you're filling up your car.

Mike: Yes, and whatever other kind of engines use fossil fuels at the moment.

[pause]

Karina: Alright, so in the last section of the presentation, what problems are we focusing on?

Mike: Well, we've already had a look at different types of pollution in the first section, so we can leave that out, but the biggest issue related to biofuels is that land is now being used to grow biofuels crops – and that's contributing to global hunger.

Karina: Indeed. It doesn't seem right we're using corn to run cars when people can't afford to buy it to eat. Yes, let's talk about that. The other thing is that in some countries, the way that biofuel crops are grown and harvested still produces a great deal of pollution – really damaging to the atmosphere.

Mike: OK, that's definitely an issue we should look at.

Karina: Let's not finish on a negative note, though. Why don't we talk about the potential new sources of biofuel – so rather than corn and sugar cane – what other plants could be used?

Mike: Good. Some companies are exploring the possibility of using wood, and seeing how that can be used to make ethanol.

Karina: Yes, and algae is another possibility. You can grow it in any water and it absorbs pollutants, too.

Mike: I read that. And grasses. They're another plant that researchers are investigating as a biofuel.

Karina: And these kind of plants aren't used as food, which is why …

Listening Section 4

▶ 62

Good morning. Today we're thinking about the way that technology is influencing our social structures and the way we interact with one another. Humans, as we know, have always lived in groups; without this arrangement, our species would have died out long ago. But now, the way we see and define our group is changing.

I'd like to start by mentioning the research of American sociologist Mark Granovetter in 1973. It was Granovetter who first coined the term 'weak-ties', which he used to refer to people's loose acquaintances – in other words, friends-of-friends. His research showed that weak-ties had a significant effect on the behaviour and choices of populations – and this influence was something highly important in the fields of information science and politics, and as you can imagine, marketing also. So, these friends-of-friends, people we might spend time with at social or work gatherings, might not be like us but they can still have a positive influence because we share the same sort of interests. That's enough to make a connection – and this connection can turn out to be more beneficial than we might suspect. An example of this, an example of how the connection can influence us, is when our weak-ties get in touch and pass on details about jobs they think might be suitable for us. Well, since Granovetter first came up with this theory, his work has been cited in over 19,000 papers. Some of these studies have looked at how weak-tie networks are useful to us in other ways, and one thing that seems to improve as a result of weak-tie influence is our health.

[pause]

Today, our number of weak-tie acquaintances has exploded due to the Internet – to the phenomenon of online social networking. This is still a relatively new way of communication – something that has a huge amount of potential – but also, as with any invention, it brings with it a new set of problems. Let's start with the benefits. Without question, online social networking allows us to pass on the latest news – to be up-to-date with local and global events – and for many, this information comes from sources more trustworthy than local media. So, this is one clear point in favour of online social networking. I know that it's also being used by students – as a means of increasing their chances of success – in the way that lecture notes can be shared and ideas discussed. I think, personally speaking, that we need some further research before we can definitively say whether it helps or not. There's also been a great increase in the number of networking sites devoted to sharing advice on health issues but there are as yet no studies to prove the reliability of that advice. Now, what we *do* have clear evidence for is that people are developing friendships and professional networks in a way that wasn't possible before – the process is faster. I'm not talking about *quality* here, but simply that they exist. And it's debatable whether the number of online friends that you have increases your level of self-confidence – that's perhaps an area of research some of you might be interested in following up.

Turning to the problems, there are any number of articles connecting online activity to falling levels of physical fitness – but it's too easy to blame the Internet for our social problems. The poor grades of school children are also frequently linked to the time spent on social networking sites, but it would be naive to believe there are no other contributing factors. One real concern, however, is the increase in the amount of fraud. Where for example, people are using the personal data of others, which they've put online, for criminal purposes. This kind of activity seems likely to continue. And then, certainly for employers, online social networking sites have provided a great time-wasting opportunity – reducing productivity like never before, and I doubt they can put a stop to this habit, no matter what restrictions are in place.

We'll come back to these issues in a minute, but I'd like to say something about the theories of Robin Dunbar – an anthropologist at Oxford University. Dunbar has found that the human brain has evolved in a way that means we can only give real attention to a particular number of people. 150, apparently. So, for example, if the number of friends on your online network is greater than that, according to Dunbar, this would imply the relationships are only superficial. Dunbar is not *against* online relationships, but he maintains that face-to-face interaction is essential for the initial *creation* of true friendship and connections. He's concerned that for young people – if their only experience of forming relationships is online – this doesn't allow them to form the ability or acquire the strategies for maintaining relationships, for example, in situations where negotiation or diplomacy is required, or where it's essential for ...

Practice Test 7

Listening Section 1

63

Julie: Hi Nick. It's Julie. Have you managed to find any information about accommodation in Darwin?

Nick: Hi. I was just going to call you. I've found some on the Internet. There are quite a few hostels for backpackers there. The first possibility I found was a hostel called Top End Backpackers.

Julie: OK.

Nick: It's pretty cheap, you can get a bed in a dormitory for nineteen dollars per person. Private rooms cost a bit more, but we'll be OK in dormitories, won't we?

Julie: Sure.

Nick: So that hostel has parking, though that doesn't really matter to us as we'll be using public transport.

Julie: Yeah. Are there any reviews on the website from people who've been there?

Nick: Well, yes. They aren't all that good though. Some people said they didn't like the staff, they had an unfriendly attitude.

Julie: Mmm. That's quite unusual in a hostel, usually all the staff are really welcoming.

Nick: That's what I thought. People said they liked the pool, and the fact that the rooms had air-conditioning, but the problem with that was that it was very noisy, so they were kept awake. But it was too hot if they turned it off, so they had to put up with it.

Julie: Someone told me there's another hostel called Gum Tree something.

Nick: Gum Tree Lodge. It costs a bit more, forty-five dollars a person.

Julie: What?

Nick: Oh, no, that's for private rooms, it's twenty-three fifty for the dorms.

Julie: That's more like it.

Nick: It looks to be in quite a good location, a bit out of town and quiet but with good transport, and quite near a beach.

Julie: Has it got a pool?

Nick: Yes, and its own gardens. The reviews for that one are mostly OK except for one person who said they couldn't sleep because there were insects flying around in the dormitories.

Julie: Not for me then. And I'd rather be somewhere central really.

Nick: Right. There's a place called Kangaroo Lodge. They've got dorms at twenty-two dollars. And it's downtown, near all the restaurants and clubs and everything, so that should suit you. And it doesn't close at night.

Julie: So there's always someone on reception. That sounds good.

Nick: The only criticism I saw was that the rooms were a bit messy and untidy because people just left their clothes and stuff all over the beds and the floor.

Julie: Don't hostels usually have lockers in the bedrooms where you can leave your stuff?

Nick: Yeah, they do usually, but apparently they don't here. Still, hostels are never particularly tidy places, so that doesn't bother me. And the same person said that the standard of cleanliness was pretty good, and especially the bathrooms, they were excellent as far as that went.

Julie: Right. Yeah, I reckon Kangaroo Lodge sounds the best.

Nick: Me too. Quite a lot of people reviewing it said it was really fun there, like every night everyone staying there got together and ended up having a party. So it sounds like it's got a really good atmosphere.

Julie: OK, let's go for that one.

[pause]

Julie: Did you get the address of Kangaroo Lodge?
Nick: Yes ... it's on Shadforth Lane.
Julie: Can you spell that?
Nick: S–H–A–D–F–O–R–T–H. It's near the transit centre where the intercity buses and the airport buses drop you off.
Julie: Cool. I'm really looking forward to this. I've never stayed in a hostel before. Do they provide bed linen – sheets and things?
Nick: Yeah. And you can usually either bring your own towel, or hire one there, but they don't usually provide those for free.
Julie: OK. And what happens about meals?
Nick: Well, you don't have to pay extra for breakfast. It varies a lot in different places but generally it's OK. And there's usually a café where you can buy a snack or a hot meal for lunch. But actually if you're really travelling on the cheap, usually for every five or six rooms there's a kitchen where you can knock up a snack, and that saves a lot of money.
Julie: Great. Right, well shall I go ahead and book that ...

Listening Section 2

64

Hello everyone and welcome to the Anglia Sculpture Park. Right, well, the idea behind the sculpture park is that it's a place where works of art such as large sculptures and carvings can be displayed out of doors in a natural setting.

As you'll have noticed when you drove here, most of the land around the park is farmland. The park itself belonged to a family called the De Quincies, who had made a lot of money from manufacturing farm machinery, and who also owned substantial stretches of forest land to the north of the park. They built a house in the centre of the park, not far from where we're standing now, but this burnt down in 1980 and the De Quincies then sold the land.

The Anglia Sculpture Park isn't the only one in the country; several of the London parks sometimes display contemporary sculptures, and there are a couple of other permanent sculpture parks in England. But we're unique in that some of our sculptures were actually created for the sites they occupy here, and we also show sculptures by a wider range of artists than anywhere else in the country.

For example, at present we have an exhibition by Joe Tremain, of what he calls 'burnt' sculptures. These are wood and stone sculptures that he's carved and marked with fire to illustrate the ferocity and intensity of the forces that have shaped our planet over millions of years. They look really dramatic in this rural setting.

To see some of the sculptures, you'll need to follow the path alongside the Lower Lake. We had to renovate this after the lake overflowed its banks a couple of months ago and flooded the area. The water level's back to normal now and you shouldn't have any trouble, the path's very level underfoot.

You should be back at the Visitor Centre at about four o'clock. If you have time it's worth taking a look at the Centre itself. It's not possible to go upstairs at present as builders are working there adding another floor, but the rest's well worth seeing. The architect was Guy King. He was actually born in this part of England but he recently designed a museum in Canada that won a prize for innovation in public buildings.

If you want to get something to eat when you get back, like a snack or a sandwich, the Terrace Room is currently closed, but you can go to the kiosk and buy something, then sit on one of the chairs overlooking the Lower Lake and enjoy the view as you're eating.

[pause]

Now, let me just tell you a bit about what you can see in the Sculpture Park. If you look at your map, you'll see the Visitor Centre, where we are now, at the bottom, just by the entrance. Since we only have an hour, you might not be able to get right around the park, but you can choose to visit some of the highlights.

You might like to take a look at the Joe Tremain sculptures which are displayed on this side of the Upper Lake, just behind the Education Centre and near the bridge. They're really impressive, but please remember not to let your children climb on them.

One of our most popular exhibitions is the Giorgio Catalucci bird sculptures – they're just across the bridge on the north side of Lower Lake. I love the way they're scattered around in the long grass beside the lake, looking as if they're just about to take to their wings.

You could also go to the Garden Gallery. It's on this side of the Upper Lake – from the Visitor Centre you go to the Education Centre, then keep on along the path, and you'll see it on your right. There's an exhibition of animal carvings there which is well worth a look.

We also have the Long House – that's quite a walk. From here, you go to the bridge and then turn left on the other side. Soon you'll see a winding pathway going up towards the northern boundary of the park – go up there and you'll find it at the top. They have some abstract metal sculptures that are well worth seeing if you have time.

OK well now if you're ...

Listening Section 3

65

Leo: Anna, I wanted to ask you about my marketing report. I'm not sure about it ...
Anna: That's OK, Leo. So what do you have to do?
Leo: Choose a product or service then compare two organisations that produce it. I'm doing instant coffee.
Anna: But haven't you got a weekend job in a clothing store? Why didn't you choose clothing?
Leo: That was my first thought, because I thought it'd give me some practical examples, but when I searched for men's clothing on the Internet there were hardly any articles. So then I looked for coffee and I found there were tons.
Anna: Yeah, there are so many brands on the market now. OK, so how much have you actually written?

Leo: I've done part one, on economic and technological factors. I found some good data on technological changes, how in Australia fewer people are buying instant coffee because of cheap coffee percolators that they can use to make real coffee at home.

Anna: But there's also a movement away from drinking coffee …

Leo: … switching to things like herbal teas instead because they think it's healthier? But that's not really to do with technology, it's more cultural. Anyway, for part two I'm comparing two instant coffee companies, CoffeeNow and Shaffers, and I've made this table of products.

Anna: Right. Let's see … so you've got the brand names, and prices and selling size, and descriptions. OK, the table looks good, you'll get marks for research there. Where will it go?

Leo: In the section on the marketing mix, under 'Product'.

Anna: Not in the appendix?

Leo: No.

Anna: OK, but it's too factual on its own, you need to add some comment in that section about the implications of the figures.

Leo: Right, I'll do that. Now I want to say that I think that Shaffers is more of a follower than a leader in the coffee industry. Now, I'm putting that in the section on market share. Does that seem OK?

Anna: Let's see … so you've begun by explaining what market share is, that's important, but you've got to be careful how you give that opinion.

Leo: Do you think it should go in another section?

Anna: Well, it's fine where it is but you've got to back it up with some data or they'll say your report lacks weight.

Leo: OK. One thing I'm worried about is finding anything original to say.

Anna: Well, since this is your first marketing report, you're not expected to go out and do interviews and things to collect your own data, you're just using published data. So the analysis you do might not throw up anything that people didn't know before. But the focus is more on how you *handle* the data – I mean, you might take something like a graph of sales directly from a website, but what makes your work original is the perspective you provide by your interpretation of it.

Leo: Oh. You know, it's all so different from business studies assignments at school. It's really surprised me.

Anna: What, how much research you have to do?

Leo: I expected that. It's more … I knew exactly what I had to do to get a good grade at school – and I knew I'd be expected to go more deeply into things here, but I haven't got information on how the lecturer is going to grade my work – what he's looking for.

[pause]

Anna: Well, one thing you have to remember is that in a marketing report you've got to have what they call an executive summary at the beginning. I forgot that and I got marked down.

Leo: Yeah, I've drafted it. I've got an overview.

Anna: Have you got something about the background there?

Leo: Yeah.

Anna: Good.

Leo: So I've just made a summary of the main points. I wasn't sure whether or not I should have my aims there.

Anna: No, that's too personal. The executive summary is just, like, what a manager would read to get a general idea of your report if he was in a hurry.

Leo: Right. Then I'm OK for the first main part, all of the macroenvironment stuff, but it's when I get onto the problems section … I've listed all the problems that CoffeeNow and Shaffers are facing, but then what?

Anna: Well you have to prioritise, so indicate the main problems, and then you analyse each one by connecting it with a theory … that's where your reading comes in.

Leo: OK.

Anna: Have you done your implementation section yet?

Leo: I've thought about it – so that's where I write about what could be done about the problems.

Anna: Yes, and it's got to be practical so don't forget to specify things like who would be involved, and the cost, and the order that things would be done in.

Leo: Right. Well that shouldn't take long.

Anna: You'd be surprised. Actually that's the bit that tends to get badly done because people run out of time. That and the conclusion …

Leo: Any hints for that?

Anna: Well, it's got to draw out the main points from your report, so it's got to be quite general. You need to avoid introducing new stuff here, it's got to sum up what you've said earlier.

Leo: OK. Thanks Anna. That's been a big help.

Listening Section 4

66

An interesting aspect of fireworks is that their history tells us a lot about the changing roles of scientists and technicians in Europe. Fireworks were introduced from China in the 13th century. Up to the 16th century they were generally used for military purposes, with rockets and fire tubes being thrown at the enemy, but they were also sometimes a feature of plays and festivals where their chief purpose was related to religion.

By the 17th century, the rulers of Europe had started using fireworks as a way of marking royal occasions. Technicians were employed to stage spectacular shows which displayed aspects of nature, with representations of the sun, snow and rain. These shows were designed for the enjoyment of the nobility and to impress ordinary people. But fireworks also aroused the interest of scientists, who started to think of new uses for them. After seeing one firework display where a model of a dragon was propelled along a rope by rockets, scientists thought that in a similar way, humans might be able to achieve flight – a dream of many scientists at the time. Other scientists, such as the chemist Robert Boyle, noticed how in displays one firework might actually light another, and it occurred to him that fireworks might provide an effective way of demonstrating how stars were formed.

Scientists at the time often depended on the royal courts for patronage, but there was considerable variation in the relationships between the courts and scientists in different countries. This was reflected in attitudes towards fireworks and the purposes for which they were used. In London in the middle of the 17th century there was general distrust of fireworks among scientists. However, later in the century scientists and technicians started to look at the practical purposes for which fireworks might be employed, such as using rockets to help sailors establish their position at sea.

It was a different story in Russia, where the St Petersburg Academy of Science played a key role in creating fireworks displays for the court. Here, those in power regarded fireworks as being an important element in the education of the masses, and the displays often included a scientific message. Members of the Academy hoped that this might encourage the Royal Family to keep the Academy open at a time when many in the government were considering closing it.

In Paris, the situation was different again. The Paris Academy of Sciences played no role in staging fireworks displays. Instead the task fell to members of the Royal Academy of Painting and Sculpture. As in Russia, the work of the technicians who created the fireworks was given little attention. Instead, the fireworks and the spectacle they created were all designed to encourage the public to believe in the supreme authority of the king. However, science was also enormously popular among the French nobility, and fashionable society flocked to demonstrations such as Nicolas Lemery's display representing an erupting volcano. The purpose of scientists was basically to offer entertainment to fashionable society, and academicians delighted in amazing audiences with demonstrations of the universal laws of nature.

[pause]

In the course of the 18th century, the circulation of skills and technical exchange led to further developments. Fireworks specialists from Italy began to travel around Europe staging displays for many of the European courts. The architect and stage designer Giovanni Servandoni composed grand displays in Paris, featuring colourfully painted temples and triumphal arches. A fireworks display staged by Servandoni would be structured in the same way as an opera, and was even divided into separate acts. Italian fireworks specialists were also invited to perform in London, St Petersburg and Moscow.

As these specialists circulated around Europe, they sought to exploit the appeal of fireworks for a wider audience, including the growing middle classes. As in the previous century, fireworks provided resources for demonstrating scientific laws and theories, as well as new discoveries, and displays now showed a fascinated public the curious phenomenon of electricity. By the mid-18th century, fireworks were being sold for private consumption.

So the history of fireworks shows us the diverse relationships which existed between scientists, technicians and the rest of society …

Practice Test 8

Listening Section 1

▶ 67

Cathy: Hello, Hilary Lodge retirement home, Cathy speaking.

John: Hello, my name's John Shepherd. Could I ask if you're the manager of the home?

Cathy: That's right.

John: Oh, good. Hello, Cathy. A friend of mine is a volunteer at Hilary Lodge, and I'd like to help out, too, if you need more people. I work part-time, so I have quite a lot of free time.

Cathy: We're always glad of more help, John. Shall I tell you about some of the activities that volunteers get involved in?

John: Please.

Cathy: Well, on Monday evenings we organise computer training. We've got six laptops, and five or six residents come to the sessions regularly. They're all now fine at writing and sending emails, but our trainer has just moved away, and we need two or three volunteers who can help the residents create documents. Just simple things, really.

John: I'd certainly be interested in doing that.

Cathy: Great. Then on Tuesday afternoons we have an informal singing class, which most of the residents attend. We've got a keyboard, and someone who plays, but if you'd like to join in the singing, you'd be very welcome.

John: I work on Tuesdays at the moment, though that might change. I'll have to give it a miss for now, I'm afraid.

Cathy: OK. Then on Thursday mornings we generally have a session in our garden. Several of our residents enjoy learning about flowers, where they grow best, how to look after them, and so on. Is that something you're keen on?

John: I'm no expert, but I enjoy gardening, so yes, I'd like to get involved. Do you have your own tools at the home?

Cathy: We've got a few, but not very many.

John: I could bring some in with me when I come.

Cathy: Thank you very much. One very important thing for volunteers is that we hold a monthly meeting where they all get together with the staff. It's a chance to make sure we're working well together, and that everyone knows how the residents are, and what's going on in the home.

John: Uhuh.

[pause]

Cathy: Now obviously we'd need to get to know you before you become one of our volunteers.

John: Of course.

Cathy: Could you come in for an informal interview – later this week, maybe?

John: I'm busy the next couple of days, but would Saturday be possible?

Cathy: Certainly. Just drop in any time during the day. I won't be working then, so you'll see my assistant, Mairead.

John: Sorry, how do you spell that?

Cathy: It's M–A–I–R–E–A–D. Mairead.

John: OK, got that. It's not a name I'm familiar with.

Cathy: It's an Irish name. She comes from Dublin.

John: Right. And the road that Hilary Lodge is in is called Bridge Road, isn't it?

Cathy: That's right. Number 73.

John: Fine.

Cathy: Oh, one other thing you might be interested in – we're holding a couple of 'open house' days, and still need a few volunteers, if you're available.

John: What are the dates?

Cathy: There's one on April 9th, and another on 14th May. They're both Saturdays, and all-day events.

John: I can certainly manage May 14th. I've got another commitment on April 9th, though.

Cathy: That would be a great help. We're having several guest entertainers – singers, a brass band, and so on – and we're expecting a lot of visitors. So one possibility is to help look after the entertainers, or you could spend an hour or so organising people as they arrive, and then just be part of the team making sure everything's going smoothly.

John: Well, shall I show people where they can park?

Cathy: Lovely. Thank you. One reason for holding the open house days is to get publicity for Hilary Lodge locally. So you may find you have someone from a newspaper wanting to interview you. They'll want to find out from two or three people why they volunteer to help at the home. We're trying to get a TV station to come, too, but they don't seem very interested.

John: I don't mind being interviewed.

Cathy: Good. Well, if you come in for a chat, as we arranged, we'll take it from there. Thank you very much for calling.

John: My pleasure. Goodbye.

Cathy: Bye.

Listening Section 2

▶ 68

Hello. As some of you know, I'm Elaine Marriott, the head of the college's Learning Resource Centre. We've invited all of you taking evening classes and leisure activities to come and see the changes we've made to the Centre in the last month.

One major change we've made here on the ground floor is to the layout – as you can see from looking around you. I'm sure you'll recognise the desk – that's still in the same place, as it has to be just inside the door. But you'll see that there are now periodicals on the shelves in the corner behind the desk. We've brought them nearer the entrance because so many people like to come in just to read magazines. We now stock a far wider range of periodicals than we used to, so we've decided to separate them from newspapers. This means the newspapers are now just the other side of the stairs, near the study area.

Now, another thing is that we've brought the computers downstairs – people used to complain about having to go upstairs to use them. So they're now at the far side of the building on the right, in the corner overlooking the car park.

We've now got an extra photocopier, so as well as the one upstairs, there's one down here. You can see it right opposite the entrance, by the wall on the far side.

The biggest change, though, and one I'm sure many of you will welcome, is that we now have a café at last – we've been asking for one for years. If you turn right as soon as you get past the desk, you'll see the door ahead of you. It became possible to have a café because the building has been extended, and we've now got a new office and storeroom area.

What else should I tell you about before we walk round? Oh yes, we've had so many requests for books on sport that we've bought a lot more, and they're all together immediately to the right of the entrance.

[pause]

OK, that's enough on the new layout. We'll walk round in a moment, but before we do, something about the people who are here to help you. Of course all the staff will do their best to answer your questions, but now we're each going to specialise in certain areas. So if you ask a staff member about something, and they don't think they can help you enough, they'll direct you to our specialist.

Jenny Reed is the person to see if there are any films you'd like us to stock, as she's taken over responsibility for purchasing those. I'd better warn you that our budget is limited, so I'm afraid we can't promise to buy everything you ask for!

Phil Penshurst can help you to improve your writing if you need to produce reports for your course. You can book a half-hour session with Phil to start with, then if you want more help, he'll arrange follow-up sessions with you.

I must mention Tom Salisbury. Many people are interested in doing research or just reading about this region – the people, occupations, changes over the years, and so on. Tom is a specialist in this particular field, so if you want any help, he can point you in the right direction – we've got a large collection of relevant documents, from old maps to studies of the wildlife.

We have a new member of staff, Saeed Aktar. I'm sure you'll meet him soon, and will find him very helpful. If you're unemployed and want some advice on the practical aspects of looking for a job, Saeed is the person to talk to. He's also written a very useful book on the subject, which of course we've got on our shelves!

Many of you will know Shilpa Desai, who's been working here for about five years. Shilpa now has the additional responsibility of giving information and advice on anything to do with housing, such as finding out what's available, or whether you're eligible for financial help.

Right, well that's quite enough from me, so let's walk round the library.

Listening Section 3

▶ 69

Tutor: Right Stewart, well I've read your draft report on your work placement at the Central Museum Association. Sounds as if you had an interesting time. So you ended up making a film for them?

Stewart: Yeah. It was a film to train the employees in different museums in the techniques they should use for labelling ancient objects without damaging them. Some of them are really fragile.

Tutor: OK. So in your report you go through the main stages in making the film. Let's discuss that in a little more detail. You had to find a location – somewhere to shoot the film.

Stewart: That took quite a few days, because I had to look at different museums all over the country, but I'd allowed time for it. And even though it was the middle of winter, there wasn't any snow, so I didn't have any transport problems.

Tutor: Right. Did you have to decide what equipment you'd need for the filming?

Stewart: Yes. I think they were quite surprised at how well I managed that. It was just the luck of the draw actually, I'd done that project with you last year …

Tutor: Oh, on recording technology? So you knew a bit about it from that, right.

Stewart: Yeah. What I found really hard was actually writing the script. I had a deadline for that but the Association had to extend it. I couldn't have done it otherwise.

Tutor: Would it have helped if you'd had some training there?

Stewart: I think you're right, I probably needed that, yeah.

Tutor: Right. Now from your draft report it sounds as if you had one or two problems deciding who was going to actually appear in the video.

Stewart: The casting? Yeah. I'd expected that the people who worked for the Association would be really keen on taking part …

Tutor: But they weren't?

Stewart: The thing was, they were all so busy. And it did mean some of them had to travel. But Janice King, who I was reporting to for the project, she was great. She arranged for people to have time off and for their work to be covered. So that was a big help for me.

Tutor: Right. And it sounds like the filming itself went well. I gather you found a company who provided an online introduction to the techniques.

Stewart: Yeah. It was really informative, and very user-friendly. I learned a lot from it.

Tutor: And then the editing?

Stewart: For that, the Association put me in touch with someone who works for one of the big movie companies and I went down to the studio and sat with him in front of his computer for a day, learning how to cut and paste, and deal with the soundtrack and so on.

Tutor: So was that all?

Stewart: No, I didn't include this in my draft report but I had to design the cover for the DVD as well … the lettering and everything.

Tutor: Have you done any of that sort of design work before?

Stewart: No, but I did a rough draft and then talked it through with a couple of my mates and they gave me some more ideas, and when I'd finished it, I showed it to the people who worked at the Association and they really liked it.

Tutor: Excellent.

[pause]

Tutor: Now as well as your own draft report, I've also received some written evaluation from the Association on the work you did during your placement, and how it was of benefit to them. I noticed that you haven't included anything on that in your report yet.

Stewart: How my project benefited the Association, you mean? So do I have to include that?

Tutor: Yes.

Stewart: Well, let's think … I suppose if I hadn't made the film for them, they'd have had to get an outside company to do it. But because I was actually working for the Association, I'd got much more of a feeling for what their aims are. Things like their responsibility for the conservation of the exhibits. I don't think an outside company would have had that understanding, they'd have been more detached.

Tutor: Right. And the Association also said that because of your background, you had a good idea of where to go to get the best deal for the equipment you needed. They said the saving in expense made it worthwhile even though sourcing it took quite a bit of time.

Stewart: Yes, that's true.

Tutor: The Association also said making the film had a very positive effect in getting staff to work together more closely.

Stewart: Oh. I hadn't heard that. That's good. And certainly, people weren't afraid to tell me what they thought about it as I was making it, so I was able to get lots of feedback at every stage. That was useful for me but it also meant the final product worked better for them.

Tutor: Can you think of any other benefits?

Stewart: Well, I don't think they'd really thought out what they'd do with the film once it was made. I made quite a few suggestions for the distribution – other people we could send it to as well as museum staff.

Tutor: Yes, they mentioned that. OK, good, well it sounds like they certainly …

Listening Section 4

70

I'm going to talk today about research into a particular species of bird, the New Caledonian crow, whose natural habitat is small islands in the Pacific Ocean. And it seems that these crows are exceptionally resourceful.

Using sticks or other tools to find food isn't unknown among birds and animals. Some chimpanzees, for example, are known to bang nuts on stones, in order to break the shell and get at the edible kernel inside. One New Caledonian crow, called Betty, bent some straight wire into a hook and used it to lift a small bucket of her favourite food from a vertical pipe. This experiment was the first time she'd been presented with wire, which makes it very impressive. Another crow, called Barney, has demonstrated his skill at using sticks to forage for food.

In one research project, scientists from New Zealand and Oxford set captive New Caledonian crows a three-stage problem: if they wanted to extract food from a hole, the crows first had to pull up a string to get a short stick, then use that short stick to remove a long stick from a toolbox, and finally use the long stick to reach the food. Amazingly, they worked out how to do this successfully.

Further experiments carried out at Oxford suggest that crows can also use sticks as tools to inspect all sorts of objects, possibly to assess whether or not they present a danger. The idea for the experiment came from observing the birds using tools to pick at random objects, such as a picture of a spider that was printed on some cloth. In this research, five pairs of crows – including Barney – underwent tests to see how they would react to a variety of objects, which were carefully chosen so the birds wouldn't be tempted to view them as a possible source of food. As a further precaution, all the crows had been fed beforehand.

On eight occasions, a bird's first contact was by using a tool. In all three trials, Barney began by using a stick for inspection. One involved a rubber snake. First he approached it, but didn't touch it, then retreated to pick up a stick. He then prodded it with the stick. After some more investigation, he discarded the stick and carried on pecking at the snake more confidently – apparently convinced that it wouldn't move.

In other experiments, two different birds, called Pierre and Corbeau, also made a first approach with tools on three separate occasions. Pierre used a short piece of woodchip to touch a light which was flashing, and Corbeau was seen prodding a metal toad with a stick.

Significantly, the crows tended to use the sticks only to make their first contact with the object. Subsequently, they either ignored the object or dropped the tool and pecked at the object – which is very different from using the tool to get access to food.

[pause]

So what conclusions can be drawn from the research? Evidence is building up from experiments such as these that the birds are able to plan their actions in advance, which is very interesting for understanding their cognition. They don't seem to be responding in a pre-programmed sort of way: it may even be possible that they're able to view a problem and work out what the answer is. However, a major difficulty is assessing whether this tool-using behaviour is a sign of intelligence. To some extent, this is related to the ecological circumstances in which the animal is found.

So scientists want to find out much more about how the crows behave in their native habitat, and a team from Exeter and Oxford universities is carrying out research in New Caledonia. They're looking into whether the birds' way of searching for food gives them any possible evolutionary advantage. The birds are hard to observe, as they live in a region of mountainous forest, so the researchers have attached tiny cameras to the tails of some birds, as one method of investigating their behaviour.

The birds are masters at using sticks to find their food, in particular beetle larvae from the trees. It's possible that the birds can derive so much energy from these grubs that they only need to eat a few each day. This would mean that they wouldn't have to spend most of their waking time searching for food, as most animals do.

The beetle larvae have a distinct chemical make-up, which can be traced through the feathers and blood of birds that eat them. Scientists have collected samples from crows in order to estimate the proportion of larvae in their diet. They should then be able to gauge the extent to which individual birds depend on using sticks to feed themselves.

We've learnt a great deal about the ability of New Caledonian crows to use tools, and some very interesting research is being carried out into them.

Answer key

Listening skills

1 Getting ready to listen

1 Understanding the context

1.1

1 C **2** E **3** B **4** D

(Contexts A and F are not needed.)

1.2

1 two speakers (a man and his daughter)
2 one speaker (a woman)
3 three speakers (two students and their lecturer)
4 one speaker (a student)

2 Using the correct spelling

2.1

1 F
2 LL
3 M
4 T, C
5 CH, SH

2.2

1 Browne
2 Beeton
3 kickers
4 Rose
5 HLP 528

2.3

Conversation 1
a Is that spelt the same as the colour?
b Yes, but with an E at the end.
Conversation 2
c Sorry, was that last letter N or M?
Conversation 3
d That's right, all one word and all lower case.
Conversation 4
e Oh, it's the Rose Hotel, like the flower.
Conversation 5
f It's just three letters and three numbers. It's HLP 528.

3 Writing numbers

3.1

a 3rd
b $10.50
c 6th
d 70
e 19
f 15
g 62
h £110
i 31st
j 27th

3.3

1 £95
2 $15
3 width: 3.5 / three and a half / 3½
height: 2½ / two and a half / 2.5
4 B $55
5 29th July / 29 July / 29.7 / 7.29

3.4

Suggested answers

	other numbers	reason incorrect
1	£80 £105	this is the amount she paid last time this is the full price
2	$10 $5	this is what regular students pay this is the extra fee charged for equipment
3	1.5 (metres) 1 (metre) 3 (metres)	this is the width of his car this is how much space you need between cars this is the height he would prefer
4	$25 $45	this is a child's fare this is an adult's fare
5	14th July 1st August	this is the first available date this is her father's birthday

3.5

1 B **2** C **3** B **4** A

2 Following a conversation

1 Identifying the speakers

1.1

	people	description	information wanted
1	travel agent	older female	The customer would like information about (good offers on) skiing trips.
	customer	younger male	
2	hotel receptionist	younger female	The receptionist needs to find out the guest's personal details.
	guest	older male	
3	interviewer	older male	The applicant would like to know about travel and working hours.
	job applicant	younger male	

1.2

Conversation 1
1 coach
2 insurance

Conversation 2
1 C
2 B

Conversation 3
1 America
2 marketing

1.3
Conversation 1
1 travel agent
2 customer
Conversation 2
1 both people give the answer
2 hotel receptionist
Conversation 3
1 interviewer
2 job applicant

2 Identifying function
2.1
1 **What about** getting her a new bike?
2 **That's right**. We arrive on 22nd July.
3 That sounds great. **Let's do that**.
4 **I don't think** I'd enjoy that one.
5 You said you'd prefer to have the party outside, **is that right**?
6 **Actually**, it's just gone up to $250.
7 **Now, what about** accommodation? Where would you like to stay?

2.2
1 D **2** E **3** A **4** C **5** G **6** B **7** F

2.3
1 A **2** C **3** B **4** C

2.4
a 1	**e** 1	**i** 2	**m** 1
b 2	**f** 2	**j** 2	**n** 1
c 1	**g** 1	**k** 2	**o** 2
d 2	**h** 2	**l** 2	**p** 1

3 Understanding categories
3.1
accommodation	tent cabin flat
transport	tram ferry coach
entertainment	theatre cinema concert
food	picnic barbecue buffet
drink	juice lemonade coffee

3.2
250 computer/two hundred and fifty computer

3.3
- two hundred and fivety computer ✗ (the number is spelt incorrectly)
- 250 computer ✓
- two hundred and fifty computers ✗ (there should be no 's' on *computer* – it's an adjective here)
- over 250 computer ✗ (this is two words not one; *over* is not necessary because *more than* is already in the sentence.)
- 250 computer experts ✗ (this is two words not one; *experts* is not necessary because it is already in the sentence)
- over 250 experts ✗ (this is two words not one; the words *over* and *experts* are not necessary)
- two hundred and fifty computer ✓
- 250 ✓

3 Recognising paraphrase
1 Identifying distractors
1.1
1 18th July
2 Wednesday
3 recycling
4 funds

1.2
The distractors are:
1 19th, 20th, 21st
2 Tuesday, Thursday, Friday
3 environment, pollution
4 equipment, volunteers

2 Recognising paraphrase
2.1
1 d **2** e **3** a **4** f **5** h **6** b **7** c **8** g

2.2
1 A **2** A **3** C **4** B

2.3
1 A	a place to stay	accommodation /hotel	✓
B	their airfares	flights	They'll do it in the morning.
C	car hire	transport	They'll borrow a car.
2 A	improve the shade	plant trees	✓
B	remove plants	take out	They don't want to do this.
C	add a water feature	pond	They already have one.
3 A	do more research	(find) information	They have plenty.
B	make some cuts	reduce any of it	They don't want to do this at all.
C	add some visual effects	include graphics	✓

4 A	how snow forms in different conditions	process; is created	They already know this.
B	the effect that snow has on our climate	influences weather patterns	✓
C	the effect different clouds have on snow	impact	They want to do the opposite – see if snow affects clouds.

3 Selecting from a list

3.1

(The key information is underlined.)

What TWO disadvantages of the new mobile phone does the speaker mention?

A it isn't very user-friendly
B it is very expensive
C it can't take photographs
D it has a short battery life
E it is quite big

3.2

A	it isn't very user-friendly	4
B	it is very expensive	5
C	it can't take photographs	2
D	it has a short battery life	3
E	it is quite big	1

3.3

A it isn't very user-friendly
✗ (it is easy to use)
B it is very expensive
✓
C it can't take photographs
✗ (it can take very good photos)
D it has a short battery life
✓
E it is quite big
✗ (it has a big screen but this is not a disadvantage – it still fits in your pocket)

(B and D are the two correct options.)

4 Places and directions

1 Describing a place

1.1

A an escalator
B a fountain
C a hill
D a pond
E traffic lights
F a roundabout

1.3

1 a market
2 a tree, a fountain, a play area (swings)
3 at the bottom on the left
4 a tree

1.4

1 A **2** B **3** C **4** A

1.5

1 lifts, entrance, toilets	• The entrance is over there on your left • Then go straight ahead • The shop you want is opposite the toilets • Next to the lifts
2 circular courtyard, entrance, tree	• In the middle of the resort, you'll see a • To the right of the courtyard, you'll find a • It's just behind the tree
3 river, motorway	• I was thinking of putting it right in the middle • I think it would be better if it's at the eastern end of the motorway
4 bushes, pond, tree	• … it is unable to live in the area of a pond • … it does need to live in fairly close proximity to water • … in a tiny burrow surrounded by bushes

2 Following directions

2.1

B

2.2

Some useful phrases are underlined in the script below.

A: Can you tell me how to get to the supermarket?
B: Sure, let me have a think. We're in Bridge Street now and it's in Queens Road.
A: Oh, the only street I know is Riverside Street, I know my hotel's on the corner there.
B: That's right. You need to go up Bridge Street as far as the traffic lights, then turn right. That's Riverside Street.
A: I see.
B: Then you walk along there to the next set of traffic lights and you'll be at Queens Road. You turn left there and it's the second shop on your left.
A: Thanks very much!

3 Labelling a map

3.1

Useful landmarks: information, the entrance, the toilets, the barbecue, the tree and the playground.

3.2

1 F **2** B **3** D **4** A

The following are incorrect:

C ticket booth (it is complimentary now so there is no need to pay; complimentary = free)
E second-hand book stall (there are no books or second-hand goods for sale)

5 Listening for actions and processes

1 Understanding mechanical parts

1.1

1 a pipe
2 a wheel
3 a pump (handle)
4 a spring/coil
5 (storage) tank/s
6 a grill / grille / filter

1.2

A 5 **B** 4 **C** 1 **D** 3 **E** 6 **F** 2

1.3

1 two

1.4

1 D **2** E **3** B **4** C

1.5

The incorrect answers are:
F (he wanted to put one on but he couldn't find a way to attach it);
A (a cooling fan is not necessary because it is elevated and so doesn't overheat).

1.6

turn, pop, hold, wind, generate, wrap, pull, explode, push, rotate, activate

2 Describing an action or process

2.1

2 through

3 upside down

4 along

5 beneath

6 around

7 upwards

8 diagonally

2.2

A thermometer (it is used to measure temperature)
B calculator (it is used to calculate / work out figures)
C scales (they are used to weigh things)
D speedometer (it is used to measure / calculate speed)

3 Describing a process

3.2

Here's how to wrap a present. First, gather together all of the things you need: wrapping paper, sticky tape, scissors, some ribbon and, of course, a present. Then, **1 place** your present on the opened wrapping paper and **2 cut** a suitable amount using the scissors. Next, **3 wrap** the paper around the present and **4 stick** it down with sticky tape. Then, neatly **5 fold** up each of the ends of the paper and **6 stick** them down. Finally, **7 tie** the ribbon around your present. It's now ready to present!

6 Attitude and opinion

1 Identifying attitudes and opinions

1.1

1 b **2** a **3** b **4** a **5** b **6** c **7** b **8** c

1.2

1 agree up to a point
2 really valid point
3 not so sure
4 absolutely right
5 hard to believe
6 highly unlikely
7 doubtful
8 sound of that at all

1.3

1 d **2** g **3** e **4** f **5** c **6** b **7** a

1.4

C

1.5

surprising: astonishing; amazing; alarming
unsurprising: to be expected; typical

2 Persuading and suggesting

2.1

3 The presentation sections will be in order. The decisions in the box will not be in order.

2.2

1 D **2** A **3** B **4** F

2.3

reduce the length = cut (something); leave (something) out
method = way
write some more = include something else
interesting = grab (someone's) attention; enjoyable; exciting
check = verify
current data = the very latest information
advantages = benefits
disadvantages = negatives

2.4

(Suggested answers)

make a suggestion: *let's … shall we?; Why don't we …; maybe we should …; perhaps we could …; I'd like to propose …; I think we should …; Should we …?*

agree with an idea: *Of course; Great idea; I agree; Agreed; that would be better; let's give it a try; Absolutely*

disagree: *I don't think we should …*

3 Reaching a decision

3.1

(Suggested answers)

Section 1: distance, cost, convenience, availability

Section 3: to get help, to find out more, to make it presentable

3.2

Section 1: C
Section 3: C

3.3

(Suggested answers)
Section 1:
... but the fare is so expensive.
That's true.
It might be cheaper but ...
That would be great.
Yes. I'm sure she ...

Section 3:
I don't think we need to ...
You're right.
But I'd rather do that after ...
I don't want to show him that.
OK. Let's ...

7 Following a lecture or talk

1 Identifying main ideas

1.1

- The very first field trip I went on (5)
- It's an ancestor of the modern Australian wombat (3)
- I found a funny-looking piece of rock (6)
- an old professor studying dried-up dinosaur bones (1)
- I immediately changed courses (4)
- I had to do a compulsory unit on extinction (2)

1.2

b

1.3

These points are directly related to the main purpose of the talk:

- I had to do a compulsory unit on extinction (this was how he first became interested in palaeontology)
- I immediately changed courses (this is when he first began to study palaeontology)
- I found a funny-looking piece of rock (this was what encouraged him to continue his palaeontology studies)

These points give additional information that is not directly connected to the main purpose of the talk:

- an old professor studying dried-up dinosaur bones (this is how many people picture palaeontologists)
- It's an ancestor of the modern Australian wombat (an explanation of what a Diprotodon is)
- the very first field trip I went on (nothing happened on this trip)

1.4

(Suggested answers)

1 Why did Paul take an ecology course? / What was Paul interested in?
2 What did the course include?
3 What are the conditions usually like when working in palaeontology?
4 What did Paul find/discover? / How did Paul know he had made the right choice?

1.5

1 environment
2 extinction
3 extreme
4 tooth

1.6

1 Yes, the information will always be in the same order in the questions and the recording.
2 2 As a part of my degree course, I had to do a compulsory unit on 3 an interesting lecture
4 I immediately changed courses 5 the discovery of a
6 a tooth from a giant kangaroo

2 Understanding how ideas are connected

2.1

1 C **2** A **3** E **4** D

2.2

1 a date
2 a grant//funds
3 climate change
4 humans, nature

3 Understanding an explanation

3.1

1 mice
2 cells, diet, exercise
3 pigeons
4 new
5 Earth's magnetic field
6 beak(s), ears

3.2

1 A **2** C

3.3

1 B is incorrect because in both types of mice, cells showed some change – their cells either deteriorated or showed less change.
C is incorrect because there is no information about diet.
2 A is incorrect because this has been known for decades, so is not new.
B is incorrect because this has been proven to be false.

8 Contrasting ideas

1 Signposting words

1.1

1 OK, **let's move on to** the late 19th century, when a great deal of changes were taking place.
2 Now, **first of all**, I wanted to give you some background information.
3 So, **let's have a look at** some possible reasons for this.
4 **And finally**, I'd like to talk about some future projects.
5 So, **what conclusions** did we reach?
6 I'll **begin by explaining** what this machine can do.

1.2

1 B **2** A **3** B **4** C **5** C **6** A

1.3

1 D	**3** H	**5** B	**7** C
2 F	**4** A	**6** G	**8** E

2 Comparing and contrasting ideas

2.1

1 C
2 a place
3 the third column
4 the last column
5 the name of a plant

2.2

1 Europe	**5** starvation	**9** tax(es)
2 diet(s)	**6** cash	**10** trade
3 lives	**7** war	
4 poor	**8** tea	

3 Using notes to follow a talk

3.1

1 It's organised chronologically (by year) and it takes a historical view.
2 You can listen for the dates to help you follow the talk.
3 prehistory
4 Question 6

3.2

1 food	**4** religions	**7** vitamins
2 silver	**5** gunpowder	**8** disease
3 silk	**6** Spanish	**9** emigration

Reading skills

1 Reading strategies

1 Using the features of a Reading passage

1.1

1 E **2** B **3** G **4** D **5** F **6** A

1.2

A 2 **B** 5 **C** 1 **D** 3

1.3

1 C **2** A **3** C **4** A **5** B **6** D

1.4

1 B **2** A **3** D **4** F **5** C

1.5

1 B (*Tea leaves contain tannins, a loose collection of chemicals that give tea … its flavour*)
2 B (*that astringent puckering effect in the mouth*)
3 A (footnote 1)
4 A (footnote 2)
5 C (*All tannins are soluble in water, but how much of them can dissolve in a given amount of water*)

2 Skimming a passage and speed reading

2.2

1 B **2** C **3** A

2.3

1 B, C **2** D **3** A

3 Global understanding

3.1

B

3.2

A

2 Descriptive passages

1 Scanning for detail

1.1

B

2 Using words from the passage

2.1

1 (ochre) engravings / (the) engravings
2 100,000 years ago
3 earth, rock (in either order but you must have both)

2.2

(The words that will help you locate the information in the passage are underlined here.)
4 What did the ancient people use to keep their ochre mixture in?
5 Nowadays, who makes use of ochre?
6 Apart from painting, what else might ancient humans have used ochre for?
(The details you need to find in the passage are underlined here.)
4 What did the ancient people use to keep their ochre mixture in?
5 Nowadays, who makes use of ochre?
6 Apart from painting, what else might ancient humans have used ochre for?

(Answer Questions 4–6.)
4 (two) shells / (abalone) shells
5 indigenous communities
6 skin protection

3 Notes/flow-chart/diagram completion

3.1

1 stored in **2** modern **3** functioned as

3.3

1 *ingredients = (raw) materials*
2 *tools = equipment; make = produce; paint = pigment*
3 *scientists = Henshilwood and his team; work out how = deduce*

3.4

(The words in brackets in the answer are allowed but not necessary.)
1 (mammal) bone (samples / pieces); charcoal
2 grindstones; hammerstones
3 signs of wear

3.5

(Suggested answers)
1 a noun – something colourful that is created by rubbing ochre against quartzite
2 a verb – something that was done to animal bones before they were crushed and added to ochre
3 a noun – something that researchers believe was added to the mixture
4 a noun – something the mixture was poured into
5 a noun – a way of using the mixture on walls
6 a noun – a way of using the mixture on the body

3.6

1 *colourful = red; created = produced; pieces of = slabs*
2 *crushed = ground up*
3 *other solids = charcoal, stone chips, quartz grains; the researchers = Henshilwood and his team*
4 *poured into = transferred; mixed = stirred*
5 *the body = skin*

3.7

1 powder **3** liquid / water **5** decoration
2 heated **4** shells **6** sunscreen

3.8

(Suggested answers)
2, 3, 4 nouns – types of ancient objects found in the area
5 a noun – the name of a substance used to provide colour
6 a plural noun – something recently found in the area, something linked to animal bone and charcoal
7 a noun – something the researchers have concluded about early humans and what they knew about

3.9

1 1992
2, 3, 4 (in any order) beads; tools; engravings
(N.B. Because of the word limit, if you write 'bone tools' or 'ochre engravings', your answer will be marked as wrong.)
5 ochre
6 materials
7 chemistry

3.11

Most hydropower plants rely on a <u>dam</u> that holds back water, creating a large <u>reservoir</u> behind it. Often, this <u>reservoir</u> is used as a recreational lake and is also known as the intake. <u>Gates</u> on the <u>dam</u> open and gravity pulls the water through the penstock, a line of pipe that leads to the <u>turbine</u>. Water builds up pressure as it flows through this pipe. The water strikes and turns the large blades of a <u>turbine</u>, which is attached to a <u>generator</u> above it by way of a shaft. As the <u>turbine</u> blades turn, so do a series of magnets inside the <u>generator</u>, producing alternating current (AC) by moving electrons. The <u>transformer</u>, located inside the powerhouse, takes the AC and converts it to higher-voltage current.

3.12

1 intake **3** powerhouse **5** penstock
2 magnets **4** shaft

3.13

1 helps contain = holds back; produces = creates
2 moves = flows; increases in = builds up
3 rotates = turns; connected = attached
4 changes into = converts to

3 Understanding the main ideas

1 Identifying the main idea

1.1

The topic they all have in common is urban planning – this is the overall topic of the Reading passage.
i <u>The future of</u> urban planning <u>in America</u>
ii <u>Conflicting ideas through</u> the <u>history</u> of urban planning
iii Urban planning has <u>a long and varied history</u>
iv <u>Financial problems helped spread</u> an urban planning <u>concept</u>
v <u>The background to one particular</u> planned <u>community</u>
vi <u>Political change obstructs progress</u> in urban planning
vii An urban <u>plan to reduce traffic</u>

1.3

B

1.4

1 Headings iv, vi and vii feature money, politics and traffic (none of these are mentioned in Paragraph A, so they can be crossed off the list).
2 iii (the whole paragraph provides an overview of the long and varied history of urban planning)

1.5

shortlists
Paragraph B: ii, iii, iv, v
Paragraph C: i, ii, iii, v, vii
Paragraph D: i, ii, iv, v, vi

final answers

Paragraph B: v – the main topic is to explain what led to (*the background*) Letchworth, the first garden city (*one particular planned community*)

Paragraph C: vii – the main topic is the design of the city of Radburn, America (*An urban plan*) which was built with the aim of creating a safe environment for children (*to reduce traffic*)

Paragraph D: iv – the main topic is the impact the stock market crash, unemployment and a lack of affordable housing (*financial problems*) had in America and how the president dealt with these by creating more garden cities (*helped spread an urban planning concept*)

1.6

i – Although Paragraphs A, C and D all refer to America (or places in America), none of these paragraphs mention the future of urban planning.

ii – Although Paragraphs A, B, C and D all contain historical references, none of the paragraphs mention 'conflicting ideas'.

vi – Paragraphs A and D refer to political places or people, but neither of these mentions progress being stopped because of politics.

2 Understanding the main points

2.2

B (A is incorrect because the passage makes no comparison between theoretical and actual designs; C is incorrect because no advice is given about who should carry out the planning, though several professionals are mentioned; D is incorrect because there is no comparison between ancient and modern planned cities. Although A, C and D all mention ideas that are in the passage, they do not accurately reflect the information in the text.)

2.3

2

A *arose in the latter part of the 19th century as a reaction to the pollution and crowding of the Industrial Revolution*

B *After the First World War, the second town built following Howard's ideas, Welwyn Garden City, was constructed*

C *Howard believed that these towns should be limited in size and density*

D *arose in the latter part of the 19th century as a reaction to the pollution and crowding of the Industrial Revolution*

3

A *inspired by Howard's ideas and the success of Letchworth and Welwyn, created the city of Radburn*

B *Conceived as a community which would be safe for children,*

C *designed so that the residents would not require automobiles … including the separation of pedestrians and vehicles*

D *'superblocks', each of which shared 23 acres of commonly held parkland*

4

A *In America, following the stock market crash of 1929*

B *employment for workers who had lost their jobs*

C *These towns contained … a 'green belt' of undeveloped land surrounding the community.*

D *in 1935 President Roosevelt created the Resettlement Administration*

answers

2 D **3** B **4** C

3 Identifying information in a passage

3.2

1 False – he was the first to identify the phenomenon but it is only '*now*' that we use this term.

2 True – it occurs in winter and summer.

3 Not Given – there is no information in the text about experts attempting to create heat-reflecting materials.

3.3

(the corresponding parts of the text are in brackets)

4 Not Given. We know the weather there has been affected but the text does not compare Atlanta with other cities.

5 False (*Officials there are advising builders to use light-coloured roofs in a bid to reduce the problem.*)

6 False (*These metal constructions …*)

7 Not Given. We are not given any information about alternative plans that the designers had (*These … are made to resemble very tall trees … Their structure allowed the designers to create an immediate rainforest canopy without having to wait for trees to reach such heights*)

8 False (*They contain … containers to collect rainwater, making them truly self-sufficient*)

3.4

5 Light-coloured roofs help address the issue. // Dark-coloured roofs create the problem / issue.

7 They are manufactured from metal.

9 They are self-sufficient. // They don't need any maintenance.

4 Locating and matching information

1 Identifying types of information

1.1

B

1.2

1 a whole idea

2 *Meerkats devote a significant part of their day to foraging for food*

1.3

1 F **2** D **3** G **4** E **5** C **6** A **7** B **8** H

2 Locating and matching information

2.1

D

2.2

3 the method
4 the researcher's opinion
5 a mention of the different environments
6 the contrast between
7 the definition of

2.3

1 B
2 C
3 Paragraph D (*The toes are* *super-hydrophobic, (i.e. water repellent)* *explains Stark,* *who could see* *a silvery bubble of air around their toes*)

2.4

2 E 3 C 4 C 5 A 6 B 7 D

2.5

2 *the team is keen to understand how long it takes geckos to recover from a drenching*
3 *Fitting a tiny harness around the lizard's pelvis and gently lowering the animal onto a plate of smooth glass, Stark and Sullivan allowed the animal to become well attached before connecting the harness to a tiny motor and gently pulling the lizard until it came unstuck.*
4 *'In my view, the gecko attachment system is over-designed,' says Stark*
5 *they appear to be equally happy scampering through tropical rainforest canopies as they are in urban settings*
6 *she and her colleagues Timothy Sullivan and Peter Niewiarowski were curious about how the lizards cope on surfaces in their natural habitat. Explaining that previous studies had focused on the reptiles clinging to artificial dry surfaces*
7 *'The toes are super-hydrophobic,' (i.e. water repellent)*

3 How ideas are connected

3.1

1 C 2 F 3 A 4 E 5 B

3.2

1 The text says: *A lot of gecko studies look at the very small adhesive structures on their toes to understand how the system works at the most basic level.* So, the best sentence ending is B.
2 D (*she and her colleagues Timothy Sullivan and Peter Niewiarowski were curious about how the lizards cope on surfaces in their natural habitat. Explaining that previous studies had focused on the reptiles clinging to artificial dry surfaces*)
3 F (*Therefore geckos can walk on wet surfaces, as long as their feet are reasonably dry*)
4 E (*the team is keen to understand how long it takes geckos to recover from a drenching*)

5 Discursive passages

1 Discursive passages

1.1

to add more / clarify a point	to show contrast / present the opposite view	to give an example	to draw a conclusion / introduce a result
moreover furthermore indeed in addition similarly in fact	although though despite in spite of nonetheless whilst	such as for instance to illustrate this	therefore consequently thus as a result hence

1.2

in fact; although; whilst;
in addition; furthermore; though; thus; therefore; despite

1.3

1 D 2 F 3 A 4 C 5 B 6 H

1.4

1 in fact
2 although
3 whilst
4 thus
5 despite
6 therefore

2 Identifying theories and opinions

2.1

believes

2.2

verbs: speculate, remarked, noted
preposition: according to

2.3

D Rooks are as intelligent as the most intelligent of animals. (*Corvids are remarkably intelligent, and in many ways rival the great apes in their physical intelligence and ability to solve problems*)
F The ability of rooks is surprising, given the lack of similarities between the brains of birds and animals. (*This is remarkable considering their brain is so different to the great apes*)
A We imagine that the rooks were soon able to appreciate the advantage of using different-sized tools. (*The scientists speculate that the birds quickly realised that the larger stones displaced more water and they were thus able to obtain the reward more quickly than by using small stones.*)
C Using tools in their natural habitat is simply not necessary for rooks. (*Rooks do not use tools in the wild because they do not need to*)
E In their natural setting, rooks can obtain food without using tools. (*Rooks do not use tools in the wild because … They have access to other food that can be acquired without using tools*)
B Tool use in rooks demonstrates a common English saying. (*As Bird noted, that fits nicely with Aesop's maxim, demonstrated by the crow: 'Necessity is the mother of invention.'*)

3 Matching features

3.2

1 A (*Pagel … points out that this likely explains "why we can instinctively recognise words in other Indo-European languages, just from their sounds"*)
2 C (*Russell Gray … was impressed by both findings. "Despite all the vagaries and contingencies of human history, it seems that there are remarkable regularities in the processes of language change," he commented*)
3 B (*Lieberman … found that the more an irregular verb is used, the longer it will remain irregular*)
4 A (*"Throughout its 8,000-year history, all Indo-European-language speakers have used a related sound to communicate the idea of 'two' objects – duo, due, deux, dos, etc.," Pagel commented*)
5 B (*Lieberman … performed a quantitative study of the rate at which English verbs such as 'help' have become more regular with time. Of the list of 177 irregular verbs they took from Old English, only 98 are still irregular today*)

3.3

1 – 5 We focused on the historical changes that have occurred in one particular language.
2 – 3 Words that don't follow a standard pattern will remain that way if they are used often.
3 – 4 Certain words have kept a similar sound across many years and many countries.
4 – 1 We are able to recognise certain words used by people in other cultures.
5 – 2 Regardless of what happens in the world, there appear to be fixed rules that govern the way words alter over time.

3.4

1 Question 5
2 *writes, commented, adds, proposed, according to, points out*

3.5

1 D *(The question of why some words evolve rapidly through time while others are preserved … has long plagued linguists.)*
2 C (*Over time, however, some irregular verbs 'regularise'. For instance, the past tense of 'help' used to be 'holp', but now it is 'helped'.*)
3 B (*Despite all the vagaries and contingencies of human history, it seems that there are remarkable regularities in the processes of language change*)

6 Multiple-choice questions

1 Understanding longer pieces of text

1.3

C *(at which stage language becomes a necessity has come under debate)*

2 Different types of multiple choice

2.2

You need to find two issues that may have caused the rise in dolphin numbers.

2.3

there were probably several related phenomena … Firstly, … Something else was going on. That something was distinctively human.
The correct options are: B and E

3 Identifying a writer's purpose

3.3

blockbuster: positive, the word is used to describe a film that is very popular; *hopelessly flawed:* negative, this phrase is used to criticise the science portrayed in the film; *revel in:* positive, this gives us a positive image of people enjoying the film

3.4

1 B (the writer says that we are happy to 'suspend our disbelief' so that we can 'revel in' the story)
2 C (the writer tells us the science is 'hopelessly flawed' but that the film was a 'successful' book and a 'blockbuster' film)

7 Opinions and attitudes

1 Argumentative texts

1.1

positive	negative
diverse	disastrous
unspoilt	biased
accomplished	vulnerable
productive	dated
realistic	confusing
sophisticated	irrelevant
efficient	harsh
thorough	catastrophic
influential	monotonous
prominent	distorted

1.2

Some adjectives you might have underlined: modernist; world-class; steep (decline); (racially) integrated; (economically) stable; enormous; unique; casual; beautiful; huge; cavernous; renowned; great; famous; austere; unappealing; strong aesthetic (preferences)

2 Identifying the writer's views/claims

2.1

1 claim 2 claim 3 view 4 view 5 view

2.2

1 No 2 Yes 3 Not Given 4 No 5 Yes

2.3

1 Hundreds were built then, it's the fact that it was designed by three famous people that made it unique.
2 *built … 1962 … While much of Detroit began a steep decline soon after, Lafayette Park … bucking the trend of suburban flight … despite the fact that Detroit has suffered enormous population loss*

3 We are only told that Mies designed Lafayette Park, there is no mention of Mies and any other part of Detroit.
4 The buildings have *a kind of austere uniformity*.
5 *Indeed, the best design doesn't force a personality on its residents. Instead, it helps them bring out their own.*

3 Identifying grammatical features

3.1

A *settled* = verb or adjective
B *adapt* = verb
C *neutral* = adjective
D *poor* = adjective or noun
E *afford* = verb
F *strongly* = adverb

3.2

(Suggested answers)

1 an adjective
2 an adjective
3 an adjective or adverb
4 a verb

3.3

1 D **2** A **3** C **4** B

3.5

1 a verb
2 an adjective
3 a noun
4 an adjective

3.7

1 rise / emerge (*while members of one meerkat troop will consistently rise very early, those of another will emerge from their burrows much later in the morning*)
2 innovative (*The tests showed that the more subordinate juvenile members of meerkat troops are the most innovative … these low-ranking males were best at solving problems*)
3 treat / scorpion (*The meerkats had to work out how to open … in order to reach the scorpion inside … these low-ranking males were best at solving problems and obtaining the treat*)
4 opaque (*The meerkats had to work out how to open the opaque lid of the container ... the meerkats didn't ever appear to work out that it was the opaque surface of the box that they should attack*)

8 General Training Reading

1 The General Training Reading paper

1.1

Section 1: B, E, H
Section 2: A, D, F
Section 3: C, G

1.2

1 D **2** C **3** B **4** G **5** A **6** F **7** H **8** E

1.3

(Suggested answers)

1 It's written by a local council.
2 residents of the area

1.4

two	3.5 million tonnes
3403 8888	160,000
13	six
500 tonnes	3467 9809

1.5

1 (13) trees
2 3.5 million (tonnes) (N.B. *3.5 million* counts as 'a number' even though it is written in words)
3 3467 9809

1.6

1 rooms (*Remember to recycle items from other rooms in your house. Try placing a separate bin in the bathroom, laundry or study*)
2 black (*Your normal household waste is collected every week and should go in the bin with the black lid*)
3 two weeks (N.B. You must use words from the text – if you write *fortnight* your answer will be marked wrong because it is not in the text.) (*Place all recyclable items in your bin with a yellow lid. This will be emptied every two weeks*)
4 collection day (*You can find out your collection day by contacting the council on 3403 8888*)

1.7

1 *put* = place; *different* = separate
2 *top* = lid
3 *will collect* = will be emptied
4 *call* = contact; *they will tell you* = you can find out

1.9

3 True – (*Tree trimmings, grass clippings and flowers are not recyclable*)
4 True (*One job is created for every 500 tonnes*)
5 False (*Paper can be recycled six times*)
6 Not Given – we are told that fibres are added but there is no information given about these fibres and where they come from.

2 Dealing with multiple texts

2.1

They are all advertising open days at colleges or universities.

2.2

1 B **2** C **3** D **4** B **5** B **6** A

2.3

1 *International food fair*
2 *Visit our working farm; Marine biology exhibit – come and find out about our fascinating sea creatures*
3 *test your skills in our flight simulator; win a free flying lesson*
4 *Digital photography – workshops*
5 *Creative arts market – crafted by our third-year students – all reasonably priced*
6 *10:00 till 21:00; All finished off with our popular fireworks display*

2.4

1 D **2** A **3** E **4** B **5** C

3 Understanding work-related texts

3.1

1 F	**4** A	**7** B	**10** E
2 D	**5** H	**8** L	**11** J
3 G	**6** K	**9** I	**12** C

3.2

B someone who would like to know about what happens when their workplace is inspected

3.3

1 C (*All inspectors complete a rigorous nine-month programme of classroom training and field experience with a qualified inspector*) (A is incorrect because they spend 9 months doing this; B is incorrect because they only learn about one industry; D is incorrect because they have to do practical work after their theoretical training (*classroom training*))

2 B (*look at any documents or records and take them from the workplace in order to make copies*) (A is incorrect because they don't take away equipment; C is incorrect because they don't concern themselves with how employees are recruited; D is incorrect because they do not warn employees about inspections (*Workplace visits by an inspector are typically unannounced*))

3 D (*If the staff concerned are not available, the inspector may continue with a limited inspection … and/or arrange a follow-up visit later*) (A is incorrect because it does not have to be postponed; B is incorrect because there is no need for a complaint to be made; C is incorrect because they will not leave without talking to some staff or completing the inspection)

3.4

The last section, under the heading: *What to expect from a workplace health and safety visit*

3.5

1 representative
2 day
3, 4 policy, poster (in any order)
5 instructions
6 videos
7 injury

3.6

identifies themselves = will introduce themselves
to meet = to speak with
absent = not available
do a job = carry out specific tasks
the premises = the workplace
you can get = can be obtained

3.8

A iv **B** v **C** iii

3.9

A The whole paragraph talks about how the mayor (*one person*) decided to ban all outdoor advertising because he thought it looked ugly (*changed a city*); ii is incorrect because the city did not vote, only the mayor decided.

B The paragraph is about the reaction of people in the advertising and marketing business (*professionals*) and their warning of what would happen (*warn of the consequences*); i is incorrect because the industry insiders did not welcome the change.

C The paragraph gives the views of a person who liked the advertisements; he argues that advertisements are also an art form and a form of entertainment; iv is incorrect because, although he is one man, he did not change the city; although he gives a warning, only one man is mentioned here, so heading v is incorrect.

3.10

2 the deadline
3 the public's reaction
4 advertising techniques
5 an action
6 examples showing the wide range

1 G (*It has also brought some unforeseen advantages. When the hoardings were removed, many locals were shocked at the state of the buildings and houses beneath. As a result, renovation work in the city has increased considerably*)

2 D (*businesses were given 90 days to take down any signs that did not meet the new regulations*)

3 G (*the scheme has worked, and surveys conducted by local newspapers indicate it is extremely popular, with more than 70% of residents showing their approval*)

4 F (*innovative methods of indoor advertising such as inside elevators and bathrooms … Big banks and stores began painting their buildings in eye-catching colours*)

5 B (*representatives drove their cars up and down in front of city hall to protest against the ruling*)

6 E (*15,000 billboards … huge outdoor video screens, and even posters and ads on the side of buses and taxis, were all quickly removed across the city … Even giving out pamphlets in public spaces was made illegal*)

3.12

1 G (*As journalist Vincenze Galvao commented … 'My old reference was a big Panasonic billboard, but now my reference is an art deco building that had been covered by it.'*)

2 F (*But, according to advertising executive Marcio Oliveira, 'The internet was the really big winner.'*)

3 C (*Advertising is both an art form and, when you're in your car or on foot, a form of entertainment that helps relieve solitude and boredom*)

4 E (*'It was really dramatic ... Big companies had to change their focus and strategies,' says Marcello Queiroz*)

5 A (*Kassab set up telephone hotlines so that citizens could report instances of advertisers breaking the law. 'Some days we had 3,000 calls on those lines,' he said proudly*)

6 D (*spokesman Roberto Tripoli said. 'Yes, some people are going to have to pay a price, but things were out of hand and the population has made it clear that it wants this.'*)

Writing skills

1 Academic Writing Task 1 – Describing a chart, table or graph

1 Understanding graphs, tables and charts

1.1

1 E **2** D **3** C **4** B **5** A **6** F

1.3

(These are examples of the types of information you should have highlighted in 1.2.)

1 traffic growth in the Netherlands measured/shown as a percentage
2 Yes, ten-year gaps from 1950 to 2000.
3 Yes, four types of transport are compared: cars, trains, bicycles, and other types of public transport.

1.4

The graph shows the increases in traffic in ~~England~~ **the Netherlands** from ~~1960~~ **1950** to ~~2010~~ **2000**. During this time, car traffic increased by ~~just over 150~~ **140%**, while train traffic increased by ~~40~~ **20%**, bicycle traffic increased by approximately ~~20~~ **15%**, and other public transport traffic ~~actually decreased~~ **increased** by about ~~20~~ **10%**.

1.5 (Statements B and C are both examples of the type of information that is inaccurate)

1 B (it tells us what proportion of journeys was made by car etc. and not how many vehicles were used)
2 A
3 B (more people travelled by train than bicycle in 2000)
4 A
5 C (we are not told any information about car ownership, only about how journeys were made)
6 A

2 More complex charts

2.1

1 C **2** B **3** C **4** B

2.2

It is telling us the actual records of sea level changes from 1870 to 2008, as well as past and future estimates.

2.3

1 It is predicted that sea levels will continue to rise.
2 It is estimated that sea levels will have increased by 200 mm by the year 2050.
3 Sea levels are forecast(ed) to rise more rapidly between 2050 and 2100.
4 By 2100, sea levels are estimated to be 500 mm higher than they are at present.

3 Improving your Task Achievement score

3.2

D is the correct answer

A (this is inaccurate as the results were not mixed)
B (this is inaccurate as we are given no information about how many people used the extra lanes)
C (this is inaccurate, as we do not know traffic figures, and it is also an isolated fact about two roads only and not a main trend)
D (this summarises the impact that the introduction of the new lanes had on all roads)
E (this is an opinion rather than a main trend)

3.3

1 A **2** B **3** B **4** A **5** A **6** A

Sentences 2 and 3 do not focus on main features or significant changes so it is not necessary to report these.

Sentences 1, 4, 5, 6 all give support for the main trend that was identified in the overview sentence and so are important details to include.

3.4

1 *From their responses, it is clear that swimming is the most popular sport among all groups, and that from these three groups, boys participated in the most sports.*
2 Main features
- *for three out of the four sports, boys were the major participants.*
- *The only sport not enjoyed by the boys surveyed was hockey …*
- *… a sport that the vast majority of the girls who were interviewed participated in.*
- *only a very small number, approximately 10 of the 100, participated in football.*

3 The word count is only 143 words, so it will lose marks for being too short.

3.5

1 The final sentence needs to be deleted (leaving only 123 words): *We can conclude from this that girls in Manchester enjoy hockey a lot and that they don't particularly like football.*
You should not try to draw conclusions like this about the data; you will lose marks if you do.
2 The data for the adults has not been mentioned at all. Missing out key details will lose marks.
3 Deleting the final line and adding details about the adults will mean a higher score for Task Achievement.
For example, *When it comes to the adults surveyed, the two most popular sports were swimming and tennis, with hockey being the least popular. In fact, the team sports of football, hockey and basketball are all played less frequently by the adults who took part.* (43 words)

2 Academic Writing Task 1 – Comparing and contrasting graphs and tables

1 Avoiding repetition

1.1

1 F **2** D **3** E **4** A **5** B **6** C

1.2

1 D **2** F; B **3** A; E; C **4** G

1.3

The other differences are the words and phrases used to replace 'show(s)' in the question:

indicates; tells us; we can see; reveal

2 Comparing and contrasting data

2.1

1 the net worth of three different sectors in the UK in billions of British pounds (£)
2 One has a positive value (above the line) and one has a negative value (below the line).
3 the UK total

2.2

1 2000–2008
2 2009–2010
3 2002, 2008, 2010
4 2002 and 2008
5 Government, UK Total and Households
6 Businesses

2.3

1 remained; began to increase; had risen
2 showed; increased
3 dropped; fell; went
4 followed
5 improved; did not last; began to worsen
6 experienced / was experiencing; returned
7 revealed / reveals; was growing; was declining / declined

2.4

A sentences 1 and 5
B sentences 2 and 4
C sentences 3, 6 and 7

3 Grammatical Accuracy – describing numbers and figures accurately

3.1

1 Percentages, years and high or complex numbers (e.g. 305,678) can be left as numerals. We often simplify complex numbers by rounding them up or down (e.g. *just under four million; a little over five million*, etc.).
2 You should write fractions and simple numbers (1–10) in words.

3.2

1 **Half** of the people who attended in 1961 had never attended a concert before.
2 They reduced the budget by **one million dollars** 40 years later.
3 60% of students report using the library in term time only and **a quarter** of those use the library at night.
4 The population rose by **three and a half billion** in the next 15 years.
5 Over 15 million planes landed at the airport in the last seven months; this is an increase of **a third**.

3.3

1 thousand cars
2 million
3 Millions
4 hundred beds
5 students

3.4

1 in
2 of
3 of; of
4 for
5 from; to

3 Academic Writing Task 1 – Describing diagrams

1 Understanding a diagram

1.2

1 tear
2 pour / add / soak / leave
3 beat / mix
4 pour / add
5 mix
6 slide
7 lift / drain
8 place / put / press
9 leave / dry

1.3

1 bowl; jug
2 electric mixer
3 tray
4 mesh
5 rolling pin

2 Describing a process – coherence and cohesion

2.1

1 D
2 E
3 H
4 B
5 I
6 F
7 A
8 G
9 C

2.2

(Suggested answer)

The diagram explains how recycled paper is made from old newspapers. First, some newspaper is torn into small pieces and put into a bowl. Then, 250 ml of water is added and it is left to soak for up to an hour. Next, using an electric mixer, the mixture is beaten for about 45 seconds until a pulp is formed. / an electric mixer is used to beat the mixture for about 45 seconds until a pulp is formed. When it is ready, the pulp is poured into a shallow tray and a further 100 ml of water is added. It is mixed together by hand. After this, a piece of mesh is used to carefully lift the pulp mixture out of the tray, allowing the water to drain. / the pulp mixture is carefully lifted out of the tray using a piece of mesh and the water is allowed to drain. Next, an old newspaper is opened up and the pulp mixture is placed inside. / the pulp mixture is placed inside an old newspaper. Then, a rolling pin is used to press the paper down and force out any excess water. / the paper is pressed down with a rolling pin and any excess water is forced out. Finally, the new paper is left to dry in a warm place for at least 24 hours.

2.3

First; Then; Next; When; After this; Finally

3 Lexical Resource – being accurate

3.1

1 government	5 countries
2 percentage	6 between
3 different	7 decreased
4 until	8 increased

3.2

1 amount	3 number	5 percentage
2 method	4 means	6 factors

3.3

1 difference	4 increase	7 sport/s
2 work	5 attendance	8 educational
3 lives	6 slight	

4 Academic Writing Task 1 – Describing maps

1 Describing a map

1.1

the hotel	It has been expanded / extended.
Steggle Farm	It's been replaced by a road.
the roads	Have been modernised and traffic lights, a roundabout and zebra crossing have been added.
the shops	There are more shops / they have been extended.
the houses	There are more houses and they are smaller.
Goode Farm	Replaced with a car park.
the house in St Peter's Lane	Replaced with a supermarket.
the stables	Replaced with a block of flats.

1.2

1 market square	3 church
2 house	4 shops

1.3

1 in the bottom left-hand corner
2 the left of
3 top left-hand corner of
4 to the right of / on the right-hand side of

2 Describing changes in a place

2.1

1 extend or expand	6 reduce
2 renovate/modernise	7 develop
3 modernise/renovate	8 add
4 replace	9 remove
5 improve	10 reconstruct

2.2

1 replaced
2 expanded / extended / developed
3 have been modernised / improved
4 have now been added; have been improved / modernised
5 have been removed

3 Grammatical Accuracy

3.1

1 allow	6 have been added
2 consisted	7 has now replaced
3 was restricted	8 are located
4 has changed	9 have been made
5 have been improved	10 has been extended

3.2

There are two clear paragraphs. The first describes the town in 1700 and the second describes modern-day changes that have taken place.

5 General Training Writing Task 1 – A letter

1 Understanding the task

1.1

	informal	semi-formal	formal
greeting	Hi Mum	Dear Mike	Dear Sir or Madam
opening statement	Thanks for the parcel, it just arrived!	I'm afraid I won't be able to attend the meeting next week.	I'm writing in response to your advertisement.
closing statement	I can't wait to see you next week.	I'm looking forward to getting back to work.	I look forward to your reply.
ending	Lots of love	Kind regards	Yours sincerely

1.2

1 F 2 A 3 D 4 E 5 B 6 C

1.4

1 formal (You do not know the person and it is a business letter.)

2 no (You should use the information in the question.)
3 no (You should not write any address.)

2 Improving your score

2.2

1 D is not relevant to the situation.
2 **A** 4 **B** 5 **C** 4 **E** 6 **F** 2

2.3

Parts 3 and 7 still need ideas.

2.4

The writer has copied several words and phrases from the question.

2.5

1 renting / living in has (got)
2 afford
3 repairs

(The paragraph fits into part 3 of the plan.)

2.6

The writer has used their imagination and filled in some extra details (e.g. the rent was increased recently; the house suits them perfectly).

2.7

Idea B.

2.8

C Yours faithfully

3 Checking and correcting

3.1

1 will
2 would
3 are
4 spent
5 would like
6 looking/hearing
7 needs
8 helps / will help
9 am writing

3.2

1 on
2 of
3 in
4 for
5 to; to
6 on; on
7 in
8 of
9 in

3.3

1 because
2 advertisement
3 society
4 available
5 library
6 business
7 restaurant
8 necessary
9 sincerely

3.4

1 I noticed …
2 However,
3 Yours sincerely,
4 to ask you about the party.
5 don't
6 I'm
7 Dear Sir,

6 Writing Task 2 – Getting ready to write

1 Understanding the task

1.1

1 E
2 G
3 H
4 C
5 F
6 B
7 D
8 A

1.2

1 D/E 2 B 3 D/E 4 B/E 5 A 6 C

2 Planning and organising your ideas

2.4

The following ideas should be cut because they are not relevant to the topic (whether the internet helps people stay connected or isolates them): 2, 3, 6, 8.

2.6

For: the internet helps us to stay connected	Against: the internet isolates us
7 My cousin travelled for a year but kept in touch with his family every day. **9** Through the internet, we can share memories with people who are far away.	**1** Instant communication (e.g. emails/text messages) means that it is difficult to escape from work. **4** A friend of mine uses a social-networking site a great deal but we rarely see her. **5** virtual friends made on the Internet cannot be compared to our actual friends and family.

2.7

We need to add more to *For: the Internet helps us to stay connected.*

2.8

A (This idea relates directly to the topic: *immediate contact provided by the internet.* It is a further argument 'for'.)

3 Getting started – writing an introduction

3.1

A 5 **B** 3 **C** 1 **D** 2

3.2

(Suggested answer)

The internet is a wonderful tool that helps us to <u>keep in touch anywhere in the world</u>. <u>However</u>, some websites <u>can become an obsession and may encourage people to stay at home instead of going out to see their friends</u>.

3.3

1 C 2 B 3 D 4 A

3.4

Sentence 2 (Sentences 1 and 3 only deal with one side of the argument. Sentence 4 is not relevant to this question.)

7 Writing Task 2 – Expressing your ideas clearly

1 Linking ideas – cohesion

1.1

- **Connecting similar ideas:** similarly, furthermore, in addition, not only … but also, also
- **Connecting different ideas:** but, in spite of, however, although, on the other hand, while, whereas, despite
- **Clarifying an idea:** in other words, that is, in fact
- **Giving examples:** for example, such as, for instance
- **Giving a reason or conclusion:** therefore, because of, as a result, consequently, so

1.2

1 Consequently
2 In fact
3 However
4 Furthermore
5 For example

1.3

1 As a result
2 In other words
3 On the other hand
4 In addition
5 For instance

2 Lexical Resource – avoiding repetition

2.1

1 these natural resources
2 these (types / kinds of) facilities
3 funding is
4 this (type of / kind of) method
5 This system

2.2

1 gonna → going to
2 & → and
3 e.g. → for example
4 OK → acceptable
5 Kids → Children
6 etc. → and so on.

2.3

1 learn
2 understand
3 find out about
4 skills
5 solve
6 money
7 employees
8 advertising

3 Expressing a personal view

3.1

1 C **2** A **3** D **4** B

3.2

(Suggested answers)

2 In my view, I don't think this is a good idea.
3 Personally, I wouldn't like to have to do a job I didn't enjoy.
4 This is probably a bad idea.
5 Life can be much more complicated for young people nowadays.
6 In my opinion, every situation is different.
7 Nowadays, young people generally use their mobile phones for multiple tasks.
8 Schools seem to be more crowded than in the past.
9 My city is less crowded now and people appear to enjoy walking through the streets.

3.3

1 A
2 B
3 B
4 C
5 A
6 C
7 A
8 C

3.4

1 In conclusion, I completely disagree **with** this view.
2 As far as I am ~~concern~~ **concerned**, this is a problem without any real solution.
3 To summarise, even **though** there is a clear downside to our dependence on technology, I honestly feel we have to find a way to cope with it, because the internet is definitely here to stay.
4 In **conclusion**, there are both negatives and positives to this system, but the negatives seem to far outweigh the positives.
5 In my ~~point of~~ **view**, education is a vital part of every child's life.

8 Writing Task 2 – Checking and correcting

1 Developing your ideas clearly

1.2

1 The writer uses these words to avoid repetition. They refer back to:

1 the internet
2 benefits
3 the internet
4 companies
5 my cousins
6 progress/the ability to keep in touch
7 some users
8 some users
9 some users
10 risks

2 a First
b However
c In addition
d For example
e Undoubtedly
f Consequently
g To summarise

3

(Possible plan)

Introduction:
agree with both points

Ideas for:
benefits of the internet
businesses use the internet every day – they can't meet customers' needs without it
in our personal lives it helps us keep in touch – e.g. my cousins backpacking

Ideas against:
the other side of the coin
it's too convenient – we can't escape work
social networking sites can make us anti-social (ironic)
feeling connected may be an illusion – it's virtual not real

Conclusion
my opinion – I agree
we can help with education
benefits outweigh drawbacks: disabled people isolated at home

2 Grammatical Accuracy

2.1

1 ~~wich~~ – which; ~~Nowdays~~ – Nowadays; ~~thier~~ – their; ~~belive~~ – believe

2 there are many who ~~is~~ **are** concerned; the Internet **has** brought; to ever ~~escaping~~ **escape**; can be ~~minimise~~ **minimised**; As far as I'm ~~concern~~ **concerned**

3 Progress comes at a price (You could cut either one: However, I do think that some people can find it quite addictive and there are many who are concerned about … / However, there is always another side to the coin)

2.3

1 According to the survey, the population will grow more and more. It is predicted that by 2050 the population will have increased by 30%.

2 Many famous film stars are American.

3 My conclusion, therefore, is that teaching children to be good members of society is the job of both parents and the school.

4 The pie chart gives us information about the causes of land degradation worldwide.

5 Many children spend hours playing video games, which can lead to health problems.

6 However, we can see that the rate of both national and international calls increased from 1995 to 2010.

7 Nowadays, in many universities around the world, university students can study any subject they like.

3 Assessing your language

3.2

A = band 8 **B** = band 4 **C** = band 6

Speaking skills

1 The Speaking Test – Part 1

1 Getting ready to speak

1.1

1 full name
2 shall I call you
3 where you're from
4 identification
5 some questions about yourself
6 where you live

1.2

some form of identification (e.g. a passport)

1.3

1 friendly, calm, confident

2 B She makes good eye contact with the examiner.
C Her body language shows she is listening carefully.

1.4

Only E should be ticked.

A & B You should not chew gum – it can be seen as impolite and the examiner will have trouble hearing you. You should not take any food or drink into the exam room.

C & D You are not allowed to take a mobile phone into the exam room.

E You do not need to dress very formally for the exam.

F The examiner cannot tell you your score, and you should not ask.

G Shrugging your shoulders instead of speaking can appear rude and shows a lack of language. Always use words to answer a question, even if it is to say 'I'm sorry, I'm not sure what you mean.'

H You are not allowed to leave the room during the test.

2 Part 1 – talking about familiar topics

2.2

If you give only a short answer and do not answer fully.

2.3

C (by including reasons for his opinions)

3 Using the right tense – Grammatical Range and Accuracy

3.1

1 of writing do you do, for example letters, emails, reports or essays?
2 writing with a pen or using a computer?
3 more now or less than you did a few years ago?
4 write stories or poems?
5 music. How often do you listen to music?

3.2

1 simple present (*I usually / generally*, etc.)
2 simple present
3 simple present and simple past, present continuous
4 simple present
5 simple present

Saida only uses the simple present and repeats *I prefer to* rather than showing a range.

3.3

1 correct

2 If you send a letter ~~by~~ yourself, it means you ~~are very~~ really appreciate this person / you are very appreciative of this person. (Saida may mean: *If you write a letter by hand …*)

3 correct

4 I think less, because technology nowadays ~~are really go fast~~ is really developing quickly.

5 Not ~~actually~~ really.

6 correct

3.6

1 Yes, I do / Not really
2 No, I didn't / Not really / Yes, I did
3 Yes, I would / No, I wouldn't / Not really
4 Not really / Yes, I do / No, I don't
5 No, I haven't / Yes, I have / Not really

3.7

1 He answers the question (*almost every day*) then expands on it by giving more detail: *I used to listen for one hour at least.*
Mistakes
1 tense: *used to* is used to talk about past habits.
2 word order: he should say *I usually listen to music for at least one hour.*

2 He explains why by explaining how it makes him feel.
Mistakes
1 verb agreement: he should say *it relaxes me / it makes me feel*
2 he needs to connect his ideas so the words are not a list: *it makes me feel at ease (and more) comfortable*

3 He answers by saying which he prefers and why.
Mistakes
1 it would be more natural to say: *you can find the song you are looking for much faster*
2 tense: *that existed in the world* – should be the present tense: *that exists*

4 He answers (*No*) and then explains about how his tastes have changed and comments on this fact.
Mistakes
He uses a good range of tenses accurately here: *When I was younger I loved … Now I have changed my mind and I prefer … It's* completely *different, I know.*

5 He talks about two instruments he learned as a child and an instrument he would like to play and also comments on that.
Mistakes
He uses a variety of tenses accurately: *When I was a child … I used to play … I studied … I would like to play. I think it will be …*
The only mistake is: *I studied two years drums.* He should say: *I studied the drums for two years.*

2 Part 2 – Giving a talk

1 Understanding the task

1.1

1 one or two minutes – **but** you should try to talk for at least two minutes
2 one minute
3 No, the examiner will give it to you.
4 no
5 The examiner will tell you when to stop.

1.3

1 Why **2** (The) Result **3** felt

1.4

Who – my friend
Why – he wanted to get a girlfriend
How – gave him advice
Result – they are now a couple
How I felt – good, useful, helpful

1.5

one minute and 40 seconds

He could have
- added more about his friend (to describe him).
- described the girlfriend and said if he knew her.
- explained more about the advice and help he gave.
- added more about his feelings.

1.6

He prompts her by asking 'Can you tell me any more about that?'.

1.7

1 As I said earlier …
2 At the beginning I mentioned / said / described …
3 I don't think I've mentioned / described / said …
4 Now, what else can I say?
5 I'd just like to add something about …
6 One thing I forgot to mention …

1.8

She didn't mention how she felt about helping this person.

1.9

1 Do you like helping other people?
2 So, do your friends help you when you have a problem?

1.10

1 Sanem keeps talking by giving examples (*like charities / old people*) and explaining why (*because they always need help*).
2 Emanuele keeps talking by giving an explanation (*it's important to have someone to help you …*) and specific examples (*for example, when I was worried … [about] university, the same friend … helped me and gave me some advice …*).

2 Improving Fluency and Coherence

2.1

1 She begins by repeating the examiner's question and stating who she has decided to talk about.
2 You asked me to describe a time when I helped someone. To that aim, I've chosen to talk about Aniseto.
3 She uses the different points in the question to organise her talk and link her ideas and signal a change in topic. E.g.
Why I wanted to do that …
How I helped this person …
What was the result …

2.2

1 H **2** A **3** D **4** C **5** B **6** G **7** E **8** F

2.4

She uses a good variety.

2.5

B I helped **him**.
C I could help **him** a little.
D **he** couldn't speak English at all.
E **it** wasn't just for **him**, **it** was also for **me**.
F **it** wasn't a good thing.
G **he** was very friendly.

2.6

1 She only uses simple connectors: *so, and, because.*
2 She could have improved her score by using a variety of connectors. Some other connectors she could have used are: *I* ***also*** *had to …,* ***as well as*** *that …,* ***because of*** *that …, and* ***as a result*** *…,* ***consequently*** *… .*
3 Yes, she says *for her* and *me, she,* etc.
4 She is quite hesitant and says *er* … a lot.

3 Organising your notes and your talk

3.3

(Suggested ideas)

My brother

- I've decided to talk about my older brother. I've known him all of my life. He's 36 years old and he's a lawyer. Unfortunately, he lives in America so I don't see him very often.
- I chose him because, when he was young, he had a lot of problems at school because he had a lot of learning difficulties. But, it was always his dream to be a lawyer and he didn't let his learning difficulties get in his way. He failed his exams many times but he kept trying and he finally succeeded.
- I think he has influenced my life by teaching me to keep going. He also taught me that it's important to have a clear goal and to never give up. Last year, I failed an important test at school and I was very disappointed. But I thought of my brother and I decided not to give up, so I'm going to try again soon.
- When I think of my brother, I feel really grateful that I have him in my life. I also feel a lot of admiration for him and I'm very proud of what he has achieved.

My grandmother

- I've decided to talk about my grandmother. I've known her all of my life and she's an amazing person.
- I chose her because, when I was young, she looked after me a lot when my parents were busy at work. So I have a lot of strong memories of her when I was growing up.
- I think she has influenced my life by being such a calm person. She also taught me how to read and write. And I think it's because of her that I work so hard now. She also taught me a lot about my culture. For example, she taught me how to cook some traditional dishes from my country.
- When I think of my grandmother, I feel very happy. I love her very much and I feel a lot of respect and admiration for her. But I also sometimes feel worried about her because she is quite old now and still lives alone.

3 Part 3 – Talking about abstract topics

1 Talking about abstract topics

1.1

1 a time when you helped someone
2 discuss with you
3 general questions related to this
4 helping neighbours/neighbors

1.2

A Can you tell me some of the practical things that people can do to help their neighbours/neighbors?
B Why should neighbours/neighbors help each other?
C Do you think that people in small towns help each other more than people in cities?
D So why don't they do the same in cities?
E Let's go on and think about attitudes towards helping other people. Some people don't want to help other people – why do you think that is?
F Do you think that the governments have a responsibility to help people?
G But doesn't that sometimes mean that people think it's only the government's responsibility?
H So, Emanuele, do you think that some people deserve more help than others?

1.3

A 4	**C** 7	**E** 8	**G** 6
B 3	**D** 5	**F** 1	**H** 2

1.5

1 B	**3** A	**5** C
2 E / D	**4** F	**6** E

1.6

1 A	**3** E / B	**5** A	**7** A / B
2 F	**4** B	**6** A	**8** A / D

2 Agreeing and disagreeing

2.1

Strongly disagree	Disagree to some extent	Neither agree nor disagree	Agree to some extent	Strongly agree
Oh no, not at all. I completely disagree.	I think I would probably have to say no. I can see your point, but …	Well, I think there are valid points for both. Actually, I think it depends on the situation (etc.) It seems to me that there are two sides to consider.	To a certain extent, yes.	I totally agree with that. Yes, I think that's absolutely right.

3 Improving your Lexical Resource score

3.1

1 C **2** E **3** A **4** B **5** F **6** D

3.2

A My boss was a bit of a slave driver.
B My sister and I are like two peas in a pod.
C You can't judge a book by its cover.
D I felt as though I didn't have a care in the world.

E Actions speak louder than words.
F I couldn't keep a straight face.

3.3

basic vocabulary	higher-level vocabulary
holiday help small children bad house	it depends on experience attitude base (something) on create the structure personal responsibility act in the right way allow people to everybody deserves more or less

3.4

He has a wide range of vocabulary and uses higher-level vocabulary. There are some inaccuracies that prevent him from being awarded a higher score:

~~Take a look at~~ his house – take care of / look after
to ~~take up~~ a mindset – develop / create a mindset
mainly it's a ~~feature of a person~~ – private issue / our individual responsibility
but ~~by the way~~ you should always try to be helpful – anyway / in any case

4 Checking, correcting and assessing

1 Dealing with problems

1.1

1 D **2** A / D **3** C **4** C **5** C

1.2

1 B **2** A **3** C **4** C **5** C

1.3

A (It shows a lack of language. Keep talking and ask a question if you are not sure what to say.)

1.4

Extract 1: the examiner gives an example to help Emanuele.

Extract 2: the examiner rephrases the question.

1.5

A *I'm not really sure what you mean. / I'm sorry, could you repeat the question?*
B *I'm sorry, could you repeat the question? / I'm not really sure what you mean.*
C *Sorry, I meant to say …*
D *I've never really thought about that before. / I honestly have no idea.*

2 Pronunciation, intonation and 'chunking'

2.1

1 it	**11** heart	**21** breeze
2 look	**12** near	**22** defend
3 fool	**13** chased	**23** bland
4 bad	**14** cruel	**24** sort
5 workman	**15** coin	**25** close (v)
6 far	**16** could	**26** shave
7 bird	**17** fair	**27** air
8 sport	**18** bike	**28** vet
9 uncle	**19** can't	
10 stars	**20** day	

2.4

/t/ based, laughed, chased, increased, hoped, washed
/d/ played, changed, arrived, learned, poured
/ɪd/ waited, acted, wanted, decided

2.7

Saida: She has problems with *th* /ð/, which she pronounces /z/.
Melanie: She pronounces *th* /ð/ as /d/ and pronounces *uncle* as *ankle*.

2.8

contact	depend	expert
respect	develop	difficult
equal	environment	expensive
practice	technique	

2.10

Over the years I've interviewed hundreds of candidates for jobs at many different levels. The point of every job interview is to make sure a candidate has the skills necessary to do the work. Hiring the wrong person can be an expensive mistake. But, apart from references, how can you determine if the candidate actually knows what he says he knows? A very effective way to sort out the good candidates from the bad is by asking 'How did you do that?' and 'Why did you do that?' at appropriate stages in the interview.

2.11

The point of every job interview // is to make sure a candidate has the skills necessary to do the work. // Hiring the wrong person // can be an expensive mistake. But, // apart from references, // how can you determine if the candidate actually knows // what he says he knows? A very effective way to sort out the good candidates from the bad // is by asking // 'How did you do that?' // and // 'Why did you do that?' // at appropriate stages in the interview.

2.12

(Suggested answers)

Every day./I love music/yeah/I'm a fan of music/every type of music/especially rock music and classical music/and I like to search from the Internet, new groups,/new bands,/new type of genres./Yeah, every day.

2.13

1 No, she doesn't pause naturally between words or phrases and there are no examples of stress.
2 Her speech pattern is monotonous.

3 Assessing yourself and improving your score

3.2

- Fluency and Cohesion: try to improve her fluency so she hesitates less
- Lexical Resource: try to improve her accuracy
- Grammatical Range and Accuracy: try to use a wider range of grammatical structures
- Pronunciation: work on individual sounds

Practice Test 1

Listening Section 1

1 café
2 9/nine am/9/nine o'clock
3 5/five km/kilometres/kilometers
4 (a) bar(-)code/(a) barcode/bar code
5 website/web site
6 1.50
7 M–A–U–G–H–A–N
8 01444 732900
9 guiding/guide
10 taking/take photos/photographs

Listening Section 2

11 sharks
12 old fishing village/Old Fishing Village
13 shopping
14 (water) fountain
15 student card
16 fifty/50 minutes/mins
17 museum
18 tourist office
19 rain(-)wear/rainwear
20 e(-)ticket/e ticket

Listening Section 3

21 C
22 A
23 B
24 A
25 C
26 B
27 (senior) management/ managers
28 project request
29 meeting
30 conference call

Listening Section 4

31 29,000 years
32 southern/south Europe
33 water
34 minerals
35 white gold
36 china stone
37 cooling (down)
38 windows
39 volcanic ash
40 harbours

Reading Passage 1

1 road (*It was 1992. In England, workmen were building a new road …*)
2 conference (*In 2002, … the Dover Bronze-Age Boat Trust hosted a conference … Many speakers came from overseas, and debate about cultural connections was renewed.*)
3 proposals (*Detailed proposals to reconstruct the boat were drawn up in 2004.*)
4 launch (*… an official launch of the project was held at an international seminar in France in 2007.*)
5 exhibition (*Meanwhile, the exhibition was being prepared ready for opening in July 2012 …*)
6 TRUE (*The boat was not a wreck, but had been deliberately discarded, dismantled and broken. Perhaps it had been 'ritually killed' at the end of its life …*)
7 FALSE (*With hindsight, it was significant that the boat was found and studied by mainstream archaeologists who naturally focused on its cultural context. At the time, ancient boats were often considered only from a narrower technological perspective, but news about the Dover boat reached a broad audience.*)
8 FALSE (*The possibility of returning to Dover to search for the boat's unexcavated northern end was explored, but practical and financial difficulties were insurmountable – and there was no guarantee that the timbers had survived the previous decade in the changed environment.*)
9 NOT GIVEN (*Archaeological evidence was beginning to suggest a Bronze-Age community straddling the Channel, brought together by the sea, rather than separated by it.*) (Although the text implies that trade existed at the time across the Channel, there is nothing in the text to say what this particular boat was used for.)
10 six/6 metres/meters/m (*At the base of a deep shaft six metres below the modern streets a wooden structure was revealed.*)
11 (pads of) moss (*The seams had been made watertight by pads of moss, fixed by wedges and yew stitches.*)
12 (the) hull (shape) (*In 2012, however, the hull shape was at the centre of the work, …*)
13 cost and time/cost time/time cost (both needed for a mark) (*It was decided to make the replica half-scale for reasons of cost and time, …*)

Reading Passage 2

14 E (*In total, there were responses from staff at 154 airports and 68% of these answered 'yes' to the question: Does your airport own and have meetings facilities available for hire?*)
15 B (*Some of the more obvious solutions to growing commercial revenues, such as extending the merchandising space or expanding the variety of shopping opportunities, have already been tried to their limit at many airports.*)
16 G (*Average revenue per airport was just $12,959. Meeting facilities are effectively a non-aeronautical source of airport revenue. Only 1% of respondents generated more than 20% non-aeronautical revenue from their meetings facilities; none generated more than 40%.*)
17 A (*Meanwhile, the pressures to control the level of aeronautical revenues are as strong as ever due to the poor financial health of many airlines and the rapid rise of the low-cost carrier sector.*)
18 C (*Within this context, Jarach (2001) discusses how dedicated meetings facilities located within the terminal and managed directly by the airport operator may be regarded as an expansion*

of the concept of airline lounges or as a way to reconvert abandoned or underused areas of terminal buildings.)

19 security procedures (*... new security procedures that have had an impact on the dwell time of passengers.*)

20 final destination (*At this stage of facilities provision, the airport also has the possibility of taking on the role of the final destination rather than merely a facilitator of access.*)

21 airlines (*When an airport location can be promoted as a business venue, this may increase the overall appeal of the airport and help it become more competitive in both attracting and retaining airlines and their passengers.*)

22 competitive advantage (*... but clearly this will be dependent on the competitive advantage that the airport is able to achieve in comparison with other venues.*)

23 economic downturn/climate (*These are fairly high proportions considering the recent economic climate.* Also: *Moreover, the global economic downturn has caused a reduction in passenger numbers while those that are travelling generally have less money to spend.*)

24 five years (*In addition, 28% of respondents that did not have meeting facilities stated that they were likely to invest in them during the next five years.*)

25 local (people) (*Their findings show that meeting facilities provided by the majority of respondents tend to serve local versus non-local or foreign needs. 63% of respondents estimated that over 60% of users are from the local area.*)

26 flights (*16% of respondents estimated that none of the users of their meeting facilities use flights ...*)

Reading Passage 3

27 C (*Is Photography Art? This may seem a pointless question today ... But in the decades following the discovery of photography, this question reflected the search for ways to fit the mechanical medium into the traditional schemes of artistic expression.*)

28 D (*In both countries, public interest in this topic was a reflection of the belief that national stature and achievement in the arts were related.*)

29 D (*Many portrait painters ... who realized that photography represented the 'handwriting on the wall' became involved with daguerreotyping or paper photography in an effort to save their careers*) (The phrase 'writing on the wall' or 'handwriting on the wall' means that there are clear signs that something will fail or no longer exist.)

30 A (*These writers reflected the opposition of a section of the cultural elite in England and France to the 'cheapening of art' which the growing acceptance and purchase of camera pictures by the middle class represented ... This appeal to the middle class convinced the elite that photographs would foster a desire for realism instead of idealism ...*)

31 E (*From the maze of conflicting statements and heated articles on the subject ...*)

32 G (*The simplest, entertained by many painters and a section of the public, was that photographs should not be considered 'art' because they were made with a mechanical device and by physical and chemical phenomena instead of by human hand and spirit; to some, camera images seemed to have more in common with fabric produced by machinery in a mill than with handmade creations fired by inspiration.*)

33 A (*The second widely held view, ... was that photographs would be useful to art but should not be considered equal in creativeness to drawing and painting.*)

34 C (*Lastly, ... a fair number of individuals realized that camera images were or could be as significant as handmade works of art and that they might have a positive influence on the arts and on culture in general.*)

35 B (*... Lacan and Francis Wey. The latter, ... suggested that they would lead to greater naturalness in the graphic depiction of anatomy, clothing, likeness, expression, and landscape.*)

36 E (*... a more stringent viewpoint led critic Philip Gilbert Hamerton to dismiss camera images as 'narrow in range, emphatic in assertion, telling one truth for ten falsehoods'.*)

37 A (*Still other painters, the most prominent among them the French painter, Jean-Auguste-Dominique Ingres, began almost immediately to use photography to make a record of their own output ...*)

38 D (*Delacroix's enthusiasm for the medium can be sensed in a journal entry noting that if photographs were used as they should be, an artist might 'raise himself to heights that we do not yet know'.*)

39 A (*... Jean-Auguste-Dominique Ingres, began almost immediately to use photography to ... provide ... source material for poses and backgrounds ...*)

40 C (*Baudelaire regarded photography as 'a very humble servant of art and science'; a medium largely unable to transcend 'external reality'. For this critic, photography was linked with 'the great industrial madness' of the time ...*)

Writing Task 1

Sample answer

The chart examines the levels of donation among people of different ages in Britain.

Overall, a greater percentage of British people gave money to charity in 1990 than in 2010. However, across the two years, the pattern differs before and after the age of 50.

In 1990, 42% of the 36–50 age-group made charitable donations, and this figure is the highest on the chart. The 18–25s contributed the least at only 17%. By 2010, these figures had fallen significantly to 35% and 7% respectively. The level of donations from the 26–35 age-group also experienced a decrease in 2010 from 31% to 24%.

While donations up to the age of 50 declined across the two years, they rose among the 51–65 age-group from 35% to nearly 40%, which was the highest percentage for 2010. The figure for the over 65s was lower than this, at 35%, but it was still a little higher than the 1990 figure of 32%.

(157 words)

Writing Task 2

Sample answer

For most people, when they get their first job they have little idea whether or not they will remain in the same organisation throughout their working life. If they decide to change, they need to consider how this will impact on their career overall.

People who stay with the same organisation have the advantage of thoroughly understanding how it works and also becoming familiar with the staff and processes. If they work hard, their promotion prospects are good and there is likely to be greater job security, with the promise of a good pension when they retire. Employers value loyalty and may offer additional incentives to long-term employees, including bonuses and reward schemes.

However, one of the drawbacks of staying with the same organisation is that the person may get stuck doing the same job year after year. In some cases, this can lead to boredom and disillusionment. Moving from one organisation to another can be a strategic decision in order to have variety and acquire a range of skills and experience. A friend of my father started out as a sociology teacher, he then joined the Social Services and is currently managing a care home in Western Australia. This has made him incredibly knowledgeable in a range of related fields and, in my view, has provided him with a much more interesting working life.

Although there are benefits to working for one organisation, I feel that it is also valuable for an employee to be able to offer a wide range of experience having worked for different companies. As long as it is planned carefully, I feel that change is good and will ultimately benefit the employee and the employer.

(281 words)

Practice Test 2

Listening Section 1

1 3000/3,000/three thousand words
2 surprise/surprising ending
3 16/sixteen
4 August
5 COMP4SS/comp4ss
6 post
7 famous authors
8 online
9 public
10 Spain

Listening Section 2

11 world of water/World of Water
12 (the) splash ride
13 (at) noon/midday/ 12 o'clock/12 pm
14 feed (the) sharks
15 (a) birthday party
16 (the) government
17 (the/a) quiz
18 E
19 C
20 B

Listening Section 3

21&22 IN EITHER ORDER
D B
23 mathematics/math(s)
24 theory/theoretical
25 jet engines
26 seminars
27 A
28 B
29 C
30 C

Listening Section 4

31 supportive
32 pay attention
33 next steps
34 consistent
35 graphics
36 tone
37 (a) silence/silences
38 weak verbs
39 repeat it
40 predicting

Reading Passage 1

1 (retronasal) smell
2 umami
3 toxins
4 internal scents/smells
5 disciplines
6 spatial map
7 social life
8 (air) molecules
9 flavors/flavours
10 memories
11 prey
12 chocolate
13 appetites

Reading Passage 2

14 v
15 ii
16 viii
17 vii
18 i
19 iv
20 C
21 B
22 A
23 C
24 on(-)board computer
25 ultrasound signals
26 touch(-)screen

Reading Passage 3

27 NOT GIVEN
28 NO
29 NO
30 YES
31 NO
32 visual disturbance
33 (some) directions
34 a/the door
35 identification
36 (the/some) valuables
37&38 IN EITHER ORDER
A C
39&40 IN EITHER ORDER
B E

Writing Task 1

Sample answer

The data provides information on average temperatures and annual hours of sunshine in London, New York and Sydney.

The temperature patterns for London and New York are similar, although New York has warmer summers and colder winters. In both cities, peaks occur in July/August, at 23° in London and 29° in New York. In contrast, Sydney's hottest weather is in December/January when temperatures average 25°. During this period, New York's temperatures dip to an average of around 5°, compared with 8° in London. On the other hand, Sydney's lowest average temperatures in July are just over 15°.

As far as hours of sunshine are concerned, New York and Sydney have similar averages of 2,535 and 2,473 hours respectively. London, however, has a much lower average of 1,180 hours.

Clearly, London is the coldest city and has the fewest hours of sunshine. New York has the hottest summers, but Sydney enjoys the warmest overall climate.

(156 words)

Writing Task 2

Sample answer

Over the past 50 years, people have become used to the idea that they will probably live longer than their grandparents did. However, a longer life is only desirable if you can look after yourself and be independent, otherwise there can be disadvantages for everyone.

If you walk into a hospital in my country, you are likely to see a lot more elderly people than you did in the past. In fact, this is causing significant problems as there is a shortage of beds. Medical treatment is keeping the elderly alive, but at what cost to others?

On top of this, one of the biggest medical problems these days is dementia. Even if old people are still fit, they may not be able to look after themselves. They may have to live with their children or be cared for in a home, which can be expensive. Elderly people do not like to be a burden, but their children can feel obliged to care for them.

Obviously, not all old people become ill. Those who remain healthy can enjoy a happy old age as long as they have saved enough money. People are much more active in their sixties and seventies than they used to be and this can only be a good thing. They have time to enjoy their retirement and do a range of activities that they could not do when they were at work. They can also help look after their grandchildren, which is a great benefit for working parents.

To sum up, I believe that we should aim to keep people as healthy as possible so that they can enjoy their old age without having to rely on others. A longer life expectancy is obviously advantageous, but no one wants to live to be 100 if they only cause problems for their family and society.

(308 words)

Practice Test 3

Listening Section 1

1 S-Y-M-O-N-D-S/S-y-m-o-n-d-s
2 1996
3 full(-)time
4 swimming
5 monthly
6 (go/do) jogging
7 bad ankle
8 fitness level
9 charity worker
10 (on) (the) radio

Listening Section 2

11 C
12 B
13 A
14 B
15 C
16 E
17 A
18 ring a bell
19 lounge
20 speeches/speakers

Listening Section 3

21 pine forests
22 water
23 print
24 sort
25 remove ink
26 (the) introduction
27 (the) council
28 (some) data
29 first draft
30 (their/the) tutor

Listening Section 4

31 protection
32 flexible
33 elephants
34 100 000/100,000
35 products
36 cap
37 oil
38 active
39 skin
40 blue(-)berries

Reading Passage 1

1 FALSE
2 FALSE
3 NOT GIVEN
4 TRUE
5 NOT GIVEN
6 TRUE
7 C
8 A
9 E
10 scouts
11 waggle dance
12 volume
13 democratic

Reading Passage 2

14 iv
15 viii
16 ii
17 vi
18 iii
19 factory
20 flooring/floor
21 column(s)
22 concrete
23 structural revolution
24 (non-pressurized) boilers
25 power shortages
26 climate control

Reading Passage 3

27 YES
28 YES
29 NO
30 NOT GIVEN
31 NOT GIVEN
32 NO
33 (their) behavio(u)r/activities
34 turn-taking
35 interruptions
36 belong
37 distress levels
38 rejection
39 agreement
40 content

Writing Task 1

Sample answer

The diagrams show West Park School at three different stages in its development: 1950, 1980 and 2010.

In 1950, the school was built close to a main road and next to a number of houses. A large area behind the school was turned into a playground, while the area behind the houses was farmland.

By 1980, the houses had been demolished in order to make way for a small car park and an additional school building, which became the science block. In addition to the existing playground, the school also gained the farmland and converted it into a sports field.

In 2010, the school building remained unchanged but the car park was extended to cover the entire sports field. As a result of this, the original playground was divided into two so that it provided a smaller playground and a small sports field.

During this period, the school has increased in size and a car park has been created and enlarged. The combined recreational areas, however, first expanded and were then reduced in size.

(174 words)

Writing Task 2

Sample answer

Most people would agree that car ownership has increased in recent years and is causing a range of problems, particularly in built-up areas. I think there are a number of ways that governments can aim to deal with this.

Many big cities in the world have traffic problems but these problems vary. For example, it is reasonably easy to drive around my city after 10 am and before 5 pm. However, outside these hours, you have to allow double the usual time to reach your destination. In some other cities, traffic is congested at all times, and there is the continual sound of car horns as people try to get wherever they want to go.

One of the best approaches governments can take in busy cities is to encourage the use of public transport. This means the transport facilities have to be well run and people must be able to afford them. Buses, trams and trains are good ways of getting around, and if they are cheap and reliable, people will use them.

Another approach is to discourage people from actually entering the city by building car parks and shopping centres on the outskirts. Many cities around the world do this quite successfully and offer passengers bus transport into the centre, if they need it.

At peak travel periods, governments can also run campaigns to encourage people to be less dependent on their cars. Apparently, a lot of car trips involve very short journeys to, say, the supermarket or local school. These are often unnecessary, but we automatically get in our cars without thinking.

Clearly we all have a responsibility to look after our cities. Governments can do a lot to improve the situation and part of what they do should involve encouraging individuals to consider alternatives to driving.

(299 words)

Practice Test 4

Listening Section 1

1 7.30/seven thirty
2 pencils
3 top
4 August
5 instructions
6 55/fifty-five
7 beginners
8 Kahui
9 battery
10 show

Listening Section 2

11&12 IN EITHER ORDER B E
13&14 IN EITHER ORDER B C
15 G
16 I
17 B
18 E
19 C
20 A

Listening Section 3

21 C
22 A
23 B
24 C
25 A
26 G
27 A
28 D
29 C
30 E

Listening Section 4

31 food
32 hero
33 feathers
34 shells
35 diamond
36 shark
37 teeth
38 messages
39 meeting
40 escape

Reading Passage 1

1 FALSE
2 FALSE
3 TRUE
4 TRUE
5 NOT GIVEN
6 FALSE
7 NOT GIVEN
8 NOT GIVEN
9 A
10 B
11 C
12 C
13 A

Reading Passage 2

14 NOT GIVEN
15 YES
16 NO
17 NOT GIVEN
18 fertiliser / fertilizer
19 lasers
20 cereals
21 Communication
22 C
23 F
24 H
25 A
26 D

Reading Passage 3

27 E
28 D
29 C
30 E
31 A
32 B
33&34 IN EITHER ORDER C D
35&36 IN EITHER ORDER B C
37 generation
38 citizen
39 abstract
40 music

Writing Task 1

Sample answer

This bar chart illustrates the performance of Southland's primary exports in 2000 and 2013. It also indicates future projections for 2025. According to the data, it seems likely that international tourism will become the dominant industry, although dairy exports will remain strong. In 2000, we can see that tourism was the greatest exports earner of the three industries, with revenue standing at just over £8 billion. This figure has increased slightly, so that now, in 2013, it has reached almost £9 billion. It is estimated that international tourism will continue to grow, so that by 2025, it will be earning around £10 billion for the country. In 2000, dairy exports were worth around £7 billion, but since then there has been a dramatic increase, and sales for this year are approximately £10 billion. Experts are predicting that exports in this area may fall slightly, so a figure of £9.5 billion is expected for 2025. Meat products are the third key industry in Southland, but sales have dropped since 2000 and now stand at £5.5 billion. It is expected that sales will continue to decrease in the future.

(187 words)

Writing Task 2

Sample answer

The growth of the fast food industry has, without doubt, impacted on the eating habits and the health of many societies around the world. Diabetes, high cholesterol, heart and respiratory problems are all on the rise due to fatty and sugar-rich food*. However, the question is whether higher tax would improve this situation or not.

From an economic point of view, higher tax might seem sensible. In countries such as the USA, Australia and Britain*, the healthcare system spends a large part of its budget on people with diet-related health problems. It could be argued that these people have caused their own illnesses because of their choice of food. In this case, why should they expect the state to pay for their treatment? The tax could help fund the healthcare system.

However, we also need to consider which socio-economic group consumes fast food as the main part of their diet. Statistics indicate* that lower income groups eat more of this food than wealthier people. One possible reason for this is that fast food is far cheaper than fresh produce. This is because many governments offer large subsidies to farmers who provide products for the fast food industry, such as corn, wheat and beef. Fruit and vegetables, on the other hand, are not subsidised. Research suggests* that many families simply cannot afford to buy healthy food or pay higher taxes on fast food. For them, fast food is not a choice but a necessity.

In conclusion, imposing a higher tax on fast food does not seem to be the answer. If the government chose to do this, it would only lead to greater poverty and families facing further hardship.

(278 words)

Practice Test 5

Listening Section 1

1 white
2 office
3 camera
4 umbrella
5 13th May/13 May/ thirteenth May/May 13/ May 13th/May thirteenth
6 airport
7 taxi
8 Docherty
9 River
10 07979605437

Listening Section 2

11 G	**14** E	**17** A	**20** A
12 D	**15** C	**18** C	
13 A	**16** B	**19** C	

Listening Section 3

21 B	**24** C	**27** B	**30** F
22 A	**25** B	**28** G	
23 A	**26** E	**29** A	

Listening Section 4

31 migration
32 eyes
33 lizard
34 trade
35 survival
36 political
37&38 **IN EITHER ORDER** ships; horses
39&40 **IN EITHER ORDER** industry; tourism

Reading Passage 1

1 vi **2** x **3** ii **4** ix **5** iv **6** i **7** vii
8 North America **9** (super-hot) fires **10** (stored) carbon
11 winds **12** Drought **13** beetle

Reading Passage 2

14 skin/skin samples
15 noise/noise pollution
16 (around) Tasmania
17 sperm/sperm whale(s)
18 sound waves
19 nutrients
20 microbubbles
21 blood
22 NOT GIVEN
23 TRUE
24 NOT GIVEN
25 TRUE
26 FALSE

Reading Passage 3

27 B	**31** C	**35** A	**39** G
28 A	**32** D	**36** H	**40** B
29 B	**33** B	**37** D	
30 D	**34** C	**38** F	

Writing Task 1

Sample answer

The two pie charts compare the percentages of online sales across different retail sectors in New Zealand in the years 2003 and 2013. For three of the sectors, it is evident that over this time frame there was significant change in their proportion of online transactions.

At 36% we can see that the travel sector accounted for the majority of online sales in 2003, but this percentage had dropped to 29% by 2013. Across the same ten-year period, as an increasing number of people chose to purchase films and music online, we can see that transactions went from just 21% to 33%, making it the retail sector with the highest overall share of the online market.

In 2003, the clothing industry boasted an impressive 24% of total online sales in New Zealand. However, by 2013, the figure had fallen considerably to 16%. Interestingly, online sales of books eventually overtook sales of clothes, although books still represented only 22% of the market.

(162 words)

Writing Task 2

Sample answer

In recent years, advances in technology have allowed governments, the police and privately owned companies to keep the public under constant surveillance. In many major cities and towns, security cameras are recording the movements of ordinary citizens. Whenever a cellphone is used, the call is logged, so the service provider knows exactly when and where the user made the call. Invisible satellites orbit the Earth, watching us whether we like it or not. Is this, however, a development we should welcome?

Certainly there are benefits. In areas where there is a high crime rate, the use of security cameras may act as a deterrent to criminals: if they can see a camera, they may think twice about breaking into a building or stealing a car. If a crime is carried out, then a camera may provide useful evidence. The same is true for a cellphone; the police sometimes rely on call logs to help them trace the whereabouts of suspects or victims.

On the other hand, there are a number of concerns. In countries where human rights are ignored, the use of security cameras or listening devices may be harmful to society. People should be able to hold meetings and express their opinions without their privacy being invaded. There is also a very different issue we should consider. Nowadays, many people upload personal information and photographs onto social networking sites; they often do not realise how easy it is for other people to view this information or for the site owners to use the data or photographs for their own financial gain.

It seems inevitable that there will be more and more ways to monitor society in the future. However, it is our responsibility to evaluate new technology and decide whether it will do more harm than good. Surely our freedom is more valuable than technological progress?

(307 words)

Practice Test 6

Listening Section 1

1 208 613 2978
2 visiontech
3 doctor
4 garage
5 furniture
6 fridge
7 school
8 950/£950
9 quiet
10 friend

Listening Section 2

11 contact details
12 (an) emergency
13 radio
14 (spare/extra) keys
15 (window) locks
16 C
17 D
18 F
19 G
20 E

Listening Section 3

21 B
22 C
23 B
24 A
25 C
26 C
27 (global) hunger
28 pollution
29 wood
30 grass(es)

Listening Section 4

31 marketing
32 interests
33 jobs
34 health
35&36 IN EITHER ORDER C E
37&38 IN EITHER ORDER A D
39&40 IN EITHER ORDER A C

Reading Passage 1

1 vi
2 vii
3 i
4 iv
5 viii
6 ii
7 science
8 economy
9 guidelines
10 language
11 equipment/resources
12 Master's degree/Masters degree
13 respect/status

Reading Passage 2

14 F
15 E
16 A
17 E
18 B
19&20 A/C
21&22 IN EITHER ORDER A D
23 TRUE
24 NOT GIVEN
25 NOT GIVEN
26 FALSE

Reading Passage 3

27 D
28 B
29 A
30 C
31 B
32 C
33 D
34 A
35 workplace
36 acquaintances
37 conversations
38 Internet
39 cities
40 A

Writing Task 1

Sample answer

This graph illustrates how crime rates altered in Newport inner city during the period 2003–2012. We can see immediately that the greatest change occurred in the number of burglaries, while incidents of theft remained low but steady.

In 2003, we can see that burglary was the most common crime, with approximately 3,400 reported cases. The figure rose to around 3,700 in 2004, but then there was a downward trend until 2008. At this point the figure stood at just over 1,000 incidents. This rose slightly in 2009, then continued to fluctuate for the remaining period.

In 2003, the number of cars being stolen stood at around 2,800 and followed a similar trend to burglary until 2006. At this point the number rose, standing at around 2,200 in 2007. There was a marginal decrease in the following year, but from then on, the trend was generally upwards.

Finally, robbery has always been a fairly minor problem for Newport. The number of offences committed changed little over nine years. It is interesting to note that the figure of approximately 700 in 2003 is the same figure for 2012.

(187 words)

Writing Task 2

Sample answer

The pursuit of knowledge is a concept that is valued by most cultures. In the 21st century, we now have many more options regarding how and where to find that knowledge. If you are a French national, you can apply to do an economics degree in the USA, and likewise an American citizen can take a course in linguistics in France. Indeed, most universities across the world now have a good proportion of foreign students enrolled in their programmes.

Certainly, there are numerous advantages of studying in a different country. Many students choose to do this because they know that a particular university, for instance Stanford Business School, has an excellent reputation. Graduating from here, they believe, will increase their chances of securing a decent position in a company back home. Students studying abroad also have the opportunity to form friendships with people of various nationalities: in time, these may develop into useful professional networks. Furthermore, living far from family and friends can enable young people to become more independent and self-sufficient.

Unfortunately, the experience of studying abroad is not always a positive one. Research suggests that a small percentage of young people struggle to adapt to their new environment and suffer from severe culture shock. The situation can become worse if the student is not mature enough to cope by themselves. Different approaches to teaching and learning may also come as an unwelcome surprise to some students.

In essence, the key to a good experience at a foreign university is an open mind. If a student is presented with this opportunity, they should certainly seize it.

(267 words)

Practice Test 7

Listening Section 1

1 unfriendly
2 noisy
3 23.50/twenty-three fifty
4 insects
5 bathrooms
6 party
7 S–H–A–D–F–O–R–T–H/ S–h–a–d–f–o–r–t–h
8 towel
9 breakfast
10 kitchen

Listening Section 2

11 B
12 A
13 C
14 B
15 A
16 A
17 E
18 C
19 F
20 A

Listening Section 3

21 A
22 B
23 A
24 B
25 A
26 A
27 background
28 theory
29 cost(s)
30 time

Listening Section 4

31 religion(s)
32 nature
33 flight
34 stars
35 practical
36 education
37 king
38 entertainment
39 opera
40 electricity

Reading Passage 1

1 TRUE
2 FALSE
3 NOT GIVEN
4 NOT GIVEN
5 TRUE
6 FALSE
7 TRUE
8 D
9 B
10 G
11 C
12 E
13 F

Reading Passage 2

14 (the) hairs
15 (electric) charge
16 pores
17 water
18 concave
19 E
20 D
21 B
22 C
23 E
24 I
25 F
26 H

Reading Passage 3

27 i
28 x
29 ii
30 vii
31 iii
32 v
33 F
34 E
35 C
36 D
37&38 (in any order) B E
39&40 (in any order) A E

Writing Task 1

Sample answer

The diagrams below chart the development of Stokeford Village over an 80-year period from 1930 to 2010. It is apparent from the data presented that Stokeford has become increasingly populated over this time frame, with a number of new properties replacing land that was previously used for arable purposes.

In terms of specific changes to the area, two new roads have been created in the north of the village. These split off from the main road, with the eastern-facing road replacing old farmland, and with the old shops demolished to make way for the western-facing road. Both new roads are accompanied by a small number of new houses on either side. The primary school opposite the post office has been extended to include two new buildings attached to the rear of the property. A new road to the south-west of the school branches off from the main road and extends out to the river (with a series of adjoining properties), but eventually curves back into the main road a little further south. The area where the large house was previously situated has been substantially altered, with the gardens having been cut back to allow four new houses to be built, and the large house has been converted into a retirement home, with two extra buildings added to the previous three. Finally, at the southernmost edge of the map, farmland has again been converted to residential use, with a number of new properties attached to the road heading south.

Writing Task 2

Sample answer

In the media, in politics, and in academia, the impact of a massive rise in the total global population is arguably one of the most sensitive and hotly-debated topics among all of the potential threats to humanity that are currently under discussion. The current essay discusses some of the perceived causes of this rise, as well as asks the question of whether in fact an increase in the global population should be considered a serious problem, when compared to other potential threats to our existence.

That there is a global rise in the general human population is in no doubt. China now has a population of over one billion inhabitants despite the best efforts of their government to control this rise through their 'one child policy', while India now has a total number of people approaching the billion mark. The birth rate in the developing world continues to rise as families from certain countries lack access to birth control for financial, political or religious reasons, while in some cultures having a large family offers a degree of security against the impact of disease or accidents that may befall certain members of that family.

However, when discussing the seriousness of this problem compared to other pressing issues, one can find that the reported increase in population is not universal across all societies and cultures. For example, it is often reported that in far-Eastern countries such as Korea and Japan, the birth rate among the indigenous population has dropped sharply over the last few decades, and accordingly, those working in higher education worry that as the numbers of potential students looks set to drop in the coming years, some institutes may well have to close. Other European countries such as the UK or Sweden are seeing a fall in the birth rates of the native population, while this has been balanced by an increase in the immigrant population. Thus, while in some contexts population growth may appear unsustainable, in other contexts, governments are actively pushing for their populations to increase.

With the above factors in mind, as long as improvements in resource management and food technology are made, it may be possible to support an increase in the population of those in the developing world. At the same time, if developing nations can begin to reach economic parity with the developed world, one might see the increase in the global population eventually become curtailed.

General Training Reading Section 1

1 E
2 B
3 A
4 F
5 C
6 A
7 C
8 B
9 TRUE
10 NOT GIVEN
11 NOT GIVEN
12 TRUE
13 FALSE
14 FALSE

General Training Reading Section 2

15 volunteers
16 consultants
17 decisions
18 efficiency
19 confidence
20 involvement
21 aim
22 range
23 selection
24 details
25 evaluation
26 implementation
27 lessons

General Training Reading Section 3

28 C
29 A
30 C
31 C
32 A
33 A
34 B
35 Treasury
36 (commemorative) coin
37 (ornamental) stars
38 (word) Britain
39 (red) ink
40 colour/color

General Training Writing Task 1

Sample answer

Dear Sir or Madam,

I am writing this letter in support of my application to join the hospital as a volunteer worker. I would be most grateful if you would consider the following information favourably when deciding on my eligibility for this role.

I am currently a final-year college student preparing to enter medical school in the coming year, and I feel that working as a volunteer in this department will provide me with some much needed hands-on experience of the day-to-day responsibilities I might encounter while working in a medical context. As I already have taken some initial administrative and clerical roles in the past, I would be able to work on the reception desk, as well as assist the elderly, the disabled or young patients in transit to and from the various wards. I am also willing to assist medical staff with the preparation of medical equipment, and I am trained in sterilisation and general hygiene practice through an internship I took over the summer at a neighbouring hospital. I am also willing to undertake any other tasks that the management would consider suitable for my level of expertise and experience.

I will be available to accept any position if offered from early March, as I have to complete my final exams, but I am available for interview at all times throughout the week. I have enclosed my contact details, including my e-mail address and telephone number, in the resume attached to this letter.

I hope that you find my application suitable, and hope to be considered for the role.

Yours faithfully,

X

General Training Writing Task 2

Sample answer

There are a number of benefits to individuals and to society afforded by the institution of marriage. On a personal level, getting married brings with it a sense of security and commitment as the result of the solemn vows undertaken by both parties during the wedding ceremony. In the wider sense, married couples are more likely to provide stable homes for any children that might result from the union, sparing the family from undue pain and suffering and sparing the state from the financial burden of supporting single-parent families. However, the notion that there is a preferred age (suggested to be around 30) for a marriage to be regarded as optimally beneficial for both private and public interests is difficult to quantify, for the following reasons.

Firstly, there has been a change in the general health of the population as time has progressed. In the past, the life expectancy of individuals in our society hovered at around the sixty-mark. These days, due to advances in medical technology and an increased awareness of health-related issues, people are expected to live well into their eighties. In addition, due to the improvement of artificial insemination methods, women are now able to have children well into their forties. As such, it is not immediately apparent why people should hurry to settle down and get married at around the age of 30 as there is no medical or biological reason why this should be the case.

In addition, due to changing economic conditions, many couples are saddled with debt well into their thirties, as they struggle to pay off student loans, mortgages, and other payments. As modern marriages are generally very expensive affairs, the added pressure that a wedding can bring on a household's finances may in many cases be too much to bear. With this in mind, it is potentially beneficial to postpone the wedding plans until a budding couple are more financially secure in their later years, before tying the knot.

While the benefits of marriage have been in no way diminished by the claims made above, there is certainly a case to be made that there should not be any established age limit beyond which the benefits of marriage may no longer be felt

Practice Test 8

Listening Section 1

1 (simple) documents
2 keyboard
3 flowers
4 tools
5 Saturday
6 Mairead
7 Bridge
8 (the) 14(th)/fourteen(th) (of) May/May (the) 14(th)/fourteen(th)/14.(0)5/(0)5.14
9 park
10 newspaper

Listening Section 2

11 C
12 B
13 A
14 H
15 G
16 films/movies
17 reports
18 region
19 job
20 housing

Listening Section 3

21 E
22 I
23 C
24 G
25 B
26 D
27 A
28 aims/objectives/goals
29 staff
30 feedback

Listening Section 4

31 hook
32 string
33 danger
34 rubber
35 light
36 intelligence
37 tail(s)
38 energy
39 chemical
40 diet

Reading Passage 1

1 seafaring
2 merchant
3 temple
4 craftsmen
5 timber/wood/cedar
6 partnership
7 ivory
8 commission
9 TRUE
10 FALSE
11 TRUE
12 TRUE
13 NOT GIVEN

Reading Passage 2

14 iv
15 ii
16 vii
17 i
18 v
19 vi
20 FALSE
21 TRUE
22 NOT GIVEN
23 TRUE
24 vertical integration
25 movie moguls
26 divestiture

Reading Passage 3

27 D
28 C
29 E
30 B
31 environmental
32 light
33 multi tasking
34 food
35 predator
36 E
37 H
38 B
39 B
40 A

Writing Task 1

Sample answer

The number of rentals and sales in various formats of films, between 2002 and 2011 in a particular store has changed a lot. Sometimes it has been very low and sometimes very high. The number of rental since 2002 has been decreasing every year. Comparing the number of rentals in 2002 with 2011, it's possible noticing that in 2002 it was about 180,000 rentals against aproximadly 55,000 in 2011. In regarding the number of VHS sales, comparing the period between 2002 and 2005, it has happened as well. In 2002 the number of VHS sales was about 85,000 sales, against 65,000 in 2003, 40,000 in 2004 and about 10,000 sales in 2005. After that time, this store stopped to sale VHS. By another side, the number of DVD sales growed up between 2002 and 2007, from aproximadly 45,000 in 2002, more than 100,000 in 2003, to more than 200,000 in 2007. However, since 2008, it has been going down slightly. In 2011 this number was less than 180,000.

The number of Blu-Ray sales has started since 2007 and it has growing up slowly. In 2007 it was nowhere near as significant as DVD sales but I guess it will grow up drastcaly in a few years.

Actually the number of DVD sales is still very higher than another products in that place.

(222 words)

Writing Task 2

Sample answer

Nowadays we are living in a society based on consuming. As a result, some people have problems in dealing with this budget and they get into debt by buying things they don't need and can't afford.

This kind of behavior is encountered quite often in our present days, mainly because of the possibility of buying goods in leasing. Hence, people buy most of the goods using the credit card without having a clear idea on how much money they possess or they owe.

Also, another cause for this behavior could be psychological. The advertisment and the subliminal messages one encounters in a regular day in a big city has an enormous impact on one's brain. The main problem is the lack of awareness of the serious effects that advertisment can have on people.

In order to prevent people from adopting this dangerous behavior, measures should be taken so as to raise awareness among people. Also, one must learn how to manage his budget in order to get a balance between necessiting and pleasure. Keeping a record on income and monthly spendings would be very helpful and would give to the consumer an overall image on how his budget should be spent.

All summed up, the chances of becoming a victim of the consumer's society are high nowadays due to the surrounding temtations but this problem could be easily avoid by being aware of this dangers and having a rational attitude when dealing with money.

(244 words)

General Training Reading Section 1

1 F
2 C
3 B
4 A
5 C
6 F
7 E
8 FALSE
9 TRUE
10 TRUE
11 TRUE
12 FALSE
13 TRUE
14 NOT GIVEN

General Training Reading Section 2

15 duties
16 objective
17 negotiate
18 relevant
19 connection
20 modest
21 supervisor(s)
22 15 (days)/fifteen (days)
23 demolition
24 5 years/five years
25 hazards
26 practical
27 tuition

General Training Reading Section 3

28 viii
29 vi
30 iii
31 vii
32 i
33 x
34 iv
35 horses (galloping)
36 swords
37 conductor
38 machinery
39 miners
40 poverty

General Training Writing Task 1

Sample answer

Dear Michael,

I am writing to inform you that due to circumstances beyond my control, I am no longer able to continue working in my current voluntary role as a community support officer. My role as a CSO entailed regular meetings with the homeless and other impoverished members of the local community, and passing on the information gained from these meetings to the local council's liaison for social improvement. I was also responsible for maintaining adequate provision of food, blankets and stocks of other essential items for the community's homeless outreach centres.

While I found the work incredibly rewarding, I have been offered a paid position as a secretary for the Social Affairs Department, and as such, I am now unable to commit to the number of hours that are required of a CSO. However, I believe that the current deputy CSO, Mr. David Swan, would be more than willing to accept a promotion to the role of full CSO, and would be able to accept this position at the earliest opportunity. Therefore, I request that Mr. Swan be hired as my replacement for the CSO position with immediate effect, in order to minimise any potential disruption to essential services.

I look forward to your response,

General Training Writing Task 2

Sample answer

The fashion industry continues to bombard society with a non-stop stream of powerful imagery, colours, sounds and styles, in order to make us part with our hard-earned cash. Keeping up with the latest trends may feel like a full-time job at times, and what may be fashionable one minute may be out of style the next. However, this does not stop people from buying and wearing new and expensive items of clothing or jewellery in the pursuit of style, even if it is potentially to their detriment. This essay discusses why people strive to wear fashionable clothing, and why the pursuit of fashion may not always be a positive force in people's lives.

Humans are inherently social creatures, and it has often been recognised that people are able to feel 'included' if one is wearing clothes that are currently in fashion. For inclusion in certain socio-economic groups, wearing the 'appropriate' brands guarantees a sense of belonging and may act as a gatekeeper to membership within that group. With this in mind, it would be sensible to assume that there may be strong psychological factors underlying a person's choice of clothing that may have little to do with the actual garments.

However, as a corollary, people's behaviour may be strongly influenced by the perceived threat of social exclusion if one does not conform to acceptable notions of fashion. In fact, one might assume that the endless cycle of purchasing new and expensive clothes in order to remain 'fashionable' might be detrimental both to a person's bank balance as well as their sense of self, if such behaviour is driven mainly by the fear of becoming a social outcast. Such behaviour is well attested in studies on teenage girls in particular, for whom inclusion within a social structure is paramount to their developing sense of identity and self. This can cause a great deal of stress for parents who are not able to afford the latest trends and brands demanded by their children.

With the above in mind, while understandable on a basic level, one might conclude that the pursuit of fashion may well impact negatively on society as a whole, particularly if one has to manage to stay in fashion while on a budget. It would be preferable if fashion companies could promote trends that are more accessible to the wider population who may not have the time or resources to 'keep up with the Joneses'.

Sample answer sheets

BRITISH COUNCIL · idp IELTS AUSTRALIA · UNIVERSITY of CAMBRIDGE ESOL Examinations

IELTS Listening and Reading Answer Sheet

Centre number:

Pencil must be used to complete this sheet.

Please write your **full name** in CAPITAL letters on the line below:

SAMPLE

Then write your six digit Candidate number in the boxes and shade the number in the grid on the right.

0 1 2 3 4 5 6 7 8 9
0 1 2 3 4 5 6 7 8 9
0 1 2 3 4 5 6 7 8 9
0 1 2 3 4 5 6 7 8 9
0 1 2 3 4 5 6 7 8 9
0 1 2 3 4 5 6 7 8 9

Test date (shade ONE box for the day, ONE box for the month and ONE box for the year):

Day: 01 02 03 04 05 06 07 08 09 10 11 12 13 14 15 16 17 18 19 20 21 22 23 24 25 26 27 28 29 30 31

Month: 01 02 03 04 05 06 07 08 09 10 11 12 Year (last 2 digits): 09 10 11 12 13 14 15 16 17 18

Listening Listening Listening Listening Listening Listening

		Marker use only			Marker use only
1		✓ 1 ✗	21		✓ 21 ✗
2		✓ 2 ✗	22		✓ 22 ✗
3		✓ 3 ✗	23		✓ 23 ✗
4		✓ 4 ✗	24		✓ 24 ✗
5		✓ 5 ✗	25		✓ 25 ✗
6		✓ 6 ✗	26		✓ 26 ✗
7		✓ 7 ✗	27		✓ 27 ✗
8		✓ 8 ✗	28		✓ 28 ✗
9		✓ 9 ✗	29		✓ 29 ✗
10		✓ 10 ✗	30		✓ 30 ✗
11		✓ 11 ✗	31		✓ 31 ✗
12		✓ 12 ✗	32		✓ 32 ✗
13		✓ 13 ✗	33		✓ 33 ✗
14		✓ 14 ✗	34		✓ 34 ✗
15		✓ 15 ✗	35		✓ 35 ✗
16		✓ 16 ✗	36		✓ 36 ✗
17		✓ 17 ✗	37		✓ 37 ✗
18		✓ 18 ✗	38		✓ 38 ✗
19		✓ 19 ✗	39		✓ 39 ✗
20		✓ 20 ✗	40		✓ 40 ✗

Marker 2 Initials | Marker 1 Initials | Band Score | Listening Total

IELTS L-R v4.0 denote Print Limited 0121 520 5100 DP650/394

Acknowledgements

I've worked for Cambridge Exams for over 18 years now and the experience has been both a privilege and a pleasure. It feels like the right time to acknowledge the people who put their trust in me and the writing teams here in Australia and New Zealand. A very big thanks to Nick Charge for getting us all started and to Rod Burroughs, Graeme Bridges and Judith Wilson for keeping us going for so many years. To Sarah Fiddy and Coreen Doherty and to Clare McDowell and Mary Jane Hogan for their early support here in Australia, a very big warm thanks. When it comes to this book, I would like to thank Neil Holloway and Andrew Reid for their amazing efforts in turning a beast with an awful lot to say, into a coherent giant. Thank you for making us look and sound great!

Pauline Cullen

I would like to thank Liam, Georgia and Joe Keane for their love and support.

Amanda French

The author and publishers are grateful to the following reviewers and editors for their help in developing the book

Anthea Bazin, Michael Black, Jane Coates, Jill Cosh, Katie Foufouti, Judith Greet, Andrew Reid, Nik White

The authors and publishers acknowledge the following sources of copyright material and are grateful for the permissions granted. While every effort has been made, it has not always been possible to identify the sources of all the material used, or to trace all copyright holders. If any omissions are brought to our notice, we will be happy to include the appropriate acknowledgements on reprinting.

Extract on pp. 46–47 adapted from 'Kids: Gluttons or Sloths?' By Stephen Luntz, Australasian Science Aug 2006, Vol 27, Issue 7, pp.33–35. Reprinted with permission;

Extract on p. 48 adapted from 'Ochre find reveals ancient knowledge of chemistry' by Becky Crew. This extract is from an article that was first published by COSMOS, a literary science magazine based in Australia but distributed globally;

Extract on p. 56 adapted from 'Planned Communities Part 1: Garden Cities' http://www.lib.umd.edu/NTL/gardencities.html, Special Collections, University of Maryland Libraries. Reprinted with permission;

Extract on p. 61 adapted with permission, The Journal of Experimental Biology: jeb.biologists.org Inside JEB Kathryn Knight, HOW GECKOS COPE WITH WET FEET, J Exp Biol 2012 215:i. doi:10.1242/jeb.078246;

Extract on p. 65 reprinted from Current Biology Volume 19, Issue 17, page R731, Taylor, Alex H; Gray, Russell D. 'Animal Cognition: Aesop's Fable Flies from Fiction to Fact' with permission of Cell Press;

Extract on p. 69 adapted from 'Maths shows why words persist over time' by Hamish Clarke. This extract is from an article that was first published by COSMOS, a literary science magazine based in Australia but distributed globally;

Extract on p. 70 adapted from 'Baboons prove reading an ancient skill' by Greg Dash. This extract is from an article that was first published by COSMOS, a literary science magazine based in Australia but distributed globally;

Extract on p. 72 from An Australian Jurassic Park? By Brian Switek, Smithsonian Media;

Danielle Aubert, Lana Cavar and Natasha Chandani for the extract on p. 74 from Living with Mies. Reprinted with permission;

Extract on p. 80 adapted from Brisbane City Council Information Booklet: 'Guide to Recycling in Brisbane' (Text 2013) reproduced courtesy of Brisbane City Council. Reprinted with permission;

Extract on p. 85 adapted from Occupational health and safety inspections: What you should know. © Queen's Printer for Ontario: http://www.ontario.ca/government/copyright-information-c-queens-printer-ontario;

Extract on p. 152 adapted from 'The right way to conduct a job interview' by Michael Mauboussin;

Extract on p. 160 adapted from Crossing the Channel with the Dover Boat by Peter Clark, Peter Clark BA FSA MIFA FSA Scot. Reprinted with permission;

Extract on p. 163 adapted from 'Meeting Facilities at Airports' by Nigel Halpern, Anne Graham and Rob Davidson. Reprinted from Journal of Air Transport Management Volume 18, page 54, Halpern, Nigel; Graham, Anne; Davidson, Rob 'Meetings facilities at airports' with permission of Pergamon;

Extract on p. 167 adapted from 'Is photography art?' A World History of Art History of Photography, www.all-art.org;

Extract on p. 177 adapted from Food Chain – the Flavor of Pleasure by Daniel A Marano. Published by Psychology Today. Reprinted with permission of Daniel A Marano;

Extract on p. 181 adapted from 'Dawn of Robots' by Robin McKie. This extract is from an article that was first published by COSMOS, a literary science magazine based in Australia but distributed globally;

Extract on p. 184 adapted from 'It's your choice' – Or is it really? by Anna Sagana, Melanie Sauerland and Harald Merckelbach. The Inquisitive Mind Issue 14. The Inquisitive Mind/ In-Mind Foundation. Reprinted with permission;

Extract on p. 195 adapted from 'Secrets of the Swarm' by Holly Williams, The Independent 23.8.2010. Copyright © The Independent;

Extract on p. 199 adapted from 'High Speed, High Rise' by Lauren Hilgers, Wired Magazine 2012. Copyright © 2013 Condé Nast. Richard Brody. All rights reserved. Originally published in The New Yorker. Reprinted by permission;

Extract on p. 202 adapted from 'When Conversations flow' by Namkje Koudenbourg, Tom Postmes, and Ernestine Gordjin, The Inquisitive Mind, Issue 14. Inquisitive Mind/ In-Mind Foundation. Reprinted with permission;

Extract on p. 213 adapted from 'Scott, Amundsen… and Nobu Shirase' by Stephanie Pain, New Scientist 29 December 2011, 201_Reed Business Information-UK. All rights reserved. Distributed by Tribune Media Services. Reprinted with permission;

Extract on p. 216 adapted from 'Down on the robofarm: The rise of the agribots' by James Mitchell Crow, New Scientist, 12 December 2012, 201_Reed Business Information-UK. All rights reserved. Distributed by Tribune Media Services. Reprinted with permission;

Extract on p. 220 from Moonwalking with Einstein: The art and science of remembering everything by Joshua Foer, copyright (c) 2011 by Joshua Foer. Used by permission of The Penguin Press, a division of Penguin Group (USA) LLC; 949 words (p. 125–128) and Penguin Books Ltd;

Extract on p. 232 adapted from 'How the mighty are fallen' by William Laurence, New Scientist, 28 January 2012 pp. 39–41, 201_Reed Business Information-UK. All rights reserved. Distributed by Tribune Media Services. Reprinted with permission;

Extract on p. 235 adapted from 'Mass Strandings' by Cat O'Donovan. This extract is from an article that was first published by COSMOS, a literary science magazine based in Australia but distributed globally;

Extract on p. 239 adapted from 'Science on the Edge of Space' by Molly Bentley, New Scientist, July 2012 pp. 39–44, 201_Reed Business Information-UK. All rights reserved. Distributed by Tribune Media Services. Reprinted with permission;

Extract on p. 253 from Why are Finland's Schools so Successful by LynNell Hancock, Professor of Journalism, Columbia University. Reprinted with permission;

Extract on p. 257 from 'Australia's Lost Giants' by Joel Achenbach, National Geographic Creative. Reprinted with permission;

Extract on p. 259 adapted from 'The Eureka Moment' by Rebecca Mcfie, New Zealander Listener, Issue 3760 May 30 2012. Reprinted with permission.

The publishers are grateful to the following for permission to reproduce copyright photographs and material:

p.30: Jon Stanley Austin/Martin Smith Studio; p.44: Shutterstock/Hu Xiao Fang; p.59: Shutterstock/Henk Bentlage; p.61: Alamy/Martin Harvey; p.65: Shutterstock/Al Mueller; Graph on p. 102 adapted from 'Net worth of the UK by sector', http://www.ons.gov.uk/ons/dcp171766_284260.pdf, page 18. Data from the Office for National Statistics licensed under the Open Government Licence v.1.0.

Picture and photo research: Louise Edgeworth

Design: Hannah Dade, Tom Perkins

Production controller: Lucy Edwards

Text design and page make-up: Kamae Design, Oxford

Audio Producer: Leon Chambers, Soundhouse Studio, London

DVD: filmed by Tristan Estall, edited by Pete Kyle (Crank Films, Leiston), developed by Stephen Forbush (Zenergy Films, Seattle)

Terms And Conditions Of Use

This is a legal agreement between "You" (which for individual purchasers means the individual customer and, for network purchasers, means the Educational Institution and its authorised users) and Cambridge University Press ("the Licensor") for **The Official Cambridge Guide to IELTS DVD-ROM**. By placing the DVD in the DVD-ROM drive of your computer You agree to the terms of this license.

1. Limited license

(a) You are purchasing only the right to use the DVD-ROM and are acquiring no rights, express or implied, to it or the software ("Software" being the DVD-ROM software, as installed on your computer terminals), other than those rights granted in this limited license for not-for-profit educational use only.

(b) The Licensor grants You the license to use one copy of this DVD-ROM on your site and (i) to install and use the software on this DVD-ROM on a single computer if You have purchased a single-user license, or (ii) to install and use the Software simultaneously on a number of computers if You have purchased a site license. You may not install the software on this DVD-ROM on a single secure network server for access from one site or install the software via MSI installer for deployment across a network.

(c) You shall not: (i) copy or authorize copying of the DVD-ROM, (ii) translate the DVD-ROM, (iii) reverse-engineer, alter, adapt, disassemble, or decompile the DVD-ROM, (iv) transfer, sell, lease, profit from, assign, or otherwise convey all or any portion of the DVD-ROM, or (v) operate the DVD-ROM from a mainframe system, except as provided in these terms and conditions.

2. Copyright

(a) All original content ("the Original Content") is provided as part of the DVD-ROM (including text, images and ancillary material) and is the copyright of, or licensed by a third party to, the Licensor, protected by copyright and all other applicable intellectual property laws and international treaties.

(b) You may not copy the DVD-ROM except for making one copy of the DVD-ROM solely for backup or archival purposes. You may not alter, remove, or destroy any copyright notice or other material placed on or with this DVD-ROM.

(c) The DVD-ROM contains Adobe® Flash® Player.

Adobe® Flash® Player Copyright © 1996–2012 Adobe Systems Incorporated. All Rights Reserved.

Protected by U.S. Patent 6,879, 327; Patents pending in the United States and other countries. Adobe and Flash are either trademarks or registered trademarks in the United States and/or other countries.

3. Modifications and adaptations

You may be permitted to modify, adapt, supplement, and/or save certain parts of the Original Material as part of the Software functionality of this DVD-ROM. You acknowledge that any such modifications, adaptations, supplementations, and saved versions (collectively called "New Material") are not the work of the Licensor even though they may contain elements of Original Material owned by the Licensor. Any modified, adapted, or supplemented elements of the New Material are the sole responsibility of the person who collates them in their particular composite form. The Licensor does not guarantee the accuracy, quality, or integrity of such New Material.

4. Importing material

(a) You may be permitted to import material as part of the Software functionality of this DVD-ROM ("Imported Material"). You acknowledge that all such Imported Material is the sole responsibility of the importing person, who shall be solely liable for any misuse. Any Imported Material is posted without the knowledge of the Licensor.

(b) The Licensor shall have no liability to You or to another person/institution for any damage, loss, cost, claim, or expense suffered by You or by any other person/institution arising directly or indirectly from the posting of such Imported Material and the use made of it by You or any other person/institution.

(c) You undertake not to use the importing facility to:
(i) post advertising or promotional materials or transmit any "junk mail," "spam," or "chain letters," or any other form of solicitation for goods or services;
(ii) post any material that You do not have the right to post under any law or under any other obligatory relationship;
(iii) post any material that infringes any intellectual property right including without limitation patent, trademark, trade secret, copyright, or other proprietary rights of any other person;
(iv) post any material that is defamatory, libelous, unlawful, threatening, or harmful, abusive, harassing, obscene, invasive of another's privacy, hateful, or racially, ethnically, or otherwise objectionable;
(v) import any Imported Material that contains software viruses or any other computer code; files or programs designed to interrupt, destroy, or limit the functionality of any computer software or hardware or telecommunications equipment;
(vi) promote or provide instructional information about illegal activities; physical harm or injury against any group or individual.
(vii) engage in any commercial activities.

5. Liability and indemnification

(a) The DVD-ROM is supplied "as-is" with no express guarantee as to their suitability. To the extent permitted by applicable law, the Licensor is not liable for costs of procurement of substitute products, damages, or losses of any kind whatsoever resulting from the use of this product, or errors or faults in the DVD-ROM, and in every case the Licensor's liability shall be limited to the suggested list price or the amount actually paid by You for the product, whichever is lower.

(b) You accept that the Licensor is not responsible for the persistency, accuracy, or availability of any URLs of external or third-party internet Web sites referred to on the DVD-ROM and does not guarantee that any content on such Web sites is, or will remain, accurate, appropriate, or available. The Licensor shall not be liable for any content made available from any Web sites and URLs outside the Software.

(c) Where, through use of the Original Material, New Material, and Imported Material you infringe the copyright of the Licensor, you undertake to indemnify and keep indemnified the Licensor from and against any loss, cost, damage, or expense (including, without limitation, damages paid to a third party and any reasonable legal costs) incurred by the Licensor as a result of such infringement.

6. Termination

Without prejudice to any other rights, the Licensor may terminate this license if You fail to comply with the terms and conditions of the license. In such event, You must destroy all copies of the DVD-ROM.

7. Governing law

This agreement is governed by the laws of England, without regard to its conflict of laws provision, and each party irrevocably submits to the exclusive jurisdiction of the English courts.